Science and Spirituality

Science and Spirituality

Physical Completeness & Religious Belief

Leonard Angel

Lulu Publishing

Science and Spirituality

To reach the copyright holder, contact:

Leonard Angel Tel: 604 - 876 - 6925

Or Leonard Angel via the Douglas College email address.

ISBN: 978 – 0 – 557 – 07487 – 7

To the loving memory of
Eva Fogel (1953 – 2007)

Science and Spirituality

Table of Contents

Acknowledgements:

I'm glad to thank so many helpers: class students, friends, acquaintances, colleagues, family members, and all who contributed in the unsuspecting ways. Among them, I particularly want to thank: George Levy, whose knowledge of marbles on trains is wonderful; Michael Feld who, finding plenitude in thought, makes comments on *A* that lead the listener to *Z*; Ronnie de Sousa, whose insights are always into the basics; Kathy Leavens and Pat O'Brien, who usefully questioned the terminology; Eric Damer, who not only invented the term 'phystriology', but also probed warmly and productively, everywhere; Robert Light, who juggled the ancients facing the moderns; Larry Kazdan, who, beyond being the soul of politeness and wisdom, provided worthy sources of information; Barbara Sefran whose questions are as valuable as any answers ever were; Kathy Denton, whose indicators go beyond what is indicated; my philosophy colleagues at Douglas College who send epiphanies in every direction plus a few; my children for their bright insights; my wife Susan whose love is shining; so many friends; and all the participants in the humanist reflection groups, meditation groups, and secular wisdom groups whose presence glows.

Of course the errors, inaccuracies, slip ups, typos, confusions, mistakes, goofs, etc., of which there are undoubtedly, and unfortunately, many, are mine. Apologies.

I am sincerely appreciative of the Ed Leave provided by Douglas College in January to the end of April 2006, during which time the bulk of the first part of this book was adapted from a paper I had been working on. The Ed Leave project was to document the way in which the cultivation of wisdom can take place in contemporary secular culture. The first part of this book is, of course, required for the material in the rest of the book, and the official Ed Leave project, as described in the last Chapter of this book, was written afterwards. In any case, I gratefully acknowledge the time provided by the supporters of the Ed Leave project.

Chapter One: Overview

1.0 What this book is about

Obviously, this book is about two things: science and spirituality. This means, though, that it is about *three* things. First, it is about science; second, it is about spirituality; and third, it is about the relation between science and spirituality. Hence, the three parts of this book.

It also happens to be about the two topics in the subtitle. How it is about them will become clear soon enough.

1.1 Science

1.1.1 The main message

About science itself, there is one main message. Just about everyone wants to be up to date with current science. Unfortunately, though, most everyone (outside of many philosophers) is not. So part I of the book is, unsurprisingly, about the main message that puts one up to date with current science. As it happens, this main message is the most important result that the sciences reached in the last two thousand five hundred years. Why is it so important? I'll talk about that in a moment (1.1.3). But first, what is the main message?

It sounds merely technical to spell it out in a few words, but sometimes one has to sound merely technical. But don't worry. The technicality is not as bad as it might be. The most important result of the last twenty five hundred years of scientific research was reached about forty or fifty years ago. It's been referred to as *the closure of physics* since the late 1960's. It's been called *the completeness of physics*, or *physical completeness* since the 1960's, too. Since the early 1990's *physical completeness*, or *the completeness of physics* are the names the position is usually called in philosophy discussions. And it was only philosophers who first stated the result. We will see why in a moment. The position maintains two things: first, that the tiniest parts of things studied by physicists have no inherent purposes, and, second, that there is no overturning of the rules of governance, or the laws, or the forces of physics.

I would like to, but won't, call this result by an acronym taken from an exposition of its meaning. The first idea yields POPP as an acronym (Parts Of Physics-things are, sort of, Purposeless), and the second yields NOP (No Overturning of Physics). Together, alas, we get POPPNOP, which sounds a bit silly. It calls to my mind a clown popping out of a box. Perhaps we should just stick with 'physical closure' or 'physical completeness.' But some people are not happy when 'closure' is used; some people are not happy when 'completeness' is used. Both have unintended and misleading nuances. For general exposure of the concepts, it's best to avoid use of either term. Yet that acronym is inadequate. Perhaps we need to create a new term that does the job. But let's bypass the question of what the position should be called, and just look at the position itself.

The position is philosophical. So it is not the very latest result of astronomy, nor the very latest technology in genetics, nor the very latest chemical compound. And that is why it was first philosophers who stated the result. Yet although most positions in philosophy are fraught with controversy of one sort or another, this position, as we will see (in detail in Chapters Eleven and Appendix 2), is not fraught with controversy.

Incidentally, this makes for a distinct change in the role of philosophical work. Every bit of philosophical work used to be 'up for grabs;' that is, every bit of philosophical work used to be both 'up for approval' and 'up for disapproval.' A position would be given; contrary positions would then be given as well. But that, astonishingly, is no longer the case. As I will show (in detail in Chapters Eleven and Appendix 2) there are no serious counterclaims to the main result of the natural sciences we are looking at here. And we will see why, as well. Basically, the history of the natural sciences in the last few hundred years is too clear for there to be serious counterclaims.

Some will still wonder why it was philosophers who first stated the overall result. In answer, the position is found in philosophy because the position *combines* key results in physics, in chemistry, and in biology. The position cannot be stated in plain ordinary physics. The position cannot be stated in any way in chemistry. The position cannot be stated in plain ordinary biology. It can be stated in philosophy, and was stated in philosophy, because philosophy is, among other things, a combinatorial field. Philosophy looks at everything.

The two main components of the position have already been briefly stated, and are not difficult to state more fully: The first says that purposes are not fundamental elements, or are not inherent elements, of the small physical parts of any natural thing, where a natural thing is a thing that occupies space or spacetime. This doesn't say that there are no purposes in any things; it says that if there are purposes in some things, like human beings, the purposes are not properties of the invisibly small things somehow in them. On the contrary, if there are purposes in some things, like human beings, they arise on account of the properties of some *sums* of the invisibly small purposeless things.

The second says that whatever goes on does not overturn the rules, laws, or forces of physics. Why 'rules, laws or forces'? Why not just 'rules', or just 'laws', or just 'forces'? Because some people think that physical changes are governed by rules; some think they are governed by laws that are not properly thought of as rules; and some think they are governed not by laws, nor by rules, but by forces. It makes no difference to this discussion as to what one thinks about this or similar classification questions. Consequently, we will talk about the rules, laws, or forces of physics.

The key results are in the three most basic *natural* sciences, namely, physics, chemistry, and biology. The work done leading to this result was done primarily in the last four or five hundred years. More specifically, in the last four or five hundred years we saw three processes occur: the mathematization of physics, the physicalization of chemistry, and the physio-chemicalization of biology. The terms referring to these three processes already give the sense of a philosophical integration of natural science results, and, in one case, the case of physics, how applying mathematics turns out to be important.

The mathematization of physics is a simple enough process. The mathematization of physics is the process in which what had been thought to be inherently purposive changes came to be no longer thought of as inherently purposive changes; instead they were thought of, one way or another, as changes governed merely by mathematical relations. There is, however, one point of possible confusion, or possible trouble, lurking in the 'one way or another'.

We will look at two examples, and the second of the two will show this. The first example is easy enough on its own: Rocks fall to the earth. Why? There is a contrast between one ancient view and the modern view. Aristotle thought twenty three hundred years ago, and so did more or less every learned person in the European world for another 1900 or so years, but not much after, rocks are earthy things, and things, in general, want to be, or seek to be, or purposively move so as to be, where their true nature is; so, Aristotle thought, and his followers, too, if set free, rocks, in some sense purposively, head to the centre of earthiness, which is at the centre of the earth. After the mathematization of physics, though, rocks were seen as made of tiny parts that just followed mathematical formulas. The rocks, too, behaved just as the sums of the tiny parts. To put it a bit simply, there didn't need to be changes in the sums of the formulas to find out how a big rock changes its position if it is let loose. This did not produce much trouble. That summative results in inanimate things are merely summative results is not troubling.

The second example is somewhat confusing, or troubling, though. As most everyone thought a few thousand years ago, and most people think today, too, if a human apologizes, it seems that it is because there is a non-summative inherent moral structure in a mature human being, and this apparently non-summative inherent moral structure moves a mature human being to apologize in certain occasions. Hmm... 'non-summative'; what does that mean? There will be more discussion of the relationship between features an object has on the one side and on the other side parts adding together to make sums later on[1]. Here I will merely adapt a phrase used before: rocks falling to the earth, after the mathematization of physics, came to be thought of as sums of changes of very small inherently non-purposive things, where the changes follow the rules, laws, or forces expressed in mathematical relationships. A somewhat similar point can be made about humans apologizing, too. But such a transition, from believing in inherently purposive properties in human beings to believing in properties at two levels – purposeless non-sum properties and properties held by the sum of the purposeless non-sum things, would only unavoidably happen after all three processes had occurred, namely, the mathematization of physics, the physicalization of chemistry, and the physio-chemicalization of biology. Also apologies are

---

[1] In 12.2, and, with perhaps too much detail for some readers, at the end of A2.4.

psychological states, and there are many problems generating vigorous debate having to do with psychology, not biology. But that there are biological sums underlying the psychological states is clear.

That was putting the point in a somewhat complicated way. To put it simply, the mathematization of physics process is easy to grasp for inanimate objects, but hard to grasp for animate objects, especially sophisticated and psychological animate objects like human beings.

The physicalization of chemistry is the process through which it came to be discovered that chemical relations are primarily or statistically changes in electromagnetic relations between subatomic particles.

And the physio-chemicalization of biology is the process in which it came to be discovered that *no* biological changes alter, or undo, or overturn the physics-based changes.

Given the physicalization of chemistry and the physio-chemicalization of biology we have the troubling problem: the changes a human being undergoes must be, at some level, sums of physics changes. The small invisible things making physics changes have no inherent purposes. But the sum beings, apparently, have purposes. How does this happen? That is a troubling problem. But the main message of the philosophical integration of the important natural science results that have by now been reached is, put as simply as it can be put, that no natural changes overturn the merely mathematical rules, or laws, or forces of physics. (Later we will undo a simplification: the rules, laws, or forces are approximations, restricted to original research contexts, and taken only in short term time periods.)

1.1.2 A new name for the main message

Well, that gives us another way to name the position that was reached about forty or fifty years ago and is the most important result of the sciences ever reached. Given that chemistry has been physicalized, and that biology has been physio-chemicalized, we have a nesting of the three basic natural sciences; we also have a mathematization of the one at the bottom, namely, physics. We could call the result 'the nesting of the basic natural sciences'. Alternatively, we could join the names of the three basic natural sciences so as to capture the nesting of them. That yields something like *phystriology*.[2]

---

[2] The 'phys' suggests 'physics'. The 'y' in 'chemistry' becomes an 'i'; that 'i' is both the transformed 'y' of chemistry, and the 'i' of 'biology'; and the 'b' of

Indeed 'phystriology' does suggest that the nesting occurs, and when we use 'phystriology' we assume that physics has been mathematized. Accordingly, we can, and will, take phystriology to be an 'ism.' Phystriology is the position or the viewpoint in which it is taken to be the case that (a) physics-studied changes are governed by mathematically expressed rules, laws, or forces, with no purposes inherently in the (small) parts of the changing things, and that (b) in all changes of natural objects, there is no overturning of the rules, laws, or forces of physics, as properly considered.

'Phystriology,' then, is the term to be used as a substitute for the terms currently in use: 'physical closure', 'closure of physics', 'physical completeness,' 'completeness of physics', 'physical causal completeness' and 'physical causal closure.' The use of 'phystriology' is good (i) for general consumption, (ii) to avoid unintentional problems and confusions, and (iii) to avoid use of the controversial and disputable notion of 'causes' in physics. Anyway, it doesn't matter what term is used; the meaning intended here is the same, a meaning that will be clearly set out in Chapter Ten.

1.1.3 Why the main message is so important

Part I of this book reviews the ancient inherently purposive properties picture, followed by a review of the three processes: the mathematization of physics, the physicalization of chemistry, and the physio-chemicalization of biology. This occupies us from Chapter Two to Chapter Nine. There are many details in these Chapters; some of them will not be needed for the general reader; but they are included anyhow, for greater comprehensiveness. Part I of this book also reviews why the development of phystriology – let's start using the term – is so important.

Chapter Ten summarizes the story of how the phystriology view developed, defines it more carefully than was done here, shows how the evidence supports it, and shows that phystriology requires that eight very commonly found views in religious or spiritual systems are, and must be, incorrect. These eight views are: that there is an interactive God at the human (or classical) scale, that there is a conscious afterlife, that there is a physics-overturning form of human freedom or responsibility, that there is a hidden moral system at work in the universe, that there are some

---

'biology' has been dropped, because it would sound odd if it were in. Many thanks to historian Eric Damer, who invented this term in conversation one day.

mentally produced (and not grossly physically produced) parapsychological or paranormal events, that there is a mystical ascent to a higher reality beyond the grossly physical realm, that interactive dualism obtains, and that emanationism obtains. (The 'jargon terms' at the end of the list will be explained as required.) These are the eight positions each of which is logically rejected by phystriology. That phystriology is *logically inconsistent* with those eight views, and not merely in interpretive tension or dissonance with them, is important. Some of the differences between logical inconsistency and interpretive dissonance will be explained.

It will also be shown that phystriology strongly ampliatively (that is, not-strictly-logically but compellingly) eliminates the personal God, a God whose notion is a bit broader than the interactive God at the human (or classical) scale, and eliminates the existence of any supernatural intelligence. This result, relying on various features within phystriology, happens to be a good deal stronger than the interpretive or non-logical arguments typically given against the existence of a personal God or a supernatural intelligence.

Part I will further show two things. First, as already suggested, Chapter Eleven will show how people sometimes try to get away from phystriology and how these methods for trying to get away from phystriology fall very far short of being able to do the job. In fact, I will take on the task of showing that the supposed objections to phystriology are but pseudo-objections. This will be done – at the general level – in Chapter Eleven, and – at a more scholarly level – in Appendix 2. Second, Chapter Twelve shows the other side of the story: within a view of the world that accepts phystriology there can be advocacies for various views that life has meaning. More particularly, within a view of the world that accepts phystriology, there are many ways to explain the arising of consciousness, the way mental states relate to physical states, the way human beings might be free, the way ethical determinations might legitimately occur, and the way life might have meaning.

One vital and mostly unexplored question facing our time is about the relation between phystriology on the one hand, and on the other hand, spirituality as is found in, or associated with, religions. In the old way of putting it, one vital and mostly unexplored question facing our time is about the relation between phystriology (that is, physical completeness) and religious belief. The subtitle of the book makes it clear that this is the book's topic, allowing for 'religious belief' to be interpreted as broadly as it can be interpreted. However one states the book's topic, we have now looked at the main challenge that science poses to spirituality.

It is important to see that the challenge posed by phystriology does not include the claim that the basic natural sciences from physics through to biology have answers to human problems; similarly, phystriology does not include the claim that physics-talk directly explains everything. There is no such view included within any adequate statement of the phystriology challenge. According to typical exponents of phystriology, to address the central problems of human concern we need to talk as broadly as it is possible to talk. This means that we need to talk in psychological language. (Similarly, to address problems in biology, we need to talk in biological language; to address problems in chemistry, we need to talk in chemistry language.) Saying that the laws, rules, forces, or whatever, of physics are not overturned does not say that we can avoid talking in psychological language (about suffering, hopes, meaning in life, transcendent states, non-transcendent states, and so on) when we are addressing matters of central human concern. Please notice that we are only talking about psychological *language*. We are not talking about staying within the academic discipline called *psychology*; the terms we use, the language we use, is not at all limited by the contents of the discipline called psychology. Perhaps, for both reasons just mentioned – we don't need to talk in physics language, and psychological language is as encompassing as can be – it is better to avoid distractions, and simply not say that there is a sense, direct, or indirect, in which physics explains everything. That more freely allows psychological *vocabulary* to be used as broadly as psychological vocabulary can be used.

But whatever we say in psychological language must be consistent with the results of phystriology. And that means that if we accept phystriology, then whatever we say (in psychological language) cannot tell us that there is an interactive God at the human scale, say, nor can it tell us that there is a conscious afterlife, nor a strong physics-overturning freedom, nor a cosmic moral karma, nor paranormal events as usually understood, etcetera. In fact, if we are to accept phystriology, we must be willing to say that there is no interactive God at the human scale, no conscious afterlife, no strong physics-overturning freedom, no cosmic morality, no paranormal events as usually understood, etcetera. Yet many people are reluctant to say that. *That* is one way of putting the challenge posed by the evidence for phystriology.

Another way of putting the challenge posed by the evidence for phystriology is to say that first, it requires us to make a sharp and reasoned choice between phystriology on the one hand, and, on the other hand, those eight theories that are logically inconsistent with phystriology; second, it requires us to make a reasoned choice between phystriology on the one hand, and, on the other hand, those theories, such as that the personal God exists, that are strongly, though not strictly logically, rejected by phystriology; and third, it requires us to relate the result of those choices to current expositions of religion or spirituality. Phystriology poses a logical choice to us, and a strong, though not strictly logical, choice. Both choices are important to face. Neither is a gentle interpretive choice that everyone can agree can go either way. And both choices require us to face current religious and spiritual systems to see what can be satisfactory, and what cannot be satisfactory in them.

The ideas being tracked in this book are worth going through. As usual, ideas that are worth going through can be gone through at many levels. Here, the pitch is for anyone at the post-secondary level with a touch of patience. That includes undergraduate students with no philosophy background, general readers, and scholars as well. True enough, a few portions of part I are a bit difficult. They will be marked as difficult (brief) sections, and these can be skipped, on first reading at least, or merely skimmed. The story unfolds clearly enough with or without the difficult parts.

Also, the very end of the book has two appendices whose level of presentation is for upper level undergraduates in philosophy or beyond.

1.2 Spirituality

About spirituality itself, there are four main background messages and two religious phenomena classifications.

1.2.1 The four background messages

The four background messages are: First, the term 'spirituality' is so wide as to have many different meanings; we go through some of these meanings; and, given reasons presented, for the rest of the book (excluding Chapter Twenty Three) 'spirituality' is to mean 'a specifically religious-ish condition.' It is also observed that the challenge posed by phystriology is as strong to exponents of moderate or pluralist religion or spirituality as it is to exponents of literalist or fundamentalist religion or spirituality. Second, it is *not* entirely correct to think that if you're spiritual then it must be that you make certain sorts of ethical determinations. Third, parapsychological claims often associated with spirituality are not backed by scientific evidence; the claims can be readily explained naturalistically; and the claims as typically understood go against phystriology, which is backed by scientific evidence; consequently, one should not accept the parapsychological claims. And, fourth, there are many forms of religious or spiritual systems that maintain that the highly developed religious or spiritual person can experience very strong levels of joy on an ongoing basis. These four background messages are useful for Part III where we seek to understand the relation between science and spirituality.

1.2.2 The two classes

Given these four background messages, we can classify groups of spiritual (specifically religious-ish) experiences and beliefs into two classes, which we will call the exoteric class, and the esoteric class. These classifications will be useful when it comes to understanding the relation between science and spirituality.

The exoteric class - the popular class – will be subdivided into five subgroups, and these experiences and beliefs will be found to be widespread among followers of religion or spirituality. In fact they are closely related to the first five of the eight views logically incompatible with phystriology. The subgroups are experiences apparently indicating that there is a God who interacts with nature presumptively at the human scale, that there is a conscious afterlife, that human freedom allows the human being to escape (and thereby overturn) the mathematical rules, laws, or forces of physics, that there is a reward/punishment system working through the cosmos, and that there are genuine mind-over-matter paranormal or parapsychological events.

The esoteric class is divided into three subgroups. These subgroups may be seen as occurring together, and their occurrence is much more rare within followers of religious-ish spirituality than are the exoteric experiences and beliefs. The esoteric subgroups are experiences indicating that there is a particular kind of mystical view of the world (a kind that will be explained in Chapter Eighteen), that the circulation of what is often described as a special sort of light can be experienced by the mystic, and that some people achieve a state of ongoing though contrastless joy or bliss.

By the end of Part II, we are ready to pose our central question for understanding the relation between science and spirituality. It is, "Given that science results in acceptance of phystriology, as is described in Part I, and given that physriology is logically and in other ways strongly inconsistent with many important positions central in religion and spirituality, as is also outlined in Part I, and where 'religion and spirituality' are understood as is outlined in Part II, how, if at all, can spirituality or religion be consistent with current science?" To answer this question we must figure out if we are to give up on religion or specifically religious-ish spirituality or, contrary-wise, if we are to find some way of integrating phystriology with religion or religious-ish spirituality or some aspects of religion or religious-ish spirituality. If we are to do the latter, we must discover *how* and *in what respects* it can be done.

1.3 Science and spirituality

In Part III, four answers to the central question, the question just raised, are considered.

1.3.1 The four answers to the central question

First, there is the simplest answer, which is to reject religion or specifically religion-ish spirituality in favor of the phystriological picture of the world. Several expositions of a closely related view are considered (including some early views, e.g., those of Bertrand Russell, and some more recent views, the views of Paul Kurtz, Daniel Dennett, and Richard Dawkins; none talk about phystriology explicitly, so in that sense these views are 'closely related' to the phystriological picture of the world; but that they are merely closely related is ignored; it is assumed that they would agree with, or do agree with, phystriology).

This view is then questioned on the ground that it might be leaving out something of value in religion or (specifically religion-ish) spirituality.

Second, there is the natural-scientific approach to religion or spirituality. This approach can be illustrated, in two forms, presented mainly in the 1980's and '90's. The natural-scientific approach to religion or spirituality states that one should accept the natural-scientific view (including the natural selection evolutionary view) and, either, one should draw religious benefit from such views and from associated features of human distinctiveness, or one should orient toward that which cannot be understood at all, while accepting the sciences' results for beliefs about the world. These two versions were given, respectively, by Ralph Burhoe (in the 1960's, '70's, and '80s), and by Willem Drees (e.g., in the 1990s).

I comment in three ways on the resulting system in either form: first, the intellectual system (in either form) works well with current science; second, the experiential focus favors development of emotions like awe, wonder, and a sense of mystery, and as such is not specifically religious, nor specifically associated with typical descriptions of spiritual experience; and, third, the narrative interpretive practices, rituals, and so on accompanying this approach require a lot of, and perhaps too much, jumping through hoops. The narratives and liturgy one finds associated with religions and forms of contemporary spirituality are so full of the eight views logically inconsistent with phystriology and other views not strictly logically but strongly inconsistent with phystriology that if one accepts phystriology, one will not be able to easily jump through enough hoops in reading from, or reciting from, such materials.

The third approach to the conflict between phystriology and religion/spirituality is very commonly found. I dub it the "It's all okay," approach. Those who *seek to* reconcile the scientific approach with the spiritual approach often take this approach. Yet, I comment, this approach has comparatively little (sometimes, effectively, nothing) to say in regard to how any reconciliation is to be accomplished. I will suggest that the members of this group don't manage to do what they set out to do. The main problem is that advocates of this approach are unaware of the central conflict between phystriology and many views offered in spirituality-promoting systems; illustrations will be given.

The fourth approach to the challenge posed by phystriology to religion or spirituality, which I call *mystical naturalism*, is the one I favor. It attempts to provide a specific method to reconcile religion or specifically religious-ish spirituality on the one hand with science including phystriology on the other hand. The mystical naturalist view takes it that phystriology has been established, that phystriology eliminates purposes from the *fundamental* or *basic* elements of reality, and that it eliminates many views usually found in religious or spirituality promoting systems, e.g., it eliminates the exoteric views. But mystical naturalism also maintains that there is an interpretation of the esoteric experiences and beliefs that is consistent with phystriology and is even intellectually supported by phystriology. Hence the specific mystical naturalist method of reconciling phystriology with religion or spirituality is to expand the natural-scientific approach so that it includes not only attitudes of awe, wonder and mystery toward the world, however the world is adequately described, but also a new interpretation of esoteric religion or spirituality. In this program, there are opportunities not only for revisioning religious institutions, but also for complementary revisioning of humanist institutions. All in all, in such programs there are opportunities for institutionally expressing spirituality, religion, and humanism in new ways.

1.3.2 The secular wisdom institute

Finally, in the last Chapter, Chapter Twenty Three, I will review how there is also an opportunity for a new sort of public expression of spirituality, where 'spirituality' is meant as broadly as it can be meant: a public entirely secular expression of current views, whatever they might be, traditional, or non-traditional, along with a set of practices that allow for the cultivation of spirituality, however interpreted. Such a cultivation of spirituality would be best led by philosophers in our universities and colleges. Why philosophers? For a variety of reasons, including this primary one: philosophers are well trained in the variety of views that people have. Accordingly, it is philosophers, and, for precautionary reasons, we should take it that it is only PhD holders in philosophy, who are already trained to welcome exponents of all viewpoints, including exponents of strong (ancient style) skepticism, proponents of atheism, proponents of agnosticism, proponents of theism, etc., into wisdom cultivating or fulfillment cultivating workshops.

Part I

Chapter Two: The Traditional Spiritual Picture: Ancient assumptions of physical *in*completeness

2.0 In Part I of the book we will *principally* look at the key events that happened in the last four hundred or so years in three basic natural sciences, namely, physics, chemistry, and biology. But to see them as key events we need to refresh ourselves on the views that developed much earlier. We will begin as early as is possible to begin.

In the whole of the ancient period (from pre-recorded history to 300 CE or so), as we'll shortly see from some examples, it was not at all unusual to adopt a position which asserted that purposes are, one way or another, *written into* reality, that purposes are fundamental elements of reality, or are, to put it shortly, *basic* in reality. In fact, not only was it not unusual, but rather, it was the standard position found more or less everywhere. But to think that purposes are basic requires that phystriology be false. This does not mean that people in the ancient period were aware of the positions as we might think of them now. They couldn't have been; the notions of physics, chemistry, and biology had not yet matured; such fields of research had hardly even begun. At the simplest level, the mathematization of physics was at most hinted at by a few thinkers in the ancient period. And there was no notion of chemistry till the end of the ancient period; and even 'chemistry', once it was independently thought of, had two main meanings (two main meanings, not two main theories): first between roughly 300 CE, say, and, perhaps, sometime in the 20th century, and second, using that date, from sometime in the 20th century and on. The two main meanings of chemistry will be reviewed in 8.12. For these reasons, the notion underlying phystriology was not referred to at all in the ancient period. But the phystriological picture emerged by the mid or late 20th century, and so we can now more easily see anti-phystriology[1] or physical *in*completeness in the ancient worldview than people, at that time, could have seen it then.

In this Chapter, we'll review three ancient physically incomplete systems, systems that think of purposes as basic elements of reality. We'll begin with a review of 'emanationism,' a view developed in human pre-recorded history, it seems, and, in any case, found throughout human cultures in the ancient (and in the modern) world. Then we'll look briefly at Plato's incompleteness view, and then, a bit more thoroughly, at Aristotle's elaborate physically incomplete system.

2.1 Emanationism

Let's imagine ourselves living, say, twenty thousand years ago. We can very plausibly assume that there was, at that time, a hearty language already in place. Thinkers speculate that natural languages developed some hundreds of thousands of years ago[2], so it is very unlikely that anything will go wrong by assuming that there was a hearty language in place twenty thousand years ago.

It also seems clear that we would have engaged in what's now called *inter-agency attribution*. A clear example of inter-agency attribution is in the following remark: "She's on top of the hill, looking this way and that way, because she's searching for her goat." It's 'inter-agency attribution' because (not thinking of the goat) there are two agents or do-ers, one of whom is talking, and the other, the one on the hill, is being talked about. Most questions and answers would also involve inter-agency attribution. For instance, if I asked you, "Are you hungry?" and you answered, say, "No, but I'm thirsty," then I would have assumed that not only am I an agent (a do-er) but also you are an agent (a do-er), and to be an agent includes having mental states.

It is easy to say why being an agent is to have mental states (and, you're right, having mental states, as the phrase is used here, has nothing to do with being insane). Typically, I can't act unless I have a desire, a

---

[1] 'Anti-phystriology' is any view that says that the world is 'physically incomplete'. 'Anti-phystriology' as a term sounds a bit heavy, so in future, for the most part I will just use the term 'physically incomplete' or a closely related term.

[2] This runs through Parts II and III of Christine Kenneally's *The First Word*, for instance.

belief, and an intention. For instance, if I'm thirsty, I'll want some drinkable water, (that's a desire); I'll think something like, "there's drinkable water in that stream over there behind the trees," (that's a belief); and I'll form a plan like, "I'll go to that stream and get some drinkable water," (and that's an intention). Of course, a desire, a belief, and an intention are mental states (or states of mind). Accordingly, to be an agent (a do-er) is to have mental states.

To give 'inter-agency' a sort of definition, we could say that to attribute agency to another is to ascribe to the other various mental states, the sorts of mental states that any do-er would have. It is to ascribe a belief, or a desire, or an intention, or something like that (it could be an emotion, it could be a hope), to another person. Any full-fledged language uses would be chock full of inter-agency attributive statements. And, incidentally, when we consider our individual language-learning abilities, we find that inter-agency attributions fill our language from our toddler phase, and on. At the age of about five, our inter-agency attributions improve a lot, too; we distinguish what one person believes from what another person believes based on our views of what each person had observed.

Human beings, then, twenty thousand years ago or so, would have very often used inter-agency attributive language. Built into inter-agency attributive language is the view that it is the mental states that hold various kinds of power. If one wants to understand what another person is doing, one wants to attribute various desires, beliefs, and intentions to the other person. Why, for example, is that person on that hill? Because that person has the desire to find her goat, has the belief that the way the goat went is visible from the hill, and has the intention of getting her goat back somehow once her goat is spotted.

Let's come back to the view built into agency-attributions: it is that mental states hold various kinds of power. Humans have various powers, and it is their mental states – their desires, their views of the facts, their intentions, their hopes, etcetera – that set their bodies in motion. Without the mental states of desires, views, intentions, hopes, etcetera, we wouldn't to be able to act.

It would have been entirely natural to attribute similar mental states to various animals. The wolves, moose, deer, sheep, goats, felines, etcetera, would also have been seen to have various mental states. There is nothing unnatural about this at all. In fact, we still attribute mental states to animals in an entirely natural fashion. For example, we might say that the dog is sniffing about, looking for food, or for water, or to find out what other animals have been in that region. Birds, too, can be thought of as having various mental states. I recall the story told to me by a woman who said she was out gardening when two crows were, she felt, cawing at her. Only after about a half hour of being cawed at did she discover an underage baby crow in the bushes. She put out her finger. The underage baby crow hobbled onto it, and the two adult crows stopped their cawing at her; they flew off. This seemed, strongly, to confirm her feeling that she was being cawed at. (Also, incidentally, she protected the underage baby crow.) Sometimes the attributions were presented in narratives, true or fictional – for example: "the raven spread its wings, thereby blocking out the sun."

Once inter-agency attribution includes humans and non-human animals, it becomes natural to include the plants as well. After all, plants lean toward the light; they send their roots toward the water. At least, so we put it. Accordingly, it is not unusual to attribute agency of sorts to plants: plants, we say, *want* the light or the water; it is as though they know that the light, say, is over *there*; hence they lean, *that way*, to the light. Similarly, they send roots out toward the streams.

(A brief but important digression for clarity: Nowadays if we say the plant wants the light, we say this more or less metaphorically. Biochemists have found out that there is a chemical all around the edge of many plants – as it happens, a chemical related to *auxin* hormones in the plant – that expands where there is less light, which means that the opposite side of the plant, the side of the plant receiving more light, is less expansive, and so there is a bending of any plant with that chemical all around its edges toward the light. Still, metaphorically, we can now say, "The plant wants the light." But a long time ago, we said that non-metaphorically. We thought, then, non-metaphorically, that plants *want* the light, though perhaps without a clear notion of what that 'want' means. Now we can return to the imaginary position in which we, as it were, are living twenty thousand years ago.)

Our inter-agency attributions are directed to humans, to (non-human) animals, and to plants. We are now ready for a bit of a leap. We take it that it is the mental states that have the powers. So we assume that if some strong natural event happens – such as an earthquake, a sudden storm, a sudden flood, an eclipse, or a comet flying across the night sky – it must be because of some being's mental states that that unusual natural event happened. If there is an eclipse, or a comet, or an earthquake, or a sudden flood, or the abrupt occurrence of a huge thunderstorm, we take it that it is some being's mental states that produced that eclipse or earthquake or sudden flood or thunderstorm. Thereby we talk about the hidden gods or deities or powers behind everything. It is the mental states – states thought of as inherently purposive states, or states thought of as being fundamental to the structure of reality – that are taken to be the ultimate sources of power. Of course, as it turns out under this picture of the world full of gods and so on, some of the supposedly mental beings are seen only through their effects, like earthquakes, floods, and eclipses.[3]

The picture that results is that there are various levels of powers: there are the natural powers at various degrees, which we think of as their 'height'. Perhaps there is a higher power still, from which these natural powers result. Such a highest power can be thought of as a non-physical Spirit or, alternatively, as a Being of some highly subtle sort, or the one supreme God. Everything somehow comes from it; in this view, the deities, the high natural powers, perhaps the messengers or angels, or high spirits also come from it. Perhaps there are demons as well. And there would be ghosts or something like ghosts. After all, it would have been thought, the mental states have the powers, and when a person dies, the body is buried; but what happens to the mental states that have the powers? They must go somewhere, so there is an afterlife of sorts, and the mental states are the ghosts. Or the mental states go into a fetus in development, and there is reincarnation or rebirth. Also, of course, there would be humans, (non-human) animals, plants, and the rest, all, one way or another, created by, or emanations of, the gods or God – stones, rivers, mountains, and so on. The heavenly objects, too – including stars, the sun, the moon and wanderers in the skies – might well be regarded as embodiments or expressions of some very high powers. As embodiments or expressions of some very high powers, the earthly and the heavenly things are regarded as emanations, hence the term 'emanationism.'[4]

---

[3] Notice how different the explanation given here for the prevalent ancient belief in gods or a highest God is from some other explanations that have been offered. Compare this explanation with, for example, that of Sigmund Freud in *The Future of An Illusion*, where he took it that such beliefs were the products of fear of death or desire for parental protection under conditions of ambivalence about parental powers.

[4] For most readers, this note is irrelevant. This note is only for a reader who has come across the term 'emanationism' in other special contexts. 'Emanationism' is often used more specifically to refer to what is called neo-Platonism, which

From our point of view today what we particularly want to notice is that the emanationist picture is suffused with the idea that there are some purposes *inherently*, or *fundamentally*, or *basically*, in the natural order. This feature of emanationism is enough to make it a physically incomplete view of the world. The physical incompleteness arises from the fact that there are supposed to be fundamental causal relations between any two examples of any two sorts of emanating things. For instance, there are supposed to be minds fundamentally causing bodily changes, and bodily changes fundamentally causing mental changes. The minds might be understood as non-physical things, or they might be understood as very subtle physical things. The bodily things might be understood as non-mental things or as very subtle mental things. However these things are regarded, the emanationist picture is, from the contemporary point of view, a physically incomplete picture.[5]

2.2 Plato's Socrates

We'll now skip forward many thousands of years to see how an early great philosopher, Plato (c. 428-347 BCE), adopted what we'd now say was a physically incomplete view of the world. The illustration of Plato's view is taken from a passage towards the end of his dialogue *Phaedo*. *Phaedo* is about Socrates in prison in 399 BCE just before taking the poisonous hemlock that executed him. *Phaedo* is a multi-character piece, narrated by Phaedo. The contents feature the figures of Socrates, Appolodorus, Cebes, Simmias, and Criton. The words in *Phaedo* that we'll be looking at are given as Socrates' words. Socrates was an elder when

---

was developed by Plotinus about six hundred years after the career of Plato. Neo-Platonic emanationism is but one kind of emanationism as 'emanationism' is being used here.

[5] Can you explain how emanationism is, from a contemporary point of view, a physically incomplete picture? On first exposure to the idea of our world being phystriological, it is probably a difficult question to answer. If so, take modern physics to be mathematized, and pay attention to the term 'fundamental' in the above passage. In mathematized physics, the causes would be expressed in mathematical formulas; also, *A fundamentally* causes a change in *B* if and only if that change in *B* wouldn't occur unless *A* or something similar to *A* (and necessarily at the same complexity level as A and so not a mere sum of micro-things) produced it. If taking physics to be mathematical and paying attention to the term 'fundamental' don't work, reading more material in this Chapter and the next Chapter(s) might.

Plato was a learner, and Plato wrote many dialogues that feature Socrates as the central figure; but it is likely that a lot of what is given to Socrates in *Phaedo* is Plato's own thought. The scholarship yields no clear result on how much is Plato's material, and how much is Socrates's material. But that doesn't matter to us. We will just take the material as Plato's representation of Socrates.

Here is the main content of this part of Socrates' views according to Plato. Socrates said that it would be absurd to think that the cause of his physical position – his sitting on the bed – was *nothing but* the activities of the things in his body. The real cause of his position (the fundamental cause), Socrates said, was his mind, and his mind, according to his view as depicted by Plato, was not his body. Here are what are supposed to be Socrates's words, while sitting in prison, waiting to be put to death for (supposedly) corrupting the youth and disbelieving in the gods, for which he was found guilty. Socrates is commenting about reading Anaxagoras' theories of things:

> Oh, what a wonderful hope! How high I soared, how low I fell! When as I went on reading I saw the man [Anaxagoras] using mind not at all; and stating no valid causes of the arrangement of all things but giving airs and ethers and waters as causes, and many other strange things. I felt very much as I should feel if someone said, 'Socrates does by mind all he does'; and then, trying to tell the causes of each thing I do, if he should say first that the reason why I sit here now is, that my body consists of bones and sinews, and the bones are hard and have joints between them, and the sinews can be tightened and slackened, surrounding the bones along with flesh and the skin which holds them together; so when the bones are uplifted in their sockets, the sinews slackening and tightening make me able to bend my limbs now, and for this cause I have bent together and sit here; and if next he should give you other such causes of my conversing with you, alleging as causes voices and airs and hearings and a thousand others like that, and neglecting to give the real causes. These are that since the Athenians thought it was better to condemn me, for this very reason I have thought it better to sit here, and more just to remain and submit to any sentence they may give. For, by the Dog! these bones and sinews, I think would have been somewhere near Megara or Boeotia long ago, carried there by an opinion of what is best, if I had not

believed it better and more just to submit to any sentence which my city gives than to take to my heels and run.[6]

Accordingly, as it would very likely be put now, Socrates in *Phaedo* was an advocate of the idea that, somehow, the non-physical mind fundamentally causes changes in the physical system. This goes against the contemporary view that no elements of nature overturn the rules whereby (inherently purposeless) physics-things are governed, and so Socrates (as depicted by Plato) was an exponent of what we now think of as physical *in*completeness. Another way to put this is to say that Socrates thought he had purposes in staying – to be just and to accept the verdict ('guilty') and its consequences. Socrates, then, took purposes to be basic features of mental states, and he took mental states to be basic in nature. Accordingly, he took purposes to be basic in nature. And phystriology, as we will see, takes purposes not to be basic in nature. So, Socrates's position was a position advocating physical *in*completeness.

Although there was a frequent assumption of physical incompleteness in the ancient period, it was Aristotle who gave physical incompleteness a wonderfully elaborate systematic form. Aristotle (384-322 BCE) began as a student of Plato, but later differed from Plato in many crucial matters, and, in fact, he started his own philosophical school, called the *Lyceum*, as opposed to Plato's *Academy*.

2.3 Aristotle's system in physics

Aristotle's system in physics fits into Aristotle's general system, in which to understand anything one needs to understand it from four points of view. These points of view are called the four 'causes'. The term 'cause' here is very close to our term 'analysis.' Aristotle's four types of cause, then, are Aristotle's four types of analysis. These are, first, the efficient cause, second, the material cause, third, the formal cause, and fourth, the final cause. The efficient cause is the triggering cause, the cause that gets the change going – for instance, the decision of a sculptor to scrape, say, that block of marble, so that block of marble will become, gradually, a sculpture, and the initial implementing of that decision, by moving, tools in hand, to that block of marble. The material cause is the analysis of the matter in the things that are changing, for instance, the marble in the block. The formal cause is the analysis of the form in the matter. This

---

[6] *Phaedo*, 98b-99b, translated by W. H. D. Rouse.

includes the highly abstract formal properties as are given in mathematical descriptions including geometrical descriptions. It is hard for us now to understand what was specifically meant by such phrases as 'the form in the matter'; Aristotle described the properties the form would have to have (in the sculptor, for instance) to produce the sorts of results that seemed to be produced. And the final cause, or the purposive cause, is the purpose that the change is endeavoring to accomplish, for instance, the purpose a sculptor has in regard to producing the sculpture being produced.

That Aristotle's system for analysis of matters in physics was, putting it in the contemporary jargon, physically incomplete, is given in the way – the fundamental way – there are *final* causes (purposive causes) whose effects are brought about through what Aristotle took to be the formal properties of the material objects. Our focus is on understanding what we can now describe as Aristotle's physical *in*completeness, and it is the fundamentality of the purposive final causes that renders the system physically incomplete, and not consistent with the results of the last four hundred years of natural scientific work.

Aristotle's views on physics were rejected hundreds of years ago for various reasons. Often these reasons were preliminary versions of the idea that there are no basic purposes in nature; but we are not here interested in the reasons why Aristotle's physics was rejected a few hundred years ago. The point being made here is simply that although almost everything in Aristotle's physics is now rejected, it is worthwhile understanding this enormously inventive and powerful system.

Let us look at the harmony between the four kinds of Aristotelian causes in any change. The efficient cause gets the change going; the material cause is what the change is going through; the formal cause describes the formal specifics of the change (and in Aristotle's time, the formal properties would include geometrical shapes and the capacities to generate various functions, but would not be anything like the highly complex mathematically governed systems as they are now); and the purposive cause is the purpose that the change is meant to bring about. All four causes feature in producing the resulting motions or changes or developments; in Aristotle's system, the final or purposive cause is an essential element in the understanding of change. The purposes are, in this way, 'written into,' or are basic in, or fundamental in, the structures of things.

According to many interpretations of Aristotle's system in physics, Aristotle's physics was physically incomplete on the grounds that Aristotle held that active intellect – the feature of the human intellect that renders what is potentially available actually present – is immaterial and causally interacts with the material.[7] More interesting, though, and less interpretively controversial, is to see how cases of physical motions with no intervention of an immaterial cause, in Aristotle's view, put purposes right into all natural material events. Aristotle's views in physics are no longer held today, but his synthesis was profoundly inventive and comprehensive.

To explain: Aristotle thought of the earth as at the absolute center of the (finite) cosmos bounded by the distant stars. In his view, there is a sharp difference between the region below the moon, the sub-lunar realm, and a region at and beyond the moon, the super-lunar realm. Aristotle took it that motions beneath the moon are based on straight line motions. Motions of the moon and all that is on the other side of the moon are, Aristotle thought, circular motions. Aristotle took it, then, that the sun, and all the other heavenly objects turn in circles about our earth, our earth being at the absolute centre of the universe.[8]

Below the moon, said Aristotle, there are some self-moving things and some things – stones, for example – that only move through external interactions. The self-moving feature of non-human animals and humans is regarded as an essential feature of those organisms. (More technically, Aristotle took it that it is the first grade of their actuality, still a dispositional quality, but one that belongs only to all representative or healthy members of its group, and that specially yields the essential nature of the individuals; and the first grade of the actuality of animals and humans enables the animals and humans to move about in search of food, and so on.[9])

Aristotle also maintained that it is the wet/dry, hot/cold contrasts that are the bases of what he took to be the sub-lunar elements, namely, earth, air, water, and fire. It's easy to guess what Aristotle said here. Try it if you like. Very probably you'll figure out Aristotle's

---

[7] The interpretations are of *On the Soul* III: 5.

[8] Aristotle, *De Caelo* I: 7; I: 9, II: 14; V: 3; I: 2. See also, S. Sambursky, 1956: 86-88.

[9] Aristotle, *On The Soul*, II: 1. The second grade of actuality would be a property belonging to one particular or example of the group, but not another.

formulas: Cold + dry = earth; cold + wet = water; hot + wet = air; hot + dry = fire.[10]

Once Aristotle had the (somehow combinatory) earthy, airy, watery and fiery material things, he was able to show how, in his view, purposes govern the motions of all things on and around earth. He took it that purposes govern the motions of self-moving animals including humans. There were purposes also in plants – for instance, their purpose, when seedlings, to grow. And also, he said, all fiery and airy things, or, more generally, all hot things – including smoke and steam – move up from the earth, whereas earthy and watery things, or, more generally, all cold things – including stones and water – move down to the earth. The purposive reason is that each of them, as it were, wants to be where its nature is to be most fully found. In Aristotle's system, the central region for 'cold' is at the center of the earth.[11] So any cold thing, any water or any earthy thing, if not blocked, heads to the centre of the earth. Aristotle postulated that the central region of airiness is just below the central sub-lunar region for fieriness, and so airy things and fiery things rise away from the centre of the earth. As for the heavenly objects, Aristotle regarded them as self-moving objects whose movements were in a perfectly circular form. This, too, expressed, their deepest nature, whereby they expressed perfection.[12]

2.4 Aristotle's hierarchy of forms

Aristotle expressed his philosophy in many treatises composed, apparently, at different times; consequently, there are many systematizations of aspects of his philosophy. Here is one systematization about Aristotle's hierarchy of forms:

Aristotle took it that forms are found in the material world. In Aristotle's view, matter is spread throughout space, so, as Aristotle saw it, there is no vacuum. For this reason, he disagreed with the ancient Greek atomists. (The ancient Greek atomists, including Democritus, c. 460 – c. 370, held that there are invisibly tiny indivisible things, atoms; the atomists thought that the atoms move through a vacuum or empty space, and stick onto each other so as to make bigger things, such as the things

---

[10] Aristotle, *On Generation and Corruption* II: 3. See also, S. Sambursky, 1956: 91.

[11] Aristotle, *De Caelo*, I: 2; IV: 2, 3. See also, S. Sambursky, 1956: 93-4.

[12] Aristotle, *De Caelo*, *passim*.

we ordinarily perceive.[13]) According to Aristotle, the form of a material being indicates its fundamental nature. The form is not only the shape of the thing, but also indicates the key properties of the thing.

For Aristotle, the form of a stone somehow indicates that it is a cold dry thing. Of those two features, the coldness was taken to be more purposively central, so the stone heads to what Aristotle thought was the central point of coldness in the universe, the centre of the earth.

Aristotle took it that it is the form of a plant that yields the vegetative growth properties of a plant.

The form of a (non-human) animal yields not only its being earthy and watery, and not only its growth properties, but also its self-moving appetitive nature.

And, finally, the form of a human being yields its being earthy-watery, its vegetative growing, its having a self-moving appetite, and also its being rational.

One way or another, Aristotle took it that there is a hierarchy related to the inherently purposive formal properties of things. Aristotle's physical incompleteness, then – his basic purposes being realized through the activity specified in forms – was very centrally a part of his view of nature.

2.5 Some special features of Aristotle's incomplete system in physics

Aristotle's overall scheme in physics was clever, inventive, powerful and deep, even though it turned out many centuries later to be entirely wrong in almost all of the main points. (Aristotle fit his scheme in physics into a much broader scheme; it is only his scheme in the study of nature or physics that was deeply rejected hundreds of years ago; the elements in his non-physical thinking remain as subjects of important philosophical conversation now.)

Interestingly, Aristotle maintained that a heavy earthy object falls faster than a not-so-heavy earthy object toward the earth.[14] And

---

[13] Of course what we now think of as an atom is divisible; in one way of looking at an atom, an atom is made up, primarily, of protons, neutrons, and electrons; so the Greek concept of 'atom' is very different from our current concept of 'atom'. More on this in Chapter Eight.

Aristotle's theory that things head to their nature's main location works well with Aristotle's denial of a vacuum. According to Aristotle, an earthy thing let go in the air – for example, a pen let go in the air – needs to move to the earth (or the floor of the room) since that's closer to where its nature lies. However, if there is a vacuum between material things, then it cannot be indicated to the pen, or cannot be available to the pen, which way to go to be closer to the center of the earth. This may be regarded as one reason Aristotle took it that there is no vacuum between extended material objects.[15]

2.6 Summing Aristotle's incompleteness

In sum, Aristotle's physical theory was the outcome of a remarkable synthesis of many factors. Aristotle's theory, including its variants in Aristotelianism beginning later than Aristotle's lifetime, was the predominant theory of nature for about eighteen or nineteen hundred years in Europe and the Middle East, more or less until the 17th century. It was suffused with the idea that there are *inherent* purposes in the natural order. These purposes are shown in the final or purposive causes to be seen in all changes, and in the realization of the purposive drive in things through the forms that explain the difference for Aristotle between inanimate objects, plants, (non-human) animals, and humans. Aristotle also explained the purpose of everything through the first Cause, or God. In both ways purposes were taken to be basic in the inherent structure of the world, and so Aristotle's system was very much a physically incomplete system based on purposive properties in forms governing the movement from the potential to the actual.

2.7 Aristotle and Aristotelianism

Aristotle's system took deep root in the ancient world. Some of the astronomical views that Aristotle propounded, though, did not accurately

---

[14] Aristotle, *De Caelo*, IV: 4. See also, S. Sambursky, 1956: 94.

[15] See Aristotle's *Physics*, BK IV: Ch's 8, 9. Historians of ideas may say that this can be interpreted as a consequence that follows from integrating the localism of Aristotle's theory of motions on earth (aside from what Aristotle regarded as the instantaneous speed of light) and his theory of the final causes of the motions of heavy and not heavy (or light) things. For the localism, see, e.g., *Physics* VII: 5.

match observations of the skies. Accordingly, some views in Aristotle's astronomical system were modified somewhat, and the new astronomical system became known as Aristotelian astronomy.

Here is the central reason there was a shift from Aristotle's astronomy to Aristotel*ian* astronomy. According to Aristotle, things at and beyond the moon move in perfectly circular motions around the earth. But this view did not match astronomical observations.

By judgments, day to day, of successive positions of heavenly objects in the night sky, there are *some* objects that, for many days, are moving one way, and, afterwards, again for many days, are moving in the opposite way. Then they return to moving the first way. These were called 'the wanderers' or 'planets'. The explanations of the motions of the wanderers or planets couldn't be done by thinking of them as moving in perfect circles around the earth. Aristotle's system needed to be revised.

Apollonius of Perga (c. 262 – 190 BCE) and Hipparchus of Nicea (c. 190 – 120 BCE) were two of the thinkers who made such revisions to Aristotle's system. The key idea was that the planetary wanderers were moving on a perfect circle about the earth, but they were also moving in a circle about the basic perfect circle. The little circular motion on the big circular motion would account for the motions one way and then the other way in the sky. This system, with circles on circles, called 'epicycles on deferents', became known as the Aristotelian astronomical system.

The Aristotelian astronomical system was greatly developed by various astronomers, including Ptolemy (90 -168 CE). In these developments there were more than epicycles on deferents about the earth. (The centre of the deferent was not the centre of the earth.) Given the importance of Ptolemy's work, this tends to be known as the Ptolemaic astronomical system. The Ptolemaic astronomical system is also embedded within the Aristotelian picture; in the Ptolemaic system, too, there are purposes in all natural changes. Of course, the Aristotelian astronomical picture, including the Ptolemaic astronomical picture, was deeply questioned in the 16th and 17th centuries, and, since the late 17th century, has been rejected. We will overview the reasons leading to its rejection in the next two Chapters.

Chapter Three: The Mathematization of Physics: Basic ideas

3.0 It was a long time from 300 CE – the time we arbitrarily mark as the end of the ancient world – till the 16th and 17th centuries – thirteen hundred years or so. In 3.1 through 3.4 we'll review some mathematical physics in the last centuries of the ancient world; then we will skip forward to the more recent period. We'll do so partly because the Aristotelian view of the natural world persisted through those many centuries, and partly because the key novelties in physics, chemistry and biology tended to appear beginning in the 17th century.

All historians of the scientific ideas of the last few hundred years would agree that from the 17th century and on physics has been increasingly mathematized. Also, they would agree that from the 17th century and on, chemistry has been increasingly physicalized, and biology has been increasingly physio-chemicalized. Even if the point has not been put this way, once it is put this way, the point, suitably interpreted, is not controversial. The notion of the increasing mathematization of physics is fundamental, and is, in some respects, a touch more conceptually intricate than the increasing physicalization of chemistry and the increasing physio-chemicalization of biology. So here we'll explore some of the basic features of this notion, the mathematization of physics. (In Chapters Four through Seven we'll go through the many details of the mathematization of physics process itself. In Chapter Eight we'll review the development of the physicalization of chemistry process, and in Chapter Nine, the physio-chemicalization, of biology. There is no need for an introductory chapter for those latter two processes.)

The key ideas in the process whereby physics was mathematized are, first, that physical changes (changes in physics) and physical relations (relations in physics) can be best described in mathematical terms, and, second, that when one does so, one does not have purposes written into the changes nor the relations. This can be put in a way that contrasts the modern view, including work done in the late 17th century or so, and onward, with the Aristotelian view. As we saw, in the Aristotelian view, there were the four causes, including the final or purposive cause. But once the mathematical descriptions are given, there is only the efficient cause, plus the material cause and plus the formal[16] cause. The final or purposive cause simply drops away; and, unlike the Aristotelian system, no inherent purposes were written into the formal causes.

3.1 Some of the great ancient thinkers had wonderful insights into the mathematical properties of physical relations. To show this, we will look at the productive insights into the mathematical properties of physical relations as are found in some work of Archimedes, Eratosthenes, and Aristarchus. However, there were also non-productive uses of mathematical structures in thinking about things. An illustration of a non-productive use of mathematical structures can be found in Anaximander's view on the reason – as he would have put it, incorrectly, as it turned out – explaining why the earth stays, he thought, at the centre of the universe. According to Aristotle[17], Anaximander (fl. c. 550 BCE) took it that it is the indifference of the position of the earth in relation to all the edges of the cosmos that accounts for what he thought to be the permanence of the position of the earth at the absolute centre of the universe. Anaximander, then, used what we call *symmetry*, a certain kind of mathematical property[18], to explain what he thought to be true (that the earth is at the absolute centre of the universe), but, we would say, isn't true. Perhaps Aristotle, too, used symmetry non-productively, when he postulated that the heavenly objects all move in perfect circles around the earth. Undoubtedly, Aristotle thought of circles as perfect in part because of their wonderfully symmetrical properties. Yet it turned out *not* to be objectively true that there are heavenly objects whose nature leads them to move about in perfect circles.

---

[16] In contemporary work, the material and formal analyses aren't independent by any means; it is often difficult to tell the difference between the two. And, for the careful thinker, as it will turn out, the efficient cause, too, is, one way or another, a sum of things formally/materially described.

[17] Aristotle, *De Caelo*, 295b 10.

[18] For an explanation of what a mathematical symmetry is, see 6.4.

Others, though, used symmetry more productively. For example, Archimedes (287 BCE- 212 BCE) is famous for having figured out how much buoyancy a solid object has when placed in a liquid. In fact, so excited was he when he discovered some fundamental relationships, perhaps indicating buoyancy, while being in a public bath in his home town of Syracuse, that, it is said, he immediately jumped out of the bath, and ran – naked, according to the story – shouting throughout the city, "Eureka! Eureka!" ("I have found it! I have found it!")

What did he discover? The story told is that King Hiero of Syracuse ordered a laurel crown to be made from a block of gold given to a craftsman. The crown was made, but then a rumor reported that the craftsman had kept some of the gold and had replaced it by something else, for example, silver. The king asked Archimedes, a famous mathematician, to figure out whether the crown was pure gold or not. It was known that a mixture of gold with, say, silver, that weighed the same as a given block of gold would have a different volume from the block of gold. Archimedes had to figure out if the crown was pure gold or gold mixed with another metal without melting the crown down to a block to see if the size was different from the size of the block given to the craftsman. The size of the original block can be figured out because the weight of the original block was known, and a block of the same weight of gold would have a specified size. But the crown, it seems, wouldn't have been easily melted down to see what sort of size the block of its material would have, because, presumably, the king sometimes used the crown and at other times was keeping it in a safe place.

It seems that in the bath, Archimedes hypothesized that the amount of buoyancy (or upward force) on an object in water is equal to the weight of the water displaced by the object. If the weight is evenly distributed in the object in the water, then, if the weight of the water displaced by an object is less than the weight of the object, then the object sinks; if greater, then the object floats. It seems that water displacements also, independently, provided the solution to the problem of how to figure out if the crown was pure gold or not. Buoyancy, or upward force, is not itself involved. All that counts is the volume and weight of the block of gold given to the craftsman from which to make the crown, a weight that was known.

If the crown were to be put entirely into a body of water, the displaced water would show the volume of the crown. Then a block of gold weighing exactly what the block of gold given to the craftsman weighed could be put into some water. If the volume of water displaced by the crown were not the same as the volume of water displaced by the block of gold, there was some real trouble: the crown-maker had not made a crown just out of the gold. No metal was more valuable than gold, so the craftsman would have been guilty. If the volume of water displaced by the crown were equal to the volume of water displaced by the block of gold, then the volume of the crown was equal to the volume of the gold block. Very likely, the craftsman had used only the gold. And the issue can be determined. Suppose the volume of the crown equaled the volume of the gold block. Then if the weight of the crown equaled the weight of the gold block, there was equal density; that led to the conclusion that the crown was made only out of gold. If the weight of the crown didn't equal the weight of the gold block, but its volume did equal the volume of the gold block, then there was a different density, and this would indicate a different metal was used. (As the story is told, the craftsman was guilty.)

What Archimedes' discovery showed was that there is a way in which volume, weight, and density of *one* system – has implications for volume, weight, and density of another system.

Archimedes solved the king's problem at the same time, it seems, that he also, perhaps, in some sense, independently, discovered a fundamentally interesting theory: that the upward lift on an object placed in a liquid like water would be equal, but opposite-in-direction, to the weight of the liquid displaced by the object in the liquid. Perhaps it was not only Archimedes' discovery of how to solve the king's problem, but also it was how that discovery was associated with a deeply interesting truth about buoyancy – a symmetry in nature – that so excited Archimedes. And, even without a direct interest in the metal making the crown, we can share some of the excitement as well. After all, there is a beautiful symmetry in the notion that the upward force on an object in water is equal to the weight (a downward force) of the displaced water.

Archimedes has been famous for many profound discoveries. In this case, it was his insight into simple mathematical relations that enabled him to realize how to solve the king's problem; and, it seems, it was in the process of making that discovery that he hypothesized a profound symmetrical relation between the buoyancy of an object and the weight of the liquid displaced by an object in that liquid.

3.2 This was not the only instance of productive mathematizing of physical relationships that were employed in the ancient world. Far from it. In a way, every complicated building that was built employed some mathematical relations. Certainly, the formal or informal calculation of stress factors when building overhangs, bridges, arches, roofed colonnades, and so on employed or relied on mathematical notions. In fact, any agile child's running to catch a thrown ball deploys sophisticated mathematical notions, but it's entirely at the subconscious level that the calculations – or something like calculations – are done.

Similarly, to build a circular pool or circular well involved using some sophisticated mathematics. For instance, it seems as though the authors of the Biblical text Kings I: 7: 23 took the ratio of a circle's circumference to the diameter to be 3 to 1, which was a bit rough (the correct amount being 3.14159…etc.). Even if the ratio had been rough, it would still have been a step in the mathematizing of physical relationships.

In any case, as building projects, and many other projects, were undertaken, the use of mathematical truths became important in completing the projects.

3.3 Mathematical truths were also used in ancient astronomical calculations. For example, one ancient thinker, Eratosthenes (ca. 276-194 BCE), used relatively simple mathematical relations to discover the size of the earth. His method was to use two places on earth, one a good distance (more or less) due south of the other. The two places he selected were Alexandria (where he lived) and Syene, also an Egyptian city, but a fair distance (mostly) due south of Alexandria. He took the sun to be so far away from the earth that the sun's light rays could be regarded as effectively parallel to each other. Yet of course the angles of the rays to vertical posts from the earth at different spots on the earth would be different, due to the curvature of the earth.[19]

If the sun at noon were entirely overhead at Syene, then a ray from the sun would aim directly toward the centre of the earth. The angle

---

[19] That the earth is, at least roughly, globular was known to many at this time. The evidence was as follows: a person at the seashore might see only the top sails of a boat out on the sea, whereas a person high on a cliff over the sea could see the whole above-water boat. Also, it was speculated that an eclipse of the moon is caused by the earth's blocking the light from the sun onto the moon; but the shape of the earth's shadow was then seen on the moon, and it seemed to be circular in edge.

of a ray to Alexandria at noon to a pole straight up in Alexandria, given as the angle between the straight line from the top of the shadow off the pole to the top of the pole and the line from the bottom of the pole to the top of the pole, would equal the angle between a radius from the centre of the earth to Alexandria and a radius from the centre of the earth to Syene. (Once again, the sun is so far away that its rays to the earth can be taken to be parallel; and it is assumed that at some point in the day, the sun is directly overhead at Syene.) Let's call that angle *a*. Then the distance from Alexandria to Syene (which we'll call *d*) would be enough to indicate the size of the circumference of the earth, assumed to be a globe. The ratio of *a* over 360° – the amount yielding a full circle – would equal *d* over the circumference of the earth. Simple mathematics yields that *C*, the circumference of the earth = (360 *d*)/*a*. Thereby, too, the radius of the earth would be indicated, since it was known that for any circle, $C = 2\pi r$.

Eratosthenes's results are regarded as being close to the current measurements. The question of how close is unclear, though, because the exact ratio of his units of measurements (*stadia*) to contemporary units of measurements is not entirely well known. Nonetheless, it will be agreed that Eratosthenes' results were remarkably good, given the roughness of his abilities to make measurements, e.g., of whether Syene was exactly due South of Alexandria (which it was not, not quite).

3.4 By other mathematical means, Aristarchus (ca. 310 - 250 BCE) provided calculations of the distance of the earth to the sun, the size of the sun, and other astronomical features as well, including the proportion of the earth's distance to the moon in relation to the earth's distance to the sun. It is his calculation of this proportion that we will briefly look at. Aristarchus' calculation of this proportion, it seems, did not yield as good results as did Eratosthenes' calculations about the circumference and the radius of the earth. Aristarchus' mathematical conceptions were excellent; it was just the initial measurement results that were too inaccurate to allow the overall conclusions to come close to current conclusions.

His reasoning about the proportional distance of the earth to the sun in relation to the distance of the earth to the moon is easy to state. When the moon is exactly half lit by the sun (and the line dividing the light and the dark on the moon is straight and points to the earth) the angle between the line from the moon to the earth and the line from the moon to the sun is 90°. If one measures the angle between the line from the earth to the moon and the line between the earth to the sun, one then knows two out of three angles of the triangle between the earth, the moon, and the sun. And that is enough to yield the construction of such a triangle. The three angles add up to 180° and so all three angles will be known. That yields the sides of a triangle. Alternatively, given one angle and a second angle, one can simply construct a triangle by straight line extension until the three sides of a triangle are found. Either way, for any two triangles that have the same angles, the proportions of their sides will be respectively the same. Hence the proportion of the distance from the earth to the moon and the earth to the sun can be derived.

Aristarchus's measurement, however, was a bit off. The angle he measured between the line from the earth to the moon and the line from the earth to the sun was a few degrees off (roughly 2° below 89°), but those few degrees made a difference in proportions on the triangle to a factor of about twenty. Try it out and you'll quickly see why. Both 87° and 89° are close to 90°; the other angle is 90°; two lines at 90° from one line would be parallel (in a flat space, but we will ignore that feature); and so small inaccuracies of angle make an enormous difference in the length of the one line until the intersection with the other line.

3.5 In the ancient world, basic mathematical relations were used to discover important facts about physical phenomena. It was only later, mostly in the 17th century and afterwards, that there was a great enlargement of the use of mathematical notions in defining physical phenomena. One way to think of this is to take it that prior to the 17th century, it was thought that, perhaps, one didn't need the mathematical relations to describe changes in perceived objects because purposes did the job. For example, according to Aristotle, rocks fall to get to the centre of the earth, since rocks, it was thought, are earthy and earthy things are cold dry things and so, in some sense, earthy things want to get to the centre or main region of their nature, the place at the centre of coldness, which, Aristotle, thought, was the centre of the earth.

From the 17th century and on, the explanation of changes in natural objects was increasingly given through the mathematical relations of the tiny parts of these large scale objects and their sums. This switch, abandoning final or purposive causes, while using complex mathematics, constitutes the mathematization of physics. Physical motions and equilibria or balances in natural objects were not only seen as governed by mathematical relations, as they often had been since ancient times, but also these mathematical relations, came to be seen as lacking any intrinsic or inherent purposes built into them.

That there were no intrinsic purposes in the mathematical relations in basic physical interactions (beginning in the late 17th century, in the inanimate world at least) is the first of the three developments that together result in phystriology. Perhaps this is enough of an explanation of the basics of the mathematization of physics. But there is one other set of distinctions that may be useful to some, though not all, students of this phenomenon. To see how the mathematization of physics arose, we will look at the notion of mechanism, and some of the various theoretical senses of mechanism that developed from the 17th century and on. The material that follows in this Chapter will require some careful reading, but some readers will find it useful to have gone through this material in the long run. Others, who want to follow just the main lines of the story, can skim the rest of Chapter Three and continue at the beginning of Chapter Four.

3.6 The notions of 'mechanism' and 'mechanics'

In the history of what is called natural philosophy, or viewpoints on natural events, there have been many mechanical theories. A mechanics is a theory of mechanism, but, as will be reviewed again in 11.4, 'mechanism' and 'mechanics' are slippery terms. They have many meanings. The broadest meaning of 'mechanics' is any theory of motions and equilibria.[20] Its most general effective meaning is any theory of motions and changes that sees the things changing as one sees a machine in its changing conditions; the principles governing changes include no inherent purposes. Here, we'll note three of the various mechanist theories of the 17th century and afterwards: (a) billiard-ball mechanism, (b) a slightly broader material substance based mechanism, in which all events in spacetime (including apparent action at a distance ones) are entirely governed by Newton's three laws of motion – which laws will be

---

[20] This is, effectively, the definition given 'mechanics' in Ernst Mach, *The Science of Mechanics*: 1. Here is another broad notion, but this time it is of the notion of 'mechanism': any theory of natural change that employs only the first three of Aristotle's four causes or analyses, namely efficient cause, material cause, and formal cause. (This is a rough version of our third sense of mechanism, the (c) sense, as mentioned below.) Still another basic concept of mechanism is given in 9.0.

reviewed in the next chapter, and (c) still more generally, not-intrinsically-purposive basic-physical-interaction mechanism. There are other theories of, and so, other senses of, mechanism. However, these three are the only theoretical senses of mechanism being looked at in this Chapter.

3.7 *Billiard ball mechanism* maintains that basic physical things are like tiny billiard balls, and that *all* physical changes are to be explained by *contacts* between these extended masses in motion. The cumbersome slogan of billiard ball mechanism can be put as follows:

> All basic things are extended mass objects in motion through empty space; the basic extended mass objects are shaped as tiny billiard balls; it is only contacts between these extended mass objects in motion that lead to changes in motion.

Billiard ball mechanism was only rarely found, even in the 17th century.[21] Nonetheless, one of the attractive features of billiard ball mechanism is that it exhibits symmetries rather well, as can be seen, for instance in the depiction of an exchange of motion between two billiard balls, in which one hits the other. If the particulars are right, the energy is regarded as entirely transferred from one billiard ball to the other, and so there is a sort of overall symmetry in the interaction. Once again, symmetry is discussed in 6.4.

But let us continue to see how rare billiard ball mechanism was in the 17th century. Prior to Isaac Newton's major system, published in 1687, René Descartes' system (developed from about 1630 to 1650) adopted the hypothesis of a material plenum, a spatial extension in which matter filled that extension or was taken to be identical with that extension, rather than the hypothesis of tiny stuffy particles in otherwise empty space. Descartes' system, then, was not a billiard ball mechanism. And Newton's theory included the theory of the gravitational force, which, as will be shown in 3.10 and 4.6, was apparently an action-at-a-distance force. So no billiard ball mechanism could have been accepted as an underlying *assumption* of Newton's overall system.

Still, though, billiard ball mechanism might have been used to fill in the apparent gaps in the theory, where the gaps are due to the *apparent*

---

[21] In the 17th century, Christian Huygens accepted a mechanical theory with only extended atoms in contact. See, e.g., Torretti, *The Philosophy of Physics*: 30-33, 76.

action at a distance of the gravitational force. Billiard ball mechanism, then, was still a possibility for Newton. From his point of view it might have been that some extended physical particles between the two gravitationally interacting bodies, somehow, cause the *apparently* action-at-a-distance gravitational relations.[22] The uncertainty over the explanation for apparently action-at-a-distance gravitational relations set the stage for a more general notion than billiard ball mechanism. This notion is: material substance based mechanism based on Newton's laws of motion, understood as Newton understood them. This could include Newton's gravitational theory since that theory abides by Newton's three laws of motion as Newton understood them. Newton's three laws of motion will be exposed in Chapter Four.

3.8 *Material substance based mechanism accepting Newton's three laws of motion (as Newton understood them,* for which see n. 24) maintains a wide enough approach that allows that there might be forces that seem to produce action-at-a-distance, as is apparently found in Newton's gravitational theory, but along with the idea that such forces would be based only on some hidden material relations of some sort. For example, as just mentioned, it might be that tiny billiard ball-like things, somehow, put pressures on objects, creating the gravitational effects. Another theory: there might be a subtle spread out material thing, an ether, whose properties somehow create the gravitational effects. However, what those

---

[22] Newton allowed for several ways to explain gravity; one was that there were material connections; see, for instance, the option he offered in the letter to Richard Bentley, February 25, 1692/3, *Newton*, 1995: p. 337. "Gravity," he said, "must be caused by an agent acting constantly according to certain laws, but whether this agent be material or immaterial is a question I have left to the consideration of my readers." In 1749 Georges Louis Lesage published an attempt to give such an explanation. His theory had tiny particles bombarding large objects, accounting for gravitational attractions. His theory worked for two bodies, but was soon enough discovered to have big problems accounting for the gravitational attractions of three bodies on a straight line. Modifications of his theory were presented; but, of course, they were ultimately rejected as too *post hoc* (and inadequate for elasticity) to be of interest. See Max Jammer, *Concepts of Force*: 192 – 4.

properties are wouldn't be described, because nobody could think of what they might have been.[23]

3.9 In the 20th century, a still more general mechanism was retained: Not-intrinsically-purposive basic-physical interaction mechanism where all interactions are governed by mathematical relations. Other features of earlier mechanism were abandoned. *Not-intrinsically-purposive basic-physical interaction mechanism* is the simple notion that the basic interactions of fundamental physical objects have no intrinsic purposes built into them and are governed *only* by mathematical relations. It is that process, the process through which basic (micro, or very small) physical interactions came to be regarded as governed only by mathematical relations, that is being referred to by the phrase 'the mathematization of physics.'[24]

This mathematization of physics was significantly developed as early as the 17th century and it continued to be developed till it reached a continuing high steady state by some time in the 20th century. (Some would say that the mathematization of physics is still increasing due to

---

[23] George Cheyne (1671/2-1743) presented the view that a mechanistic theory simply follows Newton's three laws of motion. (See Ian Hacking, *The Emergence of Probability*: 172.) In the 18th century, as mentioned in n. 22, Georges Louis Lesage produced a gravitational theory that was independent of an ether.

[24] It is this third general notion of mechanism that could be used to refer to a process that might be called *the mechanization of physics*. However, the phrase, 'the mechanization of physics', on the surface, would make little sense, since ancient physics was only of things in motion and things in balance, and so physics has always been, in a difference sense (Mach's sense), mechanistic. That is why I will call the process *the mathematization of physics*. The latter phrase leaves out one feature of the mathematical relations, namely, the absence of intrinsic purposes, but it is hard to refer to such a negative feature in the terminology. (Also, this third type of mechanism includes field relations.) Finally, some might ask, But why is the third theory of mechanism different from the second theory of mechanism? Does the third theory of mechanism reject one of Newton's three laws of motion? In answer, the three laws of motion are explained in 4.2. As we'll see in 11.4, Newton's second law of motion has a concealed assumption, the independence of space and time, an assumption that was rejected in 20th century physics post 1905. So, post 1905 versions of the third theory of mechanism don't accept Newton's second law of motion as Newton understood it; they do accept Newton's second law of motion in a new understanding of what the words mean.

the even more purely mathematical work than ever before in current efforts to integrate quantum physics with general relativity physics. See Chapter Seven about this.)

3.10 Easy illustrations can be given for the first two sorts of mechanism. And that both are, or seem to be, mechanist in the third sense is shown through these illustrations. A good typical illustration of the application of billiard ball mechanism is the case of a perfectly hard, perfectly elastic billiard ball, *A*, at rest, and a perfectly hard, perfectly elastic billiard ball, *B*, of equal mass, approaching *A*, and transmitting its motion to *A*, while *B* comes to rest at the moment *B* hits *A*. (The center of *B* moving toward *A* is on a line that goes through the centers of both billiard balls.) As is easy to see, there are no intrinsic desire-like purposes in that motion transmission. From this we can get the sense that the first type of mechanism embodies[25] the third type of mechanism. The relation between the two billiard balls is simply a mathematical relation.

An illustration of the second kind of mechanism – material substance based mechanism with Newton's laws of motion and, incidentally, Newton's gravitational theory – can be given through an examination of the problem of apparent action-at-a-distance in Newton's theory of gravity. Newton's formula for the gravitational force between two spherical mass objects states that the gravitational force is equal to the product of the two masses divided by the square of the distance between their two centers, the result multiplied by a number, called the

---

[25] To be precise, the phrase should read 'embodies or, at the very least, suggests…' Why weaken the phrase with 'at the very least, suggests'? For the following subtle reason: Billiard ball mechanism states that all fundamental objects move as billiard balls in contact. Newton's theory includes conservation of momentum. A momentum-conserved system still allows for interactive dualism, so long as the non-physical mind acts so as to make all mind-initiated physical changes balanced by equal opposite reactions. Then a billiard ball mechanism could still exhibit immaterial mind's intrinsic purposes in the basic interactions. Yes, it is a subtle point. And it reflects no historical position, since, as far as I'm aware, no one explicitly maintained a position with such an interactive dualist billiard ball mechanism. Given Newton's apparently action-at-a-distance gravitational force, it's unlikely there was such an interactive dualist billiard ball mechanist. Even Lesage's (incorrect) theory, referred to above in n. 22, had to modify the nature of the particles, allowing for penetrations of various kinds (see Jammer, *ibid*, 193).

gravitational constant.[26] Because the force is between two masses, and the centres of the two masses can be any distance apart, there is apparent action-at-a-distance between them.

To explain such apparent action-at-a-distance was highly problematic. How can mass objects cause things to happen at a distance? For instance, how does one mass, such as planet earth, respond exactly (but non-exclusively) to the nearest light giving larger mass, in this case, the sun, as though it 'instantaneously registers' how big that nearest larger mass is? The question was difficult and puzzling. As mentioned, it was sometimes postulated that there is some material system that accounts for the gravitational relation (though how any material system could do so was not known).

However, it was also sometimes postulated that it might be a non-material spiritual entity that accounts for the gravity. Newton, as mentioned in note 22, offered both material and immaterial sources of physical interactions as potential options.[27] So he did not specifically opt only for one of the three theoretical mechanisms we're looking at here. Indeed, Newtonians took it that a spiritual force, namely, God, from time to time repaired what they regarded as the loss of energy in the interactions of inelastic bodies, bodies that stick together after collision.[28] In any case, Newton's gravitational formula *itself* does not express any intrinsically purposive relations. It's just a mathematical relation between the mass objects involved.

Thus, restricted to our illustrations, the first two types of mechanism embody the third type of mechanism, which simply states that basic physical interactions have no intrinsic purposes built into them and are governed only by mathematical relations. Put another way, the three types of mechanism illustrate or embody the mathematization of physics. But, as we'll see, it was only the third type of mechanism that survived through the 20th century. Now in the 21st century, the term

---

[26] In this discussion, the mathematical equivalence of gravitational pull from a spherical object to that from a point-like object is assumed. See Torretti, *The Philosophy of Physics*: 57-67. More general treatments abound. See, for example: Cohen, *The Birth of a New Physics*: 172; Dijksterhuis, *The Mechanization of the World Picture*: 477-480.

[27] Newton envisioned two versions of the material option. See Cohen, *Revolution in Science*: 170.

[28] Jammer, *Concepts of Force*: 168.

'mechanism' is no longer used as frequently as it used to be used, partly because of quantum results; nonetheless, there is quantum mechanics, and, as we'll see in Chapter Seven, the mathematization of physics has continued unabated.[29]

---

[29] This mathematization of physics strengthened from the late 17th century till the 19th century. It was philosophically strong in the 19th century, at which point it seemed to be no longer necessary nor helpful to suppose that there were purposes hidden in the mathematics, for which see Ernst Mach, *Science of Mechanics*, *ibid.* 420 – 433, 561 - 575. But the mathematical results also became more unusual and striking by the end of the first few decades of the 20th century. Hence, (as we'll see in Chapter Six) the mathematization of physics process took place from the 17th century through to at least one sort of culmination by around 1918.

Chapter Four: The Mathematization of Physics: 17th and 18th centuries

4.0 Hints

The mathematization of physics, in which the basic physical interactions came to be regarded as lacking intrinsic purposes and as governed only by mathematical relations, by material structure, and by efficient causes, was hinted at in the careful work in astronomy in the 16th and early 17th centuries. Copernicus (in the first half of the 16th century) maintained that the mathematical description of the earth in relation to the sun and the other heavenly objects would have greater clarity if the earth as well as the (other) wanderers or planetary objects and other heavenly objects not including the sun, at the first level of study, were taken to orbit the sun. The preference for clarity or elegance to some extent undermined Aristotle's purposive notions; the elegance or clarity would have made an improved form-based structure, and perhaps what Aristotle thought of as the final or purposive causes related to earth being at the absolute centre of the cosmos would not be required. (Still, it should be remembered that Copernicus here was only talking about a first level simplified account.)[30]

Similarly, Kepler's (early 17th century) view that the orbits were elliptical, not strictly circular, also undermined purposive Aristotelianism, and reinforced the importance of the empirical (observational) relations however the formal mathematics worked out. Aristotle (agreeing with Plato and others) thought that a circle was perfect, and so a circle was taken to express a basic purpose more than an ellipse would have; Kepler thought that it was the facts of the matter that count. Circles might be beautiful; and we can hypothesize that there are circles on circles to

---

[30] Cohen, *Revolution In Science*: 111.

preserve that beauty; we may regard circles, or even circles on circles, as embodying a kind of perfection; but, thought Kepler, circles are not ellipses, and we have to improve the Copernican theory; we have to get the mathematical descriptions of the *observed* motions of the planets, conceived of as orbits around the sun, right.[31]

4.1 Not only Kepler but also Galileo in the early 17th century began the main elements of the tradition based on quantificational, experimental, and theoretical study. Descartes continued this study in the 1630's to 1650. And Newton brought it to fruition from 1664[32] to the publication of his *Principia* in 1687. (Newton, of course, worked productively beyond that date as well; he first published *Optics* in 1704.)

One of Galileo's many projects was to find out the rate of increased motion in free fall (the rate at which a stone, say, increases its rate of motion as it falls to the earth ignoring resistance of the air). To discover this, he discovered the rates at which small spherical objects increase their speed as they roll down slopes.[33] Through experimental research, Galileo came up with his view of the single theoretical acceleration rate at which objects fall to the earth.[34] As well, Galileo had a more strictly philosophical argument to show the error in Aristotle's view that heavy objects fall faster than light or not-so-heavy objects. Galileo said that Aristotle's view made no sense. He offered a thought-experiment to show this. What would happen under Aristotle's theory if a heavy object were tied to a less heavy object, and the fall rate would be then intellectually compared to the fall rate of the heavier of the two objects? The point is that one can't answer the question, because one can't say if the heavy object, A, tied to the less heavy object, B, would go faster or slower than A, if A had been dropped alone. A joined to B should go faster than A because the two objects are tied together and are heavier than A; it should go slower because B should slow down the fall

---

[31] Cohen, *Revolution in Science*: 127-8. Nonetheless, Kepler, too, speculated on various physical implementations of purely mathematical properties.

[32] The year in which he began his first work, "Certain Philosophical Questions."

[33] Leonardo da Vinci (1452-1519) knew "the ratio of the times of descent down the slope and the height of an inclined plane" but his results were not published till the end of the 18th century (Ernst Mach, *Science of Mechanics*: 153).

[34] The equality would obtain without air resistance differences. Galileo, *Discourse on Two New Sciences*; Cohen, *Revolution in Science*: 137.

of *A*, the heavier of the two objects. Galileo concluded, then, philosophically as well as experimentally, that the free fall rate, theoretically (ignoring air resistance), should be equal between objects of differing weights.[35] What govern the fall rates are strictly mathematical relations without intrinsic purposes, especially given that the earth (in Galileo's view, since Galileo was a Copernican, and, of course, in the view of more or less everyone for the last few centuries) is no longer thought to be at the absolute center of the universe.

In defending the intelligibility of the notion that the earth moves around the sun, Galileo advocated a preliminary version of what is now called *Galilean relativity*. The basic idea of Galilean relativity is that for all objects that are moving entirely smoothly in straight line motions in respect to each other, it is impossible to say which objects are absolutely moving and which objects are absolutely at rest. To put the point another way, any object can be taken as being at rest, and all the other objects can then be assigned quantity and direction of motion, including zero motion, in regard to the object taken to be at rest. That is Galilean relativity.[36]

Galileo, once again, accepted the Copernican view; he also explained how the earth could be moving (without our intuitively or immediately knowing about its motion); and he also worked out the free fall rate to the earth. These views added a further problem to be investigated. Why do objects fall to the earth? What would a stone do if it were let loose near another large object, like the moon?[37]

4.2 Skipping Descartes' views (to which we'll return in 9.0), Newton, over a half century after the end of Galileo's work, put forward his system, which includes three laws of motion and the gravitational force. Newton's theory of the gravitational force, in one respect at least, solved the problems of the two questions just raised.

In regard to the first question, Newton replaced the purposive answer that Aristotle had given with a purely mathematical answer. Aristotle had said that a stone has the purpose of heading to its true nature, and it is a cold dry thing, and the centre of coldness is at the

---

[35] See Galileo, *Discourse*: 66.

[36] We'll come back to Galilean relativity in Chapter Six.

[37] See Mach, *Science of Mechanics*: 230-1.

centre of the earth, so it heads to the centre of the earth. Newton said that a stone let loose near the earth is one mass object, the stone, near another mass object, the earth, and any two mass objects attract each other with the force given in the gravitational equation. That's why the stone moves to the earth.

What would happen, then, if a stone were let loose just near the moon? Newton's answer would have been that the moon, too, is a mass object, a large mass object in fact, and so the stone would move toward the moon in a manner indicated by the mathematical gravitational formula.

Another way to put this is to say that Newton's system overthrew Aristotle's idea that there is a huge difference between the sub-lunar realm and the super-lunar realm. Instead, according to Newton, we live in a single universe, and the forces of physics are constant throughout the universe (at least in inanimate parts of the universe).

4.2.1 Newton also presented three laws of motion; these are powerful notions, and worth looking at. The first law of motion says that an object maintains its state of rest or its straight-line motion until that object is affected by the application of a force on it. The second law says that if a force is applied to an object, the object's change in motion will be proportional to the force acting on it, and in the straight-line direction of the force acting on it. The third law says that every force action has an equal and opposite reaction. Notice that on the surface at least there are no intrinsic or inherent purposes in these basic interactions. The interactions are governed by merely abstract, and, one can say, by mathematical[38] relations.

From the three laws of motion follows the thesis or law of the conservation of momentum, where 'conservation of x' means that the amount of x stays the same. The momentum of a mass body in motion is the mass times the velocity of the body (where the velocity is the speed in a specified direction).[39] The single momentum for many mass bodies

---

[38] The derivation of the law of conservation of momentum from the three laws of motion (which will be reviewed in 4.4) shows that the laws, though not stated in mathematical symbols, do have significant mathematical implications.

[39] Why it is mass times velocity, not mass plus velocity, nor mass divided by velocity, nor any other relation between mass and velocity? Here is a partial answer: Take any clump of matter; such a clump can be taken to be a sum of arbitrarily many units. However, the momentum of the object has to be the

moving smoothly in relation to each other in a system, at a given instant, can be found, as will be shown below in 4.3; the single momentum for many mass bodies is an amount that can be thought of as though it were a single mass times velocity in that system issuing from a single point at that instant. This would make it a single vector (a single mass-in-a-specified-direction, represented by a line in a direction in a given frame or system) at that instant issuing from a single point. At different times, there are different points, but the momentum, the mass times velocity, stays the same.

We now have the concepts of momentum, and momentum vector. And, as was just stated, Newton's three laws of motion yield the result that momentum is always conserved, or is always the same. For those who want a more detailed explanation of what exactly conservation of momentum means, and how the law of conservation of momentum follows from Newton's three laws of motion, I will now go into some details. Those who are skimming the details can proceed directly to 4.5.

4.3 We begin with a look at how a group of objects in motion have a single momentum. Suppose, for example, that we observe (through a window, if you like) a room in which there are two tennis balls rolling on the floor. One is rolling eastward at 2 mph. Another, situated exactly to the west of the first, is rolling, westward, (therefore, on exactly the same line) at 5 mph. Suppose the two tennis balls are the only moving objects in the room, and it is the momentum within the room we are looking for. Suppose the two tennis balls are of equal mass, which we'll take to be 1 unit of mass. Then we have the momentum of the first tennis ball, which is eastward on its line of motion at the rate of 2mph times 1 unit of mass. We have the momentum of the second tennis ball, which is westward at 5mph times 1 unit of mass. Then Newton would have said that the sum momentum is 3mph westward on that line. At any given moment, he could have thought of that 3mph westward momentum vector as issuing from the point at the centre of the line connecting the centres of the two objects at that moment. However, as mentioned before, the momentum of the two tennis balls over a prolonged period of time is a vector arrow

---

same regardless if it's thought of as a single object, or two (half) objects added together, or any number, *n*, of objects added together. As it happens, the only mathematical formula to give the same momentum will be the sum of each-mass-part-times-its-velocity.

that is not given a location in whatever frame of reference is being used. The momentum of a mass object or of a group of mass objects is just the amount of mass times the amount of speed in a given direction, without placement in the frame of reference (except on a line through the frame in some cases, e.g., if the motions are smooth, each on its line, in relation to each other[40]).

More generally, here is how any number of objects (in motion) have a single momentum: (For simplicity, we assume the objects to be uniform objects, objects of equally spread density, in globular shapes.) If two objects are traveling in different directions from the line joining the two centres at a given instant, then just take the two objects at the instant in question, join the two centres, and take the half way point between them. Then from that point take the two mass-speed-direction lines and extend them from that point. Then construct a parallelogram on the two lines, and the diagonal from the centre point is the momentum of the two objects at that moment. If the masses of the two objects are different, then for each mass object, take the momentum vector to be the mass of the object times the velocity vector. Then take the centre point on the line joining their two centres, and let the two momentum vectors issue from that point; and then take the diagonal of the parallelogram of the two momentum vectors as sides for the total momentum vector. Given this (and just using addition or subtraction if two are moving along a single line), any number of particles of differing masses, each traveling in any direction in space, smoothly relative to the others, can be reduced to one total momentum vector in that space.

The conservation of momentum rule says that if a system is *closed*, that is, if a system has no force-carrying objects entering or leaving the system (the door to the room is closed, so to speak) then the amount of momentum is always the same.[41]

---

[40] The vector has a length representing the mass times velocity amount, but there is no spatially placed beginning of the vector nor spatially placed end of the vector when a greater than zero period of time is given.

[41] For those who like details: A system in which a non-physically-carried-force applies in the system but in a way that preserves the action and equal reaction rule of the third law of motion, and without the sudden disappearance of the force-carrying-immaterial object – though the force-carrying immaterial object need not be placed in the space and time system – would still have been considered to be a closed system. If the application of such a non-physically-carried-force breaks the third law of motion, that system is open. Similarly, for a

4.4 Here is how conservation of momentum follows from Newton's three laws of motion. By the first law, the inertial law, a body maintains its state of smooth motion or rest (a body maintains its inertial state) until some force acts on it to change that state. It follows that in a closed system in which there are no force-actions (for example, a system without any gravitational force, and with several billiard balls floating in space along paths that never intersect) all objects will continue their smooth motion or rest (all objects will remain in their inertial conditions), and so there will be conservation of overall or total momentum.

Now, continuing the demonstration for cases in which there are force actions, we'll look at any closed system that, over time, has force actions. They might be force actions by contact, or they might be force actions at a distance. If they're force actions by contact, the change in motion of an object is indicated by the second law. By the third law, every action has an equal and opposite reaction. And so it is that every action by contact will retain the conservation of momentum: The original state of motion or rest of an object receiving a force is combined with the change in direction and change in amount of motion given by the contact-applied force. But the change in direction and change in amount of motion will have an equal and opposite reaction in the object contact-applying the force. So the total mass in motion and its overall direction will be the same as it originally was.

All that remains are forces acting (or apparently acting) at a distance. In these cases, too, the third law of motion requires that for every force action apparently at a distance (attraction, say, as in gravitational attraction), there will be an equal and opposite reaction. The forces include the directions, and so we can say that the sum of the forces = 0. So for forces that do not act by contact, too, the equal and

---

physics with the conservation of energy to be explained below, a system in which an immaterial mind operated on the physical objects of the system while preserving the action-equal-reaction rule *and* preserving a balance of total kinetic and potential energy, would be a closed system. If either the action-equal-reaction rule were broken or the balance of total realized and potential energy were not kept, the system would be an open system. After 1960 or 1970, (and some would say, after Darwinian evolution) through the evidence for phystriology (or through the evidence for Darwinian evolution), the conditions involving non-physical minds with causal influence on the parts of a brain are so implausible as to allow the simpler definition of a closed system to stand.

opposite action/reaction requirement guarantees conservation of overall momentum.

It is easier to see this for contact action forces than for forces apparently at a distance. Consider being on earth, and consider a stone falling to the earth. The stone accelerates, and so if the frame of reference is always at the earth, there appears to be violation of the law of conservation of momentum. However, as it would have been put (prior to the use of inertial geodesics in accelerative systems in 1916), the frame of reference for calculating momentum is not accelerative. Due to the action and equal reaction third law of motion there is an equal reaction on the earth; the huge-massed earth acceleratively moves a tiny amount toward the stone, while the stone accelerates toward the earth. The small accelerative motion of the earth requires that the original frame of reference is ever so slightly *not* the centre of mass of the earth itself for any time after the first instant. Consequently, given both the earth accelerative motion, and the stone accelerative motion, the law of conservation of momentum is seen to be preserved from a frame of reference (which will be non-accelerative) slightly different from that of the earth.

4.5 In Newton's system, momentum – again, which is represented as mass times velocity, symbolized by *mv* – is always the same in any closed system (of inanimate objects at least). The notion of momentum, it should be understood, is not just scalar (or dealing solely with the quantity of mass in motion); rather, the term 'velocity' is both scalar and vectorial: it includes the direction of motion as well as the amount of motion.

Once again we note that the three laws of motion and the law of conservation of momentum do not express activities of intrinsic purposes; at the surface level at least, they are expressions of merely mathematical relations. The only problem that might be raised is whether there are, in addition to the three laws of motion, intrinsically purposive non-physically initiated forces (or, alternatively, forces triggered by particular arrangements or configurations of particles) whose physical results also obey the third law of motion. We will leave that as an open question at this stage of the investigation. Indeed, it *may have been* an open question for several centuries after Newton.

The question was fully resolved, though, and against non-physically initiated forces (and configurative forces), somewhere between

1860 and 1960 or 1970, depending on one's degree of caution. By 1860 Charles Darwin had put forward the natural selection hypothesis (in *The Origin Of Species*), and this undermined any theory that maintained that human actions are generated through non-physical minds whereas other animal actions are entirely generated within the physical system. Rather, by natural selection, human beings were descendants of preceding primates. So there wouldn't be a radical difference between human beings and non-human primates. And the primates, too, descended from other animals. The members of the whole animal realm, and, indeed the members of the whole living realm, were made of the same basic sorts of things; the differences between living beings were the result of millions, and, as it turned out, billions, of years of natural selection.

After 1960 or 1970, the end of the evidence for phystriology had already been reached, and so those who prefer logic rather than what they'd think of as 'mere interpretation' of the evidence, would say that, logically, the hypothesis of *unusual* preservations of momentum in volition was eliminated. The conservation of momentum occurred through only physical methods.[42]

4.6 As we saw in 4.2, Newton's system described the gravitational force. As is readily apparent, it is very difficult to understand the apparent action-at-a-distance aspect of Newton's gravitational force. The gravitational force is found between any two mass bodies at a given moment in time, and the size of the force is a constant (the gravitational constant) times the product of the two masses divided by the distance squared between their centers (assuming each mass body is spherical, or, otherwise, their centre of masses). The gravitational force has a size dependent on how far apart the bodies are. But this apparent action-at-a-distance in the gravitational force embodies a deep intellectual problem. How can distant mass objects affect each other?

---

[42] This result can also be reached by use of Nöther's theorem first published in 1918. (For Nöther's Theorem, see 6.4. For a strong statement of this result, see 10.4 n. 172.) In addition, it can be reached by thinking of momentum conservation for inanimate objects until Darwinian evolution, and then recognizing that the physicalization of chemistry showed that the generation of life forms happened chemically based on physical relations. Then conservation of momentum would occur equally in organisms and non-organisms.

One attempt at a solution to the problem invoked one aspect possibly in the second theory of mechanism, turning it back into a first theory of mechanism, that was exposed in n. 22 in 3.7: it specified that there's a hidden material billiard-ball like contact-based connection for everything. But there were other attempts at solutions as well, focusing on other ways material bodies might relate to each other, one of which we'll now have a look at.

4.7 In the 18th century Roger Boscovich (1711-1787) worked to develop, and did develop, what can be thought of as an action-at-a-distance theory of the interactions of basic physical particles. The theory, as it turned out, was inventive but incorrect. However, before we overview the theory, let us first try to better understand what, to some thinkers, was the *appeal* of action-at-a-distance forces.

Some theorists (for example, Gottfried von Leibniz, 1646-1716) regarded abrupt contact accelerations, as would take place in (perfectly hard, perfectly elastic) billiard ball interactions, as problematic. Such sudden accelerations would not follow elegant principles of continuity.[43] After all, if two (perfectly hard perfectly elastic) bodies come into contact, it would be at an instant that they contact each other. Then (in the usual frames and conditions), a body would go, abruptly, from moving at such and such a speed to having a zero speed; and the other particle would go, equally abruptly, from having a zero speed to having such and such a speed; the transition would take place at an instant, the instant of contact. For every instant prior to the transition instant, the first body is in motion, and the second at rest. For every instant after the transition instant, the first body is at rest, and the second in motion.

To get away from such abrupt changes, Boscovich postulated that there are point particles, that is, particles that have mass but have no extension in space. Interactions between them are by forces of attraction and repulsion that increase and decrease as two bodies come increasingly

---

[43] One such principle is given in *Leibniz, Philosophical Papers and Letters*, translated, edited, and with introduction by Leroy E. Loemker, vol. 1, Chicago: University of Chicago Press: 539. In simple terms, a basic principle of continuity states that "nature does not jump". Rather, "all natural change proceeds by degrees," for which see Leibniz's *Monadology* #13.

close to each other. From the human large-scale perspective, the results could be as we observe them.[44]

Boscovich's theory was conjectural, although complex in its mathematics. As far as I know, the theory was never directly tested; and if it had been directly tested, one way or another, the theory of close proximity yet distant interactions as Boscovich put it forward would have been refuted. (It has been refuted by many other theories that have been experimentally tested and that are satisfactory and that are inconsistent with Boscovich's theory.)

The theory of action-at-a-distance forces was intriguing and important in the late 17th century, through the 18th century, and into the 19th century. Some thinkers interpreted it as requiring spiritual, that is, non-physical, forces. However, other thinkers interpreted it as requiring a subtle material thing underlying all of space.[45] Indeed, in the 19th century, what was referred to in the second half of Chapter Three as the second theory of mechanism came to play a strong role in regard to the travelling of light. We'll return to that in Chapter Five.

4.8 For understanding developments in physics in the 17th and 18th centuries we need to note another conservation notion, besides conservation of momentum, that was clearly articulated in the 18th century.[46] This conservation notion was of the conservation of mass. Antoine Laurent Lavoisier, a chemist, clearly articulated the conservation

---

[44] See Max Jammer, *Concepts of Force*: 170-178.

[45] A detailed note: Newton's "early suggestions for a theory of gravitation made use of the motions and pressures of the ether in a manner not essentially different from Cartesianism" (Mary Hesse, "Action at a Distance and Field Theory": 10b.) Samuel Clarke, Newton's disciple, may have held to a subtle but unknown material basis; (see Hesse *ibid*: 11a.) The later development of field theories supported such notions; (see Hesse *ibid*: 11-13). The medium throughout space was mathematically rendered by the properties of the field points, and these might have been regarded, alternatively, as not being expressions of any material medium. In this way they could be regarded as non-first-theoretical-sense-mechanist and non-second-theoretical-sense-mechanist. Field theories were not action-at-a-distance theories; they involve spatial continuity; but they need not be interpreted as material substance theories.

[46] We ignore still other conservation notions articulated by the 18th century, e.g., conservation of center of gravity, and conservation of area.

of mass rule at the end of the 18th century (1789): "Nothing is created in the course of artificial or natural reactions, and it can be taken as an axiom that in every reaction the initial quantity of matter is equal to the final quantity of matter."[47]

The notion of conservation of mass is highly familiar, and not in the least forbidding. If you burn a tree in a very hot fire, it may look as though the amount of matter is less after the burning, since, after the burning, there's nothing visible of the tree but ashes. But, as is well known, most of the mass of the tree has become invisible; tiny bits of the tree have been heated to the point that they have separated from other bits and are, invisibly, floating through the air, often in new combination with other bits of things.

That there is no loss of mass in the burning of a tree can be theoretically proven. Take a twig, put it on some kindling in a very large container that can be sealed. ('Very large' is putting it mildly. The container would have to be too large to allow the experiment to be easy to conduct.) Arrange for a spark to be burning in the container, and arrange a way for the spark to be dipped down into the kindling below the twig while the container is sealed. At the beginning of the experiment, the spark is above the kindling. Weigh the sealed container, with attention, if necessary, to such matters as atmospheric pressure, and the buoyancy factor or the difference between that sealed container with ordinary air, and that sealed container with its contents. Then dip the spark into the kindling below the twig. Let the kindling and the twig burn to ashes. Then weigh the still sealed container, with attention to similar matters as before. Assuming that the height of the container from the centre of the earth hasn't changed over the period of time, and, given other factors, the weight will be the same. This will indicate the amount of mass in the container. It will turn out that the amount of mass, or the amount of matter, in the container has not been altered.

Lavoisier conducted similar experiments on metals with changing properties. The metals weighed more after the change in properties, but he showed that the extra weight of the metals came from the gasses

---

[47] Quoted from Lavoisier's *Elements of Chemistry in a new systematic order* in Jammer, *Concepts of Mass*: 86. Newton articulated the elements of what some would take to be a conservation of mass notion, though the potential for infinite divisions allowed by Newton poses some problems. See Newton, *Principia*, beginning of Book III, in *Newton*, 1995: 117.

combining with them. There was no change in the overall weight of the system, and so, no change in the overall mass of the system.[48]

The conservation of mass notion, then, is a simple notion: the quantity of matter stays the same in any system in which no matter is either entering or leaving the system by crossing the boundary of the system. More briefly, in a closed system, the amount of mass stays the same.

Also, it is useful to note how Lavoisier's articulation of the conservation of mass is specifically directed toward showing that what all would consider to be a physical principle applies throughout chemical changes. This begins to show how the operation of a basic principle in physics is not overturned by chemical events. There is a hint, then, of the development of phystriology, at least from physics through chemistry, in Lavoisier's statement of mass conservation. This requires a bit of clarity on the relations between physics-events and chemistry-events, though, and there will be some discussion of those relations in Chapter Eight.

---

[48] Jaffe, *Crucibles*: 70-72.

Chapter Five: The Mathematization of Physics: 19th century

5.0 One of the remarkably important physical findings of the 19th century was the energy conservation thesis, developed, mostly from 1820 or so till 1850. As was stated in Chapter Four, to say that something is conserved is to say that the amount of it stays the same. There are several basic forms of energy, where energy, as understood at that time, is the capacity to do work; and work is the exertion of a force over a distance; and the exertion of a force over a distance during a given period of time is the change in the amount of motion of a (clump of) matter caused by the force during that period of time.

The concept of energy, as it is used in physics (and not as it is used, informally and loosely, in everyday life) is a difficult concept to grasp. In physics (again in the early 19th century), energy is defined as the capacity to do work, and work involves motion of matter produced through a force; work is not accomplished through what's called inertial motion, which is defined in Newton's first law of motion. Newton's first law of motion says that an object in straight line motion (or rest), with no force acting on it, continues to be in that state of straight line motion (or rest) forever. Obviously, then, there is nothing corresponding to what we'd want to think of as work in this sort of motion. It is only when a force operates that there can be something like work. And the force has to change not merely the direction of motion, but also the *amount* of motion of (a clump of) mass, for work to be done.

It is also important to note that when we talk of work, and we talk of the change in the amount of motion of (a clump of) mass, we are focussing on one particular (clump of) mass. The force has to come from somewhere; it often comes from a mass object; but what if it comes from a non-mass entity? At some point it was speculated that force can come from a non-physical mind; later this notion dropped away among careful thinkers, for reasons we will come to appreciate by the end of the review of Darwinian evolution in Chapter Nine. But it was also realized that force can come from a non-mind and what was regarded as a non-mass entity (for example, from light). Putting it broadly, it is the other entity from which the force comes, whether massive or non-massive, that allows there to be conservation of energy. One way to put it is to say that it is in the transition from one situation to another that energy is conserved.

Let us now look at the various forms of energy, or capacity to do work. There is kinetic (or moving) energy, since, whenever any mass body is in motion it will have the *capacity* to act with a force on another body that it, informally, collides with, say. Another kind of energy is potential energy. Potential energy can be illustrated by the potential energy of the gravitational force when an object is prevented from, say, falling to the floor. For example, a piece of chalk resting on someone's palm has potential energy, the energy of the gravitational force keeping the chalk resting on the palm. Yes, the force is acting to keep the chalk on the palm, but the palm prevents it from being in free gravitational motion, and so the energy is called *potential* energy.

One can say that there is a type of potential energy that is chemical energy, since, for example, a dry matchstick, when suitably scratched, due to its chemical composition, will create a change in the motion-states of various things. There will be a flame on the tip; after a short period of time, the matchstick will weigh slightly less than it weighed prior to being lit. And it turns out that tiny things are in motion when the flame is burning.

The flame itself has heat, and heat, too, can be thought of as a form of energy, since a hot object can change the motion properties of another object. Light a fire under a pot of water, and the water starts bubbling, and then boiling. The bubbling and the boiling show that the bits of water are moving more quickly than they had been moving previously. Heat – kinetic, from a mass object in motion, or radiant, from what was regarded as a non-mass object, e.g., light – creates motion of mass objects. Later radiant energy became particularly important for study because it involved the energy of what were regarded as non-massive objects, e.g., light.

Similarly, magnets create motion, and so there is magnetic energy as well as the others so far mentioned. Of course, there are other forms of energy, too.

The theory of conservation of energy says that however one properly measures the amount of kinetic, temperature-based, chemical, magnetic, electrical, radiative, etc., energy, including all the forms of potential energy there might be, the amount of energy can be numerically translated to the measure of any other form of energy; and there can be a conversion, too, from any one form of energy to any other. Fire at one place creates motion nearby; eventually the fire goes out, and the motions of the nearby particles continue. That is a conversion of kinetic and radiative energy in fire to some vibrational motion of things on the ground, the ashes, and more kinetic motion, although largely invisible, of bits of things in the air. The radiative energy is, in bulk, gone, but the amount of energy in such a conversion is the same. More generally, the amount of energy in all conversions is the same; that is, energy itself is conserved.[49]

This is a remarkable and powerful theory. For another illustration, again, consider a piece of chalk resting on a palm. It has some potential energy due to the gravitational attraction keeping the chalk on the palm on which the chalk rests. Rapidly move the hand to one side, and the chalk will fall. The potential energy becomes accelerative kinetic energy as the chalk accelerates towards the floor. The amount of potential energy it had on the palm equals the amount of accelerative kinetic energy it has when it is falling (discounting air resistance).

There will be a similar equality for any one form of energy in relation to any other form of energy. Once again, it is important to note that it is the mathematical equivalences that are taken to be fundamental; there don't seem to be any intrinsic purposes in the conversions, nor in the conservation in the conversions. Of course there may be purposes getting the conversions to occur; one may light a fire under water to get the water to boil so that soup can be prepared in it. But the conversion itself, and the conservation in the conversion, has no inherent purposes.

5.1 It is also good to note the $E = 1/2\ mv^2$ equation for kinetic energy (kinetic energy equals one half of mass times velocity squared) used in

---

[49] A fine, detailed review of how the law of conservation of energy developed is given in Thomas Kuhn's 1959 article, "Energy Conservation As An Example of Simultaneous Discovery".

the 19th century.[50] This formula was rejected in the 20th century due to the development of relativity theory. Relativity theory replaces this formula with a formula in which even if the mass is at rest in the given framework (and so the velocity = 0), the energy will not = 0. We will return to the notions of kinetic energy and mass objects in motion in Chapter Six.

5.2 Another important notion that developed in the mathematized physics of the 19th century is called the second law of thermodynamics (where 'thermodynamics' is, literally, the study of heat in (force-based) motion; what's called *the first law of thermodynamics* is the law of conservation of energy, which we just reviewed). The second law of thermodynamics, developed in the 1850's and '60's, then reinterpreted in various ways in the next few decades, says, in its second way of being put, that that the amount of disorder in a closed system is always increasing, or, if the system is as disordered as can be, staying the same. Since the 1880's, *the entropy* of a system has been called *the amount of disorder* in the system.

It is easy enough to explain the basic concept. If you have a drawer full of socks and underwear, it might be a well-ordered drawer. On the other hand, it might be a messy, disordered drawer (please don't look in my socks and underwear drawer). The second law of thermodynamics, in its late 19th century version, says that a closed system (we would now add something like, "of any size larger than the miniscule Planck size") that is not as disordered as it can be is always increasing in disorder. So what happens when you organize (thereby making orderly) a disordered drawer of socks and underwear? If you take the boundary of the drawer (the five wooden planes, say, plus the invisible plane that is its hypothetical ceiling) to be the boundary of the system, then, according to the entropy law, you can't have a closed system that becomes more orderly than it was before. (Your hands have to enter the boundary of the drawer if you're going to tidy it up.)

---

[50] See Roberto Torretti, *The Philosophy of Physics*: 35. In 1807 Thomas Young said that energy was mass times velocity squared. (Here he was reinforcing some 18th century experimentation of Willem s'Gravesande, confirming Leibniz' theory, and supported by Emilie de Chatelet.) The factor 1/2 was apparently introduced in 1829 by de Coriolis. This was to make sure the work done and kinetic energy achieved would be equal whatever unit measures were used. See also Peter Atkins, *Galileo's Finger*: 95.

For instance, using some more recent results than results readily available in the 19th century, if nothing enters or leaves the system, the socks will, *eventually*, after millions of years or more, disintegrate, due to a tiny amount of atomic disintegration going on during any small period of time. Alternatively, the disintegration will happen due to large scale entropy, e.g., the absorption of the earth into the sun, which, alas, will happen a few billion years from now, though the events cross the closure boundary that was given. (A much bigger closure boundary would be used.) In any case, only an open system can become more orderly. Order within planet earth is order in an open system since earth gets energy from the sun. It is that openness that allows the earth to develop more orderly systems through the evolution of living things.

Naturally enough, you can raise various questions about closed systems. For example, you can raise a question about what happens in a closed room. Suppose you are locked in a room, and you organize the room; you make it tidy. It starts as a colossal mess; but three hours later, with nothing entering or leaving the room, it is orderly. What about the second law of thermodynamics?

The answer is that from the physicist's, chemist's, and biochemist's points of view, the disorder in the room has increased, even though, from the everyday human point of view, the visible order has increased. The reason is that the scientists would look at such things as the distribution of energy-carrying-objects before and after the person cleaned up the room. Things like distribution, they would find, would show increased disorder. (For instance, if it would be distribution, it would be more spread out.) Also, by the end of the enterprise, the person would be exhausted and hungry. That's a sign of the overall increased disorder.

The main idea is that the energy used in cleaning up the room has been physically inefficient. Although the amount of energy in the room prior to cleaning up the room is the same as the amount of energy in the room after cleaning it up, various features of the room, for example, to oversimplify it, the motions of the particles in the room, are in a more diffused, or more evenly distributed, and hence a less specifically ordered state, after the clean up than before it.

Physicists, chemists, and biochemists say that it would take a lot of detail to show this, but in our context it is not necessary to show this. (We can also think of what happens if the room is sealed: the oxygen runs out and the person dies; or there's no food, and the person dies.

The body, eventually, decomposes, as does everything else in the room. Disorder increases.)

Although the second law of thermodynamics is a fundamentally important law, it does not play any direct role in the development of the evidence *for* phystriology. The second law of thermodynamics, the law of increasing entropy, is a deeply puzzling law.[51] But we needn't consider it further in this context.

Perhaps a few readers will be frustrated at such an abrupt dropping of this intriguing subject matter. But, so be it. What is mostly irrelevant to the project at hand, showing how phystriology developed, will be, unfortunately, abruptly dropped. The topic, however, was sufficiently interesting as a demonstration of the profundity of the mathematization of physics as to warrant its being (all too briefly) covered. Also, conditions arising from the law of entropy could be used as a means to supposedly get away from phystriology. For this reason, too, the notion has been exposed here, and we will return to the topic of entropy later, in 11.10.

5.3 Now we will look at the main problem at the end of the 19th century (and very first few years of the 20th century) that came with the theory about light. (A reader who read the last sections of Chapter Three carefully will see that this is a problem for what was there called the second theory of mechanism.) In the 19th century, light was regarded as a wave, and because it was thought to be a wave, it was also thought that wherever light travels, it travels through a medium. It was thought that the universe must have a medium for light to travel in as a wave, and the medium in the universe was called *the ether*. The ether was thought to be a subtle material substance underlying everything in the universe. (No one believes in the ether any more; the idea that there is an ether was undone, as we'll see in the next Chapter, by the special theory of relativity.)

How was light thought to be a wave? By observational-theoretical means. Thomas Young in 1801 found that light that is shone through two parallel slits in a wall makes wave-interferences (bands of light and dark) on a second light-receiving wall. The wave interferences showed, as

---

[51] For introductory treatments, see Peter Atkins, *The Second Law*; Brian Silver, *The Ascent of Science*: 215-232.

it would have been put then, that light is a wave[52]; and, once again, it was thought that since light is a wave, it must travel through a medium, and the medium in the universe was named 'the ether'.

Now by the 1890's, the theory that light is a wave travelling through a universal ether was challenged by a basic conflict between James Clerk Maxwell's electromagnetic theory (presented in the 1860's and 1870's) and what is called *Galileo's transformation* (which will be explained a few paragraphs below, and which is to be distinguished from *Galileo's relativity*).

In the 19th century there had been many investigations into both electricity and magnetism. These seem to be two very different sorts of things. Lightening flashes from the sky. Magnetism is shown when two special pieces of metal attract or repel each other. In 1820, however, Hans Oersted began linking the two phenomena. He noticed, and studied, how a magnetic compass needle moves in response to electricity flowing through a nearby wire.[53] This set the stage for a detailed investigation of the deep connection between the two phenomena. And because of the deep connection between the two phenomena, the two are now known, singly, as *electromagnetism*.

As mentioned, James Clerk Maxwell presented a comprehensive mathematical theory of electromagnetism in the 1860's and '70's. He found a set of equations for electricity and magnetism. In fact, he also saw that the equations govern light as well, so that light and electromagnetism are one phenomenon, differing in, for instance, wavelength. Also, it follows from Maxwell's electromagnetic theory, as Hendrick Lorentz noticed, that the speed of light in a vacuum is a constant.[54] (To define a vacuum, one ignores any ether that may have existed; or one takes it that the vacuum does not include the ether.) This effectively meant, or suggested, that it doesn't matter how fast the measurer is traveling relative to anything else while measuring the speed of light; the speed of light is a constant.

---

[52] See "Timelines" in John Gribbin's *Q is for Quantum*: 581; and Brian Silver, *Ascent of Science*, 191. (Light is now thought to be as much a particle based stream – a photon based stream – as a wave.)

[53] Toretti, *ibid.*, 82-3; Brian Silver, *ibid.*, 87.

[54] The point made by Lorentz on Maxwell's equations was important in Einstein's work. See Einstein, *Relativity*: 23.

Now there *seemed to be* only two ways to interpret the constancy of the speed of light. In one way, the speed of light in a vacuum would be constant relative to the system that generates the beam of light. In the other way, the speed of light in a vacuum would be constant relative to the medium in which the light beam travels. Under both these interpretations, though, it seems that light should be measured as having different speeds; all one needs to do is let the measurements be done from a framework moving with respect to both the light-generating system and the medium through which the light travels. The speed of light would be given relative to the source of the light, or relative to the medium in which the light traveled. But if a framework is moving with respect both to the source of the light and the ether (the supposed medium for light), a different speed should result from the speed measured by either the source frame or the ether frame. That there should be different speeds arises from what is called *Galileo's transformation* or *the Galileo transformation.*

The Galileo transformation is a simple technique *within* the early form of Galilean relativity. Galilean relativity is a theory of relativity that, in preliminary form, Galileo subscribed to and advanced.[55] Physicists since have accepted it in its more fully developed form. In its preliminary form, Galilean relativity includes the Galilean transformation; in its developed form, it does not include the Galilean transformation. In its developed form, it includes a transformation, but the transformation may or may not be the Galilean transformation. The distinction between accepting Galilean relativity with and without the Galilean transformation is what we want to look at.

In Galilean relativity, both in preliminary and fully developed form, as mentioned in the last chapter, a speed relative to one framework can be provided in another framework so long as the two frameworks are moving smoothly (non-acceleratively) in respect to each other. How would the speeds be provided? By a transformation, and the transformation used in preliminary Galilean relativity employed

---

[55] There are two aspects in which it was preliminary. First, Galileo didn't recognize the Newtonian inertial motion, in which objects always moved in straight lines. Galileo thought that an object in something like inertial motion would go around the earth; second, Galileo subscribed to the Galileo transformation. No attention is being paid here to the first aspect of the preliminary form.

elementary additive and subtractive means. It is these additive and subtractive means that are referred to as the Galileo transformation.

For example, let us assume that the earth is flat, that each body on earth can take itself to be at rest (it's not feeling any accelerative force like the jerk when a car suddenly stops, which is an accelerative jerk), and that all the speeds are judged externally as the speeds of objects moving in constant straight line motions. Under these assumptions, suppose a car, car A, is going 50 mph eastward (perfectly smoothly) on an east-west highway at a given instant in time from the framework of someone on the earth. Suppose a truck, truck B, is east of car A, and is going at 30 mph westward (perfectly smoothly) on that highway (ignoring the difference between the two lanes) at that instant also from the framework of the earth. Our illustration has two speeds in reference to the earth; but we can also figure out truck B's speed from the frame of reference of car A, in which car A is taken to be at rest and the earth moving with respect to car A. One simply adds 50 to 30, and the answer is: from car A's frame (in which someone, e.g., someone in car A, takes car A to be at rest, and takes earth to be going at 50 mph westward), truck B is going at 80 mph westward toward the frame of car A.

Now a frame of reference – we'll call it **R** – could be moving in respect to both the generating system of a specified beam of light and any medium in which the light were to be travelling. Then Galileo's transformation would find a speed of light according to the framework of **R** (as though **R** were at rest) other than that given in Maxwell's equation. In that case, though, Maxwell's equations, it would seem, would be wrong, or one would have to abandon the idea that the laws of nature in one frame will be the same as those discovered from any other frame, since the speed of light in a vacuum would be given as a law of nature. But that there are no special frames for a given law of nature is an intuitively highly appealing idea. One would prefer not to have a special frame for a law of nature.[56]

It is also important to note that Albert Michelson and Edward Morley in the 1880's failed to find any difference between the speed of light going in one direction relative to the earth, and the speed of light going in another direction relative to the earth. Yet the earth was thought to be moving in a material substratum, the ether, and light was thought to be a wave moving in that ether. The picture simply didn't make sense.

---

[56] Einstein, *Relativity*: 13-20; 21-24.

Could it be that although the earth was orbiting the sun, the earth was exactly at rest relative to the ether? That would have been absurd, especially given the earth's elliptical orbiting of the sun.[57]

The difficulty of the problem of the speed of light both being, and yet not being, relative to an inertial frame of reference was a serious problem at the end of the 19th century and the first few years of the 20th century. Anyone to whom the problem is exposed today will also be frustrated in the same way some people were frustrated then. Do you see the problem? If so, can you explain the problem to someone who has not yet heard of it? (It is good to be able to do so to understand how physics became mathematized.)

---

[57] See Torretti, *ibid.*, 251; Brian Silver, *ibid.*: 198.

Chapter Six: The Mathematization of Physics: 20th century classical physics

6.0 Albert Einstein in 1905 uncovered a way to solve the problem of the apparent conflict between the constancy of the speed of light under Maxwell's equations and the use of the Galilean transformation. After years of struggling with the problem (while still a young man) he developed the notion that one needn't take the Galilean transformation for granted. Rather, if one *generalizes* the idea of a transformation – and one can say that this was his key insight, that there was a transformation involved, and that one can generalize the idea of a transformation – one would be able to have the constancy of the speed of light from any frame of reference; however, one would no longer use the Galilean transformation. The speed of light could then be regarded as given by what one can think of as a law of nature. The non-Galilean transformation would apply to give the different speeds of a mass object as judged from different frames of reference.

Interestingly, though, the transformation yielded by the constancy of the speed of light would also give different *mass amounts* from different frames of reference for a single mass object, different *lengths* of a mass object as measured in its direction of motion from different frames of reference, different judgments as to whether two events are *simultaneous*, or *non-simultaneous* ('*non-simultaneous*' meaning that one is subsequent to the other in time), as judged in different frames of reference, and different *rates at which time passes* in different frames of reference. If A is at rest, and B is in motion, then events in B's frame of reference happen more slowly than events in A's, and vice versa. The transformation found is called *the Lorentz transformation*, and it produces those very intriguing results.[58]

---

[58] Einstein, in *Relativity*: 25-42.

These results can be regarded as direct outcomes of the mathematics used; and the mathematics used expresses an attempt to reconcile the Newtonian system with the Maxwellian equations. The results do not arise from adopting the Newtonian system and then compensating for the amount of time it takes light to travel from one point to another point. Rather, the results arise by switching from the Galilean transformation to the Lorentz transformation so that light can have a constant speed from any frame of reference for a mass object, and yet in other ways Newton's three laws of motion are preserved, except that Newton understood the second law to mean that spatial dimensions and the time dimension are independent. In special relativity, there is no such assumption; indeed, spatiotemporal judgments are relative to frames of reference.

Of course the differences between using the Galilean transformation and using the Lorentz transformation only become significant to the degree that one reference frame relative to another is moving at a high fraction of the speed of light. At the speeds of horseback-riding relative to the earth, and even at the speeds of fast airplanes relative to the earth, there are no significant effects. A thousand miles an hour relative to the earth seems fast to us; but light travels at roughly a hundred and eighty six thousand miles a *second*.

The system that Einstein developed in 1905 is called the special relativity system. It is called 'special,' because it deals only with objects moving smoothly (non-acceleratively) in relation to each other. And it is called 'relativity theory' because depictions of events as to their sequence in time, depictions of rate of time passage, depictions of length of an object in its direction of motion, and depictions of the mass size of an object are *relative* to frames of reference.

What relevance does this have to the mathematization of physics? The point it brings out is that various natural non-scientific judgements we make – for example, that two events are absolutely simultaneous – are suited to the speeds at which things travel around us at the ordinary everyday human scale of reference. They are not suited to the larger speeds of mass objects used in nature, such as being close to the speed of light from some given frame of reference. And there are special conditions that can be provided by nuclear accelerators in which subatomic particles come to have speeds close to the speed of light from our frame of reference. Our ordinary judgements fail in such cases. Instead of thinking that there are absolute judgments about events at a given moment in time, we have to think only of relative judgments,

judgments relative to a frame of reference. This emphasizes the effects of accepting the not-intrinsically-purposive basic interactions: our ordinary conceptual schemes become radically revised when we deal with events outside of our usual scales. This enables us to better grasp how different a mathematized physics is from our intuitive physics.

6.1 It was in special relativity that Einstein also showed that energy and mass cannot be regarded as two fundamentally independent sorts of things. Rather, the famous equation $E = mc^2$ followed from the first publication of his special relativity analysis, yielding an amount of kinetic energy for any mass at all, including the mass at rest. This is fundamentally different from the amount of kinetic energy in the old calculations. This result, too, was published by Einstein in 1905, just after his special relativity results were published.

The elementary meaning of the famous equation is easy to state: the amount of energy of an object is the amount of mass of the object times the speed of light squared. There are, however, many details concerning the differences between such concepts as 'mass' and 'energy' prior to special relativity theory, and subsequent to special relativity theory. In special relativity theory, the speed of light is constant relative to any mass object moving at a constant speed in any inertial frame of reference. One consequence is that given any mass in a framework in which it is at rest, that mass will have an amount of what used to be called kinetic energy equal to its mass times the speed of light squared. That is an enormous amount of what used to be called kinetic energy. Yet the mass is at rest!

Thus, there was terminological confusion. In the 19th century it was believed that a mass in motion relative to a frame of reference has an amount of kinetic energy given by the formula $E = 1/2\ mv^2$. If the mass is at rest, then its velocity, v, $= 0$, and so its kinetic energy $= 0$. But in special relativity, its kinetic energy turns out to be enormous. This was a puzzling concept, since 'kinetic' started off by meaning 'in motion'; and the Galileo transformation (in Galilean relativity) did not on its own eliminate the possibility of a specially distinguished frame of reference. In the 19th century, the ether frame of reference, for example, was often taken to be a specially distinguished frame of reference. By special relativity theory, there is no absolute, nor specially distinguished, frame of reference in which a mass object is at rest. The frame of reference in which a mass object is, or is taken to be, at rest will yield a result by the

Lorentz-transformation for a frame of reference in which the mass is in motion. And all such frames of reference, including the frame of reference in which the mass object is at rest, will have an amount of what used to be kinetic energy specified for the mass object. Now the very notion of mass seems to have – how to put it? – motion energy, and it has motion energy in infinitely many frames of reference, each of which is as good a frame of reference as any other.

But how can the very notion of mass have motion-energy even when the mass is taken to be at rest? The terms, 'kinetic', 'inertial,' 'motion,' 'rest,' 'mass,' energy,' and so on are still used post relativity theory; their new meanings may be more baldly numerical than they had been before relativity theory. In post special relativity theory it is often said that the total energy of a mass object equals its kinetic energy plus its rest energy; it might, however, be said that its kinetic energy equals its rest energy plus its motion energy; the latter would alter the old meaning of 'kinetic.' There are several ways of phrasing the mathematical results.

It was this notion that mass has, or is, a significant amount of what used to be thought of as kinetic energy that pointed to the possibility of a fundamental change within a massive object, including the possibility of a conversion of mass to non-massive energy. (For instance, light has no mass, or, in another way of putting it, has no rest mass, and so it has non-massive energy.) Conversion such as this was first shown in a thought-experimental, strictly numerical, way in an analysis by Einstein in 1906.[59] And that there was something like a conversion of mass to non-massive energy was experimentally confirmed several decades later. The special relativity mass to energy theory did not deal with the strong and weak nuclear forces used in the actual conversion discoveries; but it was consistent with them; and for that reason is often thought to have grounded the notion of practically converting some mass into non-massive energy.

6.2 It should also be mentioned that because of the energy-mass relation, it became necessary to change what had been two independent conservation rules, the mass conservation rule, and the energy

---

[59] "The Principle Of Conservation Of Motion Of The Center Of Gravity And The Inertia of Energy." A simple explanation is given in Max von Laue's "Inertia and Energy": 524-5.

conservation rule, into a single mass-energy, sometimes called 'massergy' conservation rule.[60]

6.3 Einstein's special relativity provided the basis for Hermann Minkowski's 1908 spacetime theory, which maintained that there is only spacetime, not space and time. This more concretely exhibited what Einstein had already, theoretically, showed, that what is merely a spatial relationship between two events in one framework (because the two events are simultaneous in that framework), is not only a spatial but also a temporal relationship in another framework (because the same two events in that other framework are not simultaneous, but are, rather, one after the other).[61] Einstein initially resisted Minkowski's spacetime depiction of his theory, but a few years later came to accept it.

6.4 All the physics and main mathematical results up to 1915 or so prepared the ground for Emmy Nöther's symmetry Theorem, published in 1918. A symmetry, most easily explained, is a relation between two things that from one point of view seem to be the same, yet, from another point of view, they are not the same, as there has been some sort of transformation or change in the thing from one moment in time to another. Another way to put this is to say that a symmetry is a change that doesn't seem to be a change. For example, a circle can be rotated; the circle after the rotation looks just as it did before the rotation. So there's a symmetry there, between an unrotated, and a rotated circle. Similarly, a square can be rotated just the right amount – 90 degrees – and it will look the same as it did before. Its edges are parallel to what the edges were parallel to before. There are many other symmetries, and the nature of symmetries is a topic of much mathematical exploration.[62]

---

[60] See Max Jammer, *Concepts of Mass*: Chapter Thirteen, and Brian Silver, *ibid.*: 429-30. In regard to some details: we may discount the remarks Jammer makes on Einstein's supposed fallacy pg. 177; the discounting is for reasons set out by John Stachel and Roberto Torretti in "Einstein's first derivation of mass-energy equivalence."

[61] Einstein, *Relativity*: 61-64.

[62] Often the symmetries are numerical. See *Infinite Ascent*, by David Berlinski, 2008, NY: Modern Library, Chapter Six, for more detail; and *Why Beauty is Truth*, by Ian Stewart, for still more detail, especially Chapters Six to the end, again at the popular level.

Nöther's theorems, often collectively referred to in the singular, as Nöther's Theorem, showed that conservation laws, including conservation of momentum and conservation of energy, are results of fundamental mathematical symmetry notions, together with one or another form of what is called translation.[63] Spatial translatability yields conservation of momentum; and temporal translation yields conservation of energy. The use of the required translations are, for the most part, basic in physics, and so both momentum conservation and energy conservation are mathematically to be expected in physics (larger than the Planck scale; also there are difficulties in general relativity.)[64] Nöther's Theorem shows the breadth of the mathematical governance notions in physics, and their lack of intrinsic purposes. The publication date of Nöther's Theorem, 1918, can be taken as the culmination point of three centuries of research. Pure mathematics with more or less trivial assumptions (that the world is orderly) produces singularly important results in physics. This Theorem may be taken to mark the reaching of a high plateau level in the mathematization of physics, a level that has been maintained ever since.[65]

Three important symmetries developed in 20th century physics: the symmetries of charge reversal, spatial parity (the indistinguishability of an original image of a basic thing and its mirror image), and time reversal. Evidence has been presented showing lack of symmetry in each of these cases, but an important theorem was developed, as a postulate, by Wolfgang Pauli: if all three are switched (charge particles are charge-reversed, original image becomes mirror image, and time sequence is reversed) then the results do preserve symmetry. This is called CPT symmetry. The important point from our vantage here is to observe how different are these purely mathematical relations from basic desire-fulfilling-like purposes as used in a physically incomplete system.

This shows some of the elements in the development of the mathematization of physics from the early 17th century into the 20th century. Once again, the mathematical relations that govern the interactions of basic particles have no intrinsic purposes built into them.

---

[63] 'Translation' is briefly explained in Einstein, in *Relativity*, 15. See also Roger Penrose, *The Road To Reality*: 26, 87, 207, 489.

[64] Roger Penrose, *ibid.*, 489-90; 471-475; 105-114; 247-291.

[65] That Nöther's Theorem on its own yields phystriology is shown in 10.4 n. 172.

The basic notions – billiard ball relations, apparent action-at-a-distance force based interactions, interactions with conserved momentum, changes in which mass is conserved, changes in which energy is conserved, replacing one transformation system by another, changes in which mass-energy is conserved, adopting a spacetime system, preservations and violations of time, parity, and charge symmetries – are built on basic mathematical and interaction notions that have no intrinsic purposes in them.

6.5 It should also be noticed that there being an interaction process having no intrinsic purposes does not reject the notion that in some cases many particles *add up to* a being that acts with desire-fulfilling purposes. It might, for example, be the case that it is the (mereological fusion or, more informally) assembly of many particles that, from the large-scaled point of view, is described as having purposes, while the basic particles in interaction with each other are governed merely by mathematical relations. If all three processes being reviewed here have occurred – if physics is not intrinsically purposive but is rather mathematical, and chemistry is physical, and biology is physio-chemical – then, it seems, it is the (mereological fusion or) assembly of certain particles in a certain manner, all behaving in a way that does not overturn the laws or forces or rules in physics, that makes for any purposive being, perhaps a human being, that there is.

There is a lot of power and depth in the mathematization of physics notion; yet that physics is mathematized does not in itself say whether some assemblies of particles are purposive beings or not. Most philosophers say some are, though a few say that 'purposes' are mere fictions. Nonetheless, there are many challenges that accompany the mathematization of physics notion. Some of these involve figuring out the relationship between psychological states and biological-chemical-physical states. As it turned out, these challenges provided many topics of philosophical conversation from the 1960's to the present time. These topics will be reviewed to some extent in Chapter Twelve. Still, the main point here can be quickly summarized: physics was fully mathematized by the end of the second decade of the 20th century.

Chapter Seven: The Mathematization of Physics: Quantum physics

7.0 Some readers, based, perhaps, on various popularizations, might question whether quantum physics undermines the 'no-intrinsic-purposes' mathematization of physics. If there is such undermining, it wouldn't be because there is less mathematics in quantum physics; that is obviously not the case. Rather, if there is such undermining it might be because the quantum processes are sufficiently dependent on subjective factors as to allow purposes to come back into the base of the system; or, in other ways, they might allow purposes to come back into the base of the system. That supplies a potential objection to phystriology. Does this potential objection have any strength?

In response, quantum physics does not seem, in any way, to undermine the view that there are no intrinsic purposes in basic-physics interactions. To see this, it would help to review, in as simple a way as can be done, some of the main features of quantum physics.

7.1 We begin by observing the important difference between continuous systems, called 'classical systems,' on the one hand, and, on the other hand, quantized systems. We tend to think that natural systems expressed in space and time (or spacetime) must be continuous: it would seem that any spatial distance can be halved, for example. Similarly, energy in a light ray – according to Maxwell's theory of light – spreads out over an ever-increasing volume. There should be continuity in that energy; and if there is continuity in that energy, then any amount of energy can be halved, in nature. The idea that any measure of a spacetime object can be halved, and, hypothetically, found halved in nature, gives one aspect of continuity.[66] If nature were not continuous, then energy would be a sum of basic energy units. Each such basic energy unit could not, in nature, be halved, and yet, such an energy unit would not = 0; it would be bigger. Yet it sounds mysterious if energy – or spacetime! – is to be quantized. The former is the basic notion in quantum physics, and it has led many physicists to suspect the latter.[67]

Given both relativity theory, which is a classical or continuous system theory, and some factors in non-classical quantum theory, the former notion (*energy* is quantized) has become the notion that *mass-energy* is quantized. It may seem as though the notion that mass-energy is quantized is easier to grasp than the notion that energy is quantized. This is partly true, but partly false. If energy is particulate (if energy is always carried by particles, which seems to be a plausible enough view) then, since even the 1905 form of relativity theory, each elementary particle, whether at rest or in motion, has, or is, an amount of energy. This applies both to particles with rest mass and to particles (like photons, particles of light) without rest mass. So the hyphenation of energy with mass doesn't particularly help. Given the continuous Lorentz transformation, how does one understand the quantization of apparently basic mass amounts and (in an old sense non-massive) radiative energy amounts?

In any case, the mass-energy quantization notion began as the energy quantization notion. This energy quantization notion developed in two stages. In 1900 Max Planck postulated a smallest energy amount that would solve an important mathematical problem dealing with the energy

---

[66] More details: The other aspect of continuity is that there are incommensurable units, for example, irrational units in relation to rational units. In measure theory, there need to be the real numbers if there is to be continuity; the sum of the rational numbers has measure 0. Then there must be the power set of rational numbers for a continuous system; but then there must be incommensurability between some numbers.

[67] There is a simple argument whose conclusion states that it is better to assume that spacetime is quantized than not to assume that. Consider the quantized rest masses, m_1 and m_2, of two particles, m$_1$ and m$_2$. Consider m$_2$ as moving in respect to m$_1$. If spacetime is continuous, then the mass of the particle with m_2 rest mass can be calculated from m$_1$'s rest frame. Let's suppose that it is m_2*. And let us suppose that the ratio m_2*/m_1 makes no quantized sense. It would be better, then, if such a ratio could not occur, and it seems that would only be the case if spacetime were quantized. In conclusion, then, it seems wise to assume that spacetime is quantized.

---

emitted from what is called a blackbody. As far as Planck was concerned in 1900, the solution was assumed not to reflect the way light is, but to reflect what Planck called the "resonators" in the cavity of a blackbody. In 1905, Einstein postulated (in fundamental work having nothing to do with relativity theory) that light itself could be taken to be a quantized particle, not a wave. This would explain some results, such as the then well known, but peculiar, photoelectric effects of light on a metal sheet. Einstein put this forward as a useful "heuristic point of view."[68] In 1906, Einstein claimed that Planck's work needed a *natural* discontinuity in energy states[69]. Some take it that the full notion of the quantum system was emerging with this theoretical claim made by Einstein.[70] Over the next few years, for various reasons, Planck and some other physicists came to agree with the quantum-in-nature point of view (rather than the merely mathematical and heuristic use of quanta).[71] By the period around the end of the first decade of the 20th century, then, the quantization notion had taken root.

Once energy had been quantized, and mass-energy was understood as basic, the quantization was understood as a mass-energy quantization.

7.2 A second feature of quantum physics is 'quantum jumps' or 'quantum leaps'. In the 1912-3 period, Niels Bohr presented his postulate of quantized orbits for electrons around the nucleus of atoms. (In 8.9 we'll briefly review the discovery of the existence of what were called electrons, protons, and neutrons within an atom.) In this theory, electrons were to instantaneously jump from one orbit to another; later this was discovered to be only a partial view of the subatomic system, but

---

[68] Albert Einstein, "On a Heuristic Point of View Concerning the Production and Transformation of Light." For an explanation, see John Rigden, *Einstein 1905*, "March"; or, more briefly, Brian Greene, *The Elegant Universe*: 91-99.

[69] Albert Einstein, "Zur Theorie der Lichterzeugung und Lichtabsorption," quoted in Thomas Kuhn, *Black-Body Theory and the Quantum Discontinuity 1894-1912*: 170.

[70] Thomas Kuhn, *ibid*, 170.

[71] The two stages are explained in detail in Thomas Kuhn, 1984, *ibid*. For brief reviews of the basic notion, see Brian Silver, *ibid*: 358-9, and Jim Al-Khalili, *Quantum*: 40-3.

it did inaugurate the notion of 'quantized jumps', or 'quantum leaps'.[72] We will return to the quantum leaps in discussing the fifth basic element of quantum physics in 7.5.

7.3 Third, in the early 1920's Louis de Broglie postulated that just as light seemed to be not only a wave but also a particle (for example, by Einstein's 1905 theory of light, which, again, did not use any relativity features), so, too, basic mass objects should have wave properties. Since then, basic objects are understood as having both particulate and wavelike properties.[73] However, how, or why, a quantum object shows a wavelike or a particulate property has been difficult to fathom.[74]

7.4 Fourth, between 1926 and 1927, Werner Heisenberg developed the uncertainty principle. For example, the degree to which an elementary object has a precise position is the degree to which it does not have a precise momentum; the degree to which a time is precisely assigned to a particle is the degree to which its energy is not precisely specified. The uncertainty relations are a direct result of the mathematical requirements; they are not a result of measurement disturbances. Both the uncertainty feature, and the wave-particle feature, only become significant when one is dealing with very small objects. The wave-particle feature, for instance, is so insignificant in human-scale objects that we shouldn't be surprised that we can't sensorily perceive the wave-properties of human-scaled objects.[75]

7.5 Fifth, basic equations were developed for the trajectories, or something like the trajectories, of quantized objects, including Schrödinger's wave equation in the mid 1920's. Schrödinger's wave equation was later modified to incorporate relativity features.

It is important to note that these quantum equations are generally interpreted as being, or are shown by measurements of results to be, probabilistic equations. It would typically be said that they yield a

---

[72] Roberto Torretti, *Philosophy of Physics*: 310-313; Jim Al Khalili, *ibid*, 44-47.

[73] Torretti, *ibid.*, 325-7; Jim Al-Khalili, *ibid.*, 47-51.

[74] Torretti, *ibid.*, 331-337; Jim Al-Khalili, *ibid.*, 12-25.

[75] Jim Al-Khalili, *ibid.*, 68-9.

probability, and only a probability, that if a particle is taken to be at such and such a location at such and such a time, then a measurement will reveal it to be at another location just a bit later.[76] Just as Bohr's 1913 theory of the electron orbits saw them as 'jumping' from one level to another, without the electron travelling between the two orbit levels, so too, the notion of a measurement placing a particle at one location, and its next location-measurement placing it at another location has come to be interpreted as a (probabilistically governed) quantum leap.

Indeed, there are three meanings of 'quantum leap'. First, there is Niels Bohr's 1913 early stab at the notion with his electron orbit leap. The second and third are more sophisticated notions. The second is the measurement in one outcome, e.g., a position (with only a certain degree of precision), and a subsequent measurement in another outcome of that type, in this case, position (with only a certain degree of precision), without it being the case that the particle is taken to have continuously gone through space or spacetime from the first outcome to the second outcome, in this case from the first position to the second position (both with only a certain degree of precision). The relation between the first position and the second position is that of probability or propensity. Third, the Schrödinger equation is of a wave; a measurement can give a result about the particle carrying the wave, for example, the particle's position (with only a certain degree of precision). The switch from a wave to a measurement result, for example, a position (with only a certain degree of precision) – often called the breakdown of the wave formula – is also taken to be a quantum leap.

The quantum leap problem is intimately connected to what is called the measurement problem. One difficulty is that there are many ways of stating the measurement problem. Here is one: There are quantum equations for the unfolding states of affairs. In the quantum equations, an item might be understood as a, or as b, or as $a + b$, where the $a + b$ sum, often, makes no sense in our classical notions. (For example, a cat cannot be both alive and dead. If a lot of results, including a lot of $a + b$ results, were added to each other they might make an 'alive and dead' cat.) However, if it were to be measured, it would not be measured as $a + b$; it would only be measured as either a or b. Why does the non-classical $a + b$ amount in the quantum formula disappear in

---

[76] Torretti, *ibid.*, 333; Jim Al-Khalili, *ibid.*, 64-7; 62-3. The locations are only approximate, and subject to the uncertainty relations: the more precise the location, the less precise the momentum, and so on.

measurement? Is it merely statistical, or is there something else involved? That is one way to state the measurement problem.

Another investigates whether there is a breakdown of the quantum wave when measurement is made.

Here is still another: measurements seem to be of classical objects, that is, objects, thought of in the ways we think of human-scaled objects. But not everything in the quantum formulas is given classically; some features of the quantum formulas are given in a fuzzy or spread-out-over-contraries way. Which, then, is more basic – the quantum world, or the classical world?

And this can be put still another way: not only everything being measured, but also, anything making measurements is itself supposed to be quantized, so it should be subject to the results of quantum physics, which are probabilistic results. Again, this makes it hard to understand what is more basic – a classical non-probabilistic reality, or a quantized fundamentally probabilistic reality.

These are, then, several versions of the measurement problem, and several ways of stating each version as well.

7.6 In 1935 Einstein and two other physicists, Boris Podolsky and Nathan Rosen, presented a model of distant particles that showed, they claimed, that there were hidden variables in quantum theory. The two particles at any distance could be linked by momentum conservation. The momentum of one would be amount-wise equal to that of the other, but in inverse direction. In a simplifying reformulation of Einstein, Podolsky, and Rosen's argument given by E. Schrödinger, of the two particles, the momentum of one, A, could be measured (within uncertainty conditions); and the position of the other, B, could be measured (within uncertainty conditions); but the momentum of B would be amount-wise equal to, and direction-wise inverse of, that of A; then the position *and* the momentum of B could be known in a way that the quantum formulas (due to the uncertainty relations) don't permit. Hence, Einstein, Podolsky, and Rosen argued (for a case analogous to Schrödinger's case), quantum formulas are incomplete. There are hidden variables.

Niels Bohr, however, disagreed. One way of understanding his position (Bohr's prose was difficult) is to take him as having said, effectively, that if a position measurement is made on B, then one can't merely calculate what momentum it *must have had*, since that measurement *couldn't have been made* on B.

One feature of Einstein, Podolsky and Rosen's 1935 model is that the hidden variables would all be local, or would be 'in the particles'. Indeed, Einstein clearly defended an ultimate localism: properties must be properties of locally placed things. However, in the early 1960's (after Einstein's death in 1955) John Bell mathematically discovered that there are some probabilistic relations required by quantum formulas such that there are measurements that can be made on particles at two distant regions, and that there must be unprepared correlations between the measurements made on both sides. These measurements, made on both sides, would show that there cannot be any form of *local* hidden variables – that is the way the consequence of Bell's point is usually articulated. Such measurements were made in the 1980's, and '90's, and the generally accepted view is that the quantum non-local correlations have been found.

7.7 The quantum objects are very different from classical (or everyday objects). In particular, the way they take states is not the way ordinary objects take states. We can see this through the difference between classical objects that follow classical statistics, quantum objects (including the electrons) that follow what is called the Fermi-Dirac statistics, and quantum objects (including the photons or light particles) that follow what is called the Bose-Einstein statistics.

Erwin Schrödinger (in 1934) explained the difference in roughly the following way.[77] Suppose there are two awards being distributed among three students. The awards analogize to the particles or objects of a certain type. And the students analogize to the states that the objects can take. The analogy is based on the flexibility in the nature of the awards, hence the flexibility in the nature of the particles, or the absence of the identity condition. On the other hand, we think of one student as having an identity condition distinguishing that student from any other student; for that reason, the students will not analogize to the particles.

For the classical objects, conceive of the awards as differentiable, one from the other. For instance, one has a Dante image, whereas the other has a Shakespeare image. Then, there are, in total, nine ways the

---

[77] Erwin Schrödinger, "What Is An Elementary Particle?" especially 109-113.

awards can be given: In six of them one student doesn't get an award, but the other two are differentiated as to which award goes to which student, and in three of them only one student gets both awards. In the Fermi-Dirac statistics, applying for example to electrons, the two awards cannot both go to one student. Each award is, let us suppose, a position on a single athletic team. There are two positions to be awarded on that team; but one player cannot occupy two places on that team. Accordingly, there are only, in total, three distributions, in each of which one student does not get an award. And the Bose-Einstein statistics are such that the awards are once again, as in the Fermi-Dirac cases, indistinguishable from each other, but, once again, as in the classical cases, awardable multiply to one student. The awards are like $20 bills. Accordingly, there are, in total, six distributions, in three of which each student has either exactly one award, or no award, and in three of which one student has both awards.

The analogy in Schrödinger's work deliberately ignores the fact that if, in the classical case, one student gets two awards, one award may be placed in the student's left hand, and the other award in the student's right hand, or, the first award may be placed in the student's right hand, and the other award in the student's left hand. If one student gets both awards, the analogy, according to its distribution number, ignores the difference in identity of the two awards. For one student to have two awards is for one student to have both awards; that's all. The student who obtains the award, thus, is the state of the award. Hence the identity of the award can be understood through the analogy with the one mentioned feature ignored. Of course, if the two awards are given to two different students, Schrödinger's analogy also deliberately ignores which hand the award is placed in. The student obtaining the award is just the state of the award.

What counts is that in the quantum physics system, the particle identity, given through the state the particle has, is very different from that of the classical physics system.

7.8 Finally, the overall project of many during the 20th century was to integrate general relativity – the application of relativity theory to gravitational attraction – with quantum theory. The project continues now in the 21st century. There is a basic conflict between general relativity theory and quantum theory. In general relativity theory, if there is no mass-energy, then, to whatever extent there could be spacetime,

spacetime would be flat (since it's only the massive objects that curve the spacetime). But in quantum physics, even if spacetime averages out to be flat, there is no spacetime empty of mass; rather, because of the uncertainty relations, there is an unstable vacuum, and, in the tiniest regions of spacetime, mass-energy objects pop into and out of existence.[78] In this and other ways there are difficult problems understanding how one might integrate the two very different systems; this difficulty is exacerbated by the lack of a background spacetime in general relativity theory, and the presence of a background spacetime in quantum physical analysis. The overall integration project has had some promising beginnings, but it is far from completed at this time.[79]

The integration of gravity and other apparently basic notions in physics was very much on Einstein's mind during the long last period of his work (for more than two decades). But Einstein criticized the fundamentally probabilistic features of quantum measurements. Einstein's focus was on integrating general relativity gravity and electromagnetic theory. This was not the path that first led other physicists (after Einstein's death) to partial integration. It was the weak nuclear force and electromagnetic theory that were first unified in quantum theory (in 1968, which was thirteen years after Einstein's death), and that unification left gravity (and the strong nuclear force) out. Although Einstein's contributions to physics were enormously significant (as significant as anyone's in the history of physics), he resisted the idea in quantum physics that probabilities were basic. "God does not play dice with the universe," was the snappy expression of Einstein's view, but that notion seems to have been incorrect.[80] In any case, Einstein's main positive effort after general relativity theory and the development of the

---

[78] As far as mass-energy conservation is concerned, there is the borrowing and repaying within the Planck scale—an extremely tiny spacetime scale, a scale as much smaller than the atom as the atom is smaller than our human-scale objects. All the borrowing and repaying has been done once one is outside the Planck scale.

[79] Brian Greene, *The Elegant Universe*, is a good introduction to this project. For an exposition of the integration problem, see pp. 67-8; 117-131. For a broader, and more mathematical, look, though only directed to members of the general public who are interested in working through mathematical details, see Roger Penrose, *The Road to Reality*, Chapters 30-33. For a detailed but less mathematical treatment, see Lee Smolin, *Three Roads to Quantum Gravity*.

[80] Brian Greene, *ibid.*, 105-108.

Bose-Einstein statistics – which was to find a unified electromagnetism plus gravitational relativity theory – made no measurable progress. More generally, the problem of integrating the gravitational force into quantum theory made little or no progress until the development of string theory in the 1970's; string theory received some large (mathematical) boosts in the 1980's and 1990's.[81] And there have been other, non-string approaches, as well. In the string approaches, the mathematization of physics process is not diminishing in the least; if there are any changes since the end of Einstein's life, then, if anything, the mathematization of physics process is increasing.[82]

7.9 What, then, about quantum physics in relation to what we're calling the mathematization of physics? First we will look at quantum physics in relation to the most general type of mechanism. (This is the third type of mechanism described in Chapter Three from 3.6 through 3.10.) Then we will look more generally at the mathematization in quantum physics.

Our definition of the most general type of mechanism is a theory of motion or balance in which there are no purposes in the basic interactions. The only difficulty here is in the concept of 'motion'. Our usual concept of an object moving is that its change in position is continuous. As soon as we have quantum leaps – in any of the three sorts of quantum leaps – we don't have what is called the classical notion of motion. Since 'motion' seems to mean classical motion, it seems no longer appropriate to talk of quantum mechanic motions, in our third sense of mechanics, when there are quantum leaps. Accordingly, all we are interested in is whether quantum physics undoes the mathematization of physics, where 'mathematization of physics' only means the removal of purposes from the basic interactions, and the view that basic interactions (first, only in inanimate objects, later, in all objects) are governed exclusively by abstract, non-purposive mathematical relations.

Most commentators would say that it would be extremely implausible to bring purposes back into the basic relationships here, and I'll try to indicate why they would say this. The mathematics in theoretical quantum-relativity physics is beyond the limit of anything that could be close to having purposes at the basic level. The abstractness is

[81] Brian Greene, *ibid.*

[82] Lee Smolin, *Three Roads to Quantum Gravity*, NY: Perseus Books; Roger Penrose, *The Road To Reality*: 869-1009.

remarkable, as was shown in the abstractness of the symmetry notion. The challenge in dealing with contemporary physics is to notice how deeply non-purposive in inherent desire-like features the relations are, and yet to be able, at another level entirely, the level dealing with some sums of trillions of small things, to talk about psychological creatures. But psychological creatures are all biological creatures (until we get more sophisticated robots, but never mind that possibility). And biological creatures evolved through natural selection. This goes heavily against there being basic purposes (inherent desire-like purposes for any basic things) in physics. In any case, if there are such basic purposes, they would only come in through a psychological, biological, chemical, or physical level. Because of Darwinian evolution, they won't be basic at the level of psychology. As we'll see in the next two Chapters, there are no special *fundamental* chemical nor biological laws or forces or rules governing change. And the base of the physics is abstractly mathematical. This shows how implausible it is to think that basic purposes (inherent desire-like purposes of root objects) will come back in through quantum physics. For those who are interested, this is spelled out in more detail in Appendix 2.1.

7.10 It is time for us now to look at the developments of the physicalization of chemistry and the physio-chemicalization of biology. These two developments are conceptually much simpler to review than the mathematization of physics.

Chapter Eight: The Physicalization of Chemistry

8.0 It is intriguing to notice the striking contrast between Newton's brilliant progress in mathematics and physics, and his lack of progress in chemistry despite decades of effort in that direction. In physics, among other things, Newton developed the three laws of motion, the gravitational formula, and the notion of the decomposition and composition of the colours in light. In mathematics, among other things, Newton invented the calculus (it seems, a bit before Leibniz independently invented the calculus though Leibniz published his calculus system first). And Newton was *experimentally* brilliant, too, for example in his experimental work on light. On the other hand, his work in chemistry, though he was furiously engaged in it for decades, was basically alchemical, and so he made no significant progress.[83] It seems that Newton's instincts in regard to chemical combinations were not the same as his extraordinarily fine instincts in mathematics and physics.

To understand this it will help to see the conceptual difference between physics and chemistry. Seeing that difference will also help make sense of the 'physicalization of chemistry.' Conceptually speaking, physics is supposed to be about changes in things without the things changing their basic nature. For example, examining the motions of several billiard balls on a billiard ball table is an examination in physics; it does not involve examining how objects seem to change their basic nature. On the

---

[83] Alchemy was centered on transmutations (the changing of one thing into another), and often expressed itself in the attempt to turn lead into gold. Of course not all alchemical work was specifically focused on transmutations themselves. But the basic approach was still based on the notion that there might be transmutations of the desired kind. *Newton*: 297-324; and Brian Silver, *Ascent of Science*: 113-117.

other hand, chemical changes were thought of, before some time in the early 20th century, or so, to be changes in the fundamental nature of an object or objects. Suppose there is a metal that goes rusty; that seems to be a change in the basic nature of the surface area where the rust occurred. Or suppose one has a piece of wood, and it is burnt to ashes. That, too, seems to be a change in the basic nature of the thing (its destruction, putting it one way). In this manner, we have, on the one hand, physical changes with no essential changes in the objects, and, on the other hand, chemical changes, in which the basic nature of a thing, or the basic nature of the surface of a thing if it's the surface that is being talked about, seems to change.

It took a long time a few hundred years ago for people to understand that two changes, first from ice to liquid water, and then from liquid water to steam, were not chemical changes. That is, it took a long time for it to be understood that ice, liquid water, and steam are all instances of the same thing, which we call water. For a couple of hundred years we have been saying that water is merely in different physical states, because the same thing – water – is just at different temperatures. In this way, conceptually speaking, physics is the study of changes in things without the study of things changing their basic nature; and chemistry (prior to some time in the early 20th century) was thought of as the study of changes in things in which the things seem to be changing their basic nature.

This gives us a differentiation between physics and chemistry; and it is that differentiation that enables us to get a better sense of how Newton saw the relation between physics and chemistry, and in how we can better understand the process of the physicalization of chemistry. (We will note how the concept of chemistry now, since the physicalization of chemistry process became completed around 1930, has a different meaning from the meaning it had before some time early in the 20th century, in 8.12.)

The physicalization of chemistry, then, is the process in which it came to be increasingly understood that the changes in some things (for instance, not rusty metal becoming rusty metal) that seem to be changing their basic nature are, indeed, changes in the relations between very small things that are not (or seem in no way to be) changing their basic nature.

8.1 Now let us return to Newton's physics and Newton's chemistry. Newton was a genius in mathematics and physics; he accomplished almost nothing in chemistry – 'almost,' because there was at least one contribution he made through his work in chemistry. The goal of his work here was to better understand the relation between physics and chemistry. Galileo had shown a single acceleration rate for the free fall of objects like stones down to the earth. Newton wanted to see if there would be any difference for items of different chemical composition. He experimented using pendulums of different material, and found that there wasn't. Accordingly, it became possible to use the gravitational force to define the weight of any object at a given height from the earth.[84]

This also, to a degree, showed the independence of the basic physical notions from the chemical notions; and, to a degree, it supported a sort of primacy of the physical realm in relation to the chemical realm.

8.2 In any case, on account of the largely alchemical exploration by Newton in the 1670's and on, we can see that the pioneering work done by Robert Boyle in *The Sceptical Chymist* of 1661 did not quickly transform what was then, often, an alchemical system into a non-alchemical system. Nonetheless, Boyle postulated a strong connection between physics and chemistry; he revived the notion that there are atoms (and we remember that the term 'atom' was then understood to refer to an indivisible thing) and that they compound in various ways in making chemical materials.[85] In this he was anticipating the development of a physicalization of chemistry process. Boyle's view that atoms compound or combine in different manners to make different things shows a way in which he took it that some things stay the same, even though it's the combinations of them that make for what seem to be different things to us.

8.3 Antoine Lavoisier's emphasis on quantification of experimental results in the 18th century enabled key chemical notions to be established. He postulated that there were basic chemical *elements*, and listed them, too, though his list had to be revised. Nonetheless, he postulated the interactions of basic chemical elements.[86] Lavoisier also

---

[84] Ernst Mach, *The Science of Mechanics*: 240-1.

[85] Richard Westfall, *The Construction of Modern Science*: 75-81; Brian Silver, *ibid.*, 116.

[86] Bernard Jaffe, *Crucibles*: 62-76. Also, it can be observed that the notion of a chemical element still survives, but the definition of being a chemical element

postulated the law of conservation of mass, as we saw in Chapter Four; and this specifically supported the notion of physical features underlying chemical relations.

8.4 John Dalton's work at the turn of the 19th century speculated about an even stronger connection between physics and chemistry than had Lavoisier. Dalton, like Boyle in the 17th century, put forward a basic atomic theory, according to which all things are made up of tiny indivisible particles, or atoms. In Dalton's theory, though, each element had its own type of atom, and each type of atom would have a different weight. Atoms of one type might combine with atoms of another type; elements on their own or elements in combination would be, or would make, the sorts of objects we are familiar with. This required a multiple proportion notion of how things compound with each other. Like Lavoisier, Dalton, too, was concerned with weights. But in Dalton's theory, the notion of different *atomic* weights became central, since, in Dalton's theory, an atom of one element was thought to have a different weight from an atom of a different element.[87]

It was recognized that proportions of things by weight were necessary for chemical transformations to occur. Hypothetically, take two batches, say, one of sodium, and one of chlorine, and put them together in a suitable manner, and a batch of salt may result. But then, some of the original batch of sodium or chlorine might be left over. Only the right proportions would combine. Given enough such proportional combinations, speculations on atomic weights can be made. Also, Amedeus Avogadro postulated that one volume of gas at a specified temperature and pressure will contain the same number of basic elements or molecules as another volume of gas with the same volume, temperature and pressure. This, too enabled a calculation of the relations of the atomic entities. If a volume of gas of oxygen at a given

---

has changed as chemistry has changed. (One might find one definition for Lavoisier's notion, one for Dalton's, one for the early divisible atomic theory, and one or more for later theories.)

[87] Bernard Jaffe, *ibid*: 77-92. Dalton's postulate here was correct, but not in the way Dalton thought it would be. He thought of an atom as indivisible. Now, of course, atoms are divisible items made of subatomic parts. The weight of an atom has been replaced by the mass of an atom, and the mass of an atom is, basically or roughly, the sum of the masses of its subatomic parts.

temperature and pressure weighs x, and the same volume of gas of hydrogen at the same temperature and pressure weighs y, then, given Avogadro's hypothesis, the relation of hydrogen units to oxygen units in the gas can be calculated. This would yield the result that an oxygen unit in the gas is eight times as heavy as a hydrogen unit in the gas. In this way, Avogadro's hypothesis of 1811 was an improvement on Dalton's, according to which an oxygen unit in the gas would only be (incorrectly) four times as heavy as a hydrogen unit in the gas.[88]

During the same period, the early 19th century, Humphry Davy proposed that chemical relations were basically electric. Previously, it had been thought that what allowed physical things to combine to make chemical elements or chemical things was the gravitational pull. However, given a fair amount of research in electric relations, including one experiment in which Davy electrically charged potash, and potassium emerged from it, Davy came to the conclusion that it was electric forces that accounted for chemical reactions.[89] In many ways, as we'll see, he was right, though he didn't have access to many empirical or observational and theoretical features that showed how that theory is true. Nonetheless, his having postulated that chemical relations are electric relations shows how physical notions, derived from current work in physics, were used in explaining chemical events.

8.5 Jons Berzelius in 1811 pioneered a new way of referring to the elements in chemistry. He took the first letter of each element, or, when several elements had the same first letter, enough first letters to enable one to know which element one was talking about. Then combinations would be written with the proportions added. Berzelius superscripted where we now subscript, but the system was fundamentally the same as ours.

For instance, in a paper by Edward Frankland in 1852, about forty years after Berzelius' notation system was developed, chemicals were notated as follows: ZnC_6H_7, and PH_3, where 'Zn' stood for zinc, 'C'

---

[88] This ignores the difference between atomic number and atomic masses, the difference between which will be explained below. It is now thought that oxygen atoms are about sixteen times as massy as hydrogen atoms. The relations between weights and combining properties were unclear throughout the 19th century.

[89] H. T. Pledge, *Science Since 1500*: 123.

for carbon, 'H' for hydrogen, and 'P' for phosphorus. There were, however, some differences from the contemporary notation – we no longer use numbered brackets for some chemicals as they did then. For example, Frankland there referred to $P(C_2H_3)_3$ as a methyl, and we no longer use the numbered bracket notation.

8.6 In any case, what we want to look at is the way the valence notion developed in chemistry in the middle of the 19th century; and by the end of this chapter we will come to see how fundamentally physical relations accounted for this chemical valence notion. In the paper just mentioned, Edward Frankland was working with metals combining with carbon-based groups. He postulated that certain proportions are required for such bondings to occur. Frankland's notion was that zinc, for example, would only bond with two organic (carbon based) groups. Alexander Williamson then generalized this notion for other elements in combination. A special number was found for each element as to how many units it would bond with; this combining property became known as the element's valency or valence.

In 1858, there were two important developments in valence theory. First, Friedrich Kukulé found that carbon is tetravalent, that is, that it combines with exactly four units; he also postulated a ring-like structure for carbon combinations. Second, Archibald Scott Couper used straight lines to indicate valence bonds in organic compounds. This, too, became generalized so that each element would have its valence represented by the number of lines coming from it. Today, too, we use the straight lines coming from an atom in representing the chemical bonding relations.

There were still some problems remaining for valence theory. The notion of the units entering into combination was not entirely clear; we now distinguish between atoms and combinations of atoms, which we call molecules. An atom when it is in combination with another atom can be a link to a group of atoms, that is, to a molecule that had been ripe for combination with a solo atom or an atom in a molecule.

A second problem in the mid 19th century theory of valence was the problem of apparently multiple valences. Sulfur, for example, sometimes seemed to have a valence of two, sometimes of four, and sometimes of six. This was difficult for anyone who believed that valence indicated a fundamental property of an element. However, more research was needed into these basic properties of elements to resolve the difficulty.[90]

8.7 This brings us now to the periodic table. Dalton's atomic weights theory received a significant maturation in Dmitri Medeleev's periodic table, first published in 1869.[91] There had been several other theories organizing chemicals into family groups, where the family groups were defined by what the members of the family groups had a tendency to combine with. However, Mendeleev's table was the most complete organization; his atomic table was a complete table for the evidence base at that time. In Mendeleev's table, to go along a row[92] is to progress by weights, and to go down a column is to progress down a list of members of a family defined by properties for combining with other elements. Furthermore, Mendeleev used the few blank spots in the table to predict that new elements would be found to fill those spots. His predictions were strikingly fulfilled.

It is also useful to see how the Mendeleev periodic table used physical elements to base the chemical relations. As mentioned, and this is as Mendeleev would have described it (if you altered his placement of the table on the page, for which, see n. 93), if you go rightward along a row, you go to an element with an increased weight. The weight progression is a physical progression. Mendeleev stopped each row at a point so that the next row lower would begin at the far left just a bit higher in weight than where the previous row stopped in weights at the far right, but any column would show a group of elements that behaved similarly as far as chemical relations are concerned. The columns expressed the chemical properties of the elements.[93] The first periodic

---

[90] See Jaffe, ibid., Ch. VII; also see www.chemheritage.org/explore/timeline/NOMEN.HTM; and web.lemoyne.edu/~GIUNTA/frankland.html; and www.bookrags.com/sciences/sciencehistory/valence-wsd.html.

[91] Bernard Jaffe, *ibid.*: 125-139.

[92] Medeleev first published the periodic tables using rows where we use columns, and using columns where we use rows. In the description just given, it is the contemporary depiction that is used.

[93] For the Mendeleev periodic table by weights, see www.aip.org/history/curie/periodic.htm. (For a 1956 list of elements by weights and numbers, see Bernard Jaffe, *ibid*: 204.)

table, then, uses physical characteristics, the weights, to organize the rows, but in such a way as to yield the chemical properties in columns.

However, there were some difficulties with Mendeleev's use of the atomic weights; some of them were due to incorrect measures; and some due to what turned out to be the incorrect theory that it was the weights of atoms that accounted, somehow, for their chemical properties. As we'll see, the atomic numbers, not the atomic weights, account for the chemical properties. And it was, effectively, impossible to develop the atomic numbers theory without the discovery of the subatomic particles. The discovery of the subatomic particles began in the 1890's, with the discovery of the electron.[94]

Once again, the ancient Greek term 'atom' meant 'indivisible thing'. But at the end of the 19th century, people discovered that what they had been calling atoms were, indeed, divisible, and that there were subatomic particles. In this way the word 'atom' changed its meaning. Now, of course, in everyday conversation an atom is a divisible thing; for over a hundred years, it has been understood as having subatomic parts. It is only some philosophers who, in some contexts, maintain the original (Greek-derived) meaning for 'atom' in which it is an indivisible thing. The everyday meaning of the word 'atom' has changed.

8.8 Before we review the discovery of the subatomic particles, we'll note how Svante Arrhenius (1859-1927) in his doctoral work in the 1880's developed the theory of chemical composition through ionic relations. The ion is an electrically charged particle. As just mentioned, the electron and other sub-atomic particles had not yet been discovered, so it was impossible for Arrhenius to have a clear conception of the nature of the ions. Nonetheless, he was certainly pursuing a profound theoretical investigation.

His experiments revealed to him that the chemical properties were fundamentally electrical in nature. In saying so, he was picking up an idea developed by Davy, and, also, by Berzelius, but an idea that had been dropped by the time Arrhenius was experimenting. Needless to say, despite their being revivals of some earlier ideas, Arrhenius' notions were considered as radical notions at the time he developed them.[95]

---

[94] Abraham Pais, *Inward Bound*: 10; Silver, *ibid*: 137-143.

[95] Bernard Jaffe, *ibid*: 140-154.

8.9 The electron was discovered in the 1890's, and this, of course, was a discovery within physics. However, it was a discovery that made it possible for chemical properties to begin to be understood. In 1911 Robert Millikan found the exact charge of the electron, and it was at roughly the same time that the nucleus of the atom was discovered by Ernest Rutherford.

Here is a quick explanation of Rutherford's discovery. J. J. Thomson in 1908 had proposed (incorrectly as it turned out) that an atom was something like a pudding, and in the pudding, the electrons would be scattered like raisins. The electrons were negatively charged, but the positive charge balancing the electrons would have been evenly spread throughout the pudding. However, Ernest Rutherford discovered that there was a small spot in the atom that deflected some particles sent toward the atom, and the remaining region of the atom allowed the rest of the particles to pass right through. Accordingly, he reasoned, the positive charge was to be found only at the centre, or nucleus, of the atom. What resulted was a picture of the atom as having negatively charged electrons at the outside of the atom and in the nucleus of the atom, positively charged particles, called protons. (Later, in 1932, it was observed that neutrally charged particles of roughly the same mass as the proton existed in the nucleus of the atoms. It had been predicted a few years earlier that there would be such particles. These particles were called 'neutrons.')

Rutherford's picture of the atom still didn't resolve the confusions over atomic weights, but it did allow for the development of the theory of atomic numbers.

8.10 The theory of atomic numbers was developed by Henry Moseley in 1912, and in time it yielded the atomic numbers table.[96]

The atomic numbers theory is based on the number of charged particles in the nucleus of the atom. As has been observationally confirmed since the 1930's, the nucleus of the atom has positively charged protons and uncharged neutrons. In (quantized) orbit around the nucleus are the negatively charged electrons whose mass (at rest)

---

[96] Bernard Jaffe, *ibid.*, 192-197. For the periodic table by atomic number, see Brian Silver, *ibid.* 151.

amounts are so much smaller than the mass (at rest) amounts of a proton or a neutron as to be negligible. What were called in the 19th century the atomic *weights* are now called the atomic *masses*, and these are the sum masses of not only the positively charged protons and tiny-massed negatively charged electrons in an atom, but also of the neutrons that have no charge in the nucleus of an atom but whose masses are like the masses of the protons.[97] (As mentioned in 8.9, it was in 1932 that the neutron was first observed.) It is instructive to note how the work in chemistry proceeded *through* the atomic weights table of the late 19th century. Only later, with certain developments in physics in the first few decades of the 20th century, were chemists able to develop the atomic numbers theory.

In the atomic numbers table for chemical work, we have the development of a profound hypothesis, that what underlie the chemical relations are the physical relations arising (primarily) from the charge relationships (the negative and positive electromagnetic charges of the electrons and protons, but not the neutrons, since the neutrons are neutral in charge) in the atom, and, consequently, the relations between atoms in proximity. Frederick Soddy, in 1911, observed that the same chemical relations occurred for some elements of different atomic weights, so that there was the need for a new theory of the basis of the chemical relations.[98] And it was the atomic number theory that provided that basis.

8.11 It was, further, the quantum physics results of the 1910's and 1920's, and uses of them in chemical bonding studies, that showed in detail how molecular bonding forces are the forces of micro-particle interactions in basic physics. The developments here were done by both physicists and chemists: Niels Bohr in 1913, Gilbert Lewis in 1916, M. L. Huggins in 1919, some pioneers of quantum physics in the 1920's and after, and various chemists, so that the overall group of physicists and chemists includes the above figures plus Wolfgang Pauli, Irving Langmuir, Niels Bohr again[99], Walter Heitler, Fritz London, (Heitler and London in 1927 explaining the covalence in hydrogen molecules), Robert Mulliken,

---

[97] More properly, weights are indicators of mass amounts. The phrasing here is rough.

[98] Abraham Pais, *ibid.*, 224.

[99] Via his lectures at the University of Göttingen, 1922.

Friedrich Hund, and Linus Pauling (Pauling extending the Lewis views of 1916 and the Heitler-London 1927 views). The large group applied the physics results, including the quantum physics results, to the subject of chemical bonding.[100] There are many patterns in chemical bonds. In particular, there are ionic, metallic, covalent, van der Waals, and hydrogen bonds, as well as variations and blends of them.

In ionic bonds, one atom gives up at least one electron to another atom, on account of the structures of the electron shells of the two atoms. In giving up one or more electrons, an atom becomes positively charged. In acquiring one or more electrons, an atom becomes negatively charged. Then the two atoms, originally neutral in charge, would now be ions, indeed, oppositely charged ions, and so they attract each other and are bonded.

Quantum physics developed the notion of the structure of the electron shells and orbitals. The number of protons and electrons, the exclusion principle developed by Wolfgang Pauli, and other factors, allowed for the explanation of each element's shells and electron orbitals. There is a tendency for each atom to fill its outermost shell. So if an atom whose quantum *capacity* for electrons in its outermost shell is greater than the number of electrons *actually in* its outermost shell is near an atom that *has* far fewer electrons in its outermost shell than is the *capacity* of that outermost shell, an electron transfer might take place.

To illustrate, Chlorine (Cl), matching electrons to protons, has two electrons in its first shell, eight in its second, and seven in its third shell. However, the third shell would be full at eight electrons, so, given the rules of quantum physics, there is a tendency for chlorine to pick up another electron. Suppose, a Sodium (Na) atom is nearby. A Sodium atom has two electrons in its first shell, eight in its second, and only one in its third. This would allow Sodium to give up the lone electron in its third shell, which becomes an empty shell. Its second shell would become the outermost shell. Chlorine picks up the electron, and so its outermost shell is also filled. The Chlorine is now negatively charged by one extra electron in its outermost shell, while the Sodium is positively

---

[100] See "Quantum Chemistry" in John Gribbin's *Q is for Quantum*: 363-368; and Bernard Pullman, *The Atom in the History of Human Thought*: 321-336. (Note that in the addendum in Pullman's *The Atom*, pg. 336, 'mechanical' means 'classical'; in any case, there is no suggestion that there are intrinsic purposes in the linkages.)

charged by one extra proton in its nucleus. The positive and the negative would move toward each other, and so the Chlorine would bond with the Sodium, and what would result is one molecule of NaCl, or salt.

In the metallic bond, the electrons are in one, two, or three valence shells, and it is easy for them to become free from the nuclei. The nuclei become ions, and the ions are surrounded by an electron sea. The positive ions of the nuclei without the electrons would repel each other, but being in a negatively charged electron sea, the metallic bond is formed.

In the covalent bonding, the electrons of several atoms, for example, three oxygen atoms, are shared among the three nuclei. The result is a three-atom molecule in which each atom is oxygen, and the result is ozone, or O_3. Of course, the atoms need not be of the same type in covalent bonding. For instance, there is covalent bonding between one nitrogen atom and one oxygen atom, making nitric oxide, or NO. To put it another way, quantum physics provides for covalent bonding by allowing this special way for the outer shell of some atoms to be, effectively, filled.

The van der Waals attractive force is between the positively charged nuclei of one molecule and the electrons of another molecule. This attraction is weaker than the bonding forces so far looked at, but it becomes larger in what then turn out to be large molecules, and so it is a significant feature in proteins, for example, which are large molecules.

Finally, the hydrogen bond is also a weak force: the number of protons in the nucleus of one atom attract the electron of a bound atom with much fewer protons. Then two nearby assemblies will have a positive spot on one (through, for instance, one or more revealed protons), and a negative spot on the other (the nearest electron to the positive spot), and this attracts the two assemblies to each other. This force functions in important ways in biological chemicals like DNA.[101]

8.12 This enabled the new notion of chemistry to be expressed. Originally, the difference between physics and chemistry was that a change in physics would be a change in the property of an object, while

---

[101] A good popular account of the way the physics of the electrons make the groups and periods of the periodic table, is in Peter Atkins, *Galileo's Finger*, Chapter Five.

the object stayed the same, whereas a change in chemistry would be a change in the object, so that the object did not seem to stay the same. But once the atomic number theory was developed, and once it became clear that chemical changes are changes in the relations of subatomic particles, the difference between a physics change and a chemistry change altered. A chemistry change became simply a change in molecular structure, or a change in which atoms or ions combined with atoms or ions. That allowed an object, still regarded as the same object, to have chemical changes. A human being could be the same human being, but have many chemical changes. So: a physical change remained as a change in the property or properties of an object that stayed the same, and a chemical change became a change in the molecular structure of some object or combination of objects.

Chemistry became, in a way, a part of physics. Of course, though, the university Departments of chemistry and of physics are different.

8.13 Again, it is useful to mention that quantum mysteries of wave-particles, probabilistic measurements, quantized basics, and so on, do not undo the classical (that is, theoretically measured things) picture in (almost all) chemical phenomena. Chemistry has always approached chemical items with the assumption that large enough items (though still micro-items, and so small as to be invisible, from the human scale point of view, that is, atoms, and so on) are, theoretically or hypothetically, measured. Molecular combinations are entirely invisible, but, still, large enough elements. It's true that there is atomic resonance, though these resonances are within molecules. Still, molecules are measurable, and, in the vicinity of other molecules, have measurable effects.[102]

All in all, the way in which electromagnetic forces explain the attractions of atoms to each other is a remarkably fundamental discovery

---

[102] Readers interested in details may want to note the following: quantum-hooked atom linkages, (for which, see Pullman, *ibid*: 336 Addendum) are still cases in which the physics explains the chemistry. In fact, one of the oddities in quantum physics, the quantization of the basic ingredients, reinforces the idea that it is the combinations of the ultimate physical basics that yields the bonding forces in chemistry. This is a narrower way of putting the more general point Robin Le Poidevin makes in "Missing Elements and Missing Premises," pp. 132-3.

that was essentially completed by 1930 or by some time in the 1930's. That was the period in which, we might say, the physicalization of chemistry had reached its high plateau level from which it has not dropped at all.

Naturally enough, of course, we cannot help but use chemical vocabulary and theory in our chemical work. The molecules we deal with often have very many atoms in them and for practical purposes we cannot in specific detail explain what is going on by using only the language of physics. Even if there are few atoms involved in a chemical change, using only physics' language would not summarize the relations in a way that is immediately useful to us. Also there are theoretical translation problems (you can't say what atom an electron 'belongs to') that prevent the language of chemistry to be translatable into the language of physics. Hence, we continue to use chemical language. Nonetheless, we understand that what is going on is going on through the operations of the forces or laws or rules of physics.

8.14 Another factor in the development of the physicalization of chemistry is the use of light spectra in the determination of elements. This has been of fundamental importance in astronomy. At the end of his life Sir William Herschel (1738-1822) suggested that line spectra might indicate metals in chemical analysis. In subsequent years, Kirchoff, Bunsen, Roscoe, and others used spectroscopic analysis for the determination of chemical elements.[103] The technique became basic in astronomy, since a principal access we have to very distant objects is the light sent to us from them. It is the spectral lines of the light that indicate the nature of the chemicals in the distant objects. In any case, it is the physical basis of the chemical structure that indicates the chemical structure, and this, too, shows the physicalization of chemistry. It is useful, then, to notice that the physicalization of chemistry happened at several important levels more or less simultaneously, if we think of the 19th and first third of the 20th century as a single time period.

---

[103] Pledge, *ibid.* 145.

Chapter Nine: The Physio-Chemicalization of Biology

9.0 We begin with a detailed description of the relation between Descartes' theory of human beings, of other animals, and of other things in nature, on the one hand, and, on the other hand, Newton's several decades later theory of conservation of momentum. For some readers the description will be a little too detailed. If so, one can skip forward to 9.1. But some readers are likely to appreciate a description of the way in which thinking about human behaviour, the behaviour of other animals, plants, and inanimate things, in the 17th century, affected the way the physio-chemicalization of biology occurred.

In the first half of the 17th century, René Descartes postulated that there is a mechanism in which the bodies of all living things *other than* human beings, and the bodies of all non-living things, are exclusively governed by mechanical (not intrinsically purposive)[104] relations. The motions of humans' bodily parts were thought of as governed *both* by the non-purposive interactions of the physical things, and by the purposive

---

[104] In Chapter Three, we saw that 'mechanism' has many meanings; in Descartes' views, 'mechanism' simply means 'like a machine, in which the parts' motions have no intrinsic purposes'. Descartes' mechanism was a contact-based mechanism. So it resembled what Chapter Three called *billiard ball mechanism*, but it was not billiard ball mechanism. Descartes rejected empty space and any tiny things moving in it. In his view, matter filled all of extension. (Everyone thinks that there is invisible matter, in air, for instance; and so it is not strange to think that there might be matter everywhere, in some places, invisible, in other places, visible.) Some say that Descartes was entirely a mechanist. They are not incorrect. He was, but only in his early sense of 'mechanism,' a sense that was undone by two results taken together: Newton's law of conservation of momentum and Darwinian evolution. This will be explained below.

non-physical minds' decisions that altered the directions of the motions of the physical bodies. This constituted one half of Descartes' ontological interactive dualism. (The other half is given in the notion that mechanical physical interactions, for example, the effects of light rays on eyes and then on brains, somehow make changes in the corresponding non-physical minds' perceptual experiences.)

This mechanism plus purpose (for human beings) was permitted in Descartes' theory because his mechanism, that is, his theory of motions based on parts that have no purposes inherent in their motions, was a theory that Descartes developed decades before Newton came up with his system including conservation of momentum; and Descartes' system did not yield conservation of momentum. Newton's conservation of momentum (developed in the late 17th century and described in 4.2 through 4.5) includes conservation of motion-vector, or, again, amount *and direction*, of motion. Descartes' theory only conserved the amount in a closed region, not the direction in a closed region, of motion. Descartes' mechanics, then, easily permitted non-physical mental control of directions of motion.[105]

It is not too difficult to see that there is a *pre-scientific* intuition that there are switches in overall momentum (in the overall amount of mass in motion including direction of motion) in the usual frames of reference every time there is an action resulting from a mental decision. Perhaps the easiest illustration of the *pre-scientific* intuition is the illustration of an intuition that goes against both Descartes' conservation of the amount of mass in motion, and Newton's conservation of the amount and direction of mass in motion. It will be the case we will look at first.

Consider a situation in which a person is at rest in a room in a building with no one else, and no other animal, etcetera. The person, say, is asleep. There's a bit of motion – the person is breathing, there are bits of dust floating around the rooms in the building. But there's not much motion. Then, say, the person wakes up, and gets out of bed, thinking, "Oh, I better get to work," puts on clothes, and leaves the building. There is a sense that before the person wakes up, there is very little

---

[105] The description given is standard. It is found not only in Descartes' *Principles*, but also, for example, in Leibniz's view of Descartes' system as given in Leibniz's *Monadology*, 1696 #80; see also, E. J. Dijksterhuis, 1961: 410-1, where 'velocity' means 'speed' and has no built in direction, or is scalar, not vectorial, as becomes clear pg. 411.

motion in the building. We also have the sense that once the person wakes up and begins moving around, there has come to be a significant amount of mass in motion in the building. Take the later time period in which the person is heading toward the front door of the building. That seems to be a very different state of affairs as far as mass in motion goes than the state of affairs before the alarm was ringing. Accordingly, in this scenario there seems to be both a change in the amount of mass in motion – first, very little mass in motion before the person woke up, and, second, after the person woke up, when the person was moving through the building, a lot more mass in motion, namely, more or less the same air masses in motion aside from the position of the human being *plus* the change from the resting mass of the human being to the mass of the human being moving across the room(s) of the building – and a change in the direction of mass in motion, from a bit of random directions of dust floating around, to the direction of the human body toward the door of the building. According to the *entirely pre-scientific* intuition, it seems that both Descartes and Newton were wrong in what they said was conserved. (Of course the entirely pre-scientific intuition turns out to be entirely incorrect.)

Next we'll consider a situation in which Descartes' theory seems to have been correct, and Newton's theory, interpreted to cover not only inanimate objects but also all living things including human beings, seems (according to what is ultimately a *partial pre-scientific* intuition) to have been incorrect. Consider a situation in which a man is alone in a building and walking toward the back door of the building. The man then decides that it would be better to leave by the front door, and so he moves at the same rate in a sort of circular path back toward the front door of the building. Once he's circled back to be near the front door of the building, he heads straight for the front door at the same rate of motion.

In this case, there seems to be conservation of the *amount* of motion, because he is moving at the same rate at first to the back door, then in a circular motion, and ends up moving (still at the same rate) to the front door. The *amount* of motion is or seems to be conserved, and that is what Descartes' theory requires. However, it seems that the amount of mass in motion has switched its direction of motion – first to the back door, then to go through part of a circle, then toward the front door. And so Newton's conservation of momentum theory, including direction of motion, interpreted to cover human beings, seems to be incorrect.

In this way, Descartes' system seems to embody half of what might be called the pre-scientific intuition that volitional action or, action by decision, does not allow conservation of momentum. This is because Descartes' system allows conservation of the *amount* of mass in motion, but does not allow (does not provide for) conservation of *direction* of mass in motion. (As it happens, the partial pre-scientific intuition is incorrect, too.[106])

A part of the motivation for Descartes' theory of conservation of the overall amount of mass in motion was his notion of matter as being the same as extension (or spread-out-ness) in space. He was against atomism, which takes it that there are tiny clumps of matter moving about in an empty space. Rather, he followed Aristotle's view that there is a plenum of matter, which, in Descartes' way of putting it, *is* extension, or spread-out-ness, in space. There is no empty space. What we refer to as a bunch of material objects Descartes thought of as an agglomeration of bumps as it were, some of which became small bumps from some rubbing, some of which combined in the rubbing to make large bumps. In his view, the bumps tend to form vortices (swirling groups), bringing objects to the centre of the vortices. Very large groups of them make stars and the sun; smaller ones are the earth and the planets. God directs the motions so that there is conservation of the amount of motion, thus conserving as much as is possible to conserve.[107]

There were several problems with Descartes' views about matter in motion. His preservation of the amount of motion, without his preservation of the direction of motion created shortcomings. And his theories of the vortices seemed not to work, or not to be sufficient to explain many of the goings on concerning the heavenly objects. However, we need not go into the vortices-theory difficulties. We are looking at the relation between living beings and non-living beings, or at least some living beings (humans), and other entities. For Descartes, there was the key division between human beings on the one hand and all other beings on the other hand including the non-human animals, the plants, and everything else. And Descartes' theory having the

---

[106] How are both pre-scientific intuitions incorrect? By there being equal action and reaction events. Someone gets off the bed and stands on the floor. The floor supports the person. The person puts a lot of force through the floor. Newton's third law of motion generates momentum conservation.

[107] Dijksterhuis, *ibid*: 408-410.

conservation of the amount of mass in motion, but not the conservation of the direction of mass in motion, seemed to him to be adequate.

In his theory, according to the usual interpretation of it, a mind is a substance[108] (a fundamental entity) that is not a physical substance; and the mind supplies the direction of motion to the human body. Under Descartes' theory, some revision was required from the full pre-scientific intuition to half the scientific intuition. There would have to be little bits of mass in motion, invisible bits (or invisible bumps in the extended mass) in motion, allowing for the preservation of total quantity of motion of mass objects, and, one speculates, God would ensure that conservation of amount of mass in motion.

In this way, Descartes' theory inaugurated the notion that all things, including the motions of *all biological* things (including human beings, though the contemporary notion of biology hadn't yet developed) would be consistent with the quantitative requirements governing the amounts of motions of physical parts. This retrospectively may be taken to having pointed to the possibility of phystriology, since (without conceiving of conservation of momentum including direction) it reached from physics through biology, and *one way* it might reach through physics to biology is what we are referring to as the phystriological way, applied to all biological objects including human beings, with no inherent purposes in the parts of such objects. But Descartes did not follow that route at all. Rather, Descartes' own system, in retrospective vocabulary, was as strongly physically *in*complete for human beings as a system can be, given, as it would typically be put today, two factors: Descartes did not anticipate Darwinian natural selective evolution that resulted in the inclusion of human beings in biological beings, and Descartes did not have the conservation of momentum for human beings, which suggested (though it didn't require) that there not be any changes in physical beings caused by non-physical mental beings. In Descartes' system, by contrast,

---

[108] In philosophy, a substance can be an immaterial thing just as it can be a material thing. If the discussion is a bit confusing, remember that everyone agrees that mind is either a non-physical entity or a non-physical-ish property of an entity. If it is the latter, what that entity is – what substance that entity is or is a part of – is unclear. That entity might be merely a physical thing, and so it might be that the only substance that exists would be physical without being mental; it might be mental without being physical; there are other options, too (it might be neither).

non-physical minds cause the directions of motions of some physical things, namely, human bodies.

Ontological interactive dualism – the view that non-physical mind and non-mental matter are in causal interaction[109] – was, indeed, consistent with Descartes' mechanism; indeed, it is the name typically and accurately given to Descartes' theory of mind-body relations.[110]

It is also worthwhile observing how ontological interactive dualism – the view that there are two types of things, one, non-physical and mental, the other, physical and non-mental, that are causally affecting each other – is, indeed, *also* left open by Newtonian mechanics. Prior to, say, the mid or late 1850's, it was theoretically possible that a non-physical mind would only introduce changes into the physical world that obeyed Newton's third law of motion (as well as the first two), generating action and equal reaction changes in the physical world. The non-physical mind might get a nerve to be excited, say; but then whatever motions were involved in that excitement would be counterbalanced by other motions in opposite directions by other particles. And those motions in opposite directions by other particles would not interfere with any intended effects of the excitation of the nerve.

Similarly, once conservation of energy was worked out in the 19th century, but prior to the late 1850's, say, it was theoretically possible that there would be non-physical minds causally affecting physical changes, but only if there were potential and actual energy balances perhaps including and quantifying non-physical mental amounts.

However, once again, the theory of Darwinian, or naturally selective, evolution was published in *The Origin of Species* in 1859. And that was just a decade after the end of the main development of the conservation of energy law in about 1850. Once Darwin's evolutionary theory was widely accepted, the theoretical possibility just mentioned – of Newtonian interactive ontological dualism – would not have been plausible. Once Darwinian evolution came to be regarded as a powerful, and correct theory – that all lasting changes in species happen by natural

---

[109] 'Ontological' means 'having to do with being, or things that exist'. 'Dualism' is any view about two types of things.

[110] Descartes fully adopted ontological interactive dualism. Late in his career, though, he worried about the effects of emotional states, conceived as physical states, on human beings, and this to some extent diminished from his straightforward ontological interactive dualism.

selection – the idea that human beings had non-physical minds governing the directions of motions of physical things no longer could have appeal equal to its original appeal. According to Darwinian evolution, human beings evolved by natural selection from other animal forms. So the sharp ontological difference between non-physical minds for human beings, and only physical processes for other animals no longer made sense. But this is skipping ahead in the story, so let us return to Descartes' notions.

To put it briefly, Descartes advocated the idea that a non-purposive physical mechanics is *consistent with* biological changes. In one version of such non-purposive *physical* mechanics (Descartes' version, in this case) the biological changes a human undergoes are also caused by a non-physical mind. The purposes are added consistently on top of the non-purposive mechanics. In another version, the only version plausible after the physicalization of chemistry and the physio-chemicalization of biology had occurred by some time in the 20th century, the biology is to be, somehow, understood in an entirely physics-based way. That means only that the biological changes do not overturn any of the objective physical outcomes, even if the physical outcome-processes are not directly accessible to us.[111]

9.1 In the 17th century, there were a few glimmers of the relation between a physical system and a biological system aside from those we've been considering – aside, that is, from 1) Descartes' system, including non-purposive mechanism for all bodily changes produced by a bodily change, and a human psychology in which there would be non-physically caused physical motions, and 2) Newton's system, which many take to suggest that the law of conservation of momentum covers human behaviour. For example, there was William Harvey's discovery of the circulation of the blood (1629), a discovery about liquid motions in the

---

[111] Once again, contemporary scholars sometimes say, "Oh, but Descartes was a full mechanist." This is a bit unfortunate. In one sense, he was; his 'mechanism' allowed him to be a full mechanist in the Cartesian way. But, 'mechanism' is usually taken to include Newtonian mechanism, and given Darwinian evolution, the consistency of Newtonian mechanism with Cartesian mechanism disappeared from plausibility. In other words, once again, both Newton's momentum law, and Darwin's natural selective evolution postulate, have to be included in assessing such matters as the plausibility of Descartes' view today.

organism that were entirely consistent with fluid studies that were then in place.

Moreover, Harvey used mechanical principles in his reasoning. He calculated how much blood is pushed out of a valve, and reasoned that within a very short period of time, a very small part of a day, the weight of the whole body would be pumped out by a heart. But, of course, there is no routine excretion of blood. Therefore, he concluded, there must be circulation of the blood. Also, he applied a perfect ligature to his arm, cutting off the flow of blood to the arm. Then, by loosening the ligature slightly, the blood in the arteries could get through to the arm, and the arm warmed. But the veins still swelled (purple in colour), since the venous routes remained blocked by the ligature. This showed that there was a connection between the arterial supply and the beginning of the venous return. In this way, Harvey used mechanical reasoning to arrive at his theory of the circulation of the blood.[112]

When Marcello Malpighi in 1660 completed Harvey's postulate of the circulation of the blood by microscopically discovering capillaries[113], this helped to suggest the usefulness of physical postulates in accounting for biological phenomena. Malpighi also discovered many other physical features of biological organs.

Similarly, Otto von Guericke in 1672 published his results on the vacuum; included were not only the methods whereby a vacuum can be produced, but also the effects of the vacuum on both inorganic and organic phenomena. It was striking, at that time, that a bell rung in a vacuum makes no sound; equally worth noting were the results that birds die in a vacuum, that fishes swell up and burst, and that a grape is kept fresh for over half a year in a vacuum.

It is the last result that is particularly striking in showing the close relationship between physical conditions and organic conditions. That birds die in a vacuum is easy enough to understand: birds need to breathe air, and a vacuum has no air; so they die. But that the tendency toward rotting is so greatly affected by the presence of air and its contents was especially important to observe; and it indicated further possible

---

[112] Richard Westfall, *Construction of Modern Science*: 90. It's not that prior to Harvey people thought the blood did not circulate; it's just that no one previous to Harvey asked many good questions about the heart and the blood that Harvey did ask, and answer.

[113] H. T. Pledge, *Science Since 1500*: 86.

connections between the overall physical order and the organisms or parts thereof.[114]

9.2 In 1711, Stephen Hales (1677-1761) began studying the blood pressure of animals. He published his results in 1733, and showed that there is a high blood pressure and a low blood pressure, and that smaller animals have quicker heart rates than large animals. Once again, a physical notion, this time that of pressure, played an important role in understanding the goings on in biological systems.[115]

In the mid 18th century Albrecht von Haller (1708-1777) published work showing that all the sensation that we have is associated with organs that have nerves in them. This formed the basis of the vast amount of nerve research, which, as we'll see, continued and grew through the 19th and 20th centuries, and of course, is growing now, too, in regard to the chemical processes that underlie nervous functioning. He also showed that the thyroid, thymus, and spleen put substances into circulation. This, too, supported what was to become the chemical analysis of the functioning of the biological processes.[116] It was significant to him that muscles separated from the living body would still contract when pricked[117]; this, too, supported the physical basis of organic changes. And in the early 1740's, the discovery that a polyp (hydra) chopped into pieces would regenerate in each piece was greeted with much interest.[118] That fact was a bit ambiguous in its implications. It may have supported the notion of material composition, though it may also have supported the idea of some kind of vitalism, or special force for living things.

Also in the 18th century, a major biological conundrum was explored: on what basis do living things reproduce? There were three rival hypotheses – that there is a micro-organism in the egg, that there is a micro-organism in the sperm, and that there are some special properties in a preliminary entity that was neither egg nor sperm but of roughly that

---

[114] Ernst Mach, *The Science of Mechanics*: 145.

[115] Pledge, *ibid*: 104.

[116] Pledge, *ibid*: 240.

[117] This is reported in *Science and Religion*, John Hedley Brooke: 172.

[118] John H. Brooke: 173.

size.[119] This problem remained unsolved till the middle of the 20th century. As it turned out, of course, and as had been strongly suspected for a very long time, none of the three 18th century hypotheses were right. (There were many grounds for this suspicion. For example, in 1887 it was reported that the ovum and sperm are haploid cells, not diploid cells[120]; this supported the view that it is the combination of the ovum and sperm that makes the living being. But how the haploid cells are created, and what enables their combination to occur, was not even basically known till the middle of the twentieth century.)

9.3 In 1772, Joseph Priestley, a chemist, showed that plants give off a gas that is necessary for animals' survival. This was the beginning of what turned out to be a fundamental fact in the history of planet earth – that when there were no plants on earth, there was no or little oxygen in the air; the oxygen in our air is primarily the result of billions of years of plant life on earth. Lavoisier saw respiration as a form of combustion, and this, too, supported the chemicalization part of the physio-chemicalization of biological notions.[121]

In the 1780's, the relationship between electricity and the musculo-nervous system was discovered by Luigi Galvani. Connect a basic nerve to metal and from this provide some form of electricity to a frog's leg. Then the muscles of the leg contract, even if, say, the bottom half of the frog has been cut off from the rest of the frog. There were different views as to whether the electricity in a living system was of the same type as electricity in the inanimate world. Galvani's associate, Alessandro Volta, (correctly) took the electricity to be the sort of electricity that was studied by physicists.

The connection between electricity and muscular motion was profoundly important in two ways. It indicated the electro-muscular nervous system function; and, as important for our purposes, it indicated

---

[119] Marjorie Grene, David Depew, *The Philosophy of Biology*: 83.

[120] Pledge, *ibid*: 220. The haploid cells have half of some elements of the diploid cells.

[121] Reported in David Spurrett, *The Completeness of Physics* (PhD thesis): 82; with a citation to Coleman 1987 *Biology in the Nineteenth Century* 123-7 and Antoine Lavoisier, 1952, *Elements of Chemistry, Great Books of the Western World 45* Chicago: Encyclopedia Britannica: 99-103.

possible identities between things going on in the inanimate world, and things going on in the animate world.[122]

From 1792 till 1801, Thomas Young (1773-1829) – the same Thomas Young who discovered the wave properties of light, or, as it would have been put then, that light is a wave – studied the retina. He found that there were three sorts of things in it, each of which was sensitive to one of the primary colours.[123] Here, too, a physical notion, the primacy of each primary colour, comes to play a role in understanding biological functioning, in this case, the functioning of visual perceivers.

9.4 In 1812, Russian chemist Gottlieb Kirchoff (1764-1833) took an organic material, starch, and converted it to a simple sugar, which he called glocuse, by use of an acid.[124] Here was an important simplification of a chemical important to organisms and found in organisms, by a chemical that was known outside of organisms. The simplification suggested a chemical structure to materials in living things. That living things are made out of chemical materials was also supported by the discovery in 1817 that the green of plants is chlorophyll.[125]

Also in the early 1820's the idea of a strong connection, possibly an underlying identity, between the inanimate and the animate world received a big boost in the manufacture of urea by Friedrich Woehler.[126] That materials, like urea, important in living beings, could be manufactured out of mere laboratory materials having nothing to do with living things was, for good reasons, remarkable to people at that time. Again, a big possible connection, in fact an identity, of the types of underlying structures between the inorganic and the organic worlds was supported.

9.5 In the mid 19th century, the specifics of Charles Darwin's form of evolution – evolution by natural selection – gave strong support to the

---

[122] Brian Silver, *The Ascent of Science*: 84-5.

[123] Pledge, *ibid*: 132.

[124] Pledge, *ibid*: 214.

[125] Pledge, *ibid*: 129.

[126] Bernard Jaffe, *Crucibles*: 108-110.

notion of unplanned events leading to the selection of offspring well fitted to their environments. It was a remarkably simple idea, that offspring with varying characteristics of their ancestors compete in regard to which ones are more fitted to survive, and, thus, which ones are more reproductive.[127] The ones that are more reproductive, by definition, produce more offspring of their type, and in this way there is a gradual branching of types in nature. Eventually, different species come to exist.

Darwin's success followed from his ingenious applications of a relatively simple notion to a wide variety of circumstances, so broadly and with such depth. Of course Darwin was well aware that he had no theory concerning one problem, as mentioned earlier, that had been troubling biologists for many decades, the problem of how reproduction occurs.[128] Nonetheless, the power of his simple theory sufficed to show a potential physio-chemicalization of biology. It was not known, however, what any chemical means of reproduction might have been, and, therefore, it was not known how the variety of parent-resembling properties would be generated in offspring.[129]

Still, at the level at which he was describing generational succession, finding intrinsic purposes in the tiny, invisible physical interactions would have seemed to be of no theoretical use. It was the variation in the large-scale properties of offspring in their environments that governed outcomes. And the variations went in both directions, toward success and toward failure in regard to being fitted to the

---

[127] Charles Darwin, *The Origin of Species*; see also, I. Bernard Cohen, *ibid.*, 291-294.

[128] Darwin explicitly noted the various hypotheses that biologists who had discussed the origin of species had offered in "An Historical Sketch" at the beginning of *The Origin of Species*, 3rd edition. This included Lamarck's views (physical conditions of life, crossing of forms, and habits being transmitted) (16), Patrick Matthew's views including the possibility that forms "generated 'without the presence of any mould or germ of former aggregates'" (18), the anonymous author of the 'Vestiges of Creation', including vital forces (19), the ignorance confessed to by Professor Owen (20), and chemical changes postulated by Count Keyserling (22), all pages in Darwin, bibliography edition.

[129] The problem wasn't only of a lack of knowledge; the best hypothesis included a blending inheritance model, and this seemed unworkable. See Darwin, *ibid.*, 460; and Matt Ridley, *Genome*: 43. The ability of the genetic model, especially as developed after the structure of DNA was discovered, to thoroughly solve this problem was, of course, of great importance.

---

environment. It would have made little theoretical sense to think that the variation in both directions was produced by intrinsically purposive micro-events. This supported the notion that the miniscule physical interactions would not be intrinsically purposive.[130]

Darwin's natural selection evolution was important in setting the stage for a world in which the physical conditions fixed the higher scale facts. Nature's selection was not a process in which nature acted as a deliberating agent. It was only by what remained that anything that can metaphorically be called 'selection' was accomplished. But one feature is important to remember about Darwin's views. Darwin was concerned with the way to explain the occurrence of as many kinds of organisms as were found on earth. He was not concerned with *all* the biological changes that occur. He was not concerned with whether or not there are small parts of organisms, for instance, in the brains of animals, or in the seeds of plants, that might interfere with, or alter, the rules, laws, or forces of physics. For this reason, although Darwin's notions are very important, they are only a mid-part of a longer story. And it is the longer story we are looking at.

9.6 Roughly simultaneous with Darwin's work was the work of Gregor Mendel (published 1865) on the properties of ancestors being transmitted, either dominantly, or recessively, to subsequent generations. Mendel blended varieties of peas; and he noticed the exact mathematical relations between what he called, translated into English, the *factors* (now called the *genes*) of the ancestors that would be found in the immediately succeeding, second, third, and so on generations.

Mendel's work was not, however, widely known, and, indeed, it was only re-discovered, and began to be commonly employed, in the beginning of the 20th century.[131]

---

[130] It is noteworthy that Darwin did not include ignorance about the means of passing characteristics down from parents to offspring as a main objection to the theory of natural selection (Darwin *ibid.* 458-464). He did, however, mention many other serious potential objections. Perhaps this shows that Darwin was aware that supplying anything that might be a plausible theory of characteristics-transmission would not undermine the natural selection hypothesis. If both positive and negative characteristics had to be transmitted, then whatever method was supplied would not undermine the natural selection theory.

[131] Pledge, *ibid.*, 222.

9.7 One of the long-standing controversies concerning reproduction from early days to the mid 19th century had to do with spontaneous generation, the notion that mouldy grain produced mice, mud produced frogs, sewage produced rats, rotting meat produced flies, and, later, soup produced bacteria. In 1668 Francesco Redi showed that flies were not produced from sealed meats; consequently, it came to be accepted that large objects were not produced from the sorts of objects the organisms wanted to be around. But what of bacteria, since bacteria were known from Anthony van Leeuwenhoek's discovery of them by microscope in 1673? Was there any spontaneous generation of bacteria?

In 1748, John Needham advanced the view that a life force was present in air and all bits of matter and that it spontaneously generated bacteria in soups. In 1767, Lazzaro Spallanzani replied to his views; Spallanzani showed that a one-hour boiled soup, properly sealed, would generate no bacteria. The question remained as to whether the life force had been killed by the one-hour boiling; without the life force, there would be no spontaneous generation. In 1860, a prize was offered to solve the problem. Louis Pasteur, in 1864, won the prize by showing that many days would not suffice for the spontaneous generation. His experiments showed that, roughly put (ignoring the development of first living things), it is only living things that generate similar living things.[132]

What we observe from the refutation of spontaneous generation is the need for a continuity between physical and biological processes. This, too, supported the physio-chemicalization of biology.

9.8 Cell research, was, of course, important in understanding reproduction. But it took a few centuries for the results to emerge, both for cell reproduction and for complex organism reproduction. In 1665, Robert Hooke, using the microscope, noticed, and named, cells. In 1806 Lorenz Oken speculated that all living things were made up of cells. In 1828 Matthias Schleiden showed that from all information then available, all plants are made of cells; in 1829, Theodor Schwann showed that from all information then available, all animals, too, and so all organisms (as they were then classified) are made of cells. In his theory, there are both

---

[132] *Understanding Bacteria*, Sheela Srivastava, PS Srivastava, Norwell MA: Kluwer Academic Publishers, 2003: 3-4.

internal and external functions fulfilled by cells, but it was thought that there is spontaneous generation of cells.

Rudolf Virchow in the second half of the 19th century showed that cells are generated from other cells. Hence the specific question of how cells reproduce was raised.[133]

Research in cells in the late 19th century and the 20th century showed the use of the hypothesis that cell activities can be accounted for by physical or chemical means. Strikingly, the studied properties of a cell, if they were accounted for, were accounted for by ordinary chemical or physical means. They were accounted for by showing how things do or do not pass through a membrane, how nerves are stimulated into or out of excitation by neurotransmitters, and so on, only by ordinary, though often complicated, physical or chemical means.[134] To achieve these results, there were often important methods established, and stages of research reached. For instance, in 1854, carmine was used to stain the nucleus of the cell, and this enabled the study of cell nuclei. In 1877, silver salts revealed the cell boundaries.[135] In 1872, Eduard Pfluger (1829-1910) showed that oxygen is carried by the blood to the muscles and other tissue for oxygenation.[136]

In the late 19th century, it was found that the energy emitted by a small dog corresponds exactly to that of the food that it has consumed. This was shown by Max Rubner in 1889.[137] This, too, exhibited the physics-understructure of biological changes. In a similar time period ("by 1897"), Bernard (but which Bernard??) stated that the laws of physics would obtain for all biological entities as well as for all non-biological physical entities.[138]

---

[133] Vernon Avila, *Biology*: 76; Franklin Harold, *The Way of the Cell*: 18; I Bernard Cohen, *ibid*: 316-318.

[134] Franklin Harold, *ibid*; Brian Silver, *ibid*: 325.

[135] Pledge, *ibid*: 166.

[136] Pledge, *ibid*: 199.

[137] Quoted from David Papineau, *Consciousness*: 252. Papineau cites Coleman, W., 1971, *Biology in the Nineteenth Century*, NY: John Wiley & Sons: 140-3.

[138] Quoted in Spurrett, *ibid*: 84, from W. Coleman, 1977, *Biology in the Nineteenth Century*, Cambridge: Cambridge University Press: 126. For readers interested in details, aside from "which Bernard??" note that including organisms in objects covered by large level conservation of energy, for instance, does not exclude

9.9 In 1909 Wilhelm Johannsen re-named what Mendel had called (here using English) 'factors'; Johanssen called them 'genes', and, of course, that is the name that has survived. At this stage, the genes were not understood chemically at all; they were merely understood by large-scale observation as elements that are transmitted (in a dominant or recessive way) from parents to offspring. It was also in the first decades of the 20th century that Darwin's evolutionary theory was modified by the incorporation into the theory of the power of occasional mutations (striking, though unusual, sudden novelties in an offspring's properties) as one means that might lead to rapid change in a population.[139] At the time of the discovery of mutations (the 1880's[140]), and early in the 20th century, mutations were not chemically understood; it was understood that the mutations had to come about somehow, but just how was not known.

Hermann Joe Muller in the late 1920's found that by bombarding fruit flies with X-rays, he could cause their genes to mutate. This showed that whatever was producing mutations could have an ordinary physical

---

special organism forces. Hence it does not exclude, for example, a vitalism in which a living force gets directions changed, with balanced counter-direction changes to preserve momentum conservation. Similarly, it does not exclude a causal dualism in which there is conservation of energy across the physical/mental boundary. For this reason, the large scale conservation of energy in organisms does not yield physical closure or phystriology; vitalism, British Emergentism, and causal dualism were still live options. Some thinkers in the late 19th century had their eyes focused on what would develop. Still, the conclusion published in 1897, some would say, was made too quickly. Spurrett also, it seems, too quickly, took it that physical closure was established with what is here being called the physicalization of chemistry by the late 1920's or so (Spurrett *ibid*: 87). David Papineau in his "Appendix" 2002: 248-9 in principle, and 249-252 in practice, shows that conservation of energy is and was insufficient to eliminate contraries to physical closure. The physicalization of chemistry on its own doesn't do the trick; it needs to be combined with the law of conservation of momentum and the implications of both for living things, to obtain the phystriological result; but something along those lines would have to be mentioned. Alternatively, it can be combined with other notions, for instance, the physio-chemicalization of biology, to obtain that result.

[139] Marjorie Grene and David Depew, *ibid*: 249-259.

[140] Pledge, *ibid*: 222.

---

structure. X-rays are ordinary physical emissions. The internal structure of an organism was responsive to ordinary physical stimulation, suggesting again, a deep connection between the physical system and the chemical-biological system.

However, the puzzle about how parents transmit characteristics to offspring, and how reproduction, in general, occurs, had still not been solved. This allowed some philosophers (e.g., the British Emergentists[141]) to maintain their hopes that biological changes were not all ordinary though complicated chemical changes, and, perhaps, too, that the chemical changes were not all mere-physics changes. Vitalists[142] also speculated, and hoped, one might guess, that there would be special changes or motions in living beings that could not be accounted for by ordinary chemical nor ordinary physics-based means, nor even by non-ordinary (by configuration of particles) physics-based means.

physio·chemicalization of biology

9.10 Nonetheless, the expectation or hope of vitalists and British Emergentists was soon dashed. The solution of the reproduction problem, for both cells and complex-cell organisms, came in the 1950's and early 1960's with the remarkable 'chemistry only' result of the cell-nuclear DNA reproductive structure.

The basic structure of the DNA was found in 1953 by Francis Crick and James Watson.[143] They discovered that DNA (in chromosomes in the nucleus of a cell) is a double helix structure, and that what were already called A, C, G, and T molecules existed in pairs across the helices. It was known earlier that an A molecule pairs only with a T molecule, and a G molecule pairs only with a C molecule.[144] Long chains of these molecules along one side of a helix spell 'instructions' of sorts that can be used in various ways. Molecules attach to portions of the DNA helices. When a sufficient combination of attaching molecules is reached, the clump of molecules floats off; such a clump can then be used in protein

---

[141] British Emergentists thought there would be special (large and so highly) complex arrangements of tiny physical parts governed by fundamental forces altering the physics-only motions in chemistry or biology or psychology.

[142] Vitalists thought there are special life forces. For more on vitalism and British Emergentism, see Chapter Ten and the second Appendix.

[143] James D. Watson, *The Double Helix.*

[144] James Watson, *ibid*: 130.

formation. In this way, a portion running alongside one of the helices of the DNA double helix is a gene, and a gene can now be understood as an instruction for supplying a basic bodily element or function, including, for example, a bodily protein.

Also, the double helix floats in a soup that has many individual A, T, C, and G molecules that also float about the soup. So if one helix can be separated from the other, each helix, with one of the two A, T, C, and G molecules left on each strand across the helix, then there would be a detailed way to explain the reproductive property of the DNA sequence.

To explain, if one helix is free from another by a split, and if each of the very many horizontal strands in a helix has one of the A, T, G, or C molecules, there would be free-hanging A, T, G, and C molecules down the backbone, and they would be free-hanging in a soup of floating A, T, G, and C molecules. But one such molecule bonds only to one other such molecule (through a double hydrogen link[145]). So, for example, a free-hanging A molecule would bond with a floating nearby T molecule, and similar pairings would occur for each free-hanging molecule from the backbone. After all the elements are matched, and a backbone is built up for the new elements on the other side, then, where there had been one double helix, through the splitting into two single strands, and the re-matching of each single strand, and the building up of the two other backbones, there would end up being two double helices. And this would all be done through the workings of ordinary, though complicated, chemistry.

This apparently operational-reproductive feature of the double helix was extraordinarily exciting.[146] From the point of view of our context here, we want to note that the source of the excitement was double. First, the key to the reproductive property of the sequence was built right into the physio-chemical structure; second, the system also governed the protein, and, indeed, the organ construction methods. In this way, the uncovery of the DNA structure, would, effectively, be a crucial turning point in a process that had been building for about three or four centuries concerning the relations between physics, chemistry,

---

[145] See, for instance, Watson, *ibid*: 119.

[146] See Watson, *ibid*.: 116-126, for the excitement of Watson and Crick; 131 re Lawrence Bragg's first exposure to the developing hypothesis; 138 for Linus Pauling's first exposure; and 139 for the phrasing of the important biological implications.

and biology. All that was required was the confirmation that the two helices neatly separate, and that there are details explaining the protein and organ construction.

The semiconservative reproductive process, in which one strand of a double helix is from the DNA-parent and one strand is new (assembled from the soup), was shown in 1958, by Matthew Meselson and Frank Stahl.[147] In the early 1960's further basic research completed protein construction theories on closely related RNA structure.[148] By 1966 the essential features behind the genetic coding system were known. Modern genetic theory was healthily underway.[149]

Of course genetics is both biological and yet entirely chemical. Not only the way chemistry provided the basis for reproduction, but also the way chemistry provided a blueprint for organism construction were the remarkably powerful features of uncovering the DNA system.

9.11 Once the DNA structure had been uncovered, the physio-chemicalization of biology story was effectively completed. All the basic biological processes in brain functioning, cell organization, reproduction, protein construction, body development, and so on, had complex but basic physio-chemical accounts. Biology, then, had been effectively physio-chemicalized by the end of the 1950's or the end of the 1960's. To make the matter clearer: Why 'physio'-chemicalized, rather than just 'chemicalized'? Because, for example, an organism in free fall has the physical acceleration rate. Sometimes a biological change, such as an organism free-falling, is a non-chemical physical change; and sometimes a biological change, such as an organism digesting food, is a full-fledged chemical change.

For convenience, we can say that the three processes – the mathematization of physics, the physicalization of chemistry, and the physio-chemicalization of biology – were all completed by 1970.

---

[147] David Micklos, Greg A. Freyer, 2003, *DNA Science: A First Course*, 2nd edition, Cold Spring Harbor NY: Cold Spring Harbor Laboratory Press: 37-39.

[148] An anthology with excellent reviews of the history is *The Inside Story*, edited by Jan Witkowski.

[149] Matt Ridley, *ibid*: 51, 52; and Witkowski's *The Inside Story*.

Chapter Ten: Phystriology: The sum result

10.0 The story so far

We have just gone through a short history of the mathematization of physics, the physicalization of chemistry, and the physio-chemicalization of biology. This short history was highly selective; there are many other discoveries, and steps along the process, that could be included for a fuller history.

Still, there is a main sum result: purposes were removed from what are apparently the smallest things making up big things, and there are no fundamental changes of the rules, laws, or forces of physics where there are chemical or biological changes. We also understand in a new way what, in an old way, we understood since the success of Darwinian natural selection evolution, namely, that everything that is in spacetime is biological or chemical or physical. So it can all be put together into one sentence: nothing overturns the mathematical rules, laws, or forces of physics.

It is important to note how thorough the removal of purposive elements from the basic physical interactions has been and how consistent have been the steps leading to the view that there is no over-turning of the results of physics. That is, it is important to note that none of the durable laws or rules or discoveries in the history of the last four hundred years of natural research employed anything going against the removal of purposes from small things in physics-based interactions, nor going against the physicalization of chemistry, nor going against the physio-chemicalization of biology.

Rather, all the long-lasting theoretical changes suggested that, or were consistent with the view that, the physical changes happen through purposeless mathematical formulas as found in physics, and that the chemical changes are produced through physical factors, and that the biological changes are produced through physical or chemical factors. The many long-lasting theoretical views added up, and together they yielded, and still yield, the result: no changes in nature overturn the rules, laws, or forces of physics.

This can also be put in terms of purposes: The small things in physics do not change purposively; they change only by the mathematical processes. And there is no overturning of the sums of those processes. This means that if there are any purposes in what physics studies in nature, they are not intrinsic purposes; they are only summative purposes, purposes arising in sums of not inherently purposive things, and those sums were generated natural selectively over evolutionary periods of time. And we can add in the other facts not phrased in terms of purposes. By 1930 or so chemistry was physicalized; by 1970 or so biology was physio-chemicalized. And so we can conclude that the study of physics underlies the study of all natural objects. Consequently, if there are any purposive things in nature, the purposes are not basic; they arise only from natural selectively evolutionarily reached sums.

It can all be put into four words: the world is phystriological.

This is not to say that there were no resisters. Once what is here being called phystriology became a live possibility, which was some time between 1850 or so and 1950 or so, there were resisters. (Before 1850 or so it would not be appropriate to think of those who postulated a view that was retrospectively a physically *in*complete view as 'resisters'; they were speculative theorists, however incorrect their speculations proved to be.) Aside from the ontological interactive dualists[150], the most notable resisters were the vitalists in biology, the British Emergentists[151] in

---

[150] Once again, 'ontological interactive dualism' states that there is a non-physical mind in causal interaction with the elements of a non-mental physical body.

[151] For readers curious about fine points of meaning: As note-defined in Chapter Nine, the British Emergentists said that there are special motions of things in highly complex arrangements or configurations of things; the vitalists said that there is a special life force. This difference enables us to spot further differences between some of them. One such difference is that while the British Emergentists thought of things happening through laws, forces, or rules governing physics-based parts – some fundamentally governing only low-in-complexity physics assemblies, some fundamentally governing high-in-complexity physics assemblies – they thereby thought that purposes embodied

117

scientific-philosophy, and the position-relative fideists in the theory of justified belief (who take it that there are, and, most would add, always will be, *some* cases of legitimate adoption of faith-without-evidence views, those cases being specific in some specified way – hence it is *position relative* fideism[152]). Both of the first two groups maintained that there would be forces or rules or laws (in biology at least) that would not be consistent with the sums of the micro-physics forces or rules or laws. But it was shown in the first two thirds of the 20th century that all three groups of thinkers were incorrect in their speculations.

What about the ontological interactive dualists? When this view, also called the Cartesian view (or Descartes' view), was put forward in the first half of the 17th century, it could not have been thought of as resistive against phystriology (no substantial evidence for the phystriological condition had yet come forth); but there were many exponents of the Cartesian view in the period in which the vitalists and the British Emergentists were resistive against phystriology (1850 or so to 1950 or so); and there were exponents of this view a bit afterward, too. How one describes the persistence of ontological interactive dualism until, and even, in a few cases, beyond, the mid 20th century, say, is, therefore, dependent on what part of the history one wishes to emphasize.

Nonetheless, the development of phystriology presents good reasons whereby ontological interactive dualism, vitalism, and British Emergentism disappeared from mainstream views by about 1970. And the development of phystriology presents good reasons why position-relative fideism should have lost its strength on spirituality questions by 1970, even though, for most people, including a good number of professional philosophers, it didn't.

This says what needs to be said for the general reader interested in the sum result, which is here being called phystriology. But some readers will want a bit more detail. The next batch of discussion will look at the history from a more technical point of view. All those looking only for the main lines of the account can skim the material from here till the second to last paragraph in 10.2.

---

in the latter would be, somehow, mathematically structured, whereas some vitalists thought there might be purposes that were independent of the mathematical way that physics-based parts of living things change, and that such purposes might not be embodied in mathematical principles.

[152] See 21.1.1.

The mechanical notions in the 17th century, especially from Newton's work and on, removed intrinsic purposes from the functioning of the basic physical things. How, then, could there be intrinsic (non-summative) purposes in mental things? An answer was available in the mid 19th century, and earlier, for momentum: by there being non-physical mental forces that preserved momentum conservation and energy conservation. That meant that there could be intrinsic purposes in mental things only if there were both action-and-equal-reaction implementation at the physical level (for momentum conservation), and expanded potential / kinetic / electrical / etcetera energy conservations in physical regions alone or in physical regions plus mental regions (for energy conservation). Newtonian mechanics was not technically inconsistent, then, with ontological interactive dualism. That is what could have been focused on in the middle of the 19th century; there was still no evidence that went logically against the quartet taken together: Newtonian mechanics, momentum conservation, energy conservation, and Cartesian interactive dualism.

However, the evidence reached during the next hundred years or so drastically changed that. By 1970, there had been successful Darwinian evolutionary theory (including the synthesis of Darwin's theory with genetic theory and mutation theory) for very many decades, the physicalization of chemistry, and the physio-chemicalization of biology.

As was shown above, in the late 19th century, the Darwinian evolution theory didn't *have to be* only ordinarily-physically realized. Darwinian evolution theory was consistent with vitalism, British Emergentism, position-relative fideism, and, more generally, was logically consistent with interactive ontological dualism. Many characteristics of parents are transmitted to offspring; some of the characteristics are fitness-negative, and others fitness-positive. After Darwin's theory was originally enunciated, mutations – sudden changes of characteristics – were discovered; they, too, would be sometimes fitness-negative, and sometimes fitness-positive. So whatever theory of reproduction would work, it was consistent with such positions as British Emergentism and vitalism, and it would not harm the level at which Darwinian evolution occurs.

Add Darwinian evolution alone to the physics picture reached by 1850, and the result was a bit unclear. But careful reviewers of the evidence reached by 1970, say, would have both the physicalization of chemistry by 1930, and the DNA results and related results by 1970. These made it insuperably difficult to rescue each of ontologically interactive dualism, vitalism, British Emergentism, and any form of fideism. All four became insuperably difficult given the mathematization of physics, the physicalization of chemistry and the physio-chemicalization of biology. By 1970, then, the quartet taken together – Cartesian interactive dualism, Newtonian mechanics, momentum conservation, and energy conservation – was no longer workable.

How would the non-physical mind-entities arise, or how would there be special vitalistic forces, rules, or laws, or how would there be special British Emergentist groups of physical particles, if the physical things themselves were the results of naturally selective evolution under the workings of physics? The question could have been raised from 1870 to 1970, but the retrospective look has a lot more strength to it than has the prospective look. The same is true for the next questions as well: Where would the non-physical mind-entities act on the body, or where would the division be as to where the special vitalistic rules, laws or forces would operate and where they wouldn't, or where would the special British Emergentist rules, laws, or forces be restricted as to their operations? It took awhile to find this out, but after some decades, there seemed to be no plausible answers to these questions. As far as momentum conservation and energy conservation were concerned, there was no evidence at all of any special non-physically produced or non-grossly-physically produced physical action-and-equal-reaction events for momentum conservation, or psychophysical potential / kinetic / electrical / etcetera balances of energy in the brain and elsewhere for energy conservation.

In this way, careful reviewers of the evidence to 1970 would suggest that the evidence from the 16th or 17th century to the mid or two-thirds point in the 20th century has, indeed, established the mathematization of physics, the physicalization of chemistry, and the physio-chemicalization of biology the way the evidence from the 16th to the end of the 18th centuries established for learned people that the earth is a planet, like Venus, orbiting the sun.

As we will see throughout the rest of the book, the triple nesting of biology in physio-chemistry, and chemistry in mathematized physics, was a result with important implications. Before showing the implications of phystriology, though, what we will first do is *define* phystriology. True, we've already been using the notion divided into the three processes that built it up, the mathematization of physics, the physicalization of chemistry, and the physio-chemicalization of biology. But we may as well define phystriology more carefully than it has been defined in previous

Chapters. Then we will look at how it is that establishing those three processes establishes phystriology. After that, in 10.3, focusing on religious and spirituality content, we will see how important are the implications of phystriology.

10.1 Definition of phystriology

Phystriology is defined in these three points: (1) there are no intrinsic (inherent desire-like) purposes in basic physical particle interactions; (2) chemical or biological changes do not alter or violate, or over-turn the physics-based rules or laws or forces of governance of changes, including those already discovered physics-based rules or laws or forces so long as their results are considered as approximately true for short term time periods in the contexts in which the rules, laws, or forces were discovered[153]; and (3) there are no fundamental rules, laws or forces triggered by large configurations or arrangements of particles. ((3) is already included in (2), but, to avoid what a critic might say is an ambiguity in the meaning of 'physics-based'[154], I mention it for extra clarity.)

---

[153] 'Approximately true for short term time periods in the contexts in which the rules, laws, or forces were discovered' prevents chaotic results by considering only short term time periods, and prevents what are usually called paradigm troubles by considering only approximate results in the original contexts of discovery. (Since 17th century quantification, the paradigm switches occur in novel contexts.) More detail: the assumption is made that there is no systematic objective overdetermination. One way to justify the assumption is to note the important shift: the concept of purposes was present in all natural languages for thousands of years before the nesting of the three main natural sciences of physics, chemistry, and biology was conceivable. It is that shift from the intuitive pre-scientific structure, in which purposes are thought to be basic, to the scientific nesting structure, in which purposes are thought to be non-basic through being natural-selectively summative with no violation of found processes of physics or their sums, that overturns any attraction for the systemic objective overdetermination hypothesis.

[154] If the reader is puzzled, an overview of Brian McLaughlin's scholarly article "The Rise and Fall of British Emergentism," might be of assistance. McLaughlin effectively explains how 'physics-based' could mean either micro-physics based, or, unusually, based in both micro-physics and British Emergentist physics with fundamental configurative forces. (But, for good reasons) no such British Emergentist physics developed.

10.2 A demonstration of how the definition-condition is satisfied by the triple nesting

Here is how our three processes – (a) the mathematization of physics, (b) the physicalization of chemistry, and (c) the physio-chemicalization of biology – result in the establishment of phystriology as just defined. We begin by noting that if (a) has taken place, then (1), in the definition, is true. If (b) and (c) have taken place, then (3), in the definition, is true. If (1) and (3) are true, then, since (given that (b) and (c) have occurred) there are effectively no other viable options, (2), in the definition, is true. So, showing how (a), (b), and (c) developed is sufficient to establish (1), (2), and (3), or that phystriology is established.

Let's look at this more carefully. The mathematization of physics is essentially the process in which only mathematical relations are found to govern the interactions of small physical things and that in these mathematically governed interactions there are no intrinsic (inherent desire-like) purposes being expressed.[155] So the inference from (a) having taken place to (1) is immediate.

Once we have established that chemical changes are, objectively (though not theoretically translatably[156]) physical changes, and that biological changes are objectively (though not theoretically translatably) physio-chemical changes, then we can eliminate the view that highly complex (biologically complex) configurations or arrangements of particles trigger the operations of special fundamental laws or forces or rules.

Again, the physicalization of chemistry and the physio-chemicalization of biology do all the work required. The biological

---

[155] For scholars: this is also shown by attention to the development going through Lagrange's strictly mathematical treatment as shown by Mach, *Science of Mechanics*: 420-433; 561-575, and Penrose's *The Road to Reality*, Chapter 20, to Nöther's symmetry Theorem, described there in 20.6, and beyond.

[156] This point is not necessary for what is being established, but those driven by curiosity may find it worth going through: 'Na + Cl —> NaCl' is a chemical formula. But how can you tell if an electron is a part of this Na atom or that Cl atom? There is no way. So a compositional translation, a translation based on composing parts, that can be applied to the world, is impossible. That's just one illustration of the sorts of difficulties involved in applied translation. Still, the chemical formula is extraordinarily useful; and so, unsurprisingly, we use it.

configurations of particles are highly complex; and yet these are, objectively, token to token[157], chemical configurations, which are, objectively, or token to token, classical physical states. Next, we look at how subatomic particles are token items in chemical states. The relation is unclear on account of quantum physics: one can't say whether a given electron is part of this atom or that atom. In answer to the potential problem, we have an understanding of how the objective (though not theoretically accessible) sums of physical processes are, *statistically at least*, the chemical processes, and how the objective (though not theoretically accessible) sums of physical and chemical processes are the biological processes. So there aren't any special *fundamental* laws, rules or forces at the biological level.

The precise boundary between the physical level and the chemical level doesn't any longer matter to us. Indeed, there is no such precise boundary. A human is, somehow, a biological being. Yet the biological level is, somehow, the physio-chemical level. All of the above establishes (3).

Now once (1) and (3) are established, we have all we need, effectively, to establish (2), namely, that however inaccessible the rules or laws or forces governing biological changes are to us, they do not overturn any already discovered physics-based rules for approximate truths over short term time periods in the contexts in which the discoveries were made. We don't know the micro-particle location details about anyone's brain (to any degree), for instance; so the specifics to be filled in to the rules, laws, or forces for that person's brain are not accessible to us. But it doesn't matter. Vitalism was effectively eliminated

---

[157] We need to say 'token to token' to make sure that the identity of a biological to a physio-chemical to a physics-based thing is not confused for 'type to type' identity. A token is a thing. A type is found in many places. For example, there are many cats. There's a cat; there's a cat; there's a cat. One type-term, many instances. Now a biological type might be fulfilled by many types of tokens; a thinking-thing might be either carbon-neuron based or, hypothetically, silicon computer-chip based. The same is chemically true as well; for instance, jade is a type that is present through two very different types of chemical states. But in any one token case, there will be only one token group that makes it up. However, in biology, for example, does the chemical or physical thing have the biological properties? Suppose it doesn't. Still, if there is no overturning of the rules of physics, then there is at least a thin token identity, an identity in which the chemical thing doesn't have the type-defined biological properties. Appendix 2.4, last paragraph, discusses the point further.

by the evidence for (3); so was British Emergentism; and other factors render other options not viable. (If anyone is wondering about the other factors, they will be reviewed in Chapter Eleven and Appendix 2.) Hence, effectively, once (3) has been established, then (2) has been established as well.

In this way, once we've seen how physics was mathematized, how chemistry was physicalized, and how biology was physio-chemicalized, then we have also seen how these three defining features of phystriology have been established. Once again, apologies for the fine-combed details, but these were useful to go through for anyone who has a lingering sense that the issue must be controversial. Many people hope that the issue is controversial. But, in fact, it is not. The details show that the issue is not controversial at all.

The reader who wants a quick sense of the grounds for phystriology can just think of the grounds this way: Anyone in a physics lab, or a chemistry lab, or a biology lab, on being given an assignment to explain *x*, cannot simply say, "There are purposes bringing *x* about." Why not? Put loosely, because phystriology obtains: physics is mathematized, and the mathematical things have no inherent desire-like purposes, chemistry is physicalized, meaning that the chemical changes or the molecular changes are governed by electromagnetic attractions of the subatomic particles, and biology is physio-chemicalized, meaning that each biological change is a purely physical change or a physio-chemical change. So in biological, in chemical, and in physical labs, one doesn't explain why *x* occurred just by saying, "There are purposes bringing *x* about," not even if one mentions some purposes. In the biological lab one needs something like a biochemical explanation. In the chemistry lab, one needs either a detailed chemical formula-based explanation or a physics-based account of the chemical change. And in the physics lab, one needs a non-purposive (not based in anything desire-like) mathematical account of the change.

10.3 The importance of phystriology

Discovering that the phystriology condition obtains is a powerful result. In Chapter Two we reviewed the very widely found view called emanationism. As will be elaborated in a moment, if phystriology is true, then emanationism is false. Phystriology and the usual notion of emanationism are logically[158] inconsistent. That in itself is powerful. Similarly, if phystriology is true, then ontological interactive dualism – Descartes' position is an ontological interactive dualism – is also, by logic, false. Ontological interactive dualism may or may not be included in emanationism, depending on how emanationism is defined. What we will now do is note in some detail the many positions that are *logically* rejected by anyone who accepts phystriology.

As mentioned in Chapter One, there are eight positions logically rejected (rejected through the use of logic) by phystriology. Let us review them once again: (1) that there is a non-physical God who interacts with nature at the human (or classical) scale; (2) that there is an afterlife or pre-life, (3) that there is a strong form of physics-overturning freedom, (4) that there is a hidden karma, that is, a hidden moral system of reward and punishment at work upon moral beings such as human beings, but not triggered in any way by a human agent or agents, (5) that there is a powerful form of mentally generated (non-physically generated, or only subtly physically generated) paranormal events, (6) that there is a mystical ascent that some people experience to a higher (non-physical or only subtly physical) realm, (7) that ontological interactive dualism is true, and (8) that emanationism is true.

If one accepts phystriology, then each of the eight positions just listed will be logically rejected. The first six are familiar positions; the seventh is a philosophical view that was often accepted through the ages; and the eighth, emanationism, is a philosophically named view commonly found in expressions of religious systems. Coming back for a moment to ontological interactive dualism, Descartes' form of ontological interactive

---

[158] Two statements are logically inconsistent just in case there are two contradictory statements within, or implied by, the two statements. For instance, (1) "No bachelor is married," is logically inconsistent with (2) "Frank is a married bachelor." But a detective working to solve a crime, such as, who murdered Pat, may have, say, thirty key empirical data-points, and these thirty empirical data points may indicate to the detective that, in our example case, Sam was the sole killer of Pat. Yet no mere combination of the empirical data-points would be logically inconsistent with someone else having been the killer of Pat. The killer might have, for instance, transformed into an invisible goblin, appeared at the spot as the goblin, killed the victim, and returned by a similar transformation to another location in a flash. So there is a distinction between a logical relation and an ampliative (which here means a not strictly logical) relation.

dualism was widely accepted since his time, the second quarter of the 17th century, until the middle of the 20th century. Either the Cartesian ontological interactive dualism, which employs the notion of two fundamental sorts of substances, the immaterial mental substances and the material substances, and places instances of them in causal interaction with each other, or a form of emanationism, tends to be an underlying assumption of the worldview of many who have not philosophically thought about the mind-body relation; the filling out of such a position usually includes one or more of the first six positions mentioned above.

We'll proceed now in the order just given. (Familiarity first.) The intent is to show that if one accepts phystriology and one wants to be internally consistent, then one rejects each of the positions just listed. We're now mainly doing two things. First, we're seeing how the rejection occurs. Second, we're noting how the rejection is not just an interpretive rejection. Rather, it proceeds from the *logical relations* between (a) the phystriology condition, and (b) the claims as just given. (On one occasion, we're discovering that another broader spirituality-promoting view is not strictly logically, but strongly ampliatively, rejected by phystriology.)

10.3.1 Interactive God at the human or classical scale

The almost universal assumption in monotheist religions is that not only did God create the whole universe but also that God is interactive with the world at the human scale. Both are logically inconsistent with phystriology. Changes made at creation could not have been governed by the rules, laws, or forces of physics. God the Creator is taken to be an immaterial being (aside from avatar[159]-incarnations), and, clarifying 'at the human or classical scale,' God the immaterial being is taken to interact with the world by giving prophesy to humans, presumably by making changes at the human scale in the prophet's brain, making miracles, presumably by making changes at the human scale, saving some people, presumably by making changes at the human scale, acting Providentially, presumably by making changes at the human scale, and so on. Moreover, the standard view can be expanded to mean 'at the classical scale', since the standard view of the world is classical. This view of God is, plainly,

---

[159] 'Avatar' is a familiar term from its internet use; but it is here being used in a very different sense, the original sense. Its original Sanskrit meaning is an incarnation of a Divine Being. See *'avatara'*, *Encyclopedic Dictionary of Yoga*, G. Feuerstein: 43.

logically inconsistent with acceptance of phystriology: the inconsistency comes from the immaterial being, God, creating the world, and, then, interacting with the world at the human or classical scale, thus overturning the laws (or rules, or whatever) of physics, whereas the laws (or rules, or whatever) of physics according to phystriology, are not overturned.

Why, again, 'at the classical[160] scale'? Because if God didn't act at the classical scale, but acted only at the quantum scale, God might produce changes whose consequences turned into the consequences at the human scale. But then God's actions wouldn't be at the classical scale, and such actions at the quantum scale (preserving changes at the classical scale) wouldn't logically go against phystriology.

The standard view of God is that God acts at the human or classical scale; so the standard view of God is a God whose existence is logically inconsistent with phystriology.

But what about the following non-standard views of God, first, a Deist God, an immaterial Super-personal Creator of the world that does not subsequently interact with the world at all? And, second, what about a God or supernatural intelligence who merely affects the quantum states? In response, to advocate for the existence of either sort of being would be to adopt an irrational attitude, an attitude that hangs onto an old conception of purposes – as though purposes are set by basic desire-like phenomena – though the old conception was undone by the results of the natural sciences.

Chapters Two through to the end of Nine showed the evidence for making such a shift in attitude. For scores of thousands of years, there was a pre-scientific attitude about purposes, taking purposes to be basic features of the world, features that generated changes without there being any mechanistic base; then as a result of four hundred years or so of natural science research, arose the scientific attitudes about purposes, taking purposes, if they exist at all, to be non-basic or evolutionarily summative features of the world in which no micro-changes are based on inherent purposes. That made for an important shift. (Remember, Darwin's views were only about evolution; in the history as it is reviewed here, it took two more discoveries, the physicalization of chemistry and the physio-chemicalization of biology, to expand the result for *all*

---

[160] The nature of the classical system (versus the non-classical quantum system) is given in 7.1.

changes in organisms.) Yet the Deist God and the God or supernatural intelligence who acts only at the quantum scale would be instantiations of the personal God, and the personal God is a basically purposive person or super-person. But the human notion of purposes developed to be able to have good, quick interagency attributions, and to be able to account well for changes in some human-scale natural objects. Consequently, by phystriology, no natural objects have basic purposes. Thereby, not strictly logically, but strongly ampliatively, there cannot be any basically purposive or super-purposive God or non-mechanical supernatural being. Consequently, there cannot be a personal God, nor can there be a supernatural intelligence.

Another altogether different interpretation of 'God,' different from all three we have just looked at or the gathering of them into one notion – the three we have just looked at being the interactive God at the human or classical scale, the non-interactive but super-purposive Deist Creator God, and the God or supernatural intelligence interacting only at the quantum scale – is discussed in Chapter Twenty, and still another interpretation of 'God' is discussed in Chapter Twenty Two.[161] The three we have just looked at are the most popular interpretations of 'God', and the first of the three is the standard concept of God. The other two are attempts to revise the first standard concept of God given various challenges. It is important to remember that phystriology is logically inconsistent with a God who makes changes in the world at the human or classical scale, that phystriology strongly ampliatively, meaning, not strictly logically but strongly, undermines the existence of the Deist (noninteractive) God, of the God or supernatural intelligence who makes changes only at the quantum scale, and of any supernatural intelligence, and that phystriology says nothing about still other interpretations, more unusual interpretations of 'God.'

10.3.2 Afterlife or pre-life

There are many options in the notion of an afterlife (or pre-life). Our central concern is with the conscious afterlife in any form in which it is sometimes thought to occur. Reincarnation (as in Hinduism, and many other religious or spiritual views), rebirth (as in Buddhism, which rejects the notion that there is a substantial individual self, yet which still has a rebirth system), heaven without hell, heaven-purgatory-and-hell, and so

---

[161] All four are reviewed in 22.4.

on, are the many sorts of somehow conscious afterlives that we are concerned with. All of these are logically rejected by phystriology.

How? That which is thought to have an afterlife or pre-life is typically taken to be a carrier of a non-physical or only subtly physical being (that is not found as a sum of any current physics-based things at the micro-realm) that causally interacts with the physical (or grossly physical) world. Accordingly, given the causal interactivity, once one accepts phystriology, logically, one must give up belief in any standard form of conscious afterlife or pre-life.

This could be put in another way, too. The consciousness of a human person is dependent on the brain events happening in a healthy manner. When there is an injury or another defect in the operations of a brain, that part of the brain ceases to function, and an impairment results. Some of the impairments are very peculiar, and the list of such peculiar impairments is large. Some people have everyday cognitive skills, but they can't recognize faces. Others mistake their wife for a hat. (That was the basis for the title of a well-known Oliver Sacks book.) And so on. By the results of current neuroscience, the structure of the brain is extraordinarily complex and delicate. When the brain ceases to function as a whole, the basis on which conscious processes occurs is no longer available, and so the consciousness ceases. Other evidence for phystriology reinforces this. The brain operations do not overturn the rules, laws, or forces of physics. The way the brain system disintegrates after the death of the body is a process governed only by the rules, laws, or forces of physics. There is no overturning of such rules, laws, or forces at the (supposedly clear, though not in fact clear) time of death.

A problem could be raised here. As we saw in Chapter Six, there is a law of mass-energy conservation. Couldn't the soul of the afterlife be somehow the energy of what remains after the death of the body? More generally, couldn't there be a physical basis of the conscious afterlife or pre-life, and so phystriology would be consistent with the conscious afterlife or pre-life?

Similarly, William James toward the turn of the 20th century promoted the view[162] that humans merely have a permissive or transmissive function, not a productive function, for consciousness, through the cessation of which an afterlife occurs. The trigger of a crossbow has a permissive function, permitting the bow to come back to

---

[162] In "Human Immortality" conjoined with the essays in *The Will To Believe*.

its natural shape; the pipes of an organ have a transmissive function, transmissively yielding the desired sounds. When the body dies, the permissive or transmissive function ceases. But the original condition, the transcendent life, is somehow, perhaps unimaginably to us, revealed. Couldn't James's view be true as well?

The exponent of phystriology would say, in response to both questions, that to whatever degree these notion are interesting, still, they don't tally with any analysis of how the atoms make nerves that determine brain-states, and what happens to atoms or nerves of the brain, say, when a body dies. The original argument demonstrating the logical inconsistency of a conscious afterlife and phystriology showed this. There are other ways to show this as well.

A stone sitting on a slope, for example, does not have a merely transmissive or permissive function for its state of being; yet it is not in a supposed transcendent afterlife-like state of consciousness. Why, then, would a human being go into an afterlife state of consciousness after the cessation of such functions, assuming ordinary consciousness was generated through such functions? The phystriologist would say that James seems to have been hanging onto an old notion because he had trouble seeing how deep were science's tendencies to lead away from it; and those tendencies have greatly increased, not decreased, since James's time. What was logically possible in the last few decades of the 19th century, given the results of the 20th century (consciousness is locally generated and phystriological), is no longer logically possible. So the phystriologist would say.

Similarly, on energy conservation, when a body dies there won't be hundreds of thousands, or more, of atoms, or other mass-energy units of any kind, functioning together in the living-brain-complex-pattern to preserve some form of consciousness. Their patterns are not the patterns of a consciousness-generating brain (there *is* the productive, not merely transmissive or permissive function of the brain, the phystriologists would say) once the brain has died. And any radiative energy emitted by the atoms of a decaying body would go off into space or in any case would not cohere with other things in any organized fashion. Energy is conserved, but no patterns exist for consciousness.

This can be put more generally, too. When a brain ceases to function, its cognitive capacities are gone. And there is no evidence for any kind of consciousness without a cognitive basis. If one thinks there is some form of proto-consciousness or becoming-consciousness in any subatomic particle, then, as far as an afterlife state is concerned, there is no difference between a world without any living beings, and a world with living beings. Yet no one would say that there is an afterlife, but there is no difference between a world without living beings and a world with living beings. For these reasons, phystriology is logically inconsistent with the usually presented forms of the conscious afterlife.

10.3.3 Freedom and responsibility

It is important to note that phystriology is not directly inconsistent with every notion of freedom and responsibility. (There will be more on that topic in Chapter Twelve.) It is only inconsistent with one such notion, which happens to be a commonly held notion in systems affirming religion or spirituality. This is the notion that to be free is to make decisions that *overturn* the outcomes of the operations of the merely physical rules, laws or forces. In philosophy-talk this is called *the contra-causal incompatibilist* freedom. The claim, then, is – merely, some would say, though others would assert vigorously that it's not a 'mere' claim – that contra-causal-incompatibilist freedom, and any responsibility arising from contra-causal-incompatibilist freedom, is logically inconsistent with phystriology. That logical inconsistency is obvious. By phystriology, there is no overturning of the laws, rules, or forces of physics; by contra-causal incompatibilist freedom, there is overturning. So there is logical inconsistency.

We will not here expose the strengths and weaknesses of the compatibilist notions of freedom and responsibility nor of the *non*-contra-causal-incompatibilist notions of freedom and responsibility. (Again, a brief review of such concepts is given in Chapter Twelve.) All that needs to be said is that acceptance of phystriology logically rejects the view that freedom is contra-causal-incompatibilist; phystriology is logically neutral on each of the other views. On the other hand, the view typically found within religious systems and systems endorsing spirituality amounts to the contra-causal-incompatibilist view. There is, then, a logical conflict between the view of freedom typically found within religious or spiritual systems, and phystriology.

10.3.4 Hidden cosmic karma

The way outcomes turn out are often hidden from us. Yet it was said that phystriology is logically inconsistent with the notion of *hidden* cosmic karma. The notion of hidden cosmic karma, though, may need to be more clearly rendered. The suggestion was that the question whether there is hidden cosmic karma is more or less the same question as whether or not there is a moral order in the universe, or working through the universe, rather than merely a moral order initiated by human beings (or to an extent by some non-human animals). Let's now put this a little more clearly.

The essential question is whether there is an objective (but undoubtedly numerically unavailable to us) correlation[163] between people whose actions are morally good on the one hand, and, on the other hand, 'out of the blue' good events that happen to them. ('Out of the blue' means that there are no human generated connections, apparent or unapparent, linking the person's good deeds and the good events that happened to them.) Similarly, is there a correlation between people whose actions are morally defective, on the one hand, and, on the other, 'out of the blue' bad events that happen to them? (Again, 'out of the blue' means that there are no human generated connections, apparent or unapparent, linking the person's bad deeds and the bad events that happen to them.)

The exponent of hidden cosmic karma says that such correlations exist, even if we can't put our fingers on the numbers. The denier of hidden cosmic karma says that such correlations don't happen. Exponents of phystriology would say that judging by physics-based, chemistry-based, and biology-based factors is sufficient to judge whether such correlations exist, and that judging by them, the ratio (to usual degrees of significance in large enough groups) of good people to bad people overall is the same as the ratio of good people to bad people that are likely to be, say, killed by earthquakes. This is what phystriology maintains. The evidence for phystriology plus some elementary notions of probability together constitute the evidence against there being such hidden cosmic karmic correlations.

Exponents of physical *in*completeness have the disadvantage that they don't claim to be able to quantify the correlations to begin with. Hence they can't respond easily to an argument against hidden cosmic karma based primarily on the evidence for phystriology. Nonetheless, it seems to be their job to do so; if they can't, that ground for physical incompleteness dissolves. In any case, all that counts here is that I have

---

[163] A is correlated with B in supergroup G just in case the % of the A's in G that are B > the % of the non-A's in G that are B. For a full explanation, see a basic text in Critical Thinking with a unit on correlations.

shown the logical inconsistency[164] of the claim that phystriology obtains together with the claim that there is a hidden cosmic karma tending to reward good people and punish or deprive bad people.

10.3.5. Paranormal occurrences

Whether there are paranormal occurrences is a lively topic in principle. Unfortunately, in practice, there is far too little discussion on it. There are two defects in the sociology of the current situation. First, there is very active research being done, on both sides, but, largely, it is on the margin of, or alternatively, outside of, the academic world. It would be far better if there were more active research or discussion of the phenomena inside the academic world than there is. Second, there is too little interaction between the two groups. The skeptics – those who publish in *Skeptical Inquirer* magazine, or in issues of the various magazines called *The Skeptic*, for example – present the outcomes of their skeptical investigations; those who publish in *Journal of Parapsychology* or *Journal of Scientific Exploration* present the outcomes of the investigations they claim to be scientific. But specific interactions between the two groups, and mutual reviews of materials are too rarely to be found.

I'm sure that there will be objections. "We've engaged in dialogue on such and such occasions!" will be put forward, from both sides. And there are the references to back up the remarks. All that is being said here is that the various sciences, and, more importantly, the philosophy departments, do not typically expose the issues in the way they might. It seems, perhaps, that they should do so a little more than they have been.

In any case, all that is required here is to note that the paranormal claims are often, though not always, put in such a way as to suggest that phystriology is false. It is those ways of putting paranormal claims that are standard and are being looked at here. If a mind can make a distant material object move, then it seems that there are special mental powers that are not carried by a physical system. If a mind can read the distant future, then, again, it seems that there are special mental powers that are

---

[164] One could revert to a theory in which a Deist God sets up an initial condition in a deterministic system that makes it look physically incomplete, and that would permit the genuineness of hidden karmic events. However, as already shown in 10.3.1 the Deist God is strongly ampliatively undermined by phystriology; also see 11.9 for an elaboration of the same point. And since the development of quantum physics, the physical world seems not to be a deterministic system. For both reasons, the postulate is deeply undermined.

not carried by a physical system. If one person's mind (embodied ordinarily here, say) can read the content of another person's mind (embodied ordinarily there, say) without sensory cues or hidden physical connections, then, to some at least, it will seem that there are special mental powers that are not carried by a material system.

Some paranormal claims are ambiguous. They could be read two ways. For example, Rupert Sheldrake puts forward the notion of a morphic resonance[165], and it might be that *if* – and this is a big *if* – if there is a morphic resonance, then it is not carried by a force that physics will ever measure or quantify. On the other hand, it might be that if there is a morphic resonance – the same big *if* – then it is carried by a physical force that has not yet been measured or quantified, though, in some way, it could be.

The key issue is whether there is any empirical grounding for either sort of morphic resonance; only if there is would one need to figure out if morphic resonance is physically quantifiable or not. The (scientific) skeptics have said – with good ground, I'd add – that there is no such evidence. Thus, according to what I'd say is the reasonable point of view, the question of how morphic resonance occurs (physically or non-physically) hasn't arisen. It needn't arise until there is good evidence for a point of view that requires answering that question. (For more on this topic, see 11.3, and Chapter Fifteen.)

Nonetheless, the standard interpretation of many paranormal claims takes it that there are non-physical (or only subtly physical) causally active mental powers. This has the logical consequence that phystriology is false. And, vice versa: if phystriology is true, then the standard interpretations of typical paranormal claims are, logically, false.

10.3.6 Mystical union

There are various ways experience alleged to be of mystical union can be expressed. I would take it to be the case that there are four main ways claims of full mystical union or the full mystical nature of reality have been expressed.

- I am the All

---

[165] A morphic resonance is supposed to be a sort of field in which the type of a novel event in one region can be automatically transferred to another region so that an instance of that type occurs suddenly in the other region, too. See, e.g., Rupert Sheldrake, *Seven Experiments*: 188.

- There is no self
- There is only the (partless) One
- There is only Nothingness

There are also other expressions that can be used for non-full forms of mysticism, such as:

- I merged with God.

In the second and third part of this book, especially Chapters Eighteen and Twenty Two, we will explore the first four expressions and how they express the standard strong or full philosophically mystical experiential claims.

All that is required for us to do here is to note that *in the standard interpretations* of philosophical mysticism, it is taken to be the case that there are mystical ascents: the ultimate reality is non-material (or only subtly material), it is possible to experience the non-material ultimate reality, and it is possible to report on such experiences[166]. This covers all the expressions of mysticism, such as were given above, and it requires that there be causal relations between the non-material (or only subtly material) ultimate reality and the physical world. If a mystic is to remember an experience of mystical union, then there has been a causal relation between the physical world of the atoms in a mystic's brain, and the ultimate non-physical or only subtly physical reality. If so, then phystriology is false. (If so, then the second statement in the definition of physriology is false.) Accordingly, phystriology is logically inconsistent with *typically interpreted* philosophical mysticism.

10.3.7 Ontological interactive dualism

The seventh view is ontological interactive dualism. This is the position advocated by Descartes, and it can be regarded as one main form of physical *in*completeness among philosophers during the three hundred

---

[166] For a sample of standard recent and contemporary interpretations of philosophical mysticism on this point, see Frithjof Schuon, *The Transcendent Unity of Religions*: 36, 53; Walter Stace, *Mysticism and Philosophy*: 22-3, 253, 265, 270-6; William Wainwright, *Mysticism*: Chapter Two; David Loy, *Nonduality*: 89-95, 158-61; William Alston, *Perceiving God*: 232; Ken Wilber, *A Brief History of Everything*: 73, 81; John Hick, *The Fifth Dimension*: 14, 18, 19, 167-8, 242, 245; Robert Forman, "What Does Mysticism Have to Teach Us About Consciousness?": 362, 362 n. 6, 367-8, 376; Peter Kokol "Is There More Than One Kind of Non-Constructed Mystical Experience? *Sophia* **39**: 64-77.

years or so from 1650 till about 1960 or 1970. In ontological interactive dualism it is held to be the case that there are immaterial substances that causally interact with material substances. That there are both material and immaterial substances renders the position an *ontological dualism*, that is, a dualism holding that there are two types of ontological entities. (An ontological entity is an existent entity of one sort or another.) Further, ontological *interactive* dualism holds it to be the case that there are causal relations between the immaterial entities (the minds) and the material entities (the bodies). Hence it is an ontological interactive dualism.[167]

Given that the rules, laws, or forces governing the changes in a human-scale object overturn the rules, laws, or forces as specified in physics, it is clear that ontological interactive dualism goes against phystriology. (It goes against the second statement in the definition of phystriology.) In this way, if one accepts phystriology, one is logically required to reject ontological interactive dualism. And if one accepts ontological interactive dualism, one is logically required to reject phystriology.

10.3.8 Emanationism, the view that the ultimate reality is spiritual, and manifests at many levels, the last or lowest of which is the purely or grossly physical level, and that all these levels are causally influential on each other, is a view that has been claimed by many spiritual teachers. A speculative history of the development of early emanationism was given in Chapter Two. There are many later examples as well. For instance, emanationism was the view of the leading neo-Platonist, namely, Plotinus in the 3rd c. CE; it was the view of Sri Aurobindo in the first half of the 20th century; and it is the view of Ken Wilber in our own time. It is also influential on many mystical theories.

However, emanationism is logically inconsistent with phystriology, because emanationism includes the notion that there are causal relations between the various levels. Since the highest level is spiritual, it becomes apparent that use of emanationism for spirituality is logically inconsistent with phystriology. (In general, emanationism is logically inconsistent with the second point, and, in a sense, with the first

---

[167] The careful reader will want to know that it will be not only a type ontological interactive dualism but also a token ontological interactive dualism. For an explanation of the distinction between types and tokens, see above, n. 158.

point in the three-point definition of physical completeness that we have been using.)

10.3.9 The revival of physical Aristotelianism

For the sake of comprehensiveness, we can add another position here that is inconsistent with physriology, namely the revival of some versions of Aristotelianism about physical things.

In any full revival of *physical* Aristotelianism, there would be intrinsic purposes in the basic interactions of the base level physical things that there are. There is some revival of Aristotelian physical notions, but they are not full revivals.[168] Most current revivals of Aristotelianism for microparticles do not (typically or at all) revive natural purposes in microparticle physical interactions.[169] Where, then, does one find a revival of Aristotelianism that would go against physriology? It is in views put forward in religious philosophical circles. For instance, in what is called *process theology* the idea is expressed that natural events, somehow, work out intrinsically purposively. That view is a sort of Aristotelianism that seems to be logically inconsistent with physriology; it seems to go against the first point in the definition of physriology. Process theology could also be classified as a view that is not strictly logically rejected by physriology, since its relevant claim is that there is some sort of a basically purposive being, and to reason to that conclusion is not a strictly logical reasoning.

10.3.10 All in all, the logical inconsistency between physriology and each of the eight positions, or the nine positions if we include the last mentioned, shows how philosophically significant is the thesis of physriology. Its philosophical significance comes through the logical strength of the main result: physriology is not merely in soft interpretive tension with many theses often found in religious systems; rather, it *logically excludes* the standard interpretation of these theses. The logical exclusion is the strongest sort of exclusion that there can be. And physriology strongly ampliatively, though not strictly logically, rejects other important religious or pro-spirituality views as well.

This feature of the physriology result reflects a major historical change. In the past, for a few centuries prior to about 1960 or 1970, there

---

[168] For a review of modern Aristotelian essentialism, for instance, see Brian Ellis, *The Philosophy of Nature*: 9-14.

[169] Ellis, *ibid.*, 14-19.

was a soft interpretive tension between the results of the natural sciences and the claims included in religious systems. Yet there were still several ways one could maintain the religious claims *and maintain* the natural science results. However, after 1970, say, anyone who considered carefully the natural science evidence would be aware of a logical conflict between the results of the natural sciences on the one hand and on the other many theses commonly asserted within religious systems. Accordingly, the strong conflict since 1970 became important. And this conflict became important not only because there were logical conflicts between phystriology and various religious views, but also because there were not strictly logical conflicts, but apparently strong, unavoidable conflicts, between phystriology and more general religious views such as that the personal God exists. This, too, was reviewed above, e.g., at the end of 10.3.1.

After 1970, say, it was no longer possible to be fully aware of the evidence and to adopt the same sort of view of the relations between the results of the natural sciences and the religious views as it was possible to adopt prior to 1970, say. Prior to 1970 one could say, "I accept the natural sciences and I accept spirituality; there is no logical nor otherwise strong conflict between them." After 1970, anyone well aware of the evidence had to figure things out in a new way. There is, after, say 1970, a strong logical conflict between phystriology and many religious or spiritual views; and also there is a not strictly logical but still strong inconsistency between phystriology and some religious or spiritual views. Both present a vigorous challenge. The challenge requires one to give up spirituality in favor of the natural sciences, or to give up the natural sciences in favor of spirituality, or to find some aspects of spirituality that can be retained despite the logical inconsistencies that would apply elsewhere.

It is not surprising that discussions in the newspapers, the television, on the internet, etcetera, are not informed by this result. The discussions in the general culture about the science versus spirituality conflict date from the first decades of the twentieth century, or earlier; large sub-groups of philosophers are the only ones who have assimilated the phystriology result; and, as will be clear to anyone who reviews the first Appendix, the result has not been made as clear to introductory students in philosophy as it might be. A sentence or two is sometimes made on the topic, but that won't quite be enough.

A brief illustration may help clarify this point. James O'Shea, for instance, recently noted, "As every first year student of philosophy learns, however, the soul-body dualism imported from the ancients rested uneasily (to put it mildly) with the new mechanistic ontology of the scientific image of the world, …"[170] O'Shea then went on to say, "according to which the natural universe is conceived as a causally closed physical system." That the natural universe is conceived as a causally closed system is sometimes stated to first year philosophy students, but what that means will not be clear at all to the first year students, and even then, O'Shea adds, "see Chapter 6, however," a remark that suggests that there may be important controversies concerning something like spiritual or religious beliefs. But, as I have been trying to show here, that is not the case. (O'Shea's Chapter 6, illustrates Wilfrid Sellars' lack of acceptance of phystriology – called *physical causal closure* – toward the end of Sellars' life. Sellars was born in 1912, and died in 1989. His dates set the stage for a flat denial of what we're calling phystriology. Sellars, it seems, was too influenced by the sort of thinking that was common in the first half of the 20th century to be up to date in the 1970's and '80's.) The evidence for phystriology, and the relation between phystriology and spirituality has been a topic that was only available to upper level undergraduate students in philosophy, graduate students, and professionals to think about after 1970 or so. And even there, for no substantive reason, there has been apparent uncertainty about it. Should we, in the 21st century, be in the position of thinkers who grew up and formed their worldviews during, say, the 1930's? I don't think so.

10.4 At this point it would be a good exercise to figure out why it is that all that is required for the demonstration of phystriology is the demonstration of the relation between physics, chemistry, and biology. "Why is it that biologization of psychology is *not* required?" is the question you might try to respond to. (True, the Darwinian natural selection evolution theory placed all found psychological beings, including human beings, in the biological category. But what of British Emergentism, vitalism, and position-relative fideism? And how does evidence on them relate to psychological states of mind, such as hopes, fears, and beliefs?) You can check your answer by the material in this footnote:[171].

---

[170] James O'Shea, *Wilfrid Sellars*: 19.

[171] A quick answer: Darwinian evolution rendered humans as biological beings, but it left open the possibility of British Emergentism, vitalism, and position-

It would also be a good exercise to ponder the following question: are Darwinian evolution and the mathematization of physics together sufficient to establish phystriology? You can check your answer by this footnote:[172].

---

relative fideism. However, the physicalization of chemistry by 1930 or so, and the physio-chemicalization of biology by 1970 or so undid all three positions. Then all that remained was to accept radical fideism or the phystriology view. Radical fideism doesn't work, however (see 21.1). So phystriology results. A longer answer includes the contents of psychological states: We have strong introspective intuitions that psychological states, such as of belief, desire, intention, and so forth, cause our bodies to move. Yet our bodies are biological entities, and if our biological changes do not overturn the rules, laws or forces of physics, then there are no fundamental psychologically caused changes of subatomic particles in motion. So the relations from physics through biology suffice. An additional question, irrelevant to what kind of evidence is needed to establish phystriology, arises: what, then, is the mind? These theories will be briefly described in 12.1 and 12.2.

[172] They are. Darwinian evolution put pressure against finding psychologically based physical incompleteness; but it left untouched various hypotheses such as the vitalist and British Emergentist hypotheses. Hence there was still work to be done after 1860, say. Nöther's Theorem, published in 1918, is sufficient – on its own – to establish phystriology. Some further material is required to fill in the details, but the details can be filled in. (Nöther's Theorem ampliatively implies natural selection. So Nöther's Theorem covers all natural objects. Many results in quantum physics post-dated Nöther's Theorem, but since statistically many quantum results are classical results, fundamental purposes are not brought in through quantum physics. Also, Nöther's Theorem establishes a connection between numbers and spacetime if relatively trivial assumptions are made. The physical results of Nöther's Theorem can be doubly expanded, from non-relativistic classical spacetime to classical spacetime, and then to all physical results in regions greater than the Planck scale.) And the publication of Nöther's Theorem provides a high plateau level of the mathematization of physics. Yet, it seems, although there are many remarks on the power of Nöther's Theorem, nobody noticed how strong it is, on its own, in regard to establishing phystriology.

Chapter Eleven: Some Post-1970 Questions on Phystriology

11.0 Since 1960 or 1970, various questions, problems, and objections have been put, or could be put, to exponents of phystriology. (I say "or could be put" because there has been too little explicit published discussion on the topic; I have reviewed the comic miscommunication gap elsewhere.[173]) We'll now quickly review some difficulties that have been, or that might be, raised, and the responses exponents of phystriology would offer. The objections offered here are relatively simple objections. More complex scholarly objections, and responses, will be offered in Appendix 2. The main goal here, and, at a more scholarly level of detail, in Appendix 2, is to show, once again, that although lots of questions can be raised about phystriology, still, suggesting that the issue must be controversial is not correct. Yes, there is a tendency to think that such a thesis as that the world is phystriological is controversial, but, maintaining that the world is phystriological is actually *un*controversial. In fact, it is hardly more controversial than maintaining that the earth goes around the sun.

11.1 "The evidence is too recent." It might be objected that we've had only, at most, fifty or so years since just about all mind-body philosophers and all non-postmodernist philosophers of science took it that the evidence for phystriology was established. But new evidence could still arise, and so, given merely the fifty or so year period, it would be objected, we have too short a period of time on which to base as important a result as phystriology.

---

[173] "Compositional science and religious philosophy": 130, 131.

In response, exponents of phystriology would say that it rather seems to be the case that the consensus group in mind-body philosophers and the (non-constructivist, non-postmodernist) philosophers of science are looking at the last four hundred years of research, or longer, not the last fifty years. Many would say that the results by 1953 or 1960 or 1970 or so represent the culmination of at least four hundred years of work, all the significant elements of which were moving in the phystriological direction. Further, from Emmy Nöther's Theorem, published in 1918, it follows that natural selection must be true; and from both those views, phystriology follows (as was outlined in n. 173 in Chapter Ten). In Appendix 2, the demarcation problem will be shown; and the only plausible resolution of that problem is the phystriology view. That alone makes three main ways phystriology can be shown; taking it that phystriology was established some time between 1953 and 1970 is but one way of showing phystriology. And there are still other ways, beyond these three, of showing phystriology to be true. (One was given in 9.8, n. 139.) In any case, the phystriological hypothesis is the only hypothesis in use in physics, in chemistry, and in biology.

These results are surely sufficient to establish phystriology. The recent articulation of the human genome, for example, shows the strength of the results reached by the early 1960's and signaled by the uncovering of DNA structure in 1953.[174] That's just one clear example of the way the research has been fully continuing. For an objection based on epigenetic research, see 11.12.

So we do have four and more centuries of work behind current acceptance of phystriology. And the convergence of many factors should not be ignored.

11.2 "Science keeps changing." It might be objected that science has been changing so much that we have grounds to think it will keep changing drastically again. What would an exponent of phystriology say to that problem?

In response, it's true that science changes in radical ways. However, there are objects and their properties that can be referred to by

---

[174] The results were first published in February 2001; see Jan Sapp, 2003, *Genesis: Evolution of Biology*: 323 n. 7. Since then, more work has been done, this time on genomes of single individuals.

the same terms in very old theories, in somewhat old theories, and in contemporary theories. For example, the path of Mercury as seen from the earth can be described, first, in the Aristotelian-Ptolemaic system, second, in Newton's system, and, third, in Einstein's general relativity system. All would agree that it would be more accurately described in the second than in the first, and still more accurately described in the third than in the second. In the Aristotelian-Ptolemaic system, Mercury's orbit was based on combinations of circular orbits, around the earth. In Newton's system, it was elliptical, and around the sun. In 1859, it was discovered that Mercury's orbit around the sun has a perihelion effect, an effect in which the angle of the elliptical orbit keeps shifting a bit. Einstein's general relativity system accurately retrodicted the perihelion shifts of Mercury.[175]

More simply, that science has changed dramatically in many basic ways since the 16th century is not sufficient to motivate us to give up the notion, for example, that the earth, like Venus, orbits the sun. Similarly, despite all the changes science is likely to undergo in the future, there is no reason to give up the view that the thesis of phystriology is correct. There are, of course, more detailed renderings of this response than will be given here. But all that needs to be observed here is that since 1600 or so, quantified work has at least *approximately* stuck over short term time periods in the original contexts of research, in parallel to the way much mathematical work has *exactly* stuck for thousands of years. It's not at all uncommon to find physicists noting how Newton's system still works for firing a rocket into space, or getting a spacecraft to go to the moon or through the solar system.[176] So the general principle stands: since the 1600's in physics, since some time in the 18th century in chemistry, and for a long time, centuries, anyway, in biology, stable results reached remain as at least approximately correct over short term time periods in the original contexts in which the research was done.[177]

Science will change drastically, but that does not mean that there is no progress in the sciences. The triple restriction for progress is a bit

---

[175] Einstein, *Relativity*: 144.

[176] See, for example, Martin Rees, *Before the Beginning*: 64.

[177] Even the main proponent of paradigm theory, Thomas Kuhn, implicitly, at least, shows this. See, for instance, *The Structure of Scientific Revolutions*: 27, 34, and 68 re Newton's improvements over Ptolemy, and, implicitly, Einstein's over Newton's.

elaborate, requiring results as approximations, for short term time periods, and only to be taken in original contexts of research. But that is good enough to allow the progress in the natural sciences since some time in the 17th century to be visible.

11.3 "There are grounds for belief in the paranormal." Some might object that there are experimental grounds for belief in physically incomplete paranormal phenomena.

In response, this is, clearly, an empirical (observational-theoretical) issue. Exponents of phystriology typically take the view that the empirical evidence for the paranormal is so weak as not to be plausible. That gets the blood boiling in those who think that there are good journals – scientific journals, they would say, like, as mentioned before, *Journal of Scientific Exploration* – with scientific evidence for the paranormal; and there are lively discussions to be had on those points. Here, it will, I hope, suffice to briefly follow through on what I suggested in the last Chapter, that exponents of phystriology maintain that the key is not to worry about the grand philosophical questions; the key is to follow through on the everyday empirical matters.

For example, suppose I were to inform you that highly reputable scientists confirmed the observation of various unusual physical organisms, that these organisms have been examined for their properties, and conclusions have been drawn from the examinations by notable researchers, and the conclusions have been published. Perhaps you would simply adopt the attitude that those published reports must be fine. If you were a bit more cautious, though, you would want to know what those reports were of, and who the notable researchers were.

Such caution, I would say, is well advised. In the 18th century, reports of exactly that kind were given by J. B. Robinet, a *philosophe* (an 18th century French scientist-philosopher), about the capture of sea-men and mermaids, and about the scores of observers who studied them. In a related report, one mermaid, apparently, learned to sew, but could not learn to speak.[178] However, undoubtedly, no one now believes in sea-men or mermaids. In the 19th century, there were many supposedly good endorsements of photographs of ectoplasm, fairies, elves, and such like

---

[178] Arthur Lovejoy, *The Great Chain of Being*. 172.

phenomena.[179] Undoubtedly, no one now takes those photographs seriously. In the 20th century, there were supposedly good tests on people reading face-down cards. But skeptics showed the many grounds for thinking the tests were not so good, after all.[180] Nowadays, one wants studies to be carried out very carefully indeed. References to old studies that were not properly done are taken to be references to unreliable sources.

Again, such caution is well-advised for the broad contemporary period as well. Not so long ago, a noted mathematician who had also written a book on physics lent unqualified endorsement to various paranormal claims. He even wrote a tome, *Superminds*, explaining the paranormal claims that he supported. Careful researchers embarrassed his exposition in various ways; and, some years later, he retracted his endorsements. But this illustrates how scientists, too, who are unfamiliar with prestidigitation and ordinary psychology, are sometimes more vulnerable to being tricked or confused than others.[181]

When one receives contemporary reports of observations whose interpretations go against phystriology one would be well advised not to engage in drafty philosophical inquiries, but to go after the elementary bases of the reports.

In investigating experimental claims, one would be well advised to check the procedures to see whether they adhere to the elementary provisions that are required in junior or senior level university work. I will show the need for this in Part II, Chapter Fifteen; here, a couple of examples will indicate the point. In instructions for junior or senior level work in setting up experiments, the requirement is given to define in advance exactly what one is testing for. However, reports were recently made stating that there has been a scientific confirmation that patients who were the objects of prayer from people praying at a distance, without knowing that they were being prayed for, healed better than others. The reports were transmitted copiously by newspapers, magazines, tv news shows, and so on. The exciting information spread widely. Judging from polls and, informally, from classroom discussions,

---

[179] Paul Kurtz, *Transcendental Temptation*, 407; D. H. Rawcliffe, *Illusions and Delusions of the Supernatural and the Occult*: 311 ff.

[180] Excellent studies are in C. E. M. Hansel, *The Search for Psychic Power*.

[181] See Martin Gardner, "The Extraordinary Mental Bending of Professor Taylor", in *Science Good, Bad, and Bogus*: 179-184.

these reports seem to have been quickly accepted by what seems to be a majority of the audience.

However, the media gave no similar widespread report when some careful commentators mentioned that the experiment did not select in advance the measure to be tested for. Rather, in advance of the experiment, three measures were noted as measures that could be used to test for paranormal success in this case, and only one was chosen *after the data was in*, the one that gave the positive result. (One was neutral, and one gave a negative result.) Also, in a recent proper study, with the test defined in advance, there was no significance to the result.[182] This, too, unfortunately, was not widely reported in the news.

Even in experimental work, then, there are important pitfalls one can fall into (pitfalls that one is instructed not to fall into in junior or senior level university courses). I've just given one example: failure to define in advance the measure one will use. I'll now mention another one.

Rupert Sheldrake, in *Seven Experiments That Could Change the World*, says that fundamental research can be done on a shoestring budget. He provides designs for seven experiments. These experiments, he says (xiii), "could reveal much more of the world than science has yet dared to conceive." One of them involves checking people's ability to tell when they're being stared at from behind. People tend to think they can sometimes tell when they're being stared at from behind. Sheldrake is of the view that such ordinary tendencies might indicate statistically significant results, and so he proposes a simple experiment (pp. 121-4) to find out. He also requests that results be sent to a 'Seven Experiments Project', address given on pg. 252.

Intrigued, as I often am, by such projects, I administered the experiment, as Sheldrake proposed it, in several classroom settings. The results did not seem to me to be significant.[183] My point is not to mention

---

[182] See I. Tessman and J. Tessman, "Efficacy of Prayer," and Nicholas Humphrey, "The Power of Prayer." For a report on the proper study, see Kevin Christopher, "'No effect' Prayer Study."

[183] The figure for correct results of the total group of identifications by people on whether they were being stared at from behind or not, in my investigation, was $206/400 = 51.5\%$; in the same group, $115/234 = 49.1\%$ were instances of actual staring that were correctly identified as staring instances. The group had twenty students, with coin tosses determining whether to stare from behind or

that the results do not support Sheldrake's theory, but rather to mention that (through neglect, I guess) I never sent these results to the address that Sheldrake provided, nor to any other receiver of such information. In note 183, I am recording these results for the first time. So the results that Sheldrake received cannot be taken as reliable results; there surely is a tendency for those who have results that might be supportive of Sheldrake's theory to send them on; whereas those who receive results that may not be significant, or that undermine the hypothesis, are more likely not to send them on. There is a pitfall, then, in suggesting an experiment, and asking for results to be sent in.

In any case, it should not be surprising that there is an incorrect general impression of well done scientific experiments supporting paranormalism. All in all, though, exponents of phystriology would say that the paranormal evidence is so weak as to be entirely unable to threaten the phystriology result.

The pattern has been this: one positive paranormalist result is reported, but for various reasons (often better testing), it is abandoned. Then another result is reported. It, too, is later abandoned for various (good) reasons. And so the process continues.[184]

---

not. In a second group, $143/300 = 47.6\%$ was the figure for correct results, and $62/150 = 41.3\%$ was the result for correct identification of being stared at from behind. The two dates, respectively, were Feb 9, 1998, and Feb 17, 1998 at Douglas College, British Columbia.

[184] At the time I am writing this essay, an experiment is underway to detect whether consciousness is not entirely based on brain states, by examining 'near-death-experience' states. Already it has received prominent coverage in the news; an article of about fifteen hundred words followed by another article of about a hundred words has already appeared (March 14, 2009 F1 *The Globe and Mail*). Perhaps, in a few years, the experimenters will report that the experimental results may be interpreted as being positive; I predict that if, as seems plausible, such reports are made, these will receive wide coverage in the media; it also seems to be likely that if that such reports are made, then it will turn out that the experimental methods used in the experiment would have been inadequate by usual standards, and that the latter observations, when made, would not receive wide coverage. I also predict that, if as also seems plausible, only negative results come from the experiment, no large coverage of the experiment will be given in the media. The grounds for these predictions are given in more detail in Chapter Fifteen. Whether these predictions prove to be correct will emerge in a few years.

The attitude of those who look at the long history of the studies for the paranormal – strong skepticism about them – is rejected by many in the general populace. The issue, on the face of it, is a strictly empirical one, and so some readers will want to have access to broad examinations on this point. I will try to do that in two ways. First, in this note (n. 186)[185] I give some of the many citations that can be followed. Second, in Part Two, Chapter Fifteen, I will present in more detail than I have here the very many reasons that undermine acceptance of reports of genuine paranormal occurrences.

11.4 "Recent anti-mechanism goes against phystriology." Some theorists emphasize how physics has grown beyond a mechanical view. For example, Albert Einstein and Leopold Infeld, in *The Evolution of Physics*, have a long chapter entitled, "The Decline of the Mechanical View." How is this consistent with the notion that from the 17th century and on, physics has been mathematized, chemistry physicalized, and biology physio-chemicalized? Isn't phystriology a view about the mechanization of the natural world? Doesn't the decline of the mechanical view go against the general point that has been made here about there being no overturning of the rules, laws, or forces of physics?

In response, 'mechanism' is a slippery term. It means different things in different expositions. Three theories of 'mechanism' were exposed for careful readers in the latter parts of Chapter Three, and the exposition made clear that these were only three of many mechanical theories used since the beginning of the 17th century. The mathematization of physics only amounts to the adoption of mechanism in what was called (in Chapter Three) the third theoretical sense, and even the third sense of mechanism is a touch narrower than an entirely mathematical basis of physics. So what one needs to do is notice and make explicit exactly what Einstein and Infeld meant by 'mechanical.'

---

[185] See my *Enlightenment East & West*, Chapter Eight; Thomas Gilovich, *How We Know What Isn't So*; as before, C. E. M. Hansel, *The Search For Psychic Power*; *The Hundredth Monkey and other Paradigms of the Paranormal*, ed. K. Frazier; and Susan Blackmore, *The Adventures of a Parapsychologist*. A superb, though decade old, encyclopedia is *Encyclopedia on the Paranormal*, ed. Gordon Stein, 1996, Amherst NY: Prometheus Press. I reported on a later compilation of supposedly pro-paranormal material in "Universal Self Consciousness mysticism and the physical completeness principle": 15-17.

By 'mechanical' Einstein and Infeld specifically meant any theory (a) that maintains Newton's three laws of motion and (b) in which the force equations for a pair of objects are governed instantaneously by the distance between the two objects in the force relations.[186] 'Instantaneously' expresses Newton's hidden assumption in his second law that Einstein and Infeld needed to go against. Newton thought that there was an absolute temporal simultaneity. If a force is governed *instantaneously*, in any frame of reference, by the distance between two substances, this becomes troublesome. For example, in all cases in which there is collision or mass-contact interaction, there is apparent action at a distance across the body of one or all of the objects in contact interaction, and it is that apparent action at a distance that was, and had to be, undone, especially following Maxwell's electromagnetic theory; the accomplishing of that task was part of the job of special relativity. In effect, Einstein and Infeld's 'mechanism' is a specifically Newtonian mechanism assuming absolute simultaneity, that is, simultaneity without any measuring reference frame in the system.

Einstein and Infeld pointed out how Newton's theory (roughly, our second kind of mechanism of Chapter Three) arose, and then how the electromagnetic theory of Maxwell required various features that would be difficult to integrate with the specific methods of implementing Galilean relativity. As it was put in Chapter Five, (it was put a bit differently in Einstein and Infeld's book, but that doesn't affect our concerns) the problem is how to integrate an important consequence of Maxwell's results, the constancy of the speed of light from any frame of reference used by an object with rest mass, on the one hand, and, on the other hand, Galilean relativity. Einstein and Infeld showed how an attempt to conceive of the ether in mechanical terms ('mechanical' in their sense, which is, effectively, our second sense of chapter Three) would fail. They said nothing whatever against what we're calling the third mechanism theory. And Einstein's mathematical governance of fundamental physical interactions entirely supports the third sort of mechanism, which is, aside from the rather technical question of the meaning of 'motion' that arises in the interpretations of quantum physics, the mathematization of physics. The mathematization of physics has taken place; no natural change overthrows the results of physics taken as

---

[186] Einstein and Infeld, p. 119 etc.

approximate results, in short term time periods, in original contexts of research, and that is all that counts for us in our context.[187]

To put this very simply, Einstein and Infeld do not say anything against phystriology.

11.5 "Gödel proved the world is physically incomplete." In 1931, logician Kurt Gödel demonstrated that for any axiomatic system good enough to derive the basic truths of arithmetic there will be true propositions that are not provable via the axioms and rules of inference of that system. This is called Gödel's incompleteness Theorem. Doesn't it show that no system for physics can yield the physical world, or that the physical completeness thesis, here called the phystriological thesis, cannot be true?

In response, the notion of 'completeness' used by Gödel is *not* the notion of completeness used in 'physical completeness.' Gödel's result is a result in logic, and in Gödel's logic, if a system is complete then the inferences are algorithmic, that is, do not *require* some kind of interpretive creativity in working out the results. Quantum physics' results are not algorithmic because, by all appearances, the results themselves, as measured, are not deterministic. But all that is required to show that physical completeness in the desired sense, the phystriological sense, is correct, is the notion that no chemical nor biological factors overturn the rules of governance of physics, all of which govern the changes in inherently purposeless things. To explain this: suppose, hypothetically, that physical conditions at one time are given and they do not yield all physical conditions at other times. The physics could still have probabilistic rules, laws, or forces. Still, that would be irrelevant to whether there are chemical or biological factors that overturn the rules of governance or laws or forces of physics (as physics is already understood approximately, for short term time periods, with restrictions to original contexts of research).

Some might want to continue the objection by stating that the model of the rules of governance or laws or rules or forces of physics is

---

[187] This can be put more generally, too. Einstein said that the only reliable source of truth about physical matters was to find them in mathematical simplicity. See Max Jammer, 1999, *Einstein and Religion*: 40. See also *ibid*: 37-8; and less relevantly, 43, and 48, the latter on something like mind-body unity (that some think is suggested by phystriology).

inadequate. In response, there is already overwhelming evidence at hand that fully shows that biological beings are sums of inherently purposeless-symmetry-based things that are usually regarded as tiny things. This is itself sufficient to show the power of the phystriology result: we have excellent reasons to hold that whatever is left out of a model of the world – and there is a lot left out of any model of the world, as the inconsistency of quantum physics and general relativity exhibits – will not bring purposes back into the basics or fundamentals of what exists.

In conclusion, Gödel's logical incompleteness shows that the world is not logically or algorithmically complete, but physical theories in the last century do not claim that world is logically or algorithmically complete. Gödel's incompleteness theorem does nothing to show the world to be what was called physically incomplete. To put it as simply as it can be put, Gödel's incompleteness theorem does nothing to show that a biological creature changes in such a way as to violate the laws, rules, or forces, of mathematized physics.

11.6 "There are many emergent things that show the world to be physically incomplete." An objection against phystriology is based on the concept of 'emergence,' a concept that is often used both within and outside sophisticated philosophical discussions. Many claim that there are emergent effects at the higher levels of observation (levels of observation of complex systems), and that these emergent effects cannot be specified at any lower levels. It is thought that such emergence somehow indicates that the phystriology thesis is incorrect.

In responding to this objection the important point to keep in mind is that the issue is whether the emergent effects *overturn* the physical results given by applications of the formulated laws or forces or rules at equal or lower levels. It is remarkable that no one over the last few hundred years has provided an experiment such that the operation of higher level (complex level) formulated forces or laws or rules overturn the results of sums of same context lower level (or micro-physics level) formulated laws or forces or rules over short term time periods. Nor has this even been done at equal levels. At equal levels, one sort of formula is appropriately used; others are not appropriately used. The hypothetical results of the latter, the inappropriate formulas, become irrelevant. Equally important to keep in mind is the steady strengthening of the view that the physical basics are mathematically governed, and do not exhibit intrinsic purposes. Rather whatever purposive beings there are, are, one way or another, evolutionarily sum beings, not basically purposive beings, where something would be basic if it independently (non-summatively) generated changes. Accordingly, the emergence objection does not have teeth against phystriology.

It is true that in *one interpretation* of phystriology, there would be a sound objection. Suppose that phystriology asserts the condition to obtain in which the *accessible* sums or *accessible* explanations from the micro-level (the formulas we already have from the micro-level) account for all the properties specifiable at the macro-level. No one that I can think of would hold to such a view.[188] There are too many subatomic particles to make such explanations or accounts accessible to us; and, in principle subatomic particles are strange in relation to classical items. And the theories in physics are still ongoing; no one has yet fully integrated classical physics with quantum physics, for instance. And there are emergent things, where 'emergent things' are things whose properties are not the properties of their micro-parts. It is easy to object to the view that such a phystriology has been evidentially established.

On the other hand, the thesis asserted by phystriology is that no property outcomes specified by physicists are *overturned* by the operations of rules, laws or forces at the chemical, or biological (or higher in complexity) levels, whether or not the operations of those rules, laws or forces are accessible to us given the complexity of the physics-based particles. Add on the other key element in phystriology – nothing in physics has changes governed by inherent purposes – and this is still sufficient so as to exclude the typically understood interactive God, the afterlife, the physics-overturning notions of freedom and responsibility, the physics-overturning interpretation of paranormal powers, the view that there is a hidden karmic and cosmic or supernatural punishment/reward system, the mystical ascent to a higher realm beyond the gross physical level, token ontological interactive dualism, and

---

[188] Could John Dupré be attempting to undermine such a view when he says "there is essentially no evidence for the completeness of physics" ("The Miracle of Monism" in *Naturalism in Question*, edited by Mario de Caro and David Macarthur, Cambridge Mass: Harvard University Press: 36 – 58: 50)? Probably not. But if that was the intent, that would be a major mistake, since that is not what the 'completeness of physics' is taken to be about. More likely, Dupré was just arguing against conceptual, property-wise, or theoretical reductionism, or against the unity of the sciences. Phystriology, though, is neutral on those topics.

causally interactive emanationism. And that summarizes just what is logically excluded.

The way phystriology obtains has been enshrined in a useful conceptual distinction between weak and strong emergence.[189] No changes in a weak emergent system would overturn physical laws, rules, or forces. Some changes in a strong emergent system would overturn physical laws, rules, or forces. So to say that a system is emergent is not yet to say that the changes in the system overturn the physical laws, rules, or forces. A system would have to be a strong emergent system if it were to undo the phystriological claim that no changes overturn the laws, rules, or forces of physics. And no strong emergent system has been discovered.

There is the following closely related objection to phystriology: Many philosophers are anti-reductionists; but, some say, phystriology requires reductionism. Therefore, they say, phystriology is false.

In response, it is true that many philosophers are emergentists of one sort or another, and, typically, through their emergentism, they are anti-reductionists. But what kind of anti-reductionist are they? Unfortunately for the would-be-defender of physical incompleteness, or the would-be anti-phystriologist, there are no defenders of the sort of anti-reductionism that could lead to an anti-phystriology position. This may sound a bit shocking, but it is not. To read more about this, see Appendix 2.4.

11.7 "Consciousness is not physical; so phystriology is false." Many theorists take the view that consciousness necessarily arises in any physical system like the physical system of our world. However, David Chalmers in the mid-1990's argued that there is no necessity from there being certain sorts of physics things to there being conscious things. Rather consciousness is a property that can only be given by psychophysical laws. Consciousness, then, in the view of some philosophers, is not necessarily given by the physical basics.

Let us suppose for the sake of discussion that consciousness requires psychophysical laws. Still, there is no threat against phystriology. To show this in the simplest way it can be shown, in *The Conscious Mind*, the mid 1990's book referred to above, Chalmers accepted phystriology.

---

[189] This was presented by M. A. Bedau, in 1997, in "Weak Emergence."

(He called it 'causal closure'[190], but that is just the name he used.) His more recent views doubting phystriology[191] are, as will be shown in Appendix 2.1, beset by the demarcation problem, among other problems; his earlier views are not so beset, as he accepted phystriology, calling it 'causal closure.' In any case, it follows that whether or not psychophysical laws are required, the theory that there are psychophysical laws does not imply physical incompleteness; physical incompleteness would require overturning of the rules, laws, or forces of physics, and that would not be a result of the psychophysical laws. Also, many views of consciousness other than Chalmers' are consistent with phystriology (for which see 12.1).

11.8 "Mechanism shows a purposive background; therefore phystriology is somehow false." The phystriologist maintains that the basic physical interactions have been stripped of intrinsic purposes and what were earlier called 'final causes.' But the mechanists of old frequently claimed that the beauty the mechanical principles exemplified showed the fundamental purposes realized in them. For example, Leonhard Euler in the 18th century maintained that the various mechanical principles can be derived "from their final causes as well as from their efficient ones."[192] The final causes are the purposes the effects exhibit or fulfill, and the Aristotelian language is clear. This yields the objection that the mathematics in physics expresses a fundamental purpose, and that, in some way, goes against the idea that the mathematics used by physics is not supplied by any being with inherent purposes.

In response, though, it seems that there was not much in the layering of theological structure on the mathematical forms. Ernst Mach showed that there was a transition of understanding from the time of Euler to the time of Joseph Lagrange. Lagrange used Euler's work and D'Alembert's principle to yield a mathematical physics in which the results could be directly calculated without creatively thinking about the

---

[190] David Chalmers, *The Conscious Mind*: 161.

[191] David Chalmers, 2003, "Consciousness and its Place in Nature" in *Philosophy of Mind*, ed. by S. Stich and T. Warfield: 126.

[192] Quoted in Mach, *The Science of Mechanics*, 6th ed., pg. 550, from *Methodus inveniendi lineas curvas maximi minimive propriete gaudentes*, Lausanne 1744.

material.[193] This is a good justification of the notion that there was a process from the early 17th century leading to as full a mathematization of physics as was found in the late 18th century. The results since then in the 19th and first part of the 20th century only firmed up the results that had been reached earlier. Of course they have not become less firm either. (Rather they reached a high plateau level at, say, 1918, the year of publication of Nöther's Theorem; and some would predict that they will reach a still higher plateau level at some point in the future.)

The mathematics, then, according to the reply, stands on its own. And the three processes taken together undermine the view, not that there are purposes anywhere in nature, but that there are basic purposes anywhere in nature. And the supernatural being who set up a mechanical system would be a basically purposive being. Yet that is what phystriology has undermined, logically for the standard concept of an interacting supernatural being, and strongly[194] ampliatively for any concept of a purposive supernatural being.

11.9 "Physteriology can be overturned by an omniscient, omnipotent God." It could be objected that the notion of God's existence has been present more or less throughout human culture, and that if God is supposed to be omniscient, omnipotent, omni-benevolent, and to have created the world, God could easily interact causally with the world. Why should the evidence of the last four hundred years overturn the notion of such a God? Included in this is the double question, "Why should the evidence of the last four hundred years overturn the notion of such a God, a God who doesn't interact with the world, and why should the evidence of the last four hundred years overturn the notion of such a God who does interact with the world?"

This was already answered in 10.3.1, and in 11.8, too. What was said in these two places will, again, be stated, but in still other words. The typical pre-scientific view of the world thinks of agency as a *basic or fundamental property* of some things in the world, where 'basic or fundamental property', in this case, somehow, means, retrospectively, a property that overturns the laws, or forces, or rules, or principles, or formulas, or whatever they are to be called, in mathematical physics. (In

---

[193] See Mach, *ibid.*, 420-433; 561-575.

[194] Why "strongly"? See 10.3.1.

the pre-scientific intuition, agency seems to be written into some of the basic elements of reality. This can be understood retrospectively: That agents go against, or seem to go against, the supposition of there being a law of conservation of momentum, for instance, shows the pre-scientific intuition that agency is written into some of the basic elements of reality.) If agency is not a basic nor fundamental property, then agency somehow arises in a sum of things natural selectively produced over evolutionary time, and if the physicalization of chemistry is true and the physio-chemicalization of biology is true (as both are) then all changes in a biological being do not break the rules, laws, or whatever of physics. We can summarize this in a short way: a fundamental property is a non-sum property.

Agency as a fundamental (non-sum) property of the world in some objects was central in Aristotle's theory, as it was also, earlier, in various aspects of Plato's theories expressed through Socrates in some of Plato's dialogues. It is the mathematization of physics together with the physicalization of chemistry, and the physio-chemicalization of biology (remembering that biology includes Darwinian evolution) that shows us that agency is the notion we use when we consider the result of the assembly of interactions of some large groups of particles. According to the exponents of phystriology, agency is not fundamental to the universe in the way the pre-scientific intuition thinks it is.

Yet the ordinary concept of God takes the intuition of agency given by human agency to be basic or fundamental, and to occur in a non-sum way in nature. The ordinary concept of God's agency magnifies such a supposedly basic or fundamental notion in an enormous way; but the exponent of phystriology focuses on a powerful shift from the pre-scientific intuition in which purposes are basic to the post-scientific notion that any purposes that exist are summative, and, moreover are summative as the result of a natural selection process, and so are not basic. Given the evidence of the last four hundred years, there are no grounds for thinking of a fundamental agency, so, all the more so, there are no grounds for thinking of a fundamental magnified agency.

A point earlier mentioned in 10.3.1 can now be repeated, with a touch of added clarification: The notion of 'God' has four main meanings. First, the term could refer to a personal God who interacts with the world at the human (or classical) scale; this is the standard notion of God. The second notion of God will be given in two variants: God is a non-interactive personal God (the Deist God); this view was adopted when some arguments for the interactive God seemed weak; and

God (or a supernatural intelligence) interacts with the world but only at the quantum scale; this could be presented in response to the phystriological challenge. Those two are unusual versions of the personal God and together comprise the second notion of God. The third and fourth meanings of God, both rather unusual meanings of God, will come up in Chapters Twenty and Twenty Two and are reviewed in 22.4. The evidence primarily reached in the last four or five hundred years strongly ampliatively leads to acceptance of phystriology. Acceptance of phystriology logically leads to rejection of an interactive God at the human scale; it strongly ampliatively leads to rejection of a personal God (or supernatural intelligence) interacting at the quantum scale, the non-interactive (Deist) God, and any basic supernatural intelligence at all.

The objection just considered is closely related to the objection based on the view that God works through processes everywhere. Process theology holds that God is the very subtly purposive being enacting through the world. And, somewhat similarly, John Polkinghorne argues that our world is best thought of as one with an "intertwined order and novelty"; his position, critical realism, requires a fusion of epistemology and metaphysics, both a top-down complexity causation, and a bottom-up system of governance. But, he says, the "search for a modern equivalent of the Cartesian pineal gland would be the search for a will-o'-the-wisp; it is condemned to failure."[195] God, Polkinghorne conceives, might well interact with the world "in the form of information input."[196]

There are two responses to make to this form, effectively, of anti-phystriology.

First, it assumes a kind of basically purposive being, namely God, even though God's purposes would be super-purposes, purposes grandly magnified and, perhaps, incomprehensible to us. But these purposes would not be sum-purposes of small things that had no inherent purposes. This is ampliatively rejected by the overwhelming evidence gathered over the last two thousand plus years (or the last four hundred years if one prefers).

---

[195] "Profile: Conversations with John Polkinghorne: The Nature of Physical Reality": 937.

[196] John Polkinghorne: *ibid.*

Second, not only is the contribution of information not a *basic* purposive phenomenon, but also the way in which information can weakly emerge through natural selection is ignored.

In objection to this second response, it is sometimes said that information won't weakly emerge through mere copying. An analogy is presented: copy a printed sheet of paper many times and the image gradually goes fuzzy. Yet in nature, the mutations are, occasionally, supposed to improve the information of the result. But that would be absurd; natural selection by copying, says the objection to the second response, should only produce more and more fuzzy results. No one can take it to, occasionally, add to the information structure of the organism. So, it seems, a special purposive force is needed to guarantee that information is added.

A counter-analogy, however, can be given: suppose we let monkeys randomly type, each one on its keyboard, or, by some other means, we have many typewriters and a system for random pressing of the keys on each; and suppose the results of all the typewriters are examined from time to time to see if "the quick brown fox jumps over the lazy dog," has been typed. How long would it be likely for this to occur? We can calculate an enormous number of days by simple probability theory. But suppose that once a 'q' is typed if preceded by all the letters that precede it in "the quick brown fox jumps over the lazy dog," then the 'q' is removed from the keyboard; and if an 'a' is typed preceded by all the letters that precede it in "the quick brown fox jumped over the lazy dog," then the 'a' is removed from the keyboard, and so on (allowing a repeated letter to stay till its last occurrence is typed). That vastly shortens the time in which to expect "the quick brown fox jumps over the lazy dog" to be typed at one of the keyboards. The analogous element to natural selection – the structuring of the outcomes by the dropping of (entirely) used letters – adds information to the process. The process is random, but it has a constraint, the constraint being the dropping of (entirely) used letters, and that is analogous to the rules of chemical combinations.[197]

Finally, an attempt at an objection of the following form can be made in this context (it is also based on the amount of information that is left open): Suppose one is a skeptic about the external world (or about

---

[197] The ideas in the last two paragraphs were suggested to me by Ronnie de Sousa.

substances, as Hume was). What then? Wouldn't phystriology be by-passed?

In response, the skeptic about the external world needs to find a way to deal with the equipollence (equality of justification) between the view, on the one hand, that every time I do an apparently good thing, a bad thing happens in what is the real world (and vice versa), and, on the other hand, that every time I do an apparently good thing, a good thing happens in what is the real world (and *mutatis mutandis*, changing 'good' for 'bad'). The skeptics about the external world, thank goodness, are not sent to jail. For instance, Sextus Empiricus, the main exponent of Pyrrhonian skepticism, was, it seems, a physician. So, somehow, skeptics behave as though they, one way or another, choose the latter apparently harmonious path, (doing apparently good things), pragmatically, or effectively, at least. As they put it, they *follow appearances*. One can allow them to do more than follow appearances, too; one can allow their route to be based on merely aesthetic factors. But then, grounded in the following of appearances, or grounded in aesthetic factors, they also employ the apparent results of science. And that is all that counts for us.

11.10 "High tuning of the initial condition shows phystriology to be false." Some physicists have maintained that not only is there an entropy law, as we saw in 5.2, but also the initial conditions of the early high order are amazingly fine-tuned in such a way as to allow life to be able to evolve. If there had been slight differences in initial conditions, no living things could have come to be: no stars, nor planets would have formed, no chemicals of the sort that living things have would have formed, and so on. The entropy law, then, can be realized in many ways; but the specifics of the high order of the universe's initial condition were fine-tuned; and that can only be purposively explained. The purposive explanation is that a personal God placed those finely tuned conditions there to allow life to evolve. [198]

One form of response to this objection is to deny that there was the sort of high initial order and fine-tuning; that is, the numbers as

---

[198] For six apparently fine-tuned factors, see Martin Rees, *Just Six Numbers*, and for some explicit explanations, see pp: 30-1, 49, 86-7, 114-5, 135-6. It should also be noted, though, that Martin Rees does not accept the fine-tuning argument for the existence of God. For the argument itself see Robin Collins, "A Scientific Argument for the Existence of God."

usually given are not correct; a related form of response is to state or show that the theory of a high order initial condition for our world has not been appropriately supported.[199]

But here we will assume that the fine-tuning condition is empirically found: there are special fine-tuned conditions at some early high-order state of the universe. The objection is that the presence of the fine-tuning condition allows one to infer that there are fundamental purposes underlying the physical conditions of our universe. The phystriological position must be incorrect; the fundamental purposes of the Creator are found in the initial conditions of our universe.

There are three sorts of response to this viewpoint, each of which accepts that there is a fine-tuned initial condition of our universe. The first response argues that the best explanation of the initial condition is the hypothesis of a vast number of combinations of conditions; it is no wonder that we happen to be in one like this. The landscape is so vast that of course some of them will have the initial condition that allows life to evolve.[200]

The second response has already been presented in 10.3.1 (4th and 5th paragraph), in 11.8 (toward the end), and in 11.9 (in the middle). It states that there was an enormous switch from a pre-scientific notion of purposes in which purposes are taken to be basic features of the universe to a post-scientific notion of purposes in which purposes only arise as evolutionarily produced sum features, and where chemistry is physicalized and biology physio-chemicalized, and, thus, purposes are non-basic features of the universe. As a result of this switch, it is highly implausible to think of a basically purposive placing of the original conditions of the universe as a high-order condition. The reason is that purposes do not exist as basic features of the universe, and so, ampliatively, they don't exist as basic features of any world larger than

---

[199] See Victor Stenger, *God: The Failed Hypothesis*: 117-121 for the latter hypothesis. The basic idea Stenger puts out for consideration is that in an expanding universe, maximum entropy and actual entropy begin together, but keep increasing in a split way. In that model, the universe began in total chaos, and the entropy increase results from the expansion of the universe. Stenger's point is that such an hypothesis has by no means been excluded.

[200] See Martin Rees, *Before the Beginning*, ibid.: 241-257 for this argument; also see Leonard Susskind, *The Cosmic Landscape*, 2006. Susskind's landscape theory, though, is more specific than is required by the argument.

our universe. This is the result of accepting the uncontroversial results of the last four hundred years or so of the natural sciences.

The third response is given mostly for technical reasons: The response states that the objection doesn't particularly point to physical incompleteness. It points only to some purposive creation of the high-order initial or early conditions of our spacetime. This does not imply that the purposive being who created such a spacetime system interacts with it. Phystriology, though, is only a claim about changes in the world. To go against phystriology requires pointing to changes in the world that are not permitted by it.

These responses, especially the first two, fully undermine the objection.

11.11 "Phystriology is based on non-evidential factors." Some philosophers of science, the constructivists, or postmodernists, maintain that scientists do not merely assess the evidence in some objective manner to generate a consensus on a scientific theory. Rather, the constructivists or postmodernists say, there are social, pragmatic, or other non-evidential factors that lead to the scientific consensus outcomes. It is inappropriate, then, and, perhaps, a bit arrogant, say the objectors, to think that any evidential pattern in favor of phystriology can be relied on. A closely related objection says that any coherent story of progress over the last few centuries is "Whiggish," and involves a coherent but ideology-based rewrite of, or slant on, the historical period.[201] We shouldn't need just one slant on history, says this version of the objection.

Both versions of the objection can be answered together.

The first half of the answer is as easy to state as can be: there is no constructivist and no postmodernist and no irrealist and no idealist – not one! – who maintains that the earth is at the absolute centre of the universe. Yet whether the earth is at the absolute centre of the universe was a hot controversial notion just a few hundred years ago. For instance, Galileo lived for the last eight or so years of his life in house arrest on account of his holding the Copernican notion in which the earth is not at the absolute centre of the universe. Yet the idea that the earth does not

---

[201] Richard Rorty makes this sort of statement in *Philosophy And The Mirror Of Nature*: e.g.: 341.

locate the absolute centre of the universe has entirely pervaded the culture. No commentator today – none! – this is remarkable – rejects the notion that the earth, like Venus, orbits the sun. How can this be interpreted? Surely, it can't be interpreted as the result of social or pragmatic or other non-evidential merely ideological slants or factors. There are so many disputes in the world. If the spread of this view were social or pragmatic or otherwise non-evidential, surely there would be disputers here, too. But there are none.

Rather, the evidential picture has spread throughout the world. Not everyone is aware of the details of the evidence grounding the view that earth like Venus orbits the sun; but it doesn't matter. No one who is competent in dealing with the evidence thinks that there is something wrong with the evidence. So advocating the constructivist or postmodernist or irrealist or idealist picture here seems to be mere fancy-talk with no content.

The other half of the response to this objection points to the stability in mathematical research and draws the parallel for the natural sciences. Mathematical research has been enormously stable. In mathematics there have been some controversial fields at their inception, and some of these fields of research have remained as controversial fields afterwards as well. Still, though, it is not the case that there are any results in controversial or non-controversial mathematical fields that were generally accepted at one stage or generally accepted within the field, and then generally rejected afterwards or generally rejected within the field afterward. The most one has is refinements of a theorem by noting conceptual limitations, or exceptions, or revisions to properly define the contents of the theorem. This kind of stability in mathematical research goes through thousands of years. It is not, and cannot be, denied.

Similarly, in the natural sciences since the 17th century, the long-lasting theories, like Newton's theory, Coulomb's theory, Maxwell's theory, atomic composition theory, anatomy, neurophysiology, and so on, have been generally accepted, and will not be generally rejected as far as the approximate status of the results over short term time periods in original contexts of discovery are concerned. There are terms within Newton's theory that have been drastically revised. Some say the new meanings are incommensurable with the old meanings, but that is irrelevant to our concerns here. All we need to be concerned with is that the quantificational base of phystriology has rendered the natural sciences – physics, chemistry, and biology – as *approximately* stable over short term time periods in their original contexts of work as the mathematical theorems have never been overturned, even if refinements have sometimes been added.

Accordingly, this objection against phystriology does not go far at all. The evidence for phystriology remains intact.

11.12 Objections from epigenetic biology. Some might say that epigenetic biology and related fields show that the early form of the genetic revolution is incorrect. The distinction between heredity and environment, for instance, some would say, is not a sound distinction; the cell-based effects on genetic structure are enormous; mutation rates are affected by non-gene activities in the cell; and so on. Yet, the objectors would say, the phystriology result is based on the biogenetic and molecular biological revolution that happened in the 1950's and the 1960's, a revolution based on the notion of autonomous genes, a notion which has now been superceded by the epigenetic field. Consequently, it seems, the phystriological picture is undone.

In response, the epigenetic revolution presents no threat to the physio-chemicalization of biology. There is no feature of epigenetic theory that claims to isolate any biological features in which there are motions or relations that are not motions or relations of the sort found in complex chemistry or super-complex physics. The explanation of cell changes, including cell nuclear changes, as a result of epigenetics is different from that given by pre-epigenetic theorists. But the epigenetic claims do not jeopardize the physio-chemicalization of biology notion. And the physio-chemicalization of biology notion is the only notion associated with the molecular biology revolution of the 1950's and 1960's that counts in establishing phystriology. Accordingly, the epigenetic theories do not threaten phystriology in the least.

11.13 The "there's something wrong – I don't know what – with the phystriological picture" objection. Some might say, "there's something wrong, though I don't know what is wrong, with the phystriological picture." This objection has a touch of legitimate caution to it. The phystriological picture has enormous implications. To just accept the phystriological picture without careful consideration would be overly hasty.

In response, though, the depth of the triple process reviewed here – the mathematization of physics, the physicalization of chemistry, the physio-chemicalization of biology – and the depth of the abstract symmetry notion, and the power of what will be called the demarcation problem in A2.1, shows how difficult it would be to get away from the phystriological picture. The demarcation problem alone effectively presents somebody who resists accepting the phystriological picture with a challenge: conceive, even in any hypothetical or conjectural way, of any non-arbitrary region in which there might be changes overturning the inaccessible rules, laws, or forces of physics. You won't be able to do this plausibly. Nor could one have done so for hundreds of years. Accordingly, it is extremely difficult to conceive of how, given the many empirical factors culminating in the 20th century, one could get away from the phystriological picture.

Reasoning about the absence of the appropriate demarcation factors is mostly *a priori* reasoning; there is another not mostly empirical bit of reasoning too: symmetry reasoning. Once one sees the power of the symmetry notion, how it produces the conservation laws by mere mathematics plus trivial assumptions about classical spacetime, how nothing goes against the mathematization of physics in which purposes have been removed from describing how the tiny parts in physical things interact, how apparently consistent symmetry in mathematical physics is with all that has been researched in chemistry and biology, resistance to phystriology becomes less and less grounded in anything but a kind of prejudice. The symmetry principles are fundamental in nature. The complexity of chemical and biological relations rest on the symmetries of physics, and on the non-purposive nature of the constituent physics-based things. There seems to be no more use for a non-phystriological picture.

Let this be stated even more strongly: Nöther's Theorem showed how pure mathematics plus relatively trivial assumptions about (classical) spacetime yield conservation results. Nöther's Theorem depends on an undisturbable equivalence between fundamental geometrical elements, and fundamental numerical elements – points and real numbers in the continuous (classical) picture, or, moving the analysis forward a little bit, another equivalence in a discrete (non-classical or quantum) picture still to be developed. In a discrete picture the equivalence would be slightly different, but that wouldn't change the undisturbability of the equivalence.

Now, if there were special regions in which special motions occurred, those conservation results (for all regions above the Planck-scale regions in which there is no spacetime uniformity) would be, apparently, broken. So, as suggested earlier (in 10.4 n. 173), the phystriology result can be seen as deriving directly from the Nöther Theorem.

This, too, was stated earlier, in 11.1: there are, all in all, many convergent factors for phystriology.

11.14 Summary

I have briefly reviewed thirteen objections against phystriology. *All* of them, I would say, are mere pseudo-objections. Think of the evidence carefully, and the result will, I suggest, stand firmly. The questions are good, but there are solid answers to them all. The result is that no biological changes operate according to rules, forces, or laws that overturn the (inaccessible or accessible, and if the latter, approximate, short term time period, and limited in contexts) rules, forces, or laws of physics. The micro-things in physics have no intrinsic purposes. And there are no configurative forces of the sort the British Emergentists anticipated would be discovered. Nor are there vitalist forces. The leap of faith approach only works, if it works by James' reasoning (to be discussed more in Chapter Twenty One) for live forced momentous options. And given the strength of the evidence reached by 1970 or so, there is no live option here. Phystriology is not genuinely threatened by any of these objections.

Of course, there are other objections, scholarly objections, that might be put to proponents of phystriology. In Appendix 2, I review these objections and find that, as scholarly as they may be, these, too, are mere pseudo-objections. The phystriology result is as strong as any result can be.

However, acceptance of phystriology does logically require that one give up the eight views summarized in Chapter One, and again in Chapter Ten; and acceptance of phystriology does not strictly logically, but does strongly require that one give up other religious or spiritual views as well. Accordingly, there is a major clash in our time between the philosophically integrated results of the three natural sciences on the one hand, and spirituality (or religion), as standardly conceived, on the other hand.

There is a tendency, though, to think that phystriology's challenge is broader than a challenge to spirituality (and religion), because phystriology automatically goes against finding meaning in life, against accounting for the kind of consciousness we have, and such like things. But this, I suggest, is not so. It is time to look at the other side of the story, namely, what accepting phystriology leaves open.

Chapter Twelve: Phystriology, Values, and Life's Meaning

12.0 Phystriology has been established, and it strongly threatens many views that are widely held. Eight such views were mentioned in Chapter One and exposed more closely in Chapter Ten, with a ninth one added. And all of these views are found (independently mixing) in religious and spiritual systems. That problem is the *logical clash* problem. In addition there is the *not strictly logical but strong reasoning clash* between phystriology and various views found as important options in religious/spiritual systems. That is the *strong reasoning clash* problem.

It might seem, however, that the questions raised by phystriology are broader than those focusing on whether there can be an integration of phystriology on the one side with religion or spirituality on the other side. For instance, the question might be raised, "Can phystriology be integrated with the various ways we have for generating meaning in life?" Here, we'll see how acceptance of phystriology does *not* immediately nor automatically undermine the attempt to find meaning in life. It may threaten there being a *basic* meaning in life; but that is not to threaten a non-basic meaning in life. Nor does it threaten many other topics – the search for value, for interpretation of consciousness, cognition, freedom, and whether one's emotions can be integrated with other aspects of life – as will be reviewed below. In other words, it is as important to be aware of what acceptance of phystriology leaves open as it is to consider what acceptance of phystriology requires one to reject in spirituality or religion.

A broad question might be put as follows, "If phystriology maintains that there is *a sense in which* physics explains all human changes, does this mean that we are supposed to answer central human questions directly through use of the natural sciences?" I will show that the answer to this question is, "Definitely not." As earlier hinted (in 1.1.3), the phrasing of the question employs too strong a notion, the notion that there is a sense in which physics explains all human changes. Some maintain that physics does not explain all human changes. But the view that physics does, in a strong way, explain all human changes is not asserted by phystriology. Exponents of phystriology would typically say that, practically speaking, the resolutions for human problems must be given in psychological terms, not in terms of physics, chemistry, or merely biology. (By the way, the psychological terms are merely terms of language; they can refer to all sorts of things, including hopes, fears, things hoped for, things feared, and so on; the terms and references are not generated by the discipline known as psychology.) The practical answers to central human concerns are not to be found in physics-talk or chemistry-talk or biology-talk. Explaining problems is one thing. Solving problems, another. In any case, the problem all thinkers face is, "How can we answer problems of central human concern in expressions that do not logically conflict or do not strongly conflict with the results of the natural sciences?"

Those who accept phystriology agree that to address issues of central human concern is not simply to put forward the results of phystriology, nor to put forward any results within any of the three natural sciences that led to phystriology. Still, the consequences or implications of phystriology are crucially important. The efforts to address issues of central human concern cannot result in statements that are logically inconsistent, or not strictly logically, but strongly inconsistent, with the results of science, or the results of sciences put together philosophically. Since the late 1960's, those scientific results, as philosophically integrated, include phystriology. The fundamental issues that we will be concerned with in the book as a whole are, first, whether there are views that are (in some religious sense) spiritual that can be co-ordinated with the results of integrated recent natural science, namely, phystriology, and, second, in this Chapter, and through Parts I and II, too, in this book, how to use human-scale terms in our language to address issues of central human concern and yet are consistent with phystriology.

As we've already seen, acceptance of phystriology logically requires abandoning belief in: an interactive God at the human scale, a conscious pre-life and after-life, a strong freedom that overturns physics-only causation, a hidden cosmic moral karma, genuine mind-over-matter paranormal events, typically understood mysticism, Cartesian interactive dualism, and emanationism. Also, phystriology does not strictly logically but does strongly require abandoning other views, including the view that there is a personal God or supernatural intelligence of any kind. That is a significant result; and it sets up the question that will be worked on, in both aspects just mentioned, in Parts II and III. However, in this Chapter I will try to show that the search for values, for meaning in life, for interpretations of consciousness, cognition, freedom, morality, and integration of emotions are not inherently threatened by phystriology. This sets up a background for the discussion in Part III: we are either to give up on religion or spirituality, and, perhaps, do so in a way that finds meaning in life, or we are to work through a religions/spiritual system that is consistent with phystriology, and, perhaps, find meaning in life thereby.[202]

Much in what follows will present specialized material. The reader, therefore, can read lightly or skim what is not of special interest.

12.1 Consciousness

If one accepts phystriology, isn't one left entirely at a loss explaining how consciousness, with all its amazing qualitative experiences, can arise from mere atoms in the brain?

This powerful question has animated a large discussion. We are all familiar with the apparent gap between the mathematically governed bits of information, or quantized changing subatomic particles, or whatever are physically basic, on the one hand, and, on the other hand, the colors, sounds, textures, smells, tastes, thoughts, and so on, of our everyday experience. How can the former, as organized in the brain, for instance, somehow generate the latter? It seems to be impossible.

This intuition of impossibility is sometimes called *the hard problem of consciousness generation*. It has led many philosophers toward various theories about the subjective properties of the conscious world (but these theories, as will become clear in a moment, accept phystriology); other philosophers take it that the consciousness properties are not really as

---

[202] Some people adopt the view that life has no meaning. To address the question whether life has meaning is worthwhile, but it would take us far afield. Here the approach will merely be to note that just as phystriology leaves open the idea that there are some (non-basically) purposive beings, so, too, phystriology leaves fully open the idea that there is a (perhaps non-basic) meaning in life.

subjective as they seem to us to be. Here are some of the schools of thought on the matter, all of which accept phystriology.

Eliminativists like Paul Churchland maintain that our perceptions of colors and other sensory qualities arise from our registrations of the various brain states. Churchland maintains that the neuroscientific physicalistic approach to consciousness is not hostile to the ways we experience the world. There are brain neurological states we are directly familiar with, and other brain neurological states we are indirectly familiar with. But in both cases we are dealing with physicalistically based states of awareness or belief.[203] Eliminativists hope that we will eventually be able to abandon some of our folk psychological terms (the psychological terms we use everyday, like hopes, dreams, beliefs, desires, and so on), which are regarded by eliminativists as being inaccurate terms, and to substitute in their place better, more accurate terms for the folk psychological everyday terms. However, eliminativists accept phystriology.[204]

Daniel Dennett's theory of consciousness may be thought of as an *illusionist* theory of consciousness. According to Dennett, there are several angles from which we can attempt to understand the mind. We can attempt to understand the mind via understanding the brain from a strictly physical point of view; we can attempt to understand the mind by understanding our bodies from the design point of view; and we can attempt to understand the mind from the psychological point of view, in which all the intentional phenomenology appears. Applying these stances to interpreting the mind we can come to see how the subjective states of consciousness are illusions created by the system. In Dennett's *Consciousness Explained*, 1991, this approach is followed through in detail, and it is supplemented in *Sweet Dreams*, 2005. Dennett affirms the phystriological point of view.[205]

---

[203] Paul Churchland, 1996, *The Engine of Reason, The Seat of the Soul*: 202.

[204] This is not controversial. Charles Taliaferro, for instance, takes Paul Churchland, accurately, as an exponent of phystriology in "Naturalism and the Mind": 153.

[205] If one wants an explicit reference, see, for example, Dennett, Daniel, 1996, *Kinds of Minds*: 24, where he says that causal interactive dualism (Descartes' key theory that goes against phystriology) is in the trash heap of history along with astrology and alchemy. Perhaps this isn't as clear an endorsement of phystriology as one would like to see; but perhaps that is not surprising.

Some, however, are by no means convinced by either the eliminativist or the illusionist approach. They take a stronger approach. It might be a straight *functionalist* approach, or a *functionalist plus qualia* approach; it might be a *supervenience* approach; in addition, it might, or might not, be an *epiphenomenalist* approach. These theories on consciousness generation typically have a physicalistic base plus a second level or a level that somehow includes or excludes *qualia* (qualitative experiences), but one way or another, does not over-turn the rules, laws, or forces governing the non-qualitative physical changes. *Functionalism* is a theory of the second level with a functional-causal analysis, and *qualia* are the experiential qualities.

For the convenience of some readers, here is a definition of 'supervenience': a level, *B*, is *supervenient* on another level, *A*, exactly in those cases in which no change in *B* will occur without there being a corresponding change in *A*, and the changes in *A* are somehow primary, so that the *B* changes are dependent on the *A* changes.

Epiphenomenalism holds that there is no independent or fundamental causal potential of the second level or the qualitative experiences.

There are many varieties of these views.[206]

And some go further still. Colin McGinn, for example, takes it that the states of consciousness cannot be explained given the only tools of explanation that we have available to us. Consequently, we have to be *mysterians* about consciousness. It arises in a way that we can't understand; and, one way or another, we have to live with that. A mysterian, however, is prepared to accept the tough features of physics in relation to chemistry and biology, while allowing that there are crucial aspects to consciousness that will not be subsumed in our explanatory structures.[207]

Passages in Dennett's works often show that he misses the difference between soft ampliative arguments (post natural selection) on the one hand and on the other hand the logical arguments and strong ampliative arguments that follow from the phystriological result. See, for instance, *Darwin's Dangerous Idea*, Chapter Ten.

[206] A good introductory text is Jaegwon Kim's *Philosophy of Mind*, especially Chapter Seven. For a somewhat more technical book, but only about our topic, see *Consciousness*, edited by Quentin Smith and Aleksandar Jokic.

[207] Colin McGinn, *The Mysterious Flame*.

David Chalmers, and other dual property theorists, want to go, in one sense, further in the explanatory project than McGinn does. For example, in *The Conscious Mind*, Chalmers takes it that in some worlds some physical systems identical in structure to humans are zombies without consciousness but with all the behaviours of one who does have consciousness; in our world, there is a psychophysical law ensuring that we are not zombies, but conscious.

In his work in the mid 1990's including *The Conscious Mind*, Chalmers explicitly accepted physical closure, though, as mentioned, he called it 'causal closure'.[208] More recently, though, (for further, see Appendix 2.1), he suggests that we should explore physical incompleteness from a quantum point of view.[209] His suggestion is very briefly put, and, also, there was no reflection there on what I called the demarcation problem, as is explained in Appendix 2.1, nor on other enormous problems facing anyone who would like physical *in*completeness to be plausible.

One further point should be noted. Frank Jackson in 1982 held that there is a certain sort of gap between mind and body; in 1986, he exposed the notion that there is such a gap by hypothesizing that there could be a scientist, raised in an entirely black and white world, who obtains all the information there is to obtain about colors. Jackson then wanted to know whether the scientist – he called her Mary – would learn anything new if she left the black and white realm and saw a red tomato. Of course, it was thought, she would. She would learn what red looks like: she would have the qualitative experience of redness.[210]

A vast literature developed on this apparent problem for physicalism. Mary begins by knowing the physical truths about colors. Then she experientially learns about colors. Therefore she comes to knowledge she didn't have earlier. Therefore there is knowledge of a *non-physical* truth about color. Therefore, not everything is physical.

However, this doesn't directly challenge phystriology, since mysterians, and others, who accept the causal picture affirmed by phystriology hold that there are truths about colors that cannot be put in

---

[208] David Chalmers, *The Conscious Mind*: 161.

[209] David Chalmers, 2003, "Consciousness and its Place in Nature": 126.

[210] Frank Jackson, "What Mary Didn't Know."

the vocabulary of physics. But it illustrates the depth of the intuition that there are, one way or another, non-physical aspects of conscious states.

Our point of interest here is that Jackson changed his mind on the case. In 1982 and for a good time afterwards, Jackson assumed or argued that there was a problem of sorts with physicalism, but by 1996, Jackson took it that there is no problem with physicalism.[211] From our point of view, this indicates how much reflection there should be on the ways in which a phystriological system might present us with the experiences we have. The basis of the intuition against phystriology would have to have been the same basis on which Jackson assumed that there must be a non-physical aspect of conscious experience. But there is no implication from the latter (conscious experience) to the former (the view that there is, objectively, something non-physical about conscious experience). One wants to look more closely at the possible consistency of the latter and the former.

A particularly useful thought-stimulator on this topic is a single paragraph (the sixth paragraph) in a short paper by Francis Crick (one of the two discoverers of the DNA structure, who later worked on mind-body problems) and Christof Koch. They say that one can't convey with words or ideas our subjective, e.g., visual, experience. Why not? Because

> [i]n order to describe a subjective visual experience, the information has to be transmitted to the motor output stage of the brain, where it becomes available for verbalization or other actions. This transmission always involves reencoding the information, so that the explicit information expressed by the motor neurons is related, but not identical, to the explicit information expressed by the firing of the neurons associated with colour experience, at some level in the visual hierarchy.[212]

That is a simple, but stunningly powerful, observation on descriptions of non-verbally given states.

12.2 Mind-body relations

---

[211] For a full discussion, see Peter Ludlow, Yujin Nagasawa, and Daniel Stoljar's *There's Something About* Mary, an anthology about Jackson's early papers and responses to them, including Jackson's later responses.

[212] Francis Crick, and Christof Koch, "Why Neuroscience May Be Able To Explain Consciousness."

The specific problem of understanding the qualitative aspect of conscious experience gives rise to the more general question of the mind-body relations. The mind-body relations constitutes a more general area because in addition to the nature of qualitative conscious experience there is the issue of the relation between cognitive states – states of beliefs, hopes, dreams, etc., and states of the body.

As we've amply seen, mind-body theory used to be infused with various physically incomplete views: there were Platonists, who were either dualists or idealists, depending how one interprets the system, but both Platonic dualism and Platonic idealism are physically incomplete systems. There were Aristotelians, who had a physically incomplete system, though there was a lot of mental embodiment in the Aristotelian view. Nonetheless, in Aristotle's system, all changes in physical things expressed fulfillment of fundamental intrinsic purposes. And, of course, there were Cartesians who also upheld a strongly physically incomplete view. Against some aspects of the various physically incomplete schools of thought, there were a few physicalists. In the ancient world, there were the Epicureans for example. (Still, the physicalists, then, could not be called exponents of phystriology, for reasons explained at the beginning of Chapter Two.) After 1960 or 1970 or so, the vast majority of those known as the mind-body philosophers, the consensus, really, took it that the physically incomplete positions could not be maintained any longer. Does that mean that the multiplicity of pre-1960 mind-body schools – monist materialism, monist idealism, dualism, neutral monism, etc., – have turned into a single school about cognition?

No, it doesn't. Mind-body philosophy is centrally concerned with the relations of cognitive psychological states – believing, hoping, imagining, and so on – to biological, chemical, and physical states. Hence mind-body philosophy is concerned with intentional and representational type states, and so is unrestricted by the results binding token biology to token chemistry to (statistical) token physics. Indeed, there are many different ways of understanding the relation between the phystriological system and the psychological system; indeed, there are so many that philosophers of psychological states have not had to fear any lack of opportunity for debate. Some of the schools on consciousness generation have been mentioned; now we're looking at the cognitive states (with or without consciousness) in relation to the brain states.

There are very many different views of such relations, and the differences are at a reasonably high level of complexity. For thoroughness, though, we will go through some of them. Of course, many readers will skim these differentiations. In the early days following the phystriology discovery (the late 1950's and the 1960's) some philosophers postulated a type-to-type identity theory whereby the types of mental states were taken to be identical to types of physical states.[213]

But a problem soon arose for the type-to-type identity theories. If a type of mental state is identical to a type of physical state, then there couldn't be unusual creatures, extraterrestrial creatures, say, who had the same mental states we have, but different ways of physically realizing those states. Yet, we would tend to say, conceptually, there can be such creatures. (Humans have carbon-based brains; we can conceive of aliens with silicon based brains.) As a result of this problem, known as the multiple-realization problem, there were several responses. One was eliminativism, which, in another context, has been briefly mentioned. Another was to restrict the classes in which the types were to be identical to physical types. And still another was to move to token-to-token[214] identity theories.

From the token-to-token identity theories, many varieties of cognitive functionalism arose. In cognitive functionalism, the view is that the causal relations between states operate at a higher level than the level at which the states are micro-realized, and that it is the functional arrangement at the higher level that captures what needs to be captured for a theory of the (cognitive) mind.[215] Functionalist theories faced a problem in dealing with qualitative experiences. In response, some philosophers took the view that physical things have two different sorts of properties, the ontologically irreducible mental properties, and the physical properties.

Phystriology is not threatened by this position; all that phystriology requires is that there be no overturning of the rules, laws or

---

[213] JJC Smart and David Armstrong, the former in the late 1950's, and both in the 1960's, for instance, developed type-to-type identity theories.

[214] Here is another explanation of the meaning of 'type' and 'token': suppose we're in a classroom, and there are, say, twenty desks in the room. Suppose all the desks look alike. Then they are type identical. But one desk is not the same token desk as the desk that is next to it. Such desks are type identical, but token distinct.

[215] These functionalist theories are, typically, layered on supervenience theories; some say they are epiphenomenalist theories, for which, once again, see Jaegwon Kim's *Philosophy of Mind*.

forces of physics dealing with the inherently purposeless things. Other theorists, they're called anomalous monists, took the view that the physical world is causally closed or causally complete or physriological, or that there is no overturning of the rules, laws, or forces of physics, but the psychological world is saturated with normative properties, and so the psychological property level exists on a very different level from the physical level. Yet, once again, physriology is preserved.

And there are other schools as well, all of which accept physriology.[216]

A while ago, in Chapter One, I said, "Hmm… 'non-summative'; what does that mean? There will be more detail later on." There were a few other uses of terms like 'non-summative' and 'summative,' but not much detail was given in explanation. Now is a good time to provide a touch of explanation. Suppose we are all composed of tiny little (invisible) things, where every little (invisible) thing has no inherent purposes, but whose movements or changes are governed by just mathematical relations, usually based on symmetries, and on what are called spontaneous symmetry breakings through either probabilistically governed changes or the following through of mere partial symmetries.[217] Suppose also that some of the sums of these tiny things, like human beings, are apparently purposive beings. Those assumptions are very reasonable to make. In fact, since the 1960's, say, everyone has had to make them.

For all who make such suppositions, which means, effectively, for every careful thinker since approximately the 1960's, the central question arises, How do the small (invisible) things that are not inherently purposive, sum to be beings that seem to be inherently purposive beings? That apparently purposive beings are mere sums of purposeless beings seems inconsistent. Yet it cannot be inconsistent; apparently purposive beings are, by physriology, sums of purposeless beings.

---

[216] See, for example, *The Place of Mind*, ed., Brian Cooney, for the variety of views on type identity, token identity, functionalism, eliminativism, and so on. The views first published from the 1970's and on, explicitly or implicitly, accept physriology, or are neutral or unstated about it.

[217] A good explanation of spontaneous symmetry breaking through partial symmetries can be found in *Why Beauty Is Truth*, by Ian Stewart: 217 -219.

Consequently, there is a major enterprise in mind-body philosophy, an enterprise that is, in a sense, the central underlying enterprise of mind-body philosophy since around the 1960's, which is to explain, somehow, how mere inherently purposeless things, governed only by complex mathematical relations, sum to being apparently inherently purposive beings. It is this task that is being differently addressed by the many theories of mind-body relations. Yet, effectively, all of them accept phystriology.[218]

12.3 Freedom and responsibility

If phystriology is accepted, then what happens to human freedom? How can we both accept phystriology, in which there can be no overturning of the operations of the physical rules, laws or forces, and yet also accept a clear notion of human freedom and human responsibility?

The answer is built on the idea that there are two very different notions of what freedom means. According to one view, to be free is to have the capacity to choose. According to the other view, to be free is to be not-determined. Those who take the first view are called compatibilists, because for them freedom is compatible with determinism. Those who take the second view are called incompatibilists, because for them freedom is incompatible with determinism.[219]

As far as phystriology goes, there are many theories that can or do entirely accept phystriology and maintain that there is a sort of freedom. Some of these theories are compatibilist theories; and some are incompatibilist theories. All the compatibilist theories are consistent with phystriology. And only some of the incompatibilist theories, or only one type of the incompatibilist theories, as mentioned in 11.3.3, the contra-causal incompatibilist type, rejects phystriology. We will look at the compatibilists and the incompatibilists in turn.

---

[218] True, of the hundreds of main theorists about mind-body relations, a tiny handful don't accept phystriology. But these very few anti-phystriology theories have deep problems. See Appendix 2 for more.

[219] To put it another way, the compatibilist view of freedom holds that "'Event E is a determined event' is logically consistent with 'Event E constitutes a free act of agent A'. The incompatibilist view of freedom holds that these two statements are not logically consistent.

A compatibilist theory of freedom says that determinism, (or quasi-determinism, where quasi-determinism allows for more or less self-canceling quantum probabilities in highly complex states of the kind found in naturally perceivable objects including the brain) is compatible with freedom; whether determinism or quasi-determinism is true does not affect whether an action is free. There are several views about what makes a set of events a free action. One of them, the typical compatibilist view, says that a set of events constitutes a free action exactly if the set of events resulted from a strictly internal deliberative causal process, rather than an external causal process or an external/internal causal process without an internal deliberative component.

For example, if Leslie bumps into Pat, and if that bump causes Pat to knock down a vase, then Pat did not freely knock down the vase. The cause was external (Leslie's bump into Pat). But if Pat thought, "I'd like to cause trouble to Sam who owns the vase, so I'll knock it over," and then deliberately nudges into the vase with what is taken to be enough strength to knock it over, and the vase is knocked over, then that was a free action. The cause was strictly a deliberative mental process; it wasn't generated by a drug, nor was it generated by an external cause.

Compatibilists, then, can, and, since the 1960's or 1970 or so, typically, do, accept phystriology.

They also, typically or often, accept that there is a sort of quasi-determinism in the succession of psychological brain states. In this view, the brain is composed of quantum particles, but the quantum probabilities cancel themselves out from the large functional point of view of the brain. So all that's left is the functional system plus a kind of quantum noise. The functional system of the brain is taken to be classical. (The small parts, like atoms, are theoretically at least measured or measurable in the functional system; much smaller units of spacetime – including everything near, at or below the Planck scale – are, it seems, non-classical, but, as was mentioned in other words in 7.8 n. 79, they are roughly as much smaller than an atom as an atom is smaller than a tennis ball.) Whether there are special sorts of qualitative experiences at a higher level than the quantum underlying states is typically held to be irrelevant to the nature of the functional system of successions of states of the brain.

And there are other ways the compatibilist theory of freedom can accept the phystriological view.

Next, we will look at the incompatibilist theories of freedom that are consistent with acceptance of phystriology. There are some theories of incompatibilist freedom that are worded in a not entirely clear way concerning phystriology. Some readers would take the theories to go against phystriology; a close look at the theories, however, shows that the theories do not go against phystriology. Some theories of freedom, then, are incompatibilist theories of freedom, yet they do not defend physical *in*completeness. They are consistent with phystriology. One sub-class of them is non-causal and another sub-class is event-causal.[220]

And there is another view about freedom, too, the view that holds that there is no adequate concept of freedom. However, that view by no means goes against phystriology, so that it is entirely coherent to maintain that one has no adequate concept of freedom and that phystriology is to be accepted.

There is only one type of view that goes against phystriology: the contra-causal incompatibilist view. But there are several main and popular sorts of views that accept phystriology and assert human freedom: all the compatibilist views, and some of the incompatibilist views.

And there are several main and popular sorts of views that deny freedom, but accept phystriology. Consider, for instance, the incompatibilists who deny freedom. These typically recommend alteration of our mode of behaviour, but, it is important to note, some of these theorists, too, (incompatibilists who are not contra-causal incompatibilists) also accept phystriology. Finally, some thinkers say there is no freedom any more than there is non-freedom; the notion makes no sense. But they, too, will accept phystriology.

12.4 Morality and other values

The questions surrounding freedom and responsibility give rise to the more general questions about morality, and values in general, including aesthetic values. Some might put the question this way: If phystriology is true, doesn't that eliminate our evaluative capacities? According to

---

[220] For the wide variety of view on freedom, see *The Oxford Handbook of Free Will*, ed. Robert Kane. In the anthology, Randolph Clarke classifies the 'non-causal' and 'event causal' sub-groups of incompatibilist theories that, it seems, are consistent with phystriology (357ff).

phystriology, nothing that occupies spacetime changes in such a way as to overturn the operations of the physical laws or forces or rules. Doesn't that make our morals and our values a kind of self-deceptive fiction?

According to some philosophers, it does. But according to many philosophers, it doesn't. Aesthetic and other values need to be considered, but here we'll look only at moral or ethical[221] values. Parallels to aesthetic and other values can be drawn.

There are many ways to make big divides in moral traditions; here is one such divide that may be useful. (Again, some readers will prefer to skim until 12.5.) The divide is between moral naturalism and moral non-naturalism. According to moral naturalists, there are complex states of nature that intrinsically or inherently, as complex states, bear moral value. According to moral non-naturalists, there are no states of nature that intrinsically or inherently bear moral value. The moral non-naturalists will sometimes say that moral value rides on, or depends on, natural states. This riding on, or dependency on, relation is sometimes described as a supervenience relation (which was defined in 12.1). But even then the non-naturalists would say that the moral content is given by means other than the natural states, for example, either by derivation from some fundamental true moral propositions, or intuitively.

Those who adhere to moral naturalism have the basis for a moral system consistent with phystriology directly provided by the moral naturalism. It rests on there being a viable difference between tiny invisible things having no inherent purposes, and so, one would conclude, no inherent values, on the one hand, and, on the other hand, complex sum states that do have inherent values. That is the task the moral naturalists must fulfill, to show the viability of that distinction. (We can notice, also, that ethical naturalists are not committed to the view that there are any basic or fundamental purposes anywhere.)

Also, stepping aside from the division between ethical naturalism and ethical non-naturalism, virtue ethical theories are consistent with phystriology. The notion of a virtue is the notion of a dispositional quality of character (a quality or property that isn't always manifested[222]);

---

[221] In this discussion, no distinction is made between 'moral' and 'ethical'.

[222] To say "sugar is soluble" is to ascribe to sugar a dispositional quality; a dispositional quality is sometimes manifested, sometimes unmanifested. A cube of sugar in one's hand has the property or quality of being soluble, or dissolvable in water, even though one might be standing in a desert; the quality

and the relation between dispositional qualities and non-dispositional qualities is fertile. But there is no inconsistency between virtue theories and acceptance of phystriology.

Some versions of moral non-naturalism will also be consistent with phystriology. Some forms of non-naturalism require or assume an incompatibilist freedom that is inconsistent with acceptance of phystriology. However, other non-naturalisms (including other forms of either compatibilist or incompatibilist freedom) are still consistent with phystriology. Ethical intuitionism, for example – which maintains that it is our immediate intuitions or insights in which there is grounding for ethical statements – is prima facie consistent with phystriology.

Further, those who are neither naturalist nor non-naturalist about ethical judgements – those who take ethical judgements to be dependent on the states of mind of the ones making the judgements, or those who deny that ethical judgements express beliefs, or those who maintain that ethical judgements are universally false[223] – are open on the question of phystriology. Indeed, ethical conceptualists, ethical non-cognitivists, ethical universal error-theorists, from one point of view, can be seen as explaining the odd phenomenon of human beings making ethical judgements that, they say, are out-of-synch with the indifferent world. Oversimplifying a bit, the explanation could well be that the world is phystriological.

Accordingly, there are very many systems in which one accepts phystriology and accepts an independently developed view on morality; among those systems, there are many through which one can adopt moral judgements and accept phystriology: moral naturalism without dispositional states, moral naturalism with dispositional states, moral

---

or property is there, but is not being manifested. If the cube would be in water, the quality would be manifested. On the other hand, the shape an object has, its being cubical, for instance, is a property that is always manifested so long as the object has that property.

[223] Members of the first group may be naturalists; members of the latter two groups are, typically, naturalists; but this general sense of naturalism does not imply ethical naturalism. It is not conceptually true that if one is a *naturalist* then one is an *ethical naturalist* (any more than it is true that if Tibbles is a mammal then Tibbles is a dog). Whether one can be an ethical naturalist without being, in any sense, a naturalist in the general sense is a more difficult question, a question arising from the various meanings of the term 'naturalism,' but not arising from class and sub-class relations.

non-naturalism based on, or supervenient on, natural states, and ethical intuitionism. One can also accept phystriology and, independently, on one of several paths, deny that moral judgements make true statements; yet one would still find a way to make choices.[224]

12.5 Finding meaning in life

Some might say, "But if phystriology obtains, then life has no meaning. A viable sense of life's meaning must arise from one's being able to over-turn the rules, laws, or forces of purposeless parts as one finds in physics." However, the 'must' seems to go too far. For some people the sense of life's meaning is loosely tied into their thinking of themselves (or other beings) as over-turning the rules, laws, or forces of the physics of small purposeless things like electrons and photons. But there is, it seems, no need to think of things in that fashion.

The issue turns on the way in which there might be purposive beings in nature. It is important to keep clearly in mind that acceptance of phystriology does not entail the denial of the existence of purposive beings. On the contrary, most thinkers who accept phystriology also accept that there are purposive beings. Human beings, for instance, are typically regarded as purposive beings; and those who accept phystriology would typically agree. People who accept phystriology will simply say that such purposive beings are Darwinian-evolutionarily produced *sum beings*, not basically, not fundamentally, purposive beings.

There is a big difference, then, between holding that every purposive being is a fundamentally or *basically purposive being*, on the one hand, and, on the other hand, holding that every purposive being is a *sum purposive being*, a being whose purposes are the properties, or something like the properties, of the being as a large sum of purposeless (not basically purposive) things, especially as produced by natural selection evolution. A human being has trillions of subatomic particles. So a human being is a large sum of tiny particles. Most people would say that there are purposes, and, once exposed to the phystriological position, would say that it is this large sum of tiny particles that, somehow, has purposive, but non-basically purposive, qualities. In having non-basic

---

[224] For an introduction to contemporary ethical theories, see Alexander Miller, *An Introduction to Contemporary Metaethics*. For an approach to living under ethical error theory, see J. L. Mackie, *Ethics*.

purposes, a human being never overturns the processes of physics, but still behaves purposively.

Keeping this distinction between *basically purposive* and *sum purposive* or *evolutionarily sum purposive* in mind, we can see that the fulfillment of purposes is fully consistent with acceptance of phystriology. Moreover, the sense of life's meaning can be rooted in the sense of the fulfillment of (sum-generated) purposes. When we investigate the variety of views on the meaning of life, we find that for each of the many views rejected by phystriology, there are some exponents of phystriology who espouse a different view about how life can have meaning.

For instance, some people maintain that only if a personal God exists can life have meaning; however, others hold that, without a personal God's existence, life can be fully meaningful. Perhaps they will say that a person can hold to values supposedly held by the personal God but without believing in the personal God. Perhaps they will say that all moral notions are born or generated in humans anyway, so it is not impossible at all to disbelieve in God and have meaning in life through moral values. Perhaps they will say that there are no ultimate or intrinsic moral values, and yet there are various fulfillments that a person can have, though they would not involve any strong changes, or physics violating changes, in the world.

Similarly, there are many views of the meaning of life that are by no means committed to the idea of an after-life.[225] Indeed, Confucius (Kong Fu Tzu) (551 – 479 BCE), is famous for many reasons, including his insight shown in the following brief dialogue:

> Chi-lu asked how the spirits of the dead and the gods should be served. The Master [Confucius] said, 'You are not able even to serve man. How can you serve the spirits?'
>
> 'May I ask about death?'
>
> 'You do not understand even life. How can you understand death?'[226]

---

[225] A good investigation is in Paul Edwards' "Life, Meaning and Value of" in *The Encyclopedia of Philosophy*, ed Paul Edwards, vol. IV, NY: Macmillan, 1967: 467-477.

[226] Confucius, *Analects*: XI: 12, NY: Penguin, 1979, trans. D. C. Lau.

And Confucius is known not to have talked about the gods or spirits.[227] Yet he was, of course, an expositor of how to develop a sense of deep meaning in life.

Further, since moral notions in human and some animate affairs are consistent with phystriology, one doesn't need to believe in a cosmic karmic process. It seems clear, as well, that there are many views as to how life can have meaning that do not require commitment to the genuineness of paranormal phenomena. Also, it is readily apparent that there are many views as to how life has meaning that are independent of (philosophical) mysticism. Accordingly, it seems clear that acceptance of phystriology does not immediately threaten the enterprise of finding meaning in life.

One further point is worth making: many would say that if phystriology obtains, then no meaning in life is basic, or that no meaning in life requires that there be violations of physics processes. Some regard this as unchallenging; others regard this as challenging. Still, those who accept phystriology can find meaning in life.

12.6 Integrating emotions with other aspects of life

There are a great many reasons for holding that all our aspects of life are bound up with emotional states. For instance, we have inherited the amygdala structure in our brains from our millions of years ago ancestral animals, and the amygdala manages the emotional processes. The emotional processes managed by the amygdala are in deep connection with the cortical processes managed by other areas of the brain.[228] Does phystriology threaten the integration of the cognitive results with the emotional states we value?

To some extent, answering this question is best done after Part III is reviewed. But what can be immediately said at the outset is that phystriology will not adversely affect the integration of valued emotional states any more than accepting Darwinian natural selective evolution threatens such integration. Most people would say that accepting Darwinian natural selective evolution is something that we can all do. It implies that there need not have been a single designing intelligence

---

[227] Confucius, *ibid*: VII: 21.

[228] For more information, see, e.g., *Hot Thoughts*, by Paul Thagard, Cambridge Mass: Bradford MIT, 2006.

behind the creation of the species. But many denominations of religions fully allow participants in religions to accept Darwinian natural selective evolution. There are many famous scientists who have both clearly stated their acceptance of Darwinian natural science evolution, and one or another religious system. To whatever degree their emotional states were integrated with their cognitive states, one who accepts phystriology should not have any further difficulties, so long as some religious or spiritual system can be integrated with acceptance of phystriology. That is the topic of Part III, and so, in that sense, the question being looked at here is best answered after consideration of the material reviewed in Part III.

But there is one other way of immediately seeing that there should be no difficulty accepting physiology and integrating one's emotional states. There have been very many humanists who are secularists in several senses. This will be reviewed in Chapter Nineteen. These humanists integrate their emotional states with their humanism. So that strongly suggests that phystriology will present no difficulties as far as integrating emotional and intellectual states is concerned. The only outlying question is whether those disposed toward the secular humanist approach will always be a small percentage of the human community, perhaps partly for emotional reasons. But that question can be left hanging for now. (No one knows the answer to the question anyway.)

12.7 Summing it all up

The question was earlier put (in 12.0), "If phystriology maintains that there is *a sense in which* physics explains all human changes, does this mean that we are supposed to answer central human questions through the natural sciences?" The answer, I suggested, is, "Definitely not." Some reasons were earlier, briefly, given, and these reasons will now be elaborated a bit further.

We have seen in Chapter Eleven (in 11.6) that many would say there is a sort of difference between the natural way things work and the theoretically or linguistically expressible or formulated way things work. In physics we find linguistic expressions or formulations for the way things work; nothing else can be done. But nature just does what it does. The formulas represent the natural reality. In parallel, there are the principles that are, to us, anyway, inaccessible, and the principles that are accessible to us. As far as the latter goes, physicists since Newton's time (including Einstein) have found that the mathematical formulas expressing gravitational relations work only on, at most, two mass-things. But nature works with any number of mass things in interaction, for instance, gravitational interaction. In the solar system, for instance, all the planets, their moons, and the sun gravitationally affect each other. So nature has rules, laws, or forces that are only partially expressed in the mathematical formulas that we use in physics. For this reason, physicists must approximate the natural rules, or laws, or forces or whatever they are to be called. To express the difference between the way nature works, the way it is partially, but only partially (approximately) expressed in our languages, on the one hand, and, on the other hand, the way our articulations occur, we will say that there are natural truths and there are theoretical truths. Phystriology, then, can be regarded in two ways. In one, it is regarded as expressing a natural truth; in the other, it is regarded as expressing a truth using our theories as approximations.

Furthermore, as has been observed before, that chemistry is physicalized does not mean that chemists can do their work using physics-language. They must continue to use chemistry-talk for a wide variety of reasons: chemistry-talk summarizes things appropriately; it shortcuts many otherwise overly long statements; it expresses what otherwise would not be finitely expressible; it can employ type terms that can be found anywhere as well as token terms that refer to spatiotemporally specific items; it assumes a classical (continuous) picture on a reality that is quantized or non-classical; and so on. Similarly, biologists must continue to use biology-talk even though biology is understood to be physio-chemical. Further, we can now add, human beings, in addressing issues of central human concern, will continue to use psychology-talk. When we're dealing with suffering, joy, life's meaning, deep hopes, and such like matters, we are dealing with psychological issues in the broadest way possible, and so, for very many reasons, we will continue to use psychology-talk.

Whether a psychological being is token reducible to or, alternatively, identical to, a bio-chemical being is a bit controversial. But whether a token biological thing is, somehow, reducible to or identical to a token chemical thing (and whether a token chemical thing is, statistically at least, reducible to or identical to a token physical thing) is not controversial. It is. If there is difficulty with the notion of full token identity from psychology or sociology down to physics, then all one needs to do is talk of something like thin token identity. A natural object has an underlying object that (statistically at least) fills up the same spacetime but might be missing a lot of type-defined properties. A country's territory is composed of quantized particles, but, classically, the terrain can be mapped. Still, if a particular object A is an underlying object of a particular object *B*, then *A* is, statistically at least, thin-identical to *B*. (This is also exposed at the end of Appendix 2.4.)

This allows us to have token identity from any level of complexity down to chemistry and, statistically, down to physics, but it does not commit us to eliminating psychological talk in favour of natural science talk. In addition, on account of the debate between type-reductionists versus type-non-reductionists in biology, biological-talk is not to be eliminated for chemical-talk nor for physical-talk. That, too, requires us to allow psychological talk to be continued. At the very least, practically speaking, if we are to address issues of central human concern we will do so using psychological terms; we will continue to refer to psychological states such as states of suffering, joy, appreciating meanings, addressing human needs, finding sources, psychological or non-psychological, for human hopes, thinking about the objects of our needs and hopes, and so on.

All in all, there are many ways in which phystriology does not exclude important views about consciousness, mind-body relations, freedom, responsibility, morality and other values, there being some meaning of life, and integrating emotional states with cognitive states. There are strong reasons for taking it that these phenomena are not basic phenomena. That is full of challenges to us. For that reason, since 1960 or 1970, it seems, we have entered into a fundamentally new way of seeing the world. To keep up with science would be to see that human experiences are, one way or another, sum events; and how we regard human experiences is not clear. But the journey along the newly forged path is breathtakingly dramatic.

The overall question we are focusing on in this book (reaching forward into the discussion in part II a bit) is whether any specifically religious-ish spiritual teaching is consistent with the results of phystriology. Our central question is whether we can address issues of central human concern in a specifically religious-ish spiritual manner or not. This sets the stage for the examination of the main question of Part III – whether we are to abandon religious-ish spirituality, or to find a way to integrate the results of natural science with religion or religion-ish spirituality. But before we do that, we should look at a number of issues concerning the term 'spirituality,' including why we should take spirituality to be a religious-ish condition. The nature of what is called 'spirituality' is the subject matter of Part II.

Part II

Chapter Thirteen: The Many Meanings of 'Spirit' and 'Spirituality'

13.0 There is one sense of the word 'spirit' whereby everyone – and that's *everyone* – would say, "I'm for spirit." Similarly, there is one sense of the word 'spirituality' whereby more or less everyone would say, "I'm for spirituality." The word 'spirituality' is obviously based on 'spirit', but there's a touch of difference between the two words. Let's start by looking at 'spirit.' Then we'll look at 'spirituality.'

It is usually useless to employ a dictionary to discover the meaning of a word in one's fluently used language; most of the time one already knows such a word's common meanings or common uses. And when one is exploring philosophical topics, typically, one doesn't need to consult a dictionary because it is primarily a philosophical theory underlying commonly employed meanings or uses that one desires. But, occasionally, one is looking for special uses, and this is one such occasion. As it happens, there are thirteen guidance-for-use meanings of 'spirit' given in the *Concise Oxford Dictionary*[1]. They go all the way from an alinine dye soluble in alcohol to a holy spirit not connected to a material body. No wonder the world is deeply confused about spirit! Some of the meanings of 'spirit' are philosophically controversial; for instance, one meaning is "immaterial part of a person," and whether there is an immaterial part of a person, a part of a person that is not, one way or another, produced by a material part of a person, is (supposedly) philosophically controversial. But some meanings are not philosophically controversial. Alinine dye soluble in alcohol, for instance, is not philosophically controversial (unless one wants to deny the existence of

---

[1] Seventh Edition, ed., J. B. Sykes, 1982 Oxford: Clarendon Press.

the external world, but we're not looking at that sort of issue). And there is a meaning of 'spirit' that has nothing to do with picking out a chemical, and yet it seems that everybody can agree about it: a person's spirit is the person's courage, self-assertion, vivacity, energy and dash. I don't expect there will be much disagreement about whether having such spirit is a good thing.

'Spirituality,' too, has vastly many meanings. A recent secular humanist magazine listed ten ways in which a non-religious person could claim to have a kind of spirituality. One could claim to have spirituality by having: a sense of awe and wonder, a love of ritual, an appreciation of nature, a capacity for meaningful relationships, an appreciation of beauty, a sense of the arts, a desire to create in one way or another, an introspective-driven pleasure, a recognition of the self as an integral part of the universe, and a desire to grow things one way or another.[2] In this reading, there is hardly any difference between spirituality and a capacity for appreciation. In a way, everyone, including a typical secular humanist, wants to have access to something that can be called *spirituality*.

At the same time, these ten rather neutral forms of spirituality need to be placed side by side with stronger readings of the concept. It is not unusual for people familiar with interactive dualism to think of spirituality as connoting one or another sort of interactive dualism. One of the guidance-for-use meanings of 'spirit' was a holy being not connected to a material body; we saw such a definition. It is this high degree of ambiguity in the words 'spirit' and 'spirituality' that feeds the very different attitudes toward the two concepts that people have.

There is a sense in which everyone would say, "I'm for spirituality," but there is also a sense in which only some would say, "I'm for spirituality." In the second sense, some others would say, "I'm *not* for spirituality," and some of those would add, "I think that gaining what's called 'spirituality' is destructive, both for the person supposedly gaining it, and for others." This indicates a situation in which we should follow a readily available rule, to select only some tones from the many tones of the word 'spirituality'. More particularly, in this case, we should restrict ourselves to that sense of the word that makes the content of the word controversial. That sounds strange but it is not. It enables us to ask, in a meaningful way, whether the controversial sort of spirituality can be

---

[2] Terri Hope, "Spirituality Without Religion," *Canadian Humanist News*, April 2007: 5.

defended or rescued given the results of the natural sciences. By using the controversial tone or meaning of the term, we get at just the issue that we want to get at.

There is another way to see how the results of applying the rule are worthwhile. Most of the time, having an ambiguous term, for example, 'bank', does not cause much confusion. The context in which I say, "I'm going to the bank," will probably clarify whether I'm going to the place where money is deposited, or to the place where bits of dirt are deposited on a watery shore. However, if I say something like, "I'm for spirituality," even the context is unlikely to clarify what 'spirituality' is supposed to mean. Even the context, usually, wouldn't say whether I mean the term 'spirituality' in an extremely broad sense, a sense so broad that secular humanists say there are ten meanings of 'spirituality' that allow a secular humanist to practice spirituality, or if I mean 'spirituality' in a narrow sense, a sense that can be captured by 'a specifically religious-ish condition,' so that there is a debate between those who say, "I'm for spirituality," and those who say "I'm not for spirituality." It is this debate that we are interested in, so it is that sense of 'spirituality' that we want to use. Accordingly, we want 'spirituality' to mean a specifically religious-ish condition.

13.1 There is also a technical way to put the rule that generates this selection of meanings, and so, for technically minded readers, the following may be of interest. For others, it would be fine to just skip until 13.2.

The technical statement of the rule goes as follows: "If term T is ambiguous between T_1 and T_2, discover whether, for one of the senses, say, T_1, there is a term, U, which is synonymous with that sense, and no term V synonymous with the other sense, T_2. If so, if U is synonymous with T_1, and if there is no term synonymous with the other sense, T_2, then let T mean what T_2 means and use U for the other meaning. If this is not the case – if there are no terms synonymous with T_1 or T_2 – then let T be used ambiguously, hoping that context will help clarify the meaning in a given use. And if there are two terms, respectively synonymous with the two main senses of T, then, even if it is controversial as to whether one of the terms obtains, use the synonyms in place of T_1 and T_2; the ambiguity in T would be just confusing. And if U and V are compound terms, and the sense of one of T_1 or T_2 is controversial as to satisfaction, then use T in the special controversial sense, and use the uncontroversial compound synonym in the other sense."

To explain by illustration for 'spirituality': The rule says, "If 'spirituality' is ambiguous between an appreciative condition and a specifically religious-ish condition, (which it is) we discover that 'an appreciative condition' is synonymous with one sense, and 'a religious-ish condition' (meaning a specifically religious condition or a condition as is found in religions but without thinking of the many specific dogmas, rituals, etcetera, accompanying a given religion) is synonymous with the other sense. But it is controversial as to whether a specifically religious condition ever obtains, and it is not controversial as to whether an appreciative condition ever obtains. And 'a specifically religious condition' and 'an appreciative condition' are compound terms. So, our focus being on debate, we should use 'spirituality' to mean 'a specifically religious-ish condition', and we should use 'an appreciative condition' to mean just that, an appreciative condition. If we follow this rule, we are enabled to focus on a real controversy.

13.2 'Spirituality' in our discussion (with the exception of Chapter Twenty Three) will mean 'a specifically religious-ish condition'. It is also worth emphasizing, once again, though, that there are other contexts in which 'spirituality' would be best taken to have a different meaning. For example: Mark Holder, a psychologist at UBC Okanagan, and his graduate student Judi Wallace, recently conducted an investigation into the degree to which spirituality, defined very broadly, was a part of happiness.[3] The broad use of the concept of 'spirituality' – an appreciative condition – may well have been appropriate to that context. It is our focus on the relation between the results of recent sciences and what can be called spirituality that makes it best for us to take 'spirituality' to mean 'a specifically religious-ish condition.'

There are, in addition, two other considerations that support the assignment of 'a specifically religious-ish condition' to 'spirituality' for our investigation here. These are: first that spirituality is broader than religion, and, second, that phystriology offers a challenge to the moderate or pluralist[4] forms of religion that is equal to the challenge it offers to the

---

[3] UBC Reports, February 2008.

[4] Anyone who is a pluralist about religions takes it that people who like religions are following their religion's path up but one mountain. According to pluralism,

literalist or fundamentalist[5] forms of religion, yet all those forms of religion promote spirituality. Some workshops offer the cultivation of specifically religious-ish spirituality but are not parts of any organized religion. And following a moderate form of religion does not in the least provide an escape from the challenge of phystriology. The material in Chapter Ten already provided the basis for showing that; each of the eight or nine views logically inconsistent with phystriology is left open as an option in a moderate or pluralist view of religions. So, too, each view that is not strictly logically incompatible, but is strongly incompatible with phystriology, is left open as an option in a moderate or pluralist view of religion. Then the challenge posed by phystriology is as vivid for the moderate or pluralist as it is for the literalist or fundamentalist.

13.3 What makes something a religion?

To see how spirituality is broader than religion we will first have a quick look at what a religion is.

Provide a criterion for what makes something a religion, and there are likely to be controversies. Criteria that are proposed for religion tend to be too broad or too narrow. If they are broad enough to include both God-centred and non-God-centred systems, then they end up being broad enough to include various forms of Marxist state systems. If they require that only God-centred systems be thought of as religions, then they seem too narrow, since they exclude, for instance, Buddhism – which is not a God-centred system – from being a religion. Yet Buddhism, by all accounts, is a religion – it has monks and nuns, stories about the cosmic process, teachings about human beings and the cosmos, practices for realization, rituals, and so on.

Sometimes it is said that to have a religious system is to have, all at once, a doctrinal system, a ritual system, a mythic (story-based) system, an institutional system, and an experiential system.[6] If we take the

---

all religious paths are aiming for the top of the same mountain. People who are moderates about their religion tend to be pluralists about the many religions.

[5] Literalists say that the canonical or scriptural materials of their religion are, in an important sense, literally true. 'Fundamentalism' has many meanings, but in all of them, fundamentalists are literalists.

[6] Ninian Smart maintained this view. See, for instance, *Religious Experience of Mankind*: 6-12.

---

standard religious systems – tribal systems, Judaism, Christianity, Islam, Hinduism, Buddhism, Taoism, Confucianism, Shintoism, and so on – we find that all these systems do have doctrinal elements, ritual elements, mythic elements, institutional expressions, and favored experiences.

Yet so did Communist China from 1950 to some time in the 1970's, say. It had doctrinal promulgation, rituals involving study, party membership, devotion to the leaders of the state, punishment and reform, and so on, myths about forming events, (e.g., the Great March), institutions of authority of course, and various experiential transformations that were also favored. Some would say that the Communist state system in China during this period at least was, indeed, a religious system under the multi-dimensional model. Others balk at that notion.

Here we will allow our analysis of what makes for a religious system to be loose and merely paradigmatic. We accept the standard systems as listed above (tribal systems, Judaism, Christianity, Islam, etc.,) as religions, and note that they do involve all of those elements – doctrine, ritual, myth, institution, and favored experience. We will not focus on the problems surrounding borderline systems.

Some might say that a special kind of cosmic spirituality must be promoted by a system if it is to be included as a religious system, and that Communist China never promoted a cosmic spirituality, and so it was not a religious system. This might be one way out of the difficulty. On the other hand, some might say that the systems permitted by such criteria – each must have doctrine promoting cosmic spirituality, plus ritual, myth, institution, and favored experience – might be too broad still. It would permit Satanic cults as religious systems, for instance. Some would not be happy with that result. Once again, though, no effort will be made here to sort out these questions.[7]

13.4 But what of the relation between religion and spirituality?

----

[7] All those who agree with the paradigm-way of defining items would take this side-stepping maneuver to be well grounded. According to the paradigm view, no necessary and sufficient conditions need be given for a definition. All that is needed is a paradigm case and a clause that anything closely resembling the paradigm would count as well.

It seems clear that every standard religion does promote spirituality of one or another sort. It seems equally clear that some groups promote the cultivation of spirituality outside of organized religious systems. There are workshops offered for spirituality cultivation that are advertised as not being affiliated with any religious system. For instance, at the back of a recent monthly publication – and I guess that many big cities have publications like this – there is a section called "Spiritual Practices", with advertisements; one is for a talk on spiritual love; one is for a course on celebrating life; some are for regular meetings with meditations designed for all (whether they are members of organized religions or not), and there are one or two other offerings as well. In addition there are many offerings under different headings that promote various forms of spirituality, too. And, again, the workshops are not promoted as being parts of an organized religious system, though in some cases they are softly affiliated with such.

It is not crystal clear when one has a system for promotion of spirituality that ought to be thought of as a religious system, and when one has a system that is too loose or too *ad hoc* to count as a religious system. Once again, though, we will be rough and non-analytic about this. The reason for being rough and non-analytic about this is that the conflict between the results of the natural sciences and the many religious or spiritual views rejected by these results is our main focus, and this conflict would not be affected by whatever position were to be taken on this issue.

All that needs to be noticed, then, are two rather obvious points that everyone, I anticipate, will readily agree with: religions promote spirituality; and there is also religious-ish spirituality that is promoted as being outside of organized religion. It may include states that secular humanists promote; but it also promotes other states as well, states that secular humanists will be very suspicious of. It is the promotion of the latter group of states that we particularly want to look at. Promotion of such states is found not only in well known religions, but also in New Age movements, in evolving forms of practice that advertise themselves as not religions, and in some loose systems of organization for self-help, or, roughly put, for spiritual development.

Once again, we want our investigation to be about the implications of recent natural science – the implications of phystriology. So, we want a concept of spirituality that is more religious, and, in that sense, more narrow, than that used by the secular humanists or the psychologists investigating contributions to happiness. To easily approach the central focus of our investigation, from here on, except for Chapter Twenty Three, we narrow 'spirituality' to mean, 'a specifically[8] religious-ish condition.'

13.5 Pluralism, moderation, and literalism

Many promoters of spirituality emphasize that they are pluralist in their attitudes toward religions and spirituality, whereby they mean, as suggested in a note above, that the underlying sensibility of religious people is more or less in common; others insist that they are not extremist, or not fundamentalist; it may be said that they are moderates. There is, then, an alliance between pluralistic interpretations of religions and adoption of a moderate stance in one's own religion.

It is commonplace to find many Christians and Jews, for instance, not only tolerating such practices as Islamic, Hindu, and Buddhist practices, but also affirming that at heart the religious impulses underlying these different forms of religious system are, in a strong way, in common. On the other hand, some adopt the point of view that it is important not to downplay the major differences between one religious system and another. The proponents of this position are often affiliates of literalist interpretations of the canonical texts of their respective religious systems.

Literalism was briefly explained in a note above, but it would be good to go into a touch more detail now. A literalist interpretation of a canonical text in a religious system is an interpretation of the text – usually regarded by the literalists as revelatory – that takes its contents to be literally true. If a text says, for instance, that Jesus rose from the dead, then that is to be interpreted as a literal truth, and not merely as a metaphorically inspiring story. Of course, sometimes the text uses what is obviously a metaphorical statement ("in their hearts was a disease," Qur'an, 2: 10 or 11). The literal meaning ("the beating-pumping thing was physically diseased") will not be included. Sometimes the text uses language that some take to be metaphorical language, and some take to

---

[8] A 'specifically religious-ish condition' is either a condition favored by a religion or a condition favored by a group that advertises itself as not a religion, but where the group promotes experiences not favored by secular humanists. Because 'specifically religious-ish condition' is inclusive of both religions and groups representing themselves as non-religious, the word 'specifically' is sometimes dropped out; all that really counts is the 'ish' attached to 'religious'.

be literal language; that is where difficulties arise, and interpretations are required. But, ignoring those difficult sorts of cases, there is a clear difference between those who think of the uncontroversially non-metaphorical statements as being literally true and those who think of them as narrations or myths that have spiritual values, whether the narrations or myths are literally true or not. It is that difference that makes for the central difference between literalists and non-literalists.

'Literalism' is a softer term than 'fundamentalism', and it seems to pick out the same group of people as tends to be picked out by the latter term. Given the variety of very different meanings ascribed to 'fundamentalism', even if the group picked out under the different meanings is the same group, the term 'literalism' is a bit more clear in its surface meaning (its intensional meaning), and so will be used in what follows.

We have, then, the difference between religious moderates and religious literalists (ignoring the sometimes large borderline problems). Religious moderates characteristically permit people to decide for themselves which of a variety of views will be accepted literally, and which are to be regarded as metaphors, or metaphoric teachings that can be inspiring in a variety of ways. In essence, the moderates are putting forward a kind of religious pluralism, a system in which the many moderately interpreted religions are, to put it roughly, getting at the same thing, and doing so in different ways, using different metaphors, images, and stories. And it is up to each person to choose which metaphors, which images, and which stories to rely on. Dogmas are absorbed into metaphors, images, and stories.

Once again, though, our overall interest is in the conflict between phystriology and the views strongly associated with religious and spiritual systems, yet logically, or not strictly logically but strongly, excluded by phystriology. Each of these views will be included in the options permitted by the moderates or the pluralists. Moderates, accordingly, typically accept one or more of those views, including the eight or nine views logically excluded by phystriology. And so, as mentioned before in other terms, our focus is as much on what a moderate or pluralist *permits* in relation to phystriology on the one hand as on what a literalist *requires* in relation to phystriology on the other hand. The difficulty is that phystriology challenges each view that a moderate permits as much as phystriology challenges each view that a literalist requires. The challenge offered by phystriology, then, is as strong a challenge toward the moderates as it is toward the literalists. This, too, supports our assignment of the meaning 'a religious-ish condition' to 'spirituality' for the purposes of our investigation.

But, some will ask, isn't the metaphoric interpretation, the imagistic interpretation, or the narrative interpretation good enough?

In response, for many people, it is good enough.

But there are many people for whom it is not good enough. (After all, "my love is like a red red rose," is logically consistent with "my love is like a dark green eggplant.") Many people want to have a clear view on whether the world was or was not created by a grand super-personal Being, a God. Many people want to have a clear view on what happens after the body dies: Is that the end of consciousness? Or not? What of freedom? What of karma? What of mystical experience? And so on. It is to see whether there can be clear answers to such questions, answers that are well informed on the philosophical reading of current science, that this essay is written.

13.6 The new shape of religious systems

It will be useful now to look briefly at the new shape religious systems have in our time. The old view, still generally accepted, is that religion *A* has a very different doctrinal system from religion *B*. The notion of 'doctrinal system', though, is a bit unclear. One question that can be raised is what the relation is between the views of the cosmos of one religious system in relation to the views of the cosmos of another religious system.

It is clear that the literalists of the different standard religions have very different views on many points. The literalist Jews, for instance, take it (under the rabbinical system) that God commanded the seven Noahide laws for all mankind. But these laws include prohibition of idolatry. By contrast, the Hindus sometimes favor what the literalist Jews would regard as idolatrous practices. The literalist Hindus sometimes take it that one is, or may be, subtly rewarded for practices that the literalist Jews think are grievous crimes. Accordingly, the prescriptivist doctrines – the doctrines prescribing what is to be done – according to literalists, are very different from one religion to another.

On the other hand, the moderates and pluralists allow people to adopt a non-literalist interpretation of their religious systems. Accordingly, there is a shift in the nature of the doctrinal elements of religious systems. It used to be the case (in the Middle Ages in Europe, for instance) that each standard religious system (in Europe) was by and large taken to have its own set of doctrines, to the extent that each religious system was to be interpreted literally. Now, however, there is a split between the moderates or pluralists on the one side, and the literalists on the other side.

The moderates or pluralists regard the religious systems as being differentiated by the favored myths, the favored rituals, and the various binding authority systems of the different institutions; the doctrinal elements are only softly differentiable one from another. The rituals, creeds, dogmas, practices, rituals, and so on, are, as it were, for the pluralists and moderates, different costumes, each of which expresses the religious – or one might say, the spiritual – *attitudes*. On the other hand, the literalists find that the traditional view is as they see it: each religious system has its own doctrines different from the central doctrines of the other religions.

According to the moderates, religions are like costumes worn in different cultures. According to the literalists, religions are different from each other in basic doctrines. Going by differences in doctrines, this makes for a new overall organization of religious groups. The literalists belong in many camps, one for each kind of literalist. There are (1) the literalist Jews, (2) the literalist Christians, (3) the literalist Muslims, (4) the literalist Hindus, and so on. Suppose there are 10 such groups. Then there is, in addition, a very large group: (11) the moderates or pluralists. The moderates or pluralists include Jews, Christians, Muslims, Hindus, and so on. They have a more or less single, often softly interpreted, doctrine; and that doctrine is not philosophically sophisticated. The moderates or pluralists regard the differences between the religious systems as cultural costumes to be metaphorically interpreted.

One of the features of this new system is that the role for collective intellectual work among the moderate or pluralist religions has become radically constricted. The doctrines themselves have come to be regarded as dogmatic myths subject to metaphorical interpretations. But within moderate religions, practitioners, individually, still need to figure out what they think, again, individually, about some basic questions: Is there a Divine Providence, or not? Is there an afterlife of one sort or another, or not? And so on. These questions are regarded as answered, optionally, one way or the other way (often without evidential grounds). And this is the challenge provided by phystriology, since phystriology excludes each of those supposed options; the exclusion is, in addition, often a strictly logical exclusion.

13.7 Still, we need to find out a bit more conceptually about spirituality as a religious-ish condition before we can focus on the question of whether spirituality as a religious-ish condition obtains. In particular, it will be advantageous to look at some standard views about spirituality as a religious-ish condition. They are views, but I will also call them 'myths' or 'images' because they are very popularly held pictures of spirituality.

In one myth or image or picture of spirituality it is taken to be the case that "if you're spiritual, you're ethical". In another, it is taken to be the case that "if you're spiritual, you're on the road to special – paranormal – powers." In a third, it is taken to be the case that "if you're spiritual, you experience a high level of joy." These will be the subjects of our next three chapters. We'll then follow with two more studies, one of the exoteric content of religious/spirituality promoting systems, the other of the esoteric content of religious/spirituality promoting systems. Then we will be ready to pose the question for discussion in Part III.

Chapter Fourteen: "If you're spiritual, you're ethical"

14.0 Spirituality and ethics seem to be very closely related. "If you're spiritual, you're ethical," seems to be true. How could one be spiritual without being ethical?

I would suggest, though, that 'ethical' is used in different ways, and in some of the ways it is used, the view or the myth is true, but in other ways, the view or the myth is false. Being 'ethical' often means gently, in a public way, articulating that there are good and bad ways of being, right and wrong ways of acting, or virtuous and vicious ways of acting or of being. To that extent, it seems, the myth must be false. There are people who would be thought of as highly spiritual people and who do not, gently or otherwise, articulate such notions to adults. Moreover, not only do they *not* articulate such notions, as it seems, they *decidedly won't* articulate such notions to adults. That doesn't mean that they do nasty things. On the contrary, as we'll discuss a bit later on, they don't. And, sometimes, they even do things that others would describe as very noble and virtuous things. Still, though, they don't accept the view that there are ultimate intrinsic values in the world.

14.1 Let's look at the basic issues here. There are three levels at which people demonstrate ethics and morality, or might be ethical or moral. (As before, we don't make any difference here between 'the ethical' and 'the moral'.)

At the basic level, the first level, there is a person's behavior. Let's suppose we're talking about someone named Leslie. If Leslie were being (secretly) observed, would it be the case that Leslie would seem to be helping others or not? That is, centrally, a behavioral matter. To seem to be helping isn't restricted to saying nice things. Leslie might do apparently helpful things without saying anything. The behavior might be silently done when Leslie thinks no one is observing the behavior. Leslie might pick up a lost object and return it to where it should be, while thinking that no one saw this behavior. To say that Leslie was helpful would be to comment on mere behavior.

The second level at which someone can be ethical is the level at which a person either does or doesn't articulate values. Let's assume that Leslie does articulate values. Those values would have to be of one sort or another, which is a matter of further interest. But, whatever type of values Leslie articulates, Leslie verbally adheres to what is called normative ethics.

The third level at which we can think about ethics is the level at which we attempt to account for what's going on at the behavioral level and at the level of articulations of values. This third level is called the meta-ethical level, the level, literally, beyond normative ethics. At this level, we inquire into the nature of the statements that people make about ethical matters; we inquire about the relations between intention, action, and moral belief; we inquire into the relation between factual matters and evaluative matters; and so forth.

14.2 Now, if we're considering the myth, "If you're spiritual, you're ethical," we want to know whether being ethical means, first, engaging in some apparently ethical (to some hypothetical secret observer) behavior, or, second, endorsing moral or ethical viewpoints. It could mean one or both of those.

Let's look at one, the latter, the endorsing of moral or ethical viewpoints. Is it the case that people often thought to be spiritual endorse moral or ethical viewpoints? It is interesting to note that although this is often the case, nonetheless, as it appears, this isn't always the case. This is the sort of case we will focus on here, noting that spirituality is associated with moral or ethical behavior, but doesn't always lead to expressing normative ethics. Sometimes, in fact, adopting certain sorts of spiritual attitudes is logically inconsistent with expressing normative ethics.

Coincidentally, not only are there three levels at which ethics or morals might operate, but also, as it happens, there are three main theories of ethical scope, two of which presuppose that there are ultimate ethical values and then state who or what the bearers of those ultimate ethical values are, and the third of which denies, or decidedly refuses to state, that there are ultimate ethical values. We will look at these three theories of ethical scope because each of them is a theory about whether there is or isn't a (positive) normative ethics. The first two say that there is a positive normative ethics. The third says that there is no positive normative ethics.

The first view is universalist. It presupposes that there are ultimate ethical values, and holds that they arise in *all* subjects of a certain broad kind. There are, of course different views about what kinds of subjects are subjects in all of whom ultimate or intrinsic values arise; and there are different views about what sorts of things ultimate or intrinsic values are; but the universalist view would hold that as long as something is a member of a certain sort of multi-member class, then ultimate values arise for that being.

Often, universalists are universalists about persons. According to person-universalists, all persons are subjects of ultimate ethical values. Some universalists are universalists about all things in the world. The latter group, the ecological ethicists, hold that all things, all ecological systems of whatever kind, bear ultimate value. On the other hand, the former group, the person-universalists, hold that it is only to the degree that something is a person that the being bears ultimate value. Many personalists hold that some higher non-human animals are sufficiently personal as to be bearers, to a degree, of ultimate value. And some personalists would hold that there are immaterial persons who also bear ultimate value. Other personalists would deny that.

The second normative ethical view presupposes that there are ultimate values, but not all persons, or not all members of an even wider group, have ultimate value. Rather, exponents of the second normative ethical view hold that ultimate value belongs only to a narrow group of persons. For instance, *the ethical egoists* – an important group in this second class – hold that a person can only take himself or herself to be a bearer of ultimate value. All other people and all other things are bearers of merely instrumental value, where an instrumental value is merely a means to an end.

To make this a bit clearer, suppose that I am an ethical egoist. As an *ethical* egoist, I think there is ultimate value; and as an ethical *egoist*, I think the ultimate value is my own ultimate value. All other persons' values, and all values associated with non-persons, are merely instrumental toward my own ultimate value. So if someone seems to be in pain, and if I think that it is to *my* (long-term) advantage to attempt to get that person out of pain, I will help to get that person out of pain. I will do it because I take it to be in *my* (long-term) interest to do it. Perhaps people will see me doing it; or perhaps it's an "I'll scratch your back, then you will scratch my back if my back is itchy," sort of situation, or perhaps it makes me feel good to scratch the other person's back and it is that good feeling coming from scratching the other person's back that provides the ultimate reason I scratch the other person's back. On the other hand, if I don't think it is to my long-term or ultimate interest to scratch that person's back, I won't do it. The ethical egoist, then, takes himself or herself alone to have ultimate intrinsic value.

In addition to there being ethical egoists, there are also 'me-and-mine' sort of people who hold the second, narrow, normative ethical view. They would hold that I have ultimate value, and so do those very close to me – one or two friends, or my close family members. All others have merely instrumental value.

In fact there is a sort of continuum between the ethical egoists – for whom the only one who has ultimate value is the self – and the universalists. There are, at one end, the ethical egoists. Next, closest to them, are the narrow 'me and mine' folk. Next, closest to them, are the slightly broader 'me and mine' folk. (That is, the 'mine' is broader than the 'mine' of the narrow 'me and mine' folk; it includes cousins rather than merely siblings, speaking loosely.) Closest to them is the much broader 'me and mine' folk – the 'me and my neighbourhood' folk, or the 'me and my fellow nation-state citizen' folk, or the 'me and my fellow religionists' folk. Adjacent to them are the 'me and my species' folk, who are a touch narrower than the narrowest of the universalists already mentioned. (Humans don't include all animals with some proto-personal characteristics, for instance; and the question of immaterial persons and extraterrestrial persons, aside from the question of whether they exist, is also left out of the identification of the bearers of ultimate or intrinsic values with members of the human species.) A further broadening of the 'me and my....' group, focusing on persons ('me and my persons'), merges with the narrowest of the universalist class.

In fact, for the broadest of the 'me and my...' class we don't need to say 'me and my...' at all. 'All human beings' includes the thinker or the speaker. The still broader bearers would be 'all human beings, and all other persons, to the degree that a being is a person'. These have already been thought of as universalists. And then, among the group already thought of as universalists, there would be the still broader group, the ecological universalists, who would count 'all beings of whatever sort' as beings that have intrinsic value. In that way one has passed over from members of the second, 'me and my…' group, into members of the first, 'universalist,' group.

The third view of ethical scope is the negative view that there is no ultimate or intrinsic value at all. The group of espousers of the third ethical view is large; there are many ways of arriving at the conclusion that there are no intrinsic values. Although the universalist view and the 'me and mine' view are both normative ethical views and are not classified as meta-ethical views, we will not be much concerned here with the relation between the third theory as a normative ethical view, and the third theory as a meta-ethical view. The third theory can be classified as normative or as meta-ethical. All that counts is that it denies that there are ultimate or intrinsic values.

14.3 Let us now look at the many sorts of exponents of the third view that there are no ultimate or intrinsic values. First, there are the 'might is right' folk, which we find exemplified in the ancient world in the views of the figure of Callicles as depicted by Plato in his dialogue *The Gorgias*. "…[R]ight…is the advantage of the stronger over the weaker" is how it is put in W. D. Woodhead's translation; and "right consists in the superior ruling over the inferior" in Walter Hamilton's translation.[9] But both connote the well-known slogan, 'Might is right'. 'Might is right' more accurately means, 'There is only might or power; the notion of what is genuinely right disappears when one considers the way power is used in human relations.'

This point of view was adopted and developed by many others. We'll look briefly at one more example, Friedrich Nietzsche in the 19th century, who maintained, in *Beyond Good and Evil*, for instance, an elaborated version of what Plato presented some characters as having said in *The Gorgias*, that the usual moralities endorsed and promoted are expressions of weakness, a gaining of power by banding together behind the notion of the morally right. For Nietzsche, the power gained was a meaningless power. Nietzsche presented both a historical vision and a current prescription. His historical summary is of a series of steps whereby late 19th century European society, he thought, is best understood.

---

[9] "Gorgias," translated by W. D. Woodhead, in *The Collected Dialogues of Plato*: 229-307: 266; *Gorgias*, Plato, translated by W. Hamilton, NY: Penguin: 78.

First, said Nietzsche, the powerful gained the power. They judged actions by their consequences. Then, said Nietzsche, a great shift occurred through the ascension of the Christian religious sensibility: morality became intentional rather than consequential. The religious shift at first was used by the powerful in maintaining their power. But, finally, the religious morality became an ultimate morality, and this led, said Nietzsche, to a mediocre system in which the bland non-entities, without aesthetic or power merits, were regarded, in their own time, as occupying the heights of the achievable. Nietzsche ridiculed such a system, and advocated a return to the expression of full individuality. It is not unfair to think of Nietzsche's system as one in which might is right, as long as might is defined as a certain sort of powerfully-reaching individuality.

In addition to the immoralists and amoralists (often the 'might is right' thinkers: Callicles as depicted by Plato, Nietzsche, and so on), there are the moral skeptics. Sextus Empiricus (who flourished in the second or third century CE), for instance, was a moral skeptic. The English word 'skeptic' is taken directly from the ancient Greek word meaning 'inquirer'. And so the moral skeptics were moral inquirers; however, they not *only* inquired, they *merely* inquired. They never got answers for these inquiries. They inquired about morality, but they never got answers to their inquiries about morality, and so they never got what they took to be acceptable or justifiable theories about the central notions of what makes something moral. Of course they engaged in many arguments. But the upshot of the arguments, in their view, was that there was no justifiable reason to accept one point of view or another. Typically, they did not go as far as the immoralists; there might be some moral notion, they said, and there might not be. Although there were lots of arguments, when all is said and done, they were only capable of inquiring, inquiring, and inquiring about moral matters.

Socrates, who was executed at the age of 71 in 399 BCE for corrupting the youth and disbelieving in the gods, seems to have been an ongoing inquirer about moral matters. As was mentioned before, in Chapter Two, the dialogues of Plato that are usually regarded as the early or early-middle dialogues of Plato, are taken to be the most historically accurate about the figure of Socrates. In these dialogues, Socrates asks deep questions about what is the good, the virtuous, the wise, the pious, the truthful and the just, but never gets an answer that he takes to be satisfactory or justifiable.

In addition, there are the recent (primarily 20th century) non-cognitivists. (Incidentally, non-cognitivism typically sees itself as a meta-ethical view.) According to non-cognitivism about moral statements, any candidate for a central moral statement, such as "Killing a human arbitrarily, or just for fun, or just for money, is wrong," is not the sort of proposition that can be true or false. Since it is not the sort of thing that can be true or false, it is, rather, a sort of instruction or prescription, or urging. According to the non-cognitivist prescriptivists, "Do this, not that!" is the real content of a central ethical proposition. A proposition such as "It's wrong to kill a human for no reason other than pleasure," means something like "Never kill a human for no reason other than pleasure!" Non-cognitivist prescriptivists often endorse the view that moral statements are articulated "Yay this!" or "Boo that!" expressions. The non-cognitivist school in meta-ethics has a rich tradition in recent times.

There is also the universal error theory. This theory maintains that candidates for central moral statements are capable of being true or false, but, unfortunately, they're always false. There is no ultimate or intrinsic value. Nonetheless, human beings, typically, have falsely believed that there is a sort of ultimate or intrinsic value. Because there is no ultimate or intrinsic value it becomes difficult to figure out how to conduct oneself. One does need to act, though, and so the task of the general error theorists in ethics (like J. L. Mackie in *Ethics*) is to figure out what sort of strategies one can use, given that one thinks that there are no ultimate or intrinsic values.

In addition, the two-level of truth theorists among Buddhists (pioneered by Nagarjuna, fl. 150 CE), and, perhaps, among Hindus (pioneered by Sankara, 788 – 820 CE), seem to hold that, at the higher level, there are no ultimate or intrinsic moral values. At the higher level, everything is perfect or complete; consequently, there is no 'going forward' in ethical practices. Others, though, would not see it this way. "You have to understand the higher level before you can talk about it," would be used to deflect the view just presented. Nonetheless, it seems to be the case that playing down the notion that at the higher level there is nothing to be achieved *is* merely speaking at the lower level, rather than the higher level. The question remains: What does one say at the higher level? In the Buddhist vocabulary, for instance, "*Nirvana* is not essentially different from *samsara*" – a view held by Nagarjuna – means that the state of one who has extinguished the notion of the self is not essentially different from – is fundamentally the same as – the state of one in which there appears to be the usual self. For this reason it seems to be legitimate to think that the state in which nothing is to be accomplished is fundamentally the same as the state in which there is an appearance of something to be accomplished. And that means that the advocates of the two-levels of truth theory in Buddhism (or Hinduism) maintain that at the highest level, there is nothing to be achieved, and so there are no ultimate intrinsic values. And then it doesn't matter if saying that is still talking at the lower level. Rather, "Don't say that until you know what it means," seems to be not much more than a slippery way of getting out of an intellectual difficulty (at the lower level, if you like) than a clear view on the intellectual issue itself. "If nothing should be done at the higher level, why should something be done at the lower level?" is an intellectual question that seems to remain.

There is also the group that I'll call the *ethical ironists*. For instance, in the *Tao Te Ching*, which is the central philosophical foundation text in Taoism (composed, likely, sometime within the 6th to the 4th centuries BCE) we have this observation:

When the great way is abandoned,

Benevolence and rectitude arise.

When wisdom, intelligence arise,

There is great hypocrisy.

When the family is at odds,

Filial piety and kindness arise.

When the country is in confusion,

The ministers are all loyal. (XVIII)[10]

There is a deep ethical skepticism there; but it is the irony in the appearance of ethical concepts just as ethical realities vanish that shows the subtlety of the Taoist view of human language and the world.

As is apparent, then, there are (depending how one classifies) four, five, or six main sources for denying that there are ultimate or intrinsic moral values, or for abandoning positive judgements to the effect that there are ultimate or intrinsic moral values. But, as I'll show a few paragraphs below, there *do* seem to be spiritual people in this group.

Given that there are these three views in ethics, and, as I'll show below, that there seem to be spiritual people in at least some of the third

---

[10] The translation just given combines elements from several translations including that of D. C. Lau and Gregory Richter.

group in the account of moral scope, it follows that the myth (the image, the view) "If you're spiritual, then you're ethical" where that effectively means, "If you're spiritual, then you approve of ethical determinations," seems to be a false myth. (Remember, 'if...then' statements should apply to all beings centrally referred to after the 'if' and before the 'then'.)

14.4 Let's now see how some ethical immoralists, ethical skeptics, double-level-of-truth theorists, and ethical ironists, seem to have been spiritual figures.

We'll begin with the amoralists or immoralists. Some would say that Friedrich Nietzsche, for instance, had something of a creative or spiritual aspect to his views. One interesting feature of his biography is that in his youth he was very friendly with, or adulatory of, the composer Richard Wagner; then, however, he became deeply disillusioned with Wagner's stances. Wagner became avowedly Christian, for instance, and, over and above that, anti-semitic. Due to their growing philosophical differences, the association or friendship between the two men dissolved, and Nietzsche wrote explicit attacks on the philosophical standpoints he attributed to Wagner. Nietzsche referred to Wagner's anti-semitism as an attitude he (Nietzsche) despised. Indeed, Nietzsche defended the rights of the Jews and others in Europe. Despite being an immoralist, Nietzsche manifested what many would regard as a kind of individualistic courage in his personal relations with Wagner and in his vocal opposition to Wagner's public stance. The tone of the writing in his novelistic *Thus Spake Zarathustra*, too, may be regarded as exhibiting a kind of spirituality as well. Was Nietzsche's condition a religious-ish condition? It certainly wasn't a religious condition affiliated with the religions of his time. Whether it can be thought of as religious-*ish* is a controversial matter.

Next, we'll look at the skeptics. Socrates, for example, seems to have been an endless inquirer, and thus, a sort of ethical skeptic. It is difficult to know what Socrates really was like, so, as before, we use what may be the best guides, the apparently early or early-middle dialogues of Plato. Socrates, viewed this way, can be regarded as a spiritual (religious-ish) figure. In addition to endlessly asking questions about morality, he was intent on the subject, he was kind, witty, had a depth to him, both in his everyday attitudes and in his friendly but intense questions, often leading his interlocutors into contradictions, and, apparently, he did nothing that would undo his being regarded today as a fine person and one who accommodated the religious attitudes of the times. Even his last words are said to have been, "I owe a cock to Asclepius. Render it surely," and some interpreters take that to be a reference to a religious offering. Incidentally, even if some of Socrates' political views were unpopular in his own time, and might be unpopular to many observers today as well, there seems to be no ground at all to the criminal charges against him, which led to his death by judicial execution.

In addition, the ancient moral skeptics (who were even more skeptical in their position than Socrates was) can be regarded as having been spiritual figures. Consider Pyrrho (4th and 3rd c.'s BCE), for instance, who, according to the standard interpretation, *abandoned* (performed *epoché* on) all his important beliefs. Some stories have him talking as though to someone, though no one was listening. He is taken to have met gymnosophists (naked wisdom pursuers) in India when he accompanied Alexander the Great on his ventures that far, and their attitudes may have influenced him. And he is taken to have behaved indifferently in regard to cliffs, but lived a long life through being cared for by his friends.[11] If he carried on as those (unclear) stories suggested, he may well have been thought of as a sort of spiritual (religious-ish) person. But he is taken to have been an ethical skeptic, as well as a skeptic about other important beliefs as well.

The two-level of truth theorists among Buddhists, and, perhaps, Hindus, also had spiritual qualities. For one thing, anyone reputed to have achieved the higher levels of spiritual attainment through Buddhist or Hindu exercises will have a reputation as a spiritual (religious-ish) person; and the proponents of the two-level of truth views in Buddhism and Hinduism were highly trained in the disciplines. One cannot find more exalted exemplars of the class of people thought to be religious-ly spiritual than these! They may have uttered moral remarks, gently, at the lower level. But they would have been silent or cheerfully deflective in public if pressed publicly to utter remarks at the higher level. Still, they would have seemed spiritual or religious-ish.

Finally we can note that subtle Taoists, who were ethical ironists, were also regarded as highly spiritual. Living in the Way, in the Taoist view, enables one to enter the market with a deep sort of smile; and anyone reputed to have fulfilled the Taoist vision would be regarded as a highly spiritual person. Yet such a person may well have uttered

---

[11] R. J. Hankinson, *The Skeptics*: 58 – 65; 64.

paradoxical statements to the effect that one only gets ethical notions when the Way has been abandoned.

In this way, "If you're spiritual, you're ethical" seems to be a bit of a false myth.

14.5 We will now briefly consider a closely related view or myth, that "If a society is spiritual, then the society has a spiritually based value system." This view or myth is ambiguous, and what I will attempt to do here is to show that on one meaning it is incorrect.

The view or myth is ambiguous. To say that "If a society is spiritual, then it has a spiritually based value system," might mean, "If a society is spiritual, then it has an emanationist-based value system, or something similar; it has a physically-incomplete-based value system," and it might, alternatively, mean something more broad, for example, "If a society is spiritual, then, one way or another, it has an appreciation-based value system." It is only the first meaning, the first conditional, that I will try to show as false. If the first conditional is incorrect, then it will not be adequately employed even as a merely instrumental argument for supporting the exposition of physical incompleteness in society.

The easiest way to see the falsity of the view is to consider the many cases of people who were thought of as spiritual and, it may be added, were not committed to physical incompleteness. Nietzsche, for instance, was not committed to physical incompleteness. Similarly, no skeptic could be committed to physical incompleteness. Nor could any two-levels-of-truth theorist be committed to physical incompleteness at the lower level as a matter of principle. Similarly, moral ironists need not be committed to physical incompleteness as a matter of scientific analysis. Yet spirituality or something very close to spirituality is to be found among exponents of all or almost all of those views. Further, the non-cognitivists and the universal ethical error theorists could be spiritual folk entirely independently of their non-cognitivist views on ethical propositions or their universal ethical error theory. And they exhibited what can be regarded as ethical behavior. For this reason it is not correct to think that just because a group of people exhibit ethical behavior it follows that that group of people advocate an ethical view of the world. A group of ethical skeptics, immoralists, amoralists, ironists, non-cognitivists, ethical error theorists, may exhibit ethical behavior yet not make explicit positive normative ethical determinations, nor need they espouse an emanationist or any other physically incomplete view of the world.

In objection, the comment might be made that it is unrealistic to think of ethical skepticism or any of the other normative-ethics-rejecting views as spreading throughout society. The ethical skeptics were always few in number. The others, too, were rare in number. The question, then, is, "Is emanationism, or is a physically incomplete viewpoint, required as the cultural base for a broadly effective moral system?"

To answer in the affirmative, some might say that some adults at least are in the position of children, and need to hear moral determinations expressed, and since the traditional expressions of moral notions are strongly associated with emanationism or physical incompleteness, emanationism or physical incompleteness can be taken to be a required base for a moral system.

The first point, that not only children, but also adults, need to hear moral determinations expressed, is arguable both ways. For the sake of discussion, let us accept that it is so. Still, it doesn't follow that ethical determinations need to be assisted by an emanationist, or a physically incomplete, picture of the world. In Chapter Twelve it has already been shown that moral notions are consistent with an underlying view that accepts phystriology. Acceptance of phystriology is consistent with two sources of the view that there are intrinsic moral values, namely ethical naturalism and ethical intuitionism. Both these approaches to ethics could enable there to be a socially harmonious system that is not committed to physical incompleteness or anti-phystriology.

All that is left of the argument in favor of a need for emanationism or physical incompleteness accompanying moral notions is the idea that moral notions without emanationism or without physical incompleteness would be a new sort of morality, and this is too unrealistic to expect or to hope for. In this view, morality has been traditionally associated with emanationism or physical incompleteness, and so should morality stay.

On the other hand, slavery was regarded as traditional and acceptable by all for thousands upon thousands of years. Slavery is even regarded as acceptable in the Bible.[12] Yet slavery is now illegal, and entirely frowned upon. Similarly, although few lay people nowadays can

---

[12] See, for example, *Exodus*, 21: 4-6.

clearly explain why it is that the earth is not at rest, but is orbiting about the sun, everybody agrees that this is so. Similarly, it may turn out, at some point, that morality is no longer associated with physical incompleteness. Accordingly, the argument that for a society to have morality it must have an emanationist or physically incomplete base seems not to be grounded in much more than mere traditionalism. And merely traditional notions sometimes disappear.

14.6 There are, apparently, strong defects to the view that if you're spiritual then you're ethical, where to be ethical is to express ethical determinations. Still, though, we want to note that it appears that some people have more *capacity for joy* than others. Two Chapters from now we will look at claims that spiritually realizing people have access to much more ongoing joy than others. Then in Part III, especially Chapter Twenty Two, we will assess such claims. In the meantime, while looking at the different tones of spirituality, we want to look at the relationship between spirituality and belief in the genuineness of paranormal phenomena.

Chapter Fifteen: "If you're spiritual, you can access paranormal powers"

15.0 It is often thought that if a person successfully trains in spirituality then the person will gradually, step by step, acquire access to some special powers: paranormal powers, or parapsychological powers, or psychic powers. A good ancient source of this myth is the *Yoga Sutras* of Patanjali, which was written or compiled probably between fifteen hundred to twenty two hundred years ago.

Units III: 16 to 55 in the *Yoga Sutras* state that one who is well trained in Yoga gains knowledge of the past and the future, mastery of all sound systems for all beings (including animals), memory of the many past-lives, direct experience of the consciousness of others, the power to become invisible, the elephantine powers (whatever they may be, since they are interpreted differently by different commentators), knowledge of all the cosmological processes, the ability to enter another body, the ability to levitate, and in other ways, counter the law of gravity, and, on top of all that, omniscience. That's a wonderful list of the paranormal powers that a fully trained yogi is supposed to acquire! Of course the yogis say that one shouldn't go out in search of gaining such powers, and one should be entirely moral and discreet if one gains those powers, too. (No wonder, one might say, the yogis, though omniscient under the account, never gave us the general theory of relativity. Others, though, would point to some passages of the Vedas as supposedly containing the key concepts of general relativity. Oh, well; then, one might say, it's no wonder current yogis are not giving us the key concepts of the future quantum gravity theory from the Vedas.) Nonetheless, the claims, especially given the traditional and recent commentaries on the text, seem clear. The myth is affirmed. If you train well in spirituality, you will, say many exponents of spirituality, acquire various paranormal powers.

Perhaps you will be able to fly after years of training – at least that is what leading exponents of Maharishi Mahesh Yogi's meditation group claim.

Clearly, the gaining of paranormal powers, as usually interpreted, would entirely challenge the view that phystriology obtains. One cannot both believe that paranormal events, as usually interpreted, occur and that phystriology obtains. Those who believe that phystriology obtains reject that there is any non-grossly-physical mind (purely mental mind) creating changes in the physical world; those who believe that evidence for the genuineness of paranormal mental (and assumedly non-physical or only subtly physical) powers is very strong reject what the phystriologists accept; they are of the view that how and why phystriology doesn't obtain will become clear as science develops.

In 11.3 we had a brief review of some difficulties in making paranormal claims: First, I noted, there were claims of mermaids in the 18th century; then claims of photographed spirits in the 19th and early 20th century; then claims of ability to read cards when the cards were upside down or in another room later in the 20th century; then there were claims of the effectiveness of prayer when those being prayed for didn't know that they were being prayed for. Each set of claims was criticized, and then the next set of claims arose. Anyone who wants to support the paranormal has to be aware of what the phystriologist would say: that the proliferation of claims, with substitution of a new set of claims for old refuted claims, is itself an indicator of the lack of experimental evidence for the ability of some non-physical mental state to influence the physical state. In all fields other than parapsychology – for instance, in physics, in chemistry, and in biology – there are many very stable experiments first performed decades upon decades, or centuries ago, experiments that can be confirmed again and again in current learning. However, says the phystriologist, in the realm of the paranormal, there are no such experimental protocols and claims.

I also provided examples of pitfalls one can tumble into in devising supposedly rigorous experiments; and I provided citations of further readings that one can do if one is interested in this matter. Here I want to go a bit further on the nature of research into the paranormal claims. There are five further points that can, and should, be made. I am putting them forward so that anyone interested in defending the reality or genuineness of paranormal events will have access to what a phystriologist would say. These points are strong; nonetheless, a proponent of the genuineness of paranormal events needs to counter them if the view that there are genuine paranormal events is to be taken seriously. Here are the five further points:

First, it is useful to note the way in which there are subtle associative, but incorrect, and, it can be said, *merely atmospheric* (non-evidential) supports for the existence of genuine paranormal phenomena. I'll examine an example of such merely mythological or merely atmospheric (non-evidential) support and its deficiencies.

Second, it is important to recognize the many sorts of weaknesses that anecdotal, not experimental, research has.

Third, it is important to understand how even those areas in which paranormal researchers have thought that experiments cannot be made are, indeed, areas in which experiments can be made. Because the paranormal researchers have not made the tests that can be made, and have not nullified the 'ordinary chance' hypothesis (to be clarified below), there are extra reasons for thinking that the advocates of there being genuine paranormal results have not succeeded in following *the elementary rules* of scientific research.

Fourth, for comprehensiveness, a book length account, or at least a large part of a book, should be reviewed. In this case I will review one large part of a book by David Ray Griffin, and other material in that book, too, as to how paranormal research is, he says, properly grounded in evidence. The main lesson from this review is how important it is to check claims made by proponents of the paranormal against other claims made by those who doubt it. Without such checks one is liable to be much too easily taken in.

And, finally, fifth, we've already seen that phystriology is logically inconsistent with paranormal claims as usually understood; but, as we saw in Part I, there is enormous evidence in favour of phystriology. The evidence for phystriology, then, is powerful evidence against the genuineness of standardly interpreted paranormal events.

15.1 First, then, let us look at the *mere* mythological or atmospheric (non-evidential) support for the view that there are paranormal events. That is, let us look at the sort of support for paranormal events that, phystriologists would say, makes two important errors, namely, it gives no evidence whatever that there are paranormal events, and it ignores the effective implausibility of there being paranormal events under its own theory.

A good example of this is the discussion of hyperspace effects as found in the book *Surfing Through Hyperspace*, by Clifford Pickover, published in 1999. The basic idea is to consider what would happen if the world had more than the three familiar spatial dimensions. We are all familiar with three: east-west, north-south, (the world is as though flattened for those two axes of dimension) and one more axis at right angles to those two axes, which we can call 'up-down'. But what if, for example, there were a fourth spatial dimension? We can't imagine such a dimension, but we can abstractly conceive of it. And we can think of it – abstractly – as going at right angles to each of the east-west, north-south, and up-down dimensions, even though we can't *imagine* quite what that means. Pickover calls the fourth spatial dimension *upsilon-delta*. Then four-dimensional beings could manifest in our familiar three-dimensional world; they could be unified in the four dimensions, but appear, first, in scattered bits and pieces passing through our three-dimensional world, then in unified beings, passing through our three-dimensional world.

Just as a human being is a sort of continuous object in three dimensions, but would first show up passing through a two dimensional plane in pieces (first, say the two spatially separated feet would show as the human being passes through the plane), and just as only later would the pieces join up as the human being passes through the plane, and then, later still, disappear (the two feet become joined in the trunk, ignoring the arms, the shape of the trunk goes through the plane, ending in the head, a sort of circle contracting to a point and disappearing finally), so, too, a four dimensional object would appear in three dimensional pieces that join up in the three dimensional world. And just as a three dimensional being can enter a square closed on all sides in a two dimensional plane, so, too, a four dimensional being could enter any locked room. Apparently paranormal events of various kinds could happen.

Pickover discusses the possibilities as though they do happen. The whole structure of the discussion assumes that such things are happening.[13] Pickover also doesn't recognize that the hypothesis that there are such events effectively undermines phystriology, or, as it's been known since the 1960's, physical closure, and, especially since the early 1990's, the completeness of physics. To begin with, the notion that there is a very large body of evidence for phystriology is not known in the general public community. So it is not surprising that Pickover, though

---

[13] Pickover, pages xxi-xxiv, 15, 29, 38, 53, 57, etc.

writing decades after the completion of the evidence for phystriology, doesn't seem to know about it; consequently, it is not surprising that he affirms false parallels.

For instance, Pickover suggests that there is a similarity between the ten *sephirot* (emanations) of Kabbalah, and current multi-dimensional string theory.[14] However, in the following very important respect, there is no such parallel: the Kabbalah descriptions are of *sephirot* in which there are both fundamental bottom-up, *and* fundamental top-down causal relations.[15] In philosophically interpreted string theory, assuming the propriety of cause-and-effect talk (which need not be done, but then other sequence governance terms would substitute), at the fundamental level, there are *only* bottom-up cause-and-effect (or similar) relations; any top-down cause-and-effect (or similar) relations are referred to by summary terms in our language picking up on the complex goings on. Thus, any top-down causal relations are not at the fundamental level. To put it another way, there may or may not be emergent properties on some loose definition of emergence, but what phystriology maintains is that whatever properties a sum has, these will not overturn the sums, accessible or inaccessible, of the physics relations as they are understood. Yet, as was shown in Chapters Ten and Eleven, and as I'll show again below in this chapter and in Appendix 2, *fundamental* top down causal relations would overturn such physics-governed sequences. So if Pickover's parallel is correct, major revisions of rules in physics would be required. Yet, of course, Pickover nowhere mentions the revisions required. To put it more simply, the supposed parallel seems not to be a viable parallel.

Let us now look at how the more-than-three-spatial-dimensional reality relates to phystriology. The key issue is scale. If there were to be a more-than-three-spatial-dimensional explanation for the paranormal (the

---

[14] Pickover, pg. 15.

[15] For instance, the Kabbalah accepts the statements in the Torah maintaining that God spoke to Abraham or Moses etc. That's a top-down causal relation. In the Kabbalah, such revelations can be encouraged by various human acts. Those acts would embody bottom-up causal relations. The *Sefer Yetsirah*, a basic early (approximately seventeen hundred year old) Kabbalist text is supposed to have been received in a visionary (top-down) revelation of some sort. The preparatory acts of the author would have been bottom-up causal events. There are, of course, vastly many such cases and claims. For this one, see *Kabbalah* by Charles Poncé: 39.

occurrence of genuine paranormal phenomena), it would have to be at the human-scaled level. It could only be events we can perceive in everyday life that we would be interested in. We would not be primarily interested in the super-tiny events; we would not be interested in the goings on within the minute Planck-scale[16]. (For reasons already expressed in Chapter Eleven and which will be elaborated in Appendix 2.1, there would be no inherent purposes there; yet events at the human scale would exhibit purposes.) Consequently, we are not interested in the multi-dimensional aspect of string theory, since that doesn't yield effects of more than three dimensional objects at the human scale.

Let us assume that there are events at the human-scaled level involving entry of 4-D beings into our 3-D world, or effects of 4-D beings on objects in our 3-D world. To begin with, this is assuming something that is, given all the evidence we have, enormously improbable; indeed, it is so improbable that the evidence for it would have to be amazingly solid before we'd take it seriously. (Yes, in contemporary physics, there are speculations about multi-dimensional systems, but these multi-dimensions are at an amazingly tiny scale, not at the human scale, and not at anything remotely near the human scale[17].) In the case of Pickover's descriptions, there is no such evidence *at all*.

Still, for the sake of discussion, let us make that assumption. Now, what would happen if a 4-D being occupying regions of the 4-D world outside of our specified 3-D world passed through our specified 3-D world at the human scale? (This would be similar to an object in the 3-D world outside of a specified 2-D plane passing through that specified 2-D plane at the human scale.) Then there would be evidence against conservation of mass-energy within our 3-D world. There would be mass-energy appearing 'from nowhere' as it would seem. In that case, there would have to be a major rewrite of the law of conservation of mass-energy. There would, in the three dimensional world, appear to be energy coming from nowhere at the human scale. So there would have to be an account of such apparent violations of the law of mass-energy. And it would be those accounts that appeal to a higher-dimensional law of conservation of energy. Nowhere does Pickover talk about such rewrites of basic laws.

---

[16] Again, the Planck scale is as much smaller than an atom as an atom is smaller than a tennis ball.

[17] See, e.g., Brian Greene, *The Elegant Universe*, Ch. 8, e.g., 188, 191, 200.

To put it simply, that multi-dimensionality or hyperspace could explain how the paranormal might occur is merely atmospheric or mythological; it goes against phystriology as we currently have it; and Pickover gives no evidence whatever that phystriology as we currently have it should be given up or transformed. In Pickover's account, there is no empirical reason to take it that his explanatory proposal should be seriously considered. The 'explanation' is clever; but we need empirically observed events that require explanation before we propose a clever explanation. Pickover *never* presents any such empirical evidence. And, it seems, there is a reason he never does. Indeed, we are now going through five reasons additional to those given in 10.3.5 and in 11.3 for thinking that there is no such adequate evidence. The first of these five is that merely atmospheric supporters of the paranormal have no empirical evidence to reliably offer, and, it seems, that's one of the reasons why they provide merely atmospheric support.

15.2 Next, we'll look at the difficulties in doing merely anecdotal research.

In the world we live in, there are lots of things happening. Objectively, in the brain, which is the underlying object of human thinking, trillions of events take place every second or so. In our understanding, there are thousands of events happening all the time; but only a few of them surface into our direct focused consciousness. Nonetheless, that is not to say that none of the semi-conscious events are available to our memory; some may be. If so, when they appear to be especially meaningful or paranormally meaningful, they may be reported; but then no check would be made on the selection bias. Also, when it comes to anecdotal evidence for the paranormal, only a very few of the many events experienced are reported. This gives us similar cause for concern. We need to know how many events there are from which the few reported events are selected. Otherwise, we can't eliminate the 'selection bias' hypothesis.

Recently, I heard about a psychic who "may have helped police find a rapist." The description given of the psychic's activities sounded good. But the information given was not particularly helpful in getting the police to find the rapist. There was, however, one point of correspondence between what the psychic had 'seen' and the rapist found: she said he had a scar on his knee, and a limp, and the rapist did have a scar on his knee, and limped. In response to this, one wonders, how many people have given psychic reports? How many statements have been made? How unlikely is it that one of them is true? And, finally, how reconstructed was the presentation of the information that the psychic gave? This last point needs some elaboration.

There are many revisions in our memories. Accordingly, after a significant event occurs, the story will be told and re-told in many ways. When it finally comes out in a report of a purportedly paranormal phenomenon, it can, and many would say it does, come out in an embellished manner; the accurate original information is distinctly colored. Once again, it becomes very difficult to sort through anecdotal evidence to eliminate the 'mere coincidence' hypothesis.

Most importantly, though, half-correlations or partial-correlations are very frequently taken to be full-correlations. If a partial-correlation is taken to indicate a full-correlation, then already there is a failed conclusion. But in anecdotal claims for paranormal events, often partial-correlations are taken to indicate full-correlations; then a causal relation is drawn; and that causal relation is taken to have an apparently paranormal content. In such cases, all the more so, we have a failed bit of anecdotal evidence.

Here is a quick explanation of the problem. Suppose I find that each of five of my friends told me that he had a dream – an unusual dream, as each would put it – that exactly came true at some later time. I then conclude that dreams can paranormally indicate the future. But, even assuming that the dreams were accurately reported, there was not yet a correlation found between dreams and future events. Our instincts about significant parallels, and the mathematical details about significant parallels are very different. This is surprising. But we do need to get a sense of the surprising difference.

To get a correlation (check, if you like, the information in 10.3.4 and elsewhere) one needs *not only* the percent of the A's that are B's (here, the percent of the specified reported dreams that do have contents of future events) *but also* the percent of the non-A's that are B's. But what are the non-A's? The non-A's would have to be taken from a well defined supergroup; the well-defined supergroup could be all the remembered dreams, so that the reported dreams and the non-reported remembered dreams would add up to the supergroup. It could be defined in many other ways as well; but for now, we'll take this as the defined supergroup. Of course, so many of our remembered dreams go unreported! Yet to figure out how many of the non-reported remembered dreams have contents of future events is required if there's to be a proper correlation under that definition of the supergroup. But, obviously, this hasn't been done.

Let us now look at other definitions of the supergroup. The supergroup could be defined to include fantasies, stories, and so on, to see how many correspondences there are between narratives and future events. Or the supergroup could be defined to be, merely, all the recorded dreams from a specified class, for example, of one dreamer. That could be a useful supergroup to use, since it could be followed, though with some difficulties, because there would have to be a recording method, and it would have to be used, and there would have to be a way to figure out how many of the recorded dreams had elements in them that took place at later times. There would also have to be double-blind ways of implementing those criteria. And, most importantly, this definition of the supergroup has left undefined what is an 'A' dream. So some narrowing of the supergroup has to be found, in advance, to see if there is a correlation between the A dreams and future, or B, events.

In classes, I often make some remark to the effect, "If any of you have personal experiences of the paranormal, I'd like to hear about them. I might then investigate the claims a little bit further." Recently a student reported that when she was a child, and happened to be alone at the time, she saw strange changes in a statue: the eyes moved about, and so on. She also said that when she was a young adult (in 1994), she had a dream that a specific actor died. She reported it to her friend, saying, "It's too bad." "What's too bad?" asked her friend. "*So and so* died," she answered. A few days later, that actor died. She also reported having had a second 'accurate' dream. In sum, she thinks that there was a paranormal event when she saw the changes in the statue as a child, and paranormal relations between her dreams including her dream about the actor dying.

Here, though, there were two sorts of events: the first sort (the eyes moving in a statue observed alone) cannot be researched and is easily explained by the millions of events going on in the brain, allowing for a hallucinatory experience in a child, or allowing for a short term memory (or long term memory) falsely built up out of various events. The second sort is (aside from latitude of interpretation problems) of a non-correlation (or part of a correlation) that masks itself as a whole correlation.

To reason from something easily explained as hallucinatory to the genuineness of the paranormal is, in itself, insufficient as a means to get to the paranormal. To reason from what is not really a correlation to a paranormal causal explanation of the supposed correlation is incorrect reasoning.[18] To combine two individually inadequate sources of belief to yield an apparently justified belief may be persuasive. But it is itself a failed style of reasoning. The proponent of phystriology would say that when put in the light of the points made in Chapter Eleven, the points to be made in Appendix 2, and the five additional points in this Chapter, its inadequacy should become even much more apparent.

That is a sophisticated way the phystriologist might put the problem. Here is a less sophisticated, though longer, way of putting it. Anecdotal research in favor of the paranormal is built up out of selected events apparently showing the paranormal. Rarely does one find anecdotal research showing that there are no genuine paranormal phenomena. But that rarity is not because there is no such anecdotal evidence. It is because the vast number of such anecdotal cases against the paranormal just aren't (usually) reported. Then the selection fallacy explains the apparently adequate anecdotal evidence for the occurrence of genuine paranormal events.

I'll give two examples, and then a general demonstration. In the first example, we can notice how different are different responses to similar events. A friend of mine was amazed at his discovery in a town very far off from his residence, in a bookstore, of a book he had owned many years before, with his name on the first inside page. "What an incredible discovery!" he thought; "There must be some mysterious meaning to the synchronicity." On the other hand, in my morning paper recently there was a similar report, but a different attitude toward it. A woman discovered a book she had owned (proof in the book, too) in a bookstore in Toronto, hundreds of miles from Ottawa where she had owned the book. But she was not so much interested in the 'synchronicity', as in the fact that the book was *The Odyssey*, and when she asked her husband what inspired him, he said, "It is you." "To do what?" "To keep going on," he said. She took that to confirm the message of the Odyssey, that life itself is a journey. She focused on life as a journey, rather than on the 'synchronicity', which can otherwise (naturally or non-

---

[18] See Thomas Gilovich *How We Know What Isn't So,* for a good exposition of psychological slippages that take place.

paranormally) be referred to as the sort of coincidence that happens given the vast amount of information floating around and through us.[19]

Perhaps some would want an account of how much information floats around and through us. It is vast, and simple tests can reveal how vast it is. Just look at license plates with letters on them in front of you as you drive in a car, say. You can very frequently interpret such letters as acronyms, for instance. This shows how much information flows around and through us. If you resist believing this, try it out.

I just noticed some different attitudes toward similar events; but, in addition to noticing different attitudes, it would be good to give a case of anecdotal evidence *against* the paranormal. Here is one. In a recent issue of a neighbourhood paper, *The Vancouver Courier*[20], under the "Travel" Section, there was an item on the many tourists in Phoenecia in Upstate New York; they go there in search of a buried treasure hoard that gangster Dutch Schultz apparently placed there before he was scheduled to go to jail. He didn't go to jail, but was assassinated in 1935, and never got to his buried treasure hoard. The article continues with some anecdotal evidence against the genuine paranormal:

> James Schlick, a retired cartographer…had a vision in which he found himself standing next to Schultz as he buried the box… 'He picked out landmarks that he "saw". But he didn't find the treasure'.

That is a clear example of (what is too rarely attended to:) evidence against the paranormal.

I will now put these points more generally. Everyone should agree that to get rid of the selection fallacy, one would need to successfully claim a power of some sort, and the power or ability could be checked. The phystriologist adds that no such power has been found after having been properly checked.

What is perhaps the best example of the absence of successful presentations of such powers is the unanswered challenge provided by James Randi Educational Foundation. The challenge is presented to the many anecdotally based believers in the paranormal: if anyone believes he

---

[19] "An epic journey through daily life," Jeannine O'Reilly, *Globe and Mail*, May 6, 2008, L8.

[20] The article is "Catskill Mountains attract treasure hunters", Mitchell Smyth, *Vancouver Courier*, Nov 16, 2007: 39.

or she has a paranormal power, let him or her contact Randi's Educational Foundation, mention the supposed power, set up with the members of the Educational Foundation a method for checking whether the power exists, agree upon the method, follow through with the method, and if the power is demonstrated under that test, he or she would receive the million dollar award. As was just suggested, the challenge has never been met.[21]

15.3 Third, let us look at the way in which some areas of research are *taken to be* not suitable for experimental investigation, yet, I suggest, *are* suitable for experimental investigation. Yet no experimental investigations have been done. I will go through this by indicating one area of research that is frequently taken to be suitable only for anecdotal investigation, but is, I claim, not suitable only for anecdotal investigation. This is past-life memory research. The suggestions being made here are both for those who would deny the paranormal, and, to be better aware of the problem, for those who would support the genuineness of the paranormal.

Ian Stevenson was the founder of past-life memory investigation and of investigations of other past-life effects on later-life. His reports are sometimes voluminous. One of his books (*Reincarnation and Biology*) is over two thousand pages long. But, as I'll suggest now, after having done a bit of anecdotal research, he didn't follow the basic step of scientific research, which is, to put it technically, to nullify the null hypothesis.

That sounds forbiddingly fancy, but the meaning of 'the null hypothesis' is not fancy, and can be easily stated. The null hypothesis says that the elements of data conform to chance or probabilistic expectations. To nullify the null hypothesis is to say that the data go against the chance expectations. Once one has gathered a fair bit of anecdotal evidence, as happened for Ian Stevenson, for instance, by the mid 1960's, one could discover whether the anecdotal evidence goes against the null hypothesis. To do this one would have to do a little further anecdotal research, and the further anecdotal research would have to be carefully designed to match the standards used or abstracted from the first cases of anecdotal evidence. Then one would compare the two groups. The first group, for evidence on past lives, would be the cases originally studied, and it would be what is called the experimental group.

---

[21] See <www.randi.org/research/index.html>.

The second group would be cases of life-span overlapping individuals who happen to closely resemble each other in many ways, and it would be called the control group.

It is clear that there are people whose time periods are overlapping and who, in various respects, closely resemble each other in many ways. For instance, as it turns out, in over twenty respects, I (Leonard Angel, the author of this book) closely resemble Ian Stevenson. We were both born in Montreal. We both obtained the Bachelor's Degree from McGill University. We both obtained the doctoral degree. We both had large libraries in the respective homes in which we grew up. These large libraries inspired our further research. We were both married twice. Both of our mothers were interested in ethical or spiritual matters. We both have/had a sister and a brother. We both endorsed scientific method. We both had a phase in life in which we were positively impressed with the work of Sigmund Freud, but then we moved in another direction, thinking that Freud's work was too unscientific. We were both Head/Chair of our academic Departments. We both investigated specific claims about memories. We are/were both cautious when asked in public for comments on our views. The primary interest both of us have/had is in human nature. We have both developed some unusual views, given the range of views found expressed in the refereed literature. Some of our views have been quickly dismissed in a 'knee-jerk' sort of way. Still, both of us persisted in publishing the results of our thinking in journals and books. Both of us published a compendium book after many years of working on it. The publication year was the same for both of us (1997). As of the current date (in which this material is being prepared, 2008), we each published four main books, each with technical details for those inclined to pursue technical details. And so on.[22]

Now suppose we abstract from the experimental group, and say, "*A* remembers *X*. *X* is true of *B*. *A* remembers *Y*. *Y* is true of *B*," and so on. We do this for, say, ten cases of the experimental group. Then we do the same for the same number of cases of the control group. "Alpha remembers *Z*. *Z* is true of Beta. Alpha remembers *V*. *V* is true of Beta," and so on. The ten experimental (*A-B* and similar) connection cases are randomly mixed in with the control (Alpha-Beta and similar) connection

---

[22] The twenty similarities, almost all of which were taken from an extremely brief biography of Ian Stevenson, are fully reported in a dream-dialogue in *Skeptic*, published in the UK, Spring, 2008.

cases to the overall collection of cases (which now has both the *A-B* group and the Alpha-Beta group). Given a case randomly chosen from the overall collection of cases, one doesn't know whether it is one of the ten control (Alpha-Beta and similar) connection cases, or one of the experimental (*A-B* and similar) connection cases. Then one asks a group of subjects a question intended to determine whether the subjects can tell the difference between an experimental case and a control case. The question might be, "Which six of the twenty cases are most in need of a special (paranormalistic or parapsychological or psychic) sort of explanation?" If the subjects are researchers, for example, researches who positively publish on the paranormal, the question could be, "Which six cases of the twenty cases most strongly suggest a past-life memory connection or some other paranormal or parapsychological connection?" The experiment would be administered in a double-blind way – the ones administering the experiment would not know which of the twenty cases are control cases and which are experimental cases. Nor would the ones gathering and reporting on the results of the questions. Then the results would indicate whether the null hypothesis obtains or not.

My point is that this follows the basic method for doing scientific research, and, as it is usually put in texts covering experimentation for third or fourth year undergraduate students, if one does not follow this sort of method, one has failed to do the basics of scientific research. There is a vast amount of anecdotal evidence in favor of the paranormal explanation of various results. Yet the very basic step of scientific research has not been followed, which is to devise an experimental test to see if the null hypothesis itself is nullified. And in pro-paranormal presentations of anecdotal material, this was not done, but, I suggest, could be done.

15.4 What would now be useful is to have a more comprehensive look at claims for the paranormal. There are so many forums in which there are claims for the paranormal that it is insufficient to exhibit just a few of the problems. For this reason, we want to have a look at a comprehensive presentation of the ways of justifying beliefs in the paranormal. For the pro-paranormalist to have a sense of the difficulties in defending the genuineness of paranormal events, it would be good have a look at a comprehensive analysis within a book length account. Here we will look at such a comprehensive analysis given by David Ray Griffin, a prominent theorist on the subject in his book, *Parapsychology, Philosophy, and Spirituality.*[23]

In this analysis, Griffin's advocacy of psychic phenomena, mind over matter events, paranormal informational sources for afterlife evidence, thoughtography, etc., is based on four kinds of evidence, each of which is, following William James's nomenclature, a 'white crow.' Just as finding a single white crow would disprove the generalization that all crows are black, so too an individual instance of a paranormal event would refute the generalization that no paranormal events occur. This would be established, all the more so, if there were many such white crows, so that suspicions that the primary evidence was faulty could be avoided. Griffin's project is to show that there is not merely a single, or a few white crows, but that white crows abound. In fact, Griffin classifies the abundance of white crows into four kinds.

White crows of the first kind are reputable investigators, especially prominent scientists, who have investigated the paranormal, and have been convinced that some of it is genuine. White crows of the second kind are people who, it is claimed, repeatedly demonstrate their paranormal powers. White crows of the third kind are convincing examples of spontaneously occurring apparently paranormal events. And white crows of the fourth kind are replicable and replicated experimental protocols the following of which has exhibited statistically significant paranormal results. We will follow Griffin's exposition of the examples of each of the four types.

As part of his introductory material, Griffin lists nine philosophers, eight psychologists (or nine, given the repeat of William James), ten physicists, two astronomers, four biologists, ten literary figures, and three politicians as examples of white crows of the first kind (pg. 13). All of these individuals, he assures us, were not only famous and important and reputable individuals, but also persons who accepted the reality of paranormal phenomena, often based on their inquiries and investigations. Yet of course, it is not enough to have the list of such individuals. We must also look at the bases on which they accepted the reality of the paranormal. For this reason, Griffin selects a few and shows what he takes to be the persuasive basis on which they accepted the paranormal.

---

[23] Published in 1997.

In Griffin's overview, a leading example of a white crow of the first kind (one of four whom he describes, pp 44-50) is the scientist Sir William Crookes (1832 – 1919). Crookes, who invented the famous 'Crookes' tube', and was deservedly famous in his time, carefully investigated spiritualists and concluded that some of them offered genuine manifestations of the spiritual world. Griffin assures us that Crookes' endorsement is so convincing and based on such clear evidence with no mark against it that anyone who wants to doubt Crookes' judgements "can do little more than repeat the argument of the critics of the time... The events as reported by Crookes... did not occur because they could not have occurred" (pg. 62).

Griffin's saying this is, to put it mildly, puzzling. As it happens, there are many glaring marks against Crookes' research on the paranormal, yet Griffin seems not to know anything about them. As any scholar can discover with a minimum of research, Florence Cook, one of the spiritualists whom Sir William Crookes affirmed as genuine and whom he defended against the fraud charges laid against her, is reported by two independent reliable people, on unrelated occasions, as having confessed to them her use of conjuring. In particular, she is reported as having told each of them that she used plain ordinary prestidigitation to make it look as though she was the vehicle for paranormal events. Furthermore, she also confessed to them, according to these respondents, that Crookes knew about her fraud, yet affirmed her genuineness despite this knowledge.[24]

Other material shows that Annie Eva Fray, a partner of Florence Cook in the spiritualist activities, told Harry Houdini that she and Florence Cook used trickery to produce their results in general, and in particular, to make it look convincing to Sir William Crookes.[25]

And, finally, it is easy for a serious scholar to discover that Crookes, apparently, had an affair with Florence Cook and that the séances, apparently, were to provide cover for the affair.[26] This sort of connection needs to be mentioned in addition to mentions of the various apparent confessions that prestidigitation techniques were used.

---

[24] Trevor Hall, *The Medium and the Scientist*: 93, 99, 100, 102-107, 159.

[25] W. Williams, "Crookes, Sir William" *Encyclopedia of Pseudoscience*.

[26] Trevor Hall, *ibid*, 99ff., and 107.

How is it possible that Griffin alleges that the skeptic has no recourse but to claim that there is no mark whatever against Crookes' judgements? Of course it is possible that Griffin had not heard any of the readily available material concerning Florence Cook's confessions, the report of her partner, and the reports of others as well.

Astonishingly, Griffin gives the reader little else to go by wherewith to arrive at the conclusion that there is significant weight in the opinions of other white crows of the first kind. His only other cases presented in this section (pgs. 43-50) are Henry Sidgwick, Mrs. Eleanor Sidgwick, and William James. Yet Henry Sidgwick did not consider himself to be an experimental investigator. As Griffin put it:

> Although Sidgwick did not consider himself particularly good at psychical research as such, in the sense of conducting and evaluating experiments, he was involved in many investigations of Spiritualism and decided that most of the phenomena were fraudulent, or at least too ambiguous to pronounce authentic. (pg. 45)

The credit Griffin assigns to Sidgwick at the end of this brief exposition, quoting from James, is that Sidgwick had an obstinate belief that there is something yet to be brought to light, and that he drew no precipitate conclusions from the evidence at hand. This provides little indeed from which the reader can state that Sidgwick even so much as fills the bill Griffin would want for a white crow of the first kind. One would think that convincing white crows of the first kind would, among other things, have arrived at firm conclusions of the reality of some paranormal phenomena *based on evidence gathered through investigations*.

As for William James, Griffin does the reader the favour of quoting James' considered assessment: "I remain uncertain and await more facts, facts which may not point clearly to a conclusion for fifty or a hundred years" (pg. 48). Griffin goes on to quote from James's "Final Impressions of a Psychical Researcher" showing also that James reached no firm conclusions on most paranormal claims, and regarded the evidence as ambiguous (pg. 48). Since James espoused the appropriateness of evidence-less beliefs on momentous, forced, live options, even in the few areas where he accepted the paranormal, the evidence he gave is likely to be little. And this likelihood is fulfilled. He mis-reasoned several times in his first major report on psychic research.[27] And as for Eleanor Sidgwick, all that we learn from Griffin is that she studied spiritualists, and "gradually came to believe in the survival of death" (49). We will also have a brief look below at the defects in the two principal cases cited in regard to Eleanor Sidgwick, namely those of Mrs. Piper and Gladys Osborne Leonard.

In short, the exhibited evidential value of the white crows of the first kind as offered by Griffin is, putting it mildly, again, extremely low.

In any case, it is an analysis of second, third, and fourth types of purported white crows that must carry the weight. Many scientists, politicians, philosophers, astronomers, and literary figures, concluded that there are no genuine paranormal events. They could be easily cited against Griffin's list of his white crows of the first type. But neither list would establish anything. When a matter is controversial, such lists cannot be conclusive. Rather, it is the examination of the primary evidence itself that counts.

Let's look next, then, at Griffin's cited white crows of the second type. We will begin with the person whom Griffin considers to be the leading example of a convincing case of the white crows of the second type, namely, D. D. Home. Griffin lets us know that D. D. Home is "probably the most powerful white crow of his type to appear in modern times" (56).

About D. D. Home, Griffin assures us that "no fraud of any sort on his part was ever detected" (pg. 57). Once again, we have a puzzle to face. There were readily available reports to the effect that D. D. Home was caught cheating. One observer of D. D. Home's activities reported the details of the trick used. Paul Kurtz reports that "the trick was so plain to [the observer's] eyes while the company present was so reverential and adoring that he was seized with a strong impulse to

---

[27] In "Psychic Research," James misses obvious natural possibilities re apparitions and deaths (312-3); he makes mere assumptions (318); he accepted Mrs. Piper as a legitimate psychic (319), and the material below on Mrs. Piper shows the weaknesses in James' approach there too.

laugh."[28] Similarly, Gordon Stein in 1996 reported that privately he was caught in fraud several times.[29]

This is a double problem for Griffin. Not only do we have the first and most important point, the inadequacy of Griffin's canvassing the broad situation, but also there being reports of Home's cheating allow a dismissal of the other claims concerning Home as well. Of these two points, it is only the former that I wish to focus on, the apparent unreliability of Griffin's basic presentation of the issues.

Our next example of a potential contemporary white crow of the second kind mentioned on a prima facie basis by Griffin illustrates the connection between intellectual issues and moral issues. Satya Sai Baba, a contemporary Indian guru, according to Griffin, is the only person of contemporary times who may be as significant a white crow of the second type as D. D. Home was in his day in the 19th century, even though Griffin limits his claims to 'prima facie' status (pg. 63).

David Griffin goes on to offer the reader what amounts to a reassurance that Satya Sai Baba has never been caught cheating in his materializations. However, any serious researcher should know that there are many cases in which Satya Sai Baba has been, as scientific skeptics put it, "caught cheating." If Griffin had been aware of instances in which Satya Sai Baba had been caught cheating, he would not have given his prima facie assessment by quoting (pg. 63) a summary statement by Erlendur Haraldsson published in 1987 to the effect that all the investigation Haraldsson made (and, implicitly, was aware of) showed no evidence of cheating. The evidence that Satya Sai Baba has been, apparently, observed cheating many times was readily available in North America for many years prior to Griffin's book publication date. Why, then, did he quote a single inquirer of 1987, and ignore the abundance of evidence to the contrary, readily available in the 1980's and throughout the 1990's?

---

[28] Paul Kurtz, *Transcendental Temptation*: 334.

[29] Gordon Stein, *Encyclopedia of the Paranormal*: "D. D. Home" 325 – 329. Also Stein refers to Gordon Stein, *The Sorcerer of Kings: The Case of Daniel Douglas Home*, Amherst NY: Prometheus Press 1993. The conclusion of Stein's article responds to those who state that Home couldn't have been a fraud. Stein states, simply, "Home was a fraud... He was just a more clever and politically sophisticated fraud" (than others).

For example, Basava Premanand, the most well known critic of Satya Sai Baba that there is, toured North America in 1988 to make well known his exposé of Satya Sai Baba. As it happens, Premanand says that on one occasion Satya Sai Baba was caught using a thumb tip.[30] Independently, in 1992, Satya Sai Baba was video-recorded (by a state video crew) supposedly materializing a gold necklace in the presence of then PM of India P. V. Narasimha Rao. Extracts demonstrated that "[t]he videotape unambiguously shows Satya Sai Baba clandestinely being passed a necklace by his personal assistant" a short period after which the guru waves his hand and produces the necklace. Photos of the video and the video itself have been widely available.[31] There are many other examples of exposures of Satya Sai Baba's apparent cheating. In fact, if one has Haraldsson's own book on Satya Sai Baba, *On Modern Miracles*, one finds one therein. Assistants to Satya Sai Baba are quoted as acknowledging that the ash in an urn from which ash was 'produced' by Satya Sai Baba was stuck in the urn prior to the production, and so this is dismissed by Haraldsson; he took it not to be a case of materialization. However, the Satya Sai Baba promotional materials make it clear that Satya Sai Baba's production of ash from an apparently empty urn is taken as a materialization of the ash.

Coming back to the point mentioned in the first paragraph on Satya Sai Baba, although this may not be strictly relevant to our canvas of the claims and counterclaims, some followers of the controversies will want to be aware of the moral issues associated with this possible white crow of the second type. In the writings of typical proponents of the paranormal like that of Griffin, we find nothing about the voluminous moral allegations against Satya Sai Baba independently presented over decades by many youths from Malaysia, Sweden, the U.S.A., other places, and, of course, India, about sexual crimes. If these many moral allegations are true, then the paranormal claims seem to be rendered weaker.

Two other leading white crows of the second type cited by Griffin are Ted Serios, and Nina Kulagina. Griffin assures us (pgs. 65-7)

---

[30] Dale Beyerstein, "Satya Sai Baba," *The Encyclopedia of the Paranormal*: 653-657.

[31] Babu Gogineni, "Godman of India," *Skeptic*: 58. (This article would not have been available to Griffin at the time of his writing *Parapsychology, Philosophy & Spirituality*; but the event was in 1992, and there was widespread dissemination of news of the event.)

that various aspects of Serios's performances "militate against the suspicion that the pictures were produced fraudulently," and that "no sign of fraud [by Kulagina] was ever detected."

However, all you need to do is check *The Encylopedia Of The Paranormal*, edited by Gordon Stein, and published in the year before Griffin's book was published, to find out that Griffin's summary claims are highly dubious. Serios's performance, in the only occasion in which tough observers were present, strongly grounds suspicion that the pictures were produced fraudulently. Serios was caught inserting something into his gizmo, where the 'gizmo' was a device that somehow enabled him, he claimed, to produce thoughtographies. However, when a request for examination of the thing put into the gizmo was made, he wouldn't let it happen. Based on this and further experimentation, careful researchers "concluded that [Serios]...used sleight of hand."[32] How, then, can we be properly assured that the circumstances militate against suspicion that the pictures might have been produced fraudulently? At the very least, the case shows the arbitrariness of Griffin's standards. Griffin claims that Serios was properly investigated, since, according to Griffin, Serios is an established case of a white crow of the second type (not merely a prima facie case like Satya Sai Baba who wouldn't let himself be investigated experimentally). Yet when challenged to allow the device apparently inserted in the gizmo to be examined, Serios would not cooperate. Thus, it seems, Serios did not allow himself to be properly investigated.

Next, despite Griffin's assurance that "no sign of fraud [by Kulagina] was ever detected," it was reported (before the publication date of Griffin's work) that Kulagina "was caught using invisible thread and concealed magnets to perform feats of psychokinesis."[33] Once again, the contrary evidence is presented here not so much to guarantee that nothing paranormal had occurred, but rather to show that Griffin's statements about these cases to the reader shows an unacceptably low awareness of the literature on the material.

Only two other figures are covered in Griffin's section on white crows of the second kind, namely, Leonora Piper (pgs. 51-54), and Gladys Osborne Leonard (pg. 55). One of the main claims made by

---

[32] Thomas Flynn "Thoughtography" in *Encyclopedia of the Paranormal*: 522. The careful researchers are Charles Reynolds and David Eisendrath.

[33] Martin Gardner, "Eyeless Vision" *Encyclopedia of the Paranormal*: 259.

Griffin about Leonora Piper was that "She was never, in all the years she was studied, detected doing anything suspicious" (pg 52). However, there were, indeed, many grounds for suspicion. What impressed people was her apparent ability to telepathically interpret the states of others. It is important to realize, though, that she claimed that when in a trance condition she had no memory afterwards of events going on during the trance. At the same time, the conversation going on around her, by ordinary anticipation, would have contained many of the details that she delivered later. Oddly, her believing observers did not check to see how much of the later supposedly telepathically received information was already available to her through the conversation that surrounded her while she was in a supposed trance state! The article with information on her in the *Encylopedia of the Paranormal* (pg. 538) showed that there were indeed cases in which conversation around her while she was in trance later appeared in deliverances at other sessions. Why didn't Griffin at least make reference to this?

It also seems that Leonora Piper engaged in what is called 'cold reading', that is, she used what she was given, and made it look like psychic deliverance. Granville Stanley Hall gave Leonora Piper fictitious information and names. He invented a woman named 'Bessie Beals'. Leonara Piper, through her control personality, then proceeded to contact this invented woman on 'the other side.' Hall gave Piper further information of the sort that might have been true, and Piper then accepted these claims and further built on them in her spiritual deliverance. Hall "then revealed to Hodgson [Piper's 'control personality'] his many deceptions and did his best to convince" Mrs. Piper that Hodgson was only a fragment of Mrs. Piper's mind.[34] For other reasons as well, "if you read carefully between the lines, there are suggestions that in many ways Mrs. Piper practiced deceptions."[35] Once again, Griffin's assurances, for instance, "Never was any fraud, or even suspicious behavior, detected," (54), are incomplete. Given that no proper investigation was made of her reliance on cold reading, of her ready acceptance of false claims made by clients, and of information obtained while she was, or was supposedly, in trance states, the evidence about her is weak.

---

[34] Martin Gardner, "Leonara Piper", in *Encyclopedia of the Paranormal*: 539.

[35] Gardner, *ibid.*, 538.

The only other white crow of the second type offered in Griffin's section (50-67) is Gladys Osborne Leonard. Gladys Osborne Leonard, according to Griffin, engaged in 'book reports' in which she asked the client to check a book at some lines on a certain page. The client would find a reference that made particular but unusual sense to the client. Griffin reports on Eleanor Sidgwick's confirmation that 17% of the book reports were successful, 19% were somewhat successful, and gives numbers showing that roughly 18% were dubious, roughly 7.5% were almost complete failures, and roughly 38% were complete failures. There were 532 book tests in total (pg. 55). However, there was no double blindness on the evidential success appraisal, nor does Griffin seem to be interested in any basis on which to estimate the chance probability of a set of connections between a random page number, and a client's judgement of relevance. It is important to remember that there was only a 17% rate of what was judged to be a success. These are two crucial, independent issues, and both need to be discussed. Several options for a best explanation by non-paranormal means are readily available (including some not mentioned above). Thus, Griffin's quotation of both Eleanor Sidgwick's judgements and of the degree of telepathy in Gladys Osborne Leonard's deliverances is without the sort of evidence that would be required to properly establish a white crow of either the first or the second type in this case.

What about the white crows of the third kind, the many anecdotal examples of spontaneous occurrences of telepathy, clairvoyance, premonitions, and so on? Griffin devotes ten pages to some of these cases (67-77). However, as was summarized in 15.2, there are serious problems with the white crows of the third type: anecdotal reportage is hard to rely on as far as accuracy goes, and the popular imagination is prey to many cognitive fallacies in assessing the reports.

The first case reported by Griffin is about Joicey Acker Hurth (67-70), who also gave the information. In January 1949, Joicey Hurth woke up after midnight with a feeling that something was very wrong, though she had no explanation of what was wrong. Then, in the morning, she suddenly said that something was terribly wrong with her father. She then received a call in which her mother told her that her father was very ill. Griffin interprets these events as constituting good evidence that a paranormal relationship occurred between Joicey Hurth and her father.

Plainly, however, more is needed than anecdotal reports of these kinds, even if they are accurate. For one thing, there are many patterns of contact that could give people ongoing subconscious or semiconscious information of the possible problems involving other people, and sometimes, at a later date, they may turn out to be true. In that case, there could be a correlation between the earlier subconscious judgements, the later expressed judgements, and the events involving those people. There would not be anything paranormal occurring. On the other hand, there might not be a correlation, even between true judgements about distant people and facts about the distant people. For instance, there might have been no greater number of true judgements about distant people than false judgements about distant people. To gather all the information concerning contacts between Joicey Hurth and her father just before her supposedly paranormal awareness would not be an easy thing to do. For this very reason, and without any information on the frequency with which she made remarks or offered worries that did or did not correspond to external events, and without any information about contrary subconscious or semiconscious hypotheses that might have been at work, it cannot be readily or easily established that the judgement to the effect that she was feeling bad on account of something to do with her father showed a paranormal connection between them.

In general, Griffin's discussion of these cases showed no awareness of the need for proper and not partial correlation claims. In order to know whether a given case illustrates a paranormal connection between two people we need a supergroup. For instance, we need to know how frequently Joicey Hurth (and everyone like her) has contact with the relevant other person, feels bad and makes exclamatory judgements that something's wrong with that person, and how frequently the judgements turn out to be true and how frequently they turn out not to be true. Without such studies, the basic premises on which to establish the basis for a paranormal relationship cannot be made. It's not easy to design the checks for such correlations, but, in any case, without such studies, the reports are not reliable. Further, many would say that the investigations, although with some difficulties, could be done.

For example – this is another way, beyond the illustration given in 15.3 that one can turn anecdotal reports into experimental examinations – we might be able to design a study to find out how many times a day people worry about someone without calling them, how many times people worry and do call, and what the proportion is of disasters occurring to the one worried about in the two groups.

Without such studies, the premonition evidence is just succumbing to what's well known among psychologists as 'the confirmation fallacy'.[36] We could go further into Griffin's cases exemplifying anecdotal evidence, but the most serious paranormalists would want to rely on experimental work.

The white crow of the fourth type is experimental evidence, supposedly replicable and replicated. However, what we find in this source of validation is what was briefly summarized in 11.3. Decade after decade (and century after century if one wants to look more broadly than Griffin did) there is a replacement of one sort of investigation or experiment by another.

At first remarkable results are published. It is claimed that there is, for example, only a one in a billion chance that the results would occur by chance (Griffin, pg 83). Then serious efforts are made to set up protocols and to test them. When they are tested, the evidence for the paranormal vanishes, and a new type of experiment is proposed. Once again, positive results are published. Protocols are then established. A decade later, say, it is realized that the experiments don't establish any paranormal results. But, it seems, members of the public tend to remember the widely reported apparent successes, and to ignore, or never hear about, the rejection of the experiments by careful analysis and study.

For example, David Griffin's best white crow of the fourth kind consists in the 'ganzfeld' experiments of the 1970's, 1980's, and the early 1990's. However, when a careful analysis by Julie Milton and Richard Wiseman of the many studies following the protocol definitions in the 1980's was done, we learnt (in July 1999) that the results were as would be predicted by chance: "[T]he ganzfeld technique does not at present offer a replicable method for producing ESP in the laboratory."[37] This was published roughly two years *after* the publication date of Griffin's book; nonetheless, it is worth noting that Griffin seemed to be uninterested in keeping track of what happened to the issue. In 2000, up to a year or more after the Milton and Wieseman (1999) result, Griffin repeated in *Religion and Scientific Naturalism* (pg. 192) what he said in 1997 about the ganzfeld experiments. It seems he was uninterested in following the serious assessments of the evidence.

---

[36] See Paul Kurtz, *ibid*, pg. 430, and Gilovich, *ibid*, 30-37.

[37] See Griffin, *ibid*, 82-5 in support of ganzfeld efficacy. This includes his analysis of meta-results given to his date. The Milton and Wiseman quote from a study two years later is from the Abstract of their article: 387.

The 'white crows' material constitutes Griffin's comprehensive overlook that we are reviewing; after discussing the evidence of the 'white crows,' Griffin discusses a variety of other topics. It would take too long to review these other topics in the sort of detail that the 'white crows' analysis was given, but we will look for a moment at them, though here they will be organized in a different way from Griffin's organization, and, to some extent, there will be a broadening of the context of the discussion.

First, psychokinesis. There are psychokinetic mind-over-matter effects often reported in the pro-paranormal literature. An example was looked at above in the case of Nina Kulagina. Sometimes, though, experimental psychokinetic work is done. However, the statistical significance of the results of such experimental work is so marginal in terms of how far off chance the results are in any particular run of effects that it has merely hypothetical theoretical interest. Further, as of 1996, through the article in the *Encyclopedia of the Paranormal*, the results were regarded as, at best, inconclusive. More recently, we have found some statistical explanations that could make even more credible the naturalistic non-paranormal explanations of such reported results.[38]

In regard to the out of body experience (OBE) reports, taken to be genuine-paranormal claims, Susan Blackmore gives a sensible approach; she concludes that the evidence for OBE extra-sensory perception (ESP) is insufficient.[39] (Unsurprisingly, there is currently a large study of OBE results from near death experiences underway, as was referred to in 11.3 note 184.)

Third, we'll touch for a moment on memories of past life existences. Often, it has been said that as good a case as there is for the empirical confirmation of the paranormal through apparent past life memories, is a case in which Ian Stevenson himself recorded the

---

[38] See Gordon Stein (ed.) of *The Encyclopedia of the Paranormal* on psychokinesis. A general statistical analysis is "Parapsychology's File Drawer Problem" by Douglas M. Stokes in *Skeptical Inquirer*. Massimo Pigliucci's "Hypothesis Testing and the Nature of Skeptical Investigations," has useful material about the risks of standard statistical analysis and the usefulness of the Bayesian approach. See also Victor Stenger, *God: The Failed Hypothesis*: 91-93, on different values of statistical significance.

[39] Susan Blackmore, "Out of Body Experiences" *Encyclopedia of the Paranormal*, 479, 482.

memories of the child prior to the empirical check. This is the Imad Elawar case. Griffin comments on this case, about which he reaches the conclusion that "there seems to be no normal way to account for the various facts."[40]

Unfortunately, (as usual) Griffin fails to mention demonstrations that there is no positive evidential value to the supposedly distinguished case. One such demonstration concerning that case appeared in *Skeptical Inquirer* in Fall 1994.[41] Stevenson originally recorded the past life memories of Imad Elawar as memories of being an important family man, wealthy enough not to have to work, with a beautiful wife and five children. The boy originally was taken to have remembered that he was a man who moved in important circles, who met with a tragic vehicular accident in which his legs were broken, and from which he died.[42] However, this couldn't have been Ibrahim Bouhamzy (the past life identified by Stevenson as the person who matched the boy's memories). Bouhamzy was not wealthy, was a truck driver, who used his family's vehicles, without any recorded accident leading to an injury to him, and he died unmarried, probably childless, at age 25, of tuberculosis. It was primarily the way in which Stevenson reconceived the claims to be checked and then faultily and misleadingly tabulated his evidence that makes it look like he found a match. The main changes in the claims were made after the trip in search of the match.[43]

Matching fantasies or past life memories by picking, rewriting, and redoing the original claims, can always lead to an apparent 'match' but one without any evidential significance. It is puzzling that Griffin seems to rely on a supposedly open-minded postmodern approach. Either he does not want the reader to have access to contrary evidence, or he has been unfortunately narrow in his research.

---

[40] Ian Stevenson, *Twenty Cases Suggestive of Reincarnation 2nd edition*, Ch. VI, 270-320 for the Imad Elawar case; for the Griffin discussion, Griffin, *ibid.*, 186ff. The quote is on pg. 192.

[41] "Empirical Evidence for Reincarnation? Examining Stevenson's Most Impressive Case," Leonard Angel.

[42] Ian Stevenson, 1978, *ibid*: 277.

[43] See the author's article, just referred to. Also, a citation already given in Chapter Eleven can be repeated here: To see that misrepresentation in tabulation is standard in Stevenson's work, consult L. Angel, "Reincarnation All Over Again."

There is a decade by decade shift in what is experimented on. Remember, there was a recent attempt in the spirituality culture to embrace paranormal effects of prayer where the recipients of the prayer don't know that they are the objects of the prayer. But, as already mentioned in 11.3, the evidence there has failed[44]. Very likely, a new type of experiment will be widely reported in the news sometime over the next decade or so. (And the preliminary indicators of this, concerning near death experiences, seem to be already happening, as was mentioned above.)

The main result of all this is to note how weak a comprehensive analysis within a book-length review of the best available evidence for the paranormal has been, and how the other evidence within the book has inappropriate material as well. The book is roughly a decade old, but it seems to give the picture on the nature of the evidence for the paranormal. One could focus on the work of different authors, for instance the work of Charles Tart, Martin Ebon, or Dean Radin. But the evidence cited in favor of the paranormal in their work is no better, in my judgement, than that of David Ray Griffin. One who wants to support the genuineness of paranormal events needs to engage in detailed investigation and show that there is work that does not suffer from the sorts of problems that undermine David Ray Griffin's enterprise.

15.5 We've now reviewed many ways in which we can see that there are severe difficulties with the evidence for the genuineness of apparent paranormal events. One who would support the genuineness of paranormal events needs to face the problems. And there are many of them. The claims keep changing drastically as each set of claims becomes refuted; there are pitfalls researchers unfortunately fall into; there are so many cases that have been investigated and 'debunked'; there are some merely atmospheric supports without empirical or observational bases; there are very many defects in merely anecdotal accounts; anecdotal accounts that are thought to be not subject to improvement through

---

[44] As in n. 182 in Chapter 11, see, "'No effect' Prayer Study from Mayo Clinic Ignored by Media," by Kevin Christopher. For discussion of previous claims, see Irwin Tessman and Jack Tessman, *ibid*; and Nicholas Humphrey *ibid*. See also, Letters, by Ray Sutera and Jan W. Nienhuys, July/Aug. 2000 *Skeptical Inquirer* pg. 64.

---

experimental work can actually be tested by experimental work and there is no reason to think that that experimental work would be in favor of the genuineness of paranormal phenomena; and a typical comprehensive review within a book in support of the genuineness of apparent paranormal phenomena has very great errors at so many crucial turns that there is little reason to believe what's being claimed.

Here I'll mention one other point, both halves of which have been already demonstrated. First, as we saw in Part I, there is enormous evidence in favour of phystriology. Second, as we saw, again, just a bit later in Part I, phystriology is logically inconsistent with paranormal claims as standardly understood. Put these two points together and, because of the logical relations, the evidence for phystriology is evidence against the genuineness of standardly interpreted paranormal events. For this reason, it would have to be exceptionally strong empirical or observational evidence that could take one away from the results of phystriology. Yet there is no such strong empirical or observational evidence to do this. Consequently, the fifth point stands: the evidence for phystriology not only conceptually but also practically goes against there being genuine paranormal events.

Chapter Sixteen: Spirituality and Joy

16.0 The third myth or view about spirituality is that "spirituality is a highly joyful state." Here I'll suggest that this myth or view is unlike the previous one that training in spirituality leads to paranormal powers. I have suggested that that previous myth is erroneous because investigation doesn't support it and because other evidence (for phystriology) rejects it; but whether investigation supports or rejects the myth that spirituality is, in some people, a highly joyful state cannot be easily determined. That spirituality-training enables an ongoing joyful state is an empirical claim. Yet it is an unusual empirical claim in that it is both a very important claim, and yet, under current methods, a hard claim to ground. At the same time it does not contradict ordinary scientific views. Neurophysiologists have begun to investigate the neurophysiological basis of ordinary happiness, and it may become easier over the next few decades to check the claim of extraordinary bliss by neurophysiological investigations. Here I will exhibit the many suggestions that spirituality is to be associated with an ongoing state of deep pleasure or bliss. We will reserve for a later time (in Part III, Chapter Twenty Two) the effort to assess the claim.

The claim, as we'll see, affirms that an ongoing state of bliss or ecstasy is achievable; also it must be that any such state of bliss or ecstasy is stripped of its contrast value, since it is ongoing; yet, according to the claim, there is an ongoing state of high (contrastless) pleasure available to some people. It being stripped of its contrast value also makes it a difficult claim to confirm or refute by examination of external behaviour. Since it is an ongoing state, and it is not marked by strong contrasts with other experiences, it would not necessarily be marked by something like sudden jumping about with a laughing face.

And it is important to observe that this claim, that the state of trained spirituality is a highy joyful state, is a bit ambiguous. It could mean, a state in which positive values replace negative values; it could mean, a state in which there is a strong interpersonal sense of love; and it could mean something else, something more like a state in which what is usually contrastive, such as a state that typically follows healthy long running, or massage, or eating a good meal after being hungry, or drinking after being thirsty, or sexual stimulation, becomes an ongoing, and so contrastless, state. It is the latter sort of state that is meant here. And, certainly, it is conceivable that there is an aspect of ordinary pleasure states that can be present in an ongoing way without the usual contrast values.

I consider this myth, that high contrastless pleasure states are ongoing in some people, to be one of the most important theses about spirituality; yet it is a thesis that is virtually never discussed in any serious way. It is not discussed seriously by current psychologists (though they do discuss, and experiment in regard to, switching from negative to positive states, and they do discuss, and experiment in regard to, gaining a sense of an interpersonal source of love), nor by current philosophers, nor by current secular researchers of fundamental truths about human beings. Here our task is merely to exhibit the sources of the myth.

16.1 Ongoing bliss in Hinduism

One of the clearest sources of the myth is found in classical Hindu texts.

In the *Taittiriya Upanishad*, we find passages such as "he who knows that bliss of Brahman [referring back to previous claims] fears not at any time,"[45] "on getting the essence, one becomes blissful,"[46] and "he who is here in the person and he who is yonder in the Sun – he is one. He who knows this...reaches the self which consists of bliss."[47] Of course for the last quote, the preliminary claim, "he who is here in the person and he who is yonder in the Sun," is a rather strange claim; we will try to make sense of it in Chapter Twenty Two. But the subsequent claim ("he who know this...reaches the self which consists of bliss") expresses one version of the central yogic claim in which we are interested.

---

[45] II: 4: I, trans. S. Radhakrishnan.

[46] II: 7: I, trans. S. Radhakrishnan.

[47] II: 8: I, trans. S. Radhakrishnan.

The Bhagavad Gita, a central Hindu Yoga text of about twenty two hundred years ago, makes it clear that in the fulfilled state there is an ongoing peaceful contemplation of one's own nature, and that this peace is a supreme peace.[48] This claim is made explicit in VI: 21, "Supreme bliss, which is beyond the grasp of senses and yet can be comprehended by intelligence, is a truth which a yogi knows and firmly holds onto it."[49]

In the *Yoga Sutras* of Patanjali we find that "Sampradnyata Samadhi is that condition of conscious illumination, where mind is mixed up with consciousness of sentiment or consciousness of discrimination or *consciousness of joy* or consciousness of personality," (italics added)[50] that "contentment brings supreme happiness,"[51] and that one should "concentrate on friendship, mercy, *joy*, excel in them"(italics added).[52] This joy is associated with an 'inner light', e.g., "Concentrate on Inner Light."[53] In commentary on IV: 27, which states that "Sometimes in Illumination, impressions of the waking mind intervene," Shree Purohit Swami says that "The condition of Illumination is the condition of unlimited joy. Sometimes the limitations of waking mind shake the overflowing joy."[54]

In many branches of the Hindu tradition, the awakening to a state of ongoing supreme bliss is associated with what is called the awakening of the *kundalini* serpent, the serpent that is otherwise sleeping at the base of the spine. Once the *kundalini* 'snake' awakens, it is thought to pass upwards through the spine to the top of the head. In the process of this passage it is thought to awaken various spiritual centers throughout the body, allowing for the experience of what is variously called the circulation of the *shakhti* force, or the *prana*, or the illumination (and other terms are used as well). In the roughly one thousand year old *Hatha Yoga Pradipika*, the awakening of the *kundalini* and associated phenomena are described:

---

[48] *Bhagavad Gita*, VI: 15, 19, 20.

[49] Ashok Malhotra's translation.

[50] *Aphorisms of Yoga (Yoga Sutras)*, by Bhagwan Shree Patanjali, translated by Shree Purohit Swami: I: 17, italics added.

[51] *Aphorisms of Yoga, ibid*: II: 42.

[52] *Aphorisms of Yoga, ibid*: III: 23, italics added.

[53] *Aphorisms of Yoga, ibid*: III: 25.

[54] *Aphorisms of Yoga*, ibid: 59.

Kutilanga, kundalini, bhujangi, shakti, ishvari, kundali, arundhati, are all synonymous terms. Just as a door is opened with a key, similarly, the yogi opens the door to liberation with kundalini. The sleeping Parameshwari rests with her mouth closing that door, through which is the path to the knot of brahmasthana, the place beyond suffering. The kundalini shakti sleeps above the kanda. This shakti is the means of liberation to the yogi and bondage for the ignorant. One who knows this is the knower of yoga."[55]

That the awakening of the *kundalini* is a state of deep pleasure is also made clear: "The Brahma granthi being pierced, the feeling of bliss arises from the void... Whether there is liberation or not, nevertheless there is pleasure."[56]

In the contemporary interpretations of the classical texts there are also many references to ongoing bliss states that are, it is claimed, achieved by those trained in yoga.

16.2 Ongoing bliss in Buddhism

Buddhism, when it began in India, was not thought of as an exclusive or separate religious system from Hinduism; indeed, it shared central features of what we now think of as the Hindu approach; in fact 'Hinduism' originally meant something like 'India-ism'. For example, that practitioners engage in postural meditation was an expectation in the classical system(s). In any case, the classical Buddhist texts often mention the availability of an ongoing highly pleasurable state, a state of ongoing blissfulness, arising from the Buddhist practices. For instance, in the *Questions of King Milinda* we find that "by hearing the glad words of those who have seen Nirva*n*a, ...they who have not received it know how happy a state it is."[57] This is merely suggestive, but it will reinforce the more explicit quotes to come.

The Dhammapada, a classic compilation, states clearly that "those who in high thought and in deep contemplation with ever-living power

---

[55] *Hatha Yoga Pradipika*, Muktibodananda Saraswati, Swami Commentary: 104-7; 461-3.

[56] *Hatha Yoga Pradipika*, *ibid.*, verses 70 and 78, pp. 629, 638.

[57] *Questions of King Milinda*, III, 4, 7-8, T. W. Rhys Davids translation.

advance on the path, they in the end reach Nirvana, the peace Supreme, and infinite joy."[58] It also says that "Those who are watchful, in deep contemplation, reach in the end the joy supreme" (27) and other passages in the *Dhammapada* as well, namely, (89), (98, 99), (202, 204, 209), (327), make it clear that the joy of Nirvana is not to be taken to be a transient joy.

In addition, many Buddhist texts describe an ascent through the various levels of *sukha* or pleasure, and *priti* or deep rapture, so as to get beyond all pleasure states. For instance, the *Abhidamma* text describes progress through the *jhanas* (Sanskrit: *dhyanas*) in which moral states become fused with joyous states, with happiness, and, finally, with a supreme or transcendental equanimity. These imply, or seem to imply, a deep familiarity with ongoing contrastless pleasure states.

16.3 Ongoing bliss, joy or illumination in Chinese and related materials

In Chinese materials the relevant references are often to the capacity of people to awaken to *ch'i* circulation. *Ch'i* circulation is thought of in ancient Chinese culture, and in contemporary Chinese culture where it exists, as the circulation of some sort of subtle physical illuminative substance that is found both in the human body and outside of the ordinarily understood human body; there is, of course, no such subtle physical substance found in the studies of the physicists. So it is easy to dismiss all references to *ch'i* circulation as are found in Chinese thought.

However, there is no conflict between phystriology and the experience of unusual sensations in the ordinarily understood body. Such sensations may, indeed, be occurring largely as a result of changes in the brain's system of organization. An option such as this one, according to which it is possible to awaken to *experiences* of *ch'i* circulation, and that such experiences are associated with sensations of ongoing contrastless joy or bliss, will be followed further in Chapter Twenty Two.

Meng Tzu (whose Latin-based name is Mencius), a Confucian, was asked how it was to experience the circulation of the *ch'i*. His response was that "I am good at cultivating my 'flood-like *ch'i*' and that it "unites rightness and the Way... You must work at it and never let it

---

[58] *Dhammapada*: 23, translation here and below, by Juan Mascaro.

out of your mind. At the same time, while you must never let it out of your mind, you must not forcibly help it grow either."[59]

The *Kuan-tzu* text, according to A. C. Graham[60], is, possibly, the earliest of the meditative texts in Chinese culture. In the *Kuan-tzu* text, if the cultivation is deep and if one does not "let it slip,"[61] the illuminatory experience is stated to be ongoing, or, in the words of the Kuan Tzu, "an ordered heart resides within…the world will be in order".[62]

Returning to Buddhism, since it spread through China, Korea, Japan and other Asian countries, in the Japanese form of the Zen Oxherding Pictures[63] we find one in which all is forgotten; and after that, there is the depiction of the re-entering into the market place. The notion that the sage re-enters the market place is the notion of a realized being who abounds in joy, yet deals in everyday business.

In the *T'ai I Chin Hua Tsung Chih* (or *Secret of the Golden Flower*) text, a Taoist text highly influenced by Buddhism, translated into English from the German version of Richard Wilhelm, we find that the personal goal in training is "the circulation of the light".[64] Indeed, "the Golden Flower is the light… The work on the circulation of the light depends entirely on the backward-flowing movement." Such a state is regarded as a serene state; in fact the face is said to reveal its "splendour." [65]

There are also stories about a special kind of meditation illness and a recovery from such illness that allows for an ongoing clarity that can be assimilated to the cases we are looking at. For instance, the Japanese Zen Master Hakuin (1686-1769) claimed that he cured a kind of zen illness by finding out how to let the circulation of the *ki* energy ('*ki*' being Japanese for Chinese '*ch'i*') occur. *Ki* would move down from the head, and it would be stored in the belly pit. A Taoist sage instructed him as follows:

---

[59] *Mencius* 2 A, trans. D. C. Lau: 77 - 8.

[60] A. C. Graham, *Disputers of the Tao*: 100.

[61] A. C. Graham, *ibid.*, 2/101: 103

[62] A. C. Graham, *ibid.*, and also 2/102, and 2/101: 105.

[63] Kapleau, *The Three Pillars of Zen*, Boston: Beacon Books, 1967: 301-313.

[64] Richard Wilhelm, trans. (to German), *The Secret of the Golden Flower*: 7. English translation is by Cary Baynes.

[65] Wilhelm, *ibid.*: 21-22.

From the mounting of the heart-fire your grievous illness has arisen…You must know that to nourish the body it is imperative that the vital energy be made to fill its lower part.[66]

These were the remarks of a Taoist sage to a Buddhist; yet he said that there would not be any difficulty for a Buddhist to realize this. Indeed, as we have seen, the discovery of *ch'i* circulation, was apparently available to Mencius, and Mencius was a Confucian. Hakuin, after mastering the technique, remarked that:

> For the mind that is master of true meditation, the space below the navel is firm as though a huge rock were settled there, and when this mind functions in its awesome dignity, not one deluded thought may enter, not one discriminating idea can exist.[67]

16.4 The claims are widespread in India, China, Japan, and Korea.

That ongoing contrastless pleasurable illumination, or illumination of a kind of inner light, can be achieved by some people is a claim that is widespread in Hinduism, in Indian Buddhism, and in Chinese thought both influenced by and uninfluenced by Buddhism as it spread through Asia. The presence of well-developed meditation techniques in these countries may well be linked with the presence of that myth in these locations in both forms – ongoing bliss, and inner light circulation; and it is speculated here that there may well be a linking of the two forms. The myth that high ongoing bliss and circulation of inner light is available to practitioners is present in many classical texts; how to assess the myth is another matter, one we will postpone, as mentioned, till Chapter Twenty Two.

Undoubtedly some will claim that there are statements in canonical Jewish, Christian, and Islamic sources, and other sources, that parallel these claims exhibited from India and China. For instance, in the former three Abrahamic religions there is the notion of experiencing Divine Light, which can be compared with experiencing *ch'i*. Such parallels are worth pursuing; yet it is worth noting that such claims made in texts of Judaism, Christianity and Islam are usually made in slightly less clear ways than they are made in the Indian and Chinese texts. Because the Jewish, Christian and Islamic sources aren't quite as unambiguous as

---

[66] Mike Sayama, *Samadhi*: 45.

[67] Sayama, *ibid*: 48-9.

others, we can let the Indian and Chinese texts stand as representatives of the myth that religious-ish spirituality includes access to an ongoing state of contrast-less bliss or circulation of *ch'i* energy.

It is time now to look at exoteric and esoteric spirituality.

Chapter Seventeen: Exoteric Spirituality

17.0 We will now look at what may be called the exoteric content of spirituality. 'Exoteric' here means 'popular' or 'readily accessed'. (It does not mean 'external'.) And 'spirituality', again, includes the content of both named religions and un-named spirituality-promoting (religious-ish, not humanist) systems. The central task in this and the next Chapter is classificatory, to understand the kinds of religious and spirituality-promoting experiences that there are. In this Chapter, I will classify the exoteric content of religious and spirituality-promoting systems into five main sub-groups. These are: the attitudes of worship, positive attitudes toward an afterlife, an experience or theory of a strong form of (physics-overturning) human freedom, belief in hidden cosmic systems of reward, punishment, and meaning, and support for unusual (paranormal) powers. These five elements in exoteric spirituality are very much associated with the first five of the eight (or nine) views logically rejected by acceptance of phystriology.

These five exoteric elements will be presented not only in experiential terms, but also in 'view' or belief terms.

First, we will look at the layering of belief on experience. Consider, for example, exoteric content in regard to the afterlife. Suppose that a person named Pat experiences a medium (an afterlife-medium) presenting what the medium takes to be the communications of a ghost or a deceased human being. Pat would, say, hear the voice of the medium; but Pat would also interpret that voice; and Pat would have some beliefs as to whether the medium's statements, for example, "Your uncle Harry says that he is well," are true. In this way, there is a layering of belief on experience. One *can* have the experience and disbelieve in the plain interpretations of the medium's statements like, "Your uncle Harry says that he is well." But those cases will not be included in cases of exoteric spirituality; the only cases included are the cases in which a positively interpreting belief accompanies the experience. Here is another example: One can be in a cemetery, see some unusual lights, and yet not believe that those lights reflected or expressed any ghost wandering around the gravesites. On the other hand, one can be in the cemetery, see some unusual lights, and believe that those lights reflect or express some ghost wandering about the gravesites. The exoteric content of religion or spirituality is both having the experience *and* having the accompanying positively interpreting belief.

Second, it is important to note that in each subgroup of exoteric elements, the belief accompanying the experience does go against acceptance of phystriology. I will repeat this each time we consider a subgroup of what we're regarding as the exoteric content of religious or spiritual experience. The point was already made in Chapter Ten, but it is important to be aware of this point; the point relates centrally to the work coming up in Part III, especially in Chapters Twenty through Twenty Two. There we are figuring out how religious or spiritual attitudes might be rendered consistent with phystriology.

17.1 Affirming an object of worship

One of the most readily available contents of religion or spirituality is the attitude related to worship. Enter an awesome or impressively constructed religious building – such as a synagogue, a church, a mosque, a gurdwara, a temple, and so on – and an attitude of worship often follows. Many want to bow the head down, light a candle, kneel, raise the arms, or do something else that expresses devotion to an object of worship.

Not every religious system has an official God; yet even such systems without a central God, for instance, Buddhism, in just about all forms, have devotional exercises. These devotional exercises include reverence towards what are taken to be, for instance, the Buddhas, including, in that case, the founder of Buddhism, Siddartha Gautama, in the condition he was in, a state of Nivana, after the death of the body, a condition he is supposed to have achieved some twenty five hundred years ago, but is, one way or another, according to the typical Buddhist view, currently occurring as well.

The attitudes towards an object of worship include devotion, showing some degree of self-sacrifice, showing one's acknowledgement of a life-goal, or of willingness to serve what one takes to be the higher power, and showing acceptance of some doctrinal claims about the object of worship. One of the claims typically associated with the object of worship is that the object of worship, God or a god, say, often, interacts in various ways with the world. It is taken that God or a god (or a Buddha) will help some people, will answer some prayers or calls for assistance, has given instructions or prophesy to some people, will make a miracle or an unusual natural event (an event in nature that goes against some pattern of nature) to occur, and so on. It is just about always taken to be the case that the object of worship is not the sort of physical thing that a physicist studies. The God or god or Buddha is not a proton, neutron, electron, photon, nor a collection of such things.[68] Rather, the God or god or Buddha, etc., is regarded as a non-physical entity or a subtly physical entity.

Anyone who affirms such an object of worship, then, affirms that there is an interactive higher power, or God, or god, or Buddha, and so on. This shows the relation between the experiences with the attitude of worship and the beliefs about the object of worship. It also lays the ground whereby it can be seen that the typical beliefs about the object of worship are logically inconsistent with phystriology, or that the beliefs, whether typical or not, are not strictly logically but strongly inconsistent with phystriology in the way that was reviewed in Chapter Ten.

17.2 Contact with afterlife forms or pre-life forms

The experience of others dying is always highly charged as an experience; but it was unusually charged for hundreds of thousands of years. At some point, various beliefs arose in regard to the deceased person; and at some point, perhaps a few hundred thousand years ago, people started to bury dead bodies. In Chapter Two, an outline was given of how inter-agency attributions may well have led to the belief that a person survives the death of the body. But even if that is only part of the story of how belief in an afterlife began, or even if it was other factors altogether that led to the arising of that belief, all that needs to be said here is that we all go through experiences of the deaths of others, and historically, one way or

---

[68] Some people would agree for God, but might ask about a Buddha, "Why can't a Buddha be a collection of such things?" Of course, a living Buddha is supposed to be a collection of such things. The point is supposed to be about a Buddha after the death of the body.

another, there arose the belief in the reality of conscious survival after the body dies.

There are many types of contact that supposedly can occur with any of the afterlife or pre-life forms. We will classify claims about afterlife or pre-life forms into claims about unavailable ghosts, available ghosts, and pre and past life human beings of either the reincarnation or rebirth sorts.

There are different theories about what it is to be a ghost. In one of them, it is taken to be the case that no contact can occur between the afterlives in a kind of heavenly place or purgatory or worse, and living beings on earth. According to this theory, the consciousness of a human being somehow, in some way, continues after the death of the body by entering a realm that is inaccessible to us. (It is useful to note that even this theory of inaccessibility goes against the phystriology result, as was shown in Chapter Ten. Most would say that it would be mere magical thinking to hold that a soul can leave the body without making any causal changes in the brain; similarly, most would say it would be mere magical thinking to hold that a non-physical or only subtly physical soul can be the bearer of consciousness while the body is alive and yet the soul makes no causal difference in the brain, or that the soul makes no effect not already made by the physical system, while the body is alive. We already looked at this to some extent in 10.3.2.)

In other cases, it is held that, occasionally, sometimes through some suitable mediums or intercessory persons, there is contact between ghosts and living human beings. In this view, a spiritualist or psychic or, sometimes, anyone, makes contact with an afterlife, and reports on, or discovers, how the afterlife-person is, or what the afterlife person wishes to communicate to the living beings.

Finally, there are many cases of supposed past-life memory for reincarnation or rebirth beings. There also could be anticipations of future-life situations, but these are claimed less frequently. Coming back to memories, anyone who believes that he or she or anyone else remembered some past-life beings, either of the reincarnation or rebirth sort, would have some difficulty figuring out how any memory-connections could exist across the time periods involved without any physical continuity processes of the sort studied by physicists, biochemists, and psychologists. The typical view is that there is a straightforward non-physical or only subtly physical memory connection of some sort. Under this typical view, belief in access to such memories (or anticipations) logically conflicts with phystriology.

In any case, the exoteric content of religious or spiritual systems includes apparent experiences of, and beliefs that there are, afterlife entities, and, for some people, that there can be communication with some of these entities.

17.3 The view that there is strong freedom or strong responsibility

Some people take it to be the case that, as it might be put, "It can't be that changes I undergo involve nothing but the purposeless rules or forces or laws of governance of physics whose operations add up to my purposive behaviour. Rather, when I freely do something, I decide what is to be done, and I am not a mere sum of purposeless interactions! I must be overturning the inherently purposeless rules, or forces, or laws of governance, of physics."

Clearly, belief in such a strong form of freedom or responsibility explicitly goes against acceptance of phystriology. At the same time, the sense of religious or spiritual responsibility and freedom is often a powerful sense; and it is the experiences and beliefs arising from such experiences that we are primarily interested in here. Such experiences and accompanying beliefs often go to the very heart of belonging to a religious or spiritual group: one takes oneself to own a very special sort of responsibility in this matter.

17.4 Affirmation of hidden cosmic karmic laws or relations

It is striking how widespread is belief in a hidden process through which a person who has done a very specially good thing tends, apparently unconnectedly, to be rewarded, and a person who has done a particularly bad thing, tends, apparently unconnectedly, to be punished or deprived. This arises particularly in retrospect, that is, in regard to unexpected good things that have happened and unexpected bad things that have happened. Then there are thoughts that the apparently out of the blue event might be related to good or bad things the person had done in a still earlier period of time.

The tendency for such connections is technically expressed as a correlation only, though, and there are very different views about how such a hidden system of reward and punishment or deprivation takes place. Some think it's a 'karmic' process; some think it's through the activities of (an immaterial) God. Nonetheless, it is not at all unusual to find people striving for apparently hidden moral relations between bad things happening and previous bad things done, or for apparently hidden moral relations between unexpected good things occurring, and previous good deeds done.

This happens even in cases of illness. Someone, unfortunately, is diagnosed as having a terrible illness; it is not uncommon to find people saying that it is a sort of response ('punishment' would be, typically, too strong a term to use in defining the 'response'; 'deprivation' seems better) to that person's having been of a certain sort. That sort of person may be defined by a personality type, over-prone to stress, for instance – and this is not automatically objectionable on the grounds of phystriology, though acceptance of phystriology doesn't say anything one way or the other on whether there would be any correlation or, all the more so, any causal relation between the illness and the personality type.

Of course, illness is just one case in which hidden karmic relations are sought. Hidden karmic relations are typically sought and found for any sudden and unexpected good thing that occurs, or bad thing that occurs. But there being such interconnections independent of personality types or stress level types would be objectionable on ready-to-state-grounds via phystriology. The belief that there is such a hidden cosmic moral karma or divinely ordained reward/deprivation system goes against phystriology. Yet our focus here is not on the clash, but on the experiences, and beliefs based on non-naturalistic interpretations of those experiences, that proponents of exoteric spirituality have.

17.5 Positive attitudes toward special paranormal powers

All religious and spiritual systems allow for, or, in some cases, effectively require, having a positive attitude toward some people acquiring some special powers of the sort we refer to under the rubric 'paranormal' or 'parapsychological.' Here we would be particularly including belief in past-life memory, in there sometimes being contact with departed souls (both also covered in 17.2), in psychic readings, in ability to guess hidden facts of various sorts, in certain sorts of alien abductions (the ones in which the abducted person goes to a distant location and returns to earth faster than light could make such a return trip), in abilities to defy gravity and such like physical forces, in abilities to get objects to move at a distance (that is, without touching them and without using other hidden means, for instance, magnets or strings), in abilities to manufacture objects out of nothing, or alter objects in a way not explicable by physics-based means, and in reading special psychic auras, psychic auras that are not plausibly taken to be expressions of current physics-based phenomena.

It is noteworthy how full of special powers – often powers of distant communication – prophets, saints, sages, gurus, rebbes, important imams, and so on, are supposed to be in the readily available stories about them. Prophets, saints, sages, gurus, rebbes, important imams, and so on are typically taken to have been the vehicles of miracles or special powers of the sort listed above. They are taken to have given specific advice at great distances from disciples and in circumstances in which they couldn't have known the circumstances for which the highly specific advice was appropriate; they are taken to have answered prayers; they are taken to have appeared at two places at once. Examples of these kinds abound. The genuine existence of such powers, of course, is inconsistent with acceptance of phystriology.

As far as exoteric spirituality is concerned, though, all that we want to notice is that people anecdotally at least include in narratives of highly trained spiritual people accounts of many paranormal events that have supposedly occurred through those people.

17.6 Why select only the first five of the eight or nine views logically inconsistent with phystriology?

Only the first five of the eight (or nine) views, each of which is logically inconsistent with phystriology, were selected as constituents of the exoteric content of religion and spirituality. The question might be raised, why only these five? Couldn't others from the other views logically excluded by phystriology have been selected as well?

The answer to this question is that one of the other three or four logically excluded views will be selected; but it will not be selected for use in the category of exoteric experiences; it will be selected for use in the category of esoteric experiences. (It is the idea of mystical ascent as part of the having of philosophical mystical experience.) The remaining others of the logically excluded views are best not studied under religious or spiritual experiences whether exoteric or esoteric. They are ontological interactive dualism, emanationism, and process theology. These are philosophically expressed views. They are not experiences, nor primarily associated with experiences, and are not as popularly understood as are the first five. Hence they don't readily fit under the rubric of being exoteric, or popular, experiential elements in religions or spirituality-promoting systems.

And the belief in the personal God in general (strongly though not strictly logically excluded), and the belief in some supernatural intelligence, is or are effectively included already in the God to be worshipped, since the experiences one might have of such a God have to be at the human scale. The experiences of the personal God in general and of a supernatural intelligence would characteristically be of the sort that has been logically excluded by phystriology.

Chapter Eighteen: Esoteric Spirituality

18.0 We will now look at esoteric spirituality. 'Esoteric' here means the rare or unusual dimension in spirituality or religion. (It does not mean 'internal'.) I will classify esoteric content into three main interconnected phenomena: first, a strong form of apparent mystical experience; second, as we've already seen in Chapter Sixteen, an apparent circulation of an inner light sensation, sometimes called *ch'i*, or *prana*, or *shakhti*, or *kundalini*, or Divine Light; and, third, again, as we've already seen in Chapter Sixteen, an ongoing state of contrastless bliss.

18.1 Mystical experience

The terms 'mystic', 'mystical', and 'mysticism' have many meanings. Sometimes 'mysticism,' for instance, is a synonym for belief in genuine paranormal occurrences; sometimes it affirms that all experience is inexpressible; sometimes it means something like 'being fuzzy' or 'being soft-headed'; sometimes the term is restricted to mean the sort of experiential system in which any of a certain set of philosophically expressible views, such as "All is One," or, "there is no self," arise. It is in the last sense alone that the term 'mysticism' is used here, and, sometimes, we will call this 'philosophical mysticism.'

Perhaps the term 'philosophical mysticism' is a bit inappropriate. The phrase 'philosophical mysticism' as just glossed centrally covers very strong and very clear forms in the religious systems; but it is not the only term that covers them; and 'mysticism' alone has many meanings. Nonetheless, so long as 'philosophical' modifies 'mysticism', the meaning given seems clear enough.

The paradigm cases of philosophical mystics would be individuals with experience, teaching, and practice of a certain kind; it would include figures like the historical Buddha, the leading Hindu Advaita Vedantins (e.g., Sankara), some of the Taoists, Jesus in Christianity, though he was not what would usually be called a philosopher, some figures in Judaism (for example, some of the 17th or 18th century Chassids, though they too would not usually be called philosophers), and some Sufis in Islam. There are many ways to interpret these paradigm cases.

I have interpreted philosophical mysticism in the following manner[69]: there are practices claimed to produce experiences confirming teachings or doctrines or experiential expressions of four main sorts, namely, "I am the whole world," "there is no self", "there is only the partless One," and "there is Nothing." Expressions such as, "I merge with the Ultimate Reality," are taken to be partial expressions, expressions people make when it would be heretical to claim straightforward identity with the Ultimate Reality (because the Ultimate Reality is taken to be a super-person). It is only the first four sorts of full propositions we are considering.

If such propositions express teachings or doctrines, then they are interpretively inconsistent. If they merely express experiences, then, for any one person, they are synchronously experientially inconsistent (inconsistent at any given time), but diachronically experientially consistent (consistent for two distinct periods of time). On doctrinal interpretive inconsistency, obviously, for instance, if there is no self, then it cannot be the case that the self is the whole world; similarly, if there is only the partless One, then it cannot be the case that there is Nothing. On synchronous experiential inconsistency, if I am experiencing myself as the whole universe so that all the many parts of the universe are parts of me, then it is not the case that I am experiencing Nothing. And on diachronic experiential consistency, if I experience myself at time t_1 as being the whole universe, and express the thought, "I am the whole universe," and at another time, t_2, I experience things differently, and say, "There is no self," I need not be contradicting myself, so long as the reports are taken at the appearance-level. More on this in a moment.

The way doctrines and beliefs layer onto esoteric experiences is more complex than the way doctrines and beliefs layer onto exoteric experiences. For example, the way in which the esoteric doctrines that, "I am the whole world," that "there is no self," that "there is only the partless One," and that "there is Nothing", layer onto esoteric

---

[69] E.g., in *Enlightenment East & West*: Chapters Four and Five.

experiences is highly unclear; and whether the accompanying doctrines just listed are or are not inconsistent with phystriology is more difficult to discover than is the case for doctrines associated with exoteric experiences.

But if it appears to me that there is no self, this does not logically conflict with the mere appearance that the self is the whole world, so long as the two experiences or the two appearances occur at different times. In this way, the experiences of esoteric states do not appearance-wise contradict each other, so long as any one person has them at separate times.

18.2 The circulation of inner light

A central claim in many forms of esoteric spirituality is that it is possible for individuals to experience the circulation of a kind of inner light. As we've seen, the inner light is called *ch'i* in China, *ki* in Japan, *prana* or *shakhti* or *kundalini*, or by other terms (as mentioned in Chapter Sixteen) in Hinduism, *Or Ganuz* (hidden light) in Kabbalistic Judaism; there are similar references to the inner light that suffuse teachings in Christianity, Sufism, Sikhism, Sant Mat (Radhasoami), and other religions. There can be some differences of opinion as to whether these different terms refer to the same phenomena. I will not here undertake to investigate this question. The circulation of inner sensations of unusual sorts imaged as inner light or something like inner light is all that is meant in this case.

There are two sorts of claims associated with the view that there are experiences of inner light circulating. In one sort of claim, it is only within the ordinary human body that something is experienced as circulating. In the other sort of claim, it is taken to be the case that what circulates within the ordinary human body also is found moving about or circulating outside the ordinary human body in the world, and is basic in the operations of the world. The latter view, the second sort of claim, as usually interpreted, is inconsistent with phystriology. The first sort of claim is a mere representation of experience within the ordinary body, and so it is not inconsistent with phystriology. This will be useful in Chapter Twenty Three.

18.3 Ongoing contrastless bliss

We have already reviewed in 18.1 the four strong expressions associated with an enlightenment experience. There is also the claim that accompanying such experiences and views is the experience of ongoing bliss, or ongoing states of high pleasure. Not much more needs to be said here about this claim, nor about this experience, since these claims were reviewed in Chapter Sixteen. The claims are clear enough from that treatment.

As already mentioned, the claim that ongoing (contrastless) bliss experience is possible, and sometimes occurs, does not conflict with acceptance of phystriology. Once again, this is important to note for the coming examination of attempts to integrate spirituality with phystriology.

18.4 Mystical ascent versus triple philosophical mysticism

As has already been mentioned, the traditional interpretation of philosophical mysticism, according to which the philosophical mystic ascends to a higher non-gross physical level and therein experiences mystical union, is rejected by acceptance of phystriology. At the same time, the esoteric content of spirituality need not be interpreted this way. One way of expressing the difference (though there are some perspectives in which this way presents difficulties) is to say that this approach is triple, not unitary, and involves no ontological ascent; it includes (a) philosophical mysticism as expressed in sayings such as "I am the All," or "There is Nothing," (b) the experience of something like *ch'i* circulation or Divine Light, and (c) the experience of ongoing bliss or high pleasure without contrast values. It is because these two latter aspects of esoteric spirituality, (b) and (c), have no definite inconsistency with phystriology that they were not included in the eight views logically rejected by acceptance of phystriology. They are, however, included here, because they are central features associated with philosophical mysticism. Accordingly, it is only the intellectual expression of philosophical mysticism that has a traditional interpretation that goes against acceptance of phystriology. Whether there is a non-traditional interpretation of philosophical mysticism needs to be discovered; so, too, whether experience of *ch'i* circulation occurs; and whether ongoing contrastless bliss occurs also needs to be investigated. These will be explored in Chapter Twenty Two in more detail than elsewhere.

18.5 The big question remains

We are now ready to see what the responses are to the important clash between the results of natural science of the last few centuries, and the religious or spiritual beliefs accompanying literalist systems in a well-defined way, and accompanying moderate or pluralist systems as options.

One might want to hold the moderate or pluralist option as a sufficient softener within taking the pro-religion or pro-spirituality approach. But (once again) what prevents there being such a 'softening' path is that the phystriology result rejects *all* eight (or nine) of the views each of which is logically inconsistent with phystriology – the interactive God at the human scale, the afterlife, the strong physics overturning freedom, the hidden reward/punishment system, the non-physical or subtly physical mentally caused parapsychological events, the mystic ascent to the higher non-physical or subtly physical realm, interactive dualism, and emanationism. Phystriology also rejects the basic purposes of process theology. And phystriology strongly ampliatively (not strictly logically) rejects the existence of the personal God, of basic purposes, and so on. Consequently, to many at least, it will seem that no adequate option within the pro-religion or pro-spirituality system remains. This is the big question we want to look at in the next part of the book: does phystriology result in the entire rejection of religious/spiritual traditions, both literalist and moderate?

Part III
Chapter Nineteen: The Problem and the First Response

19.0 The Problem

We are facing a striking problem: There is a big gap between the integrated results of the natural sciences, on the one hand, and, on the other hand, the claims made, at one time or another, by the proponents of spirituality including the proponents of religion. And the challenge is as strong to proponents of moderate religion or spirituality as to proponents of fundamentalist or literalist religion. The natural sciences of physics, chemistry, and biology have resulted in the view that the smallest physical things interact without inherent purposes, and that there is no overturning of the rules, laws, or forces of physics. We call this view *phystriology*.

According to phystriology, every biological change that an organism goes through is a change of molecular or physical structure, according to the rules, laws, or forces of chemical and physics-based changes, and that every chemical change is a change of (primarily) electromagnetic relations between subatomic particles. The changes among subatomic particles are without inherent purposes, and are governed by highly abstract mathematical formulas based, typically, on symmetry principles. So the purposes that psychological beings like human beings apparently have occur in sums, and, as a matter of fact, in entities that are, or have underlying, natural selectively evolutionarily produced sums, of inherently purposeless events in nature.

It follows that all eight (or nine) claims, one or more of which is found (and usually many of which are found) in any religious belief system and any system of spiritual belief, must be false. Otherwise we'd allow logical inconsistency into our belief system, and we don't want to do that. Phystriology is logically inconsistent with belief in an interactive God at the human scale, an afterlife, a strong form of human freedom, a system of hidden cosmic reward and punishment, the existence of mind-over-matter paranormal or parapsychological relations, belief in a mystical realm over and above the grossly physical realm to which mystics ascend, what has been called 'interactive dualism', and what has been called 'emanationism'. We could also include process theology. In addition, many religious or spiritual views are not strictly logically but strongly rejected by phystriology, such as the existence of the personal God and the existence of a supernatural intelligence.

How do we respond to this enormously strong challenge that the natural sciences pose against religion and spirituality? There is a very strong relationship – in many cases a logical conflict relationship, and in other cases a not strictly logical but still a very strong conflict relationship – between natural science and much of what's included in spirituality. It is time now to look at the efforts to deal with this problem, both a logical problem and a not-strictly-logical, but strong, problem. That is what we will do in part III of this book.

The first response is to say that there is no adequate resolution to the problem other than rejection of religion and spirituality and acceptance of the non-religious, non-spirituality point of view. This chapter overviews this response. The response is usually given without specific reference to phystriology, but, for convenience, we will take the first response to be an explicitly phystriological response.

In the subsequent three chapters we will be interested in three other positions, positions which, aside from narrow fundamentalism or literalism, are the only other positions responding to the challenge that there are; and these three other positions do attempt to integrate results of recent natural science and religion or spirituality.

In the last chapter of the book, we will also look at an approach to the problem that would work no matter which of the four responses, or any other response, is adopted. According to this last approach to the problem, it is possible to have secular cultivation of what can be called spirituality, where spirituality is meant in its most general sense, an appreciative condition. A secular institution promoting the cultivation of appreciation-spirituality would be equally open to exponents of any views about science or spirituality (including views against any religious-ish spirituality, and including literalist views as well).

Let us come back now to the view we are considering for the rest of this chapter (except the last brief section), namely, that accepting phystriology more or less requires rejection of religion or spirituality.

19.1 The development of religious humanism

The view that we should reject religion or spirituality in favor of the results of the natural sciences is strongly associated with recent secular humanism. But the humanist movement, in general, began many centuries ago as a drive within a highly religious world for a touch more rationalism in those views. Human values were to be emphasized as opposed to the outcomes of authorities with a supposed mandate from a Divinely ordained (and old) tradition.

This can be seen in the most ancient humanists, for instance, in Confucius, who, as we saw in 12.5, did not explicitly teach about worshipping the spirits of the ancestors. Another example would be the teachings of the Greek Epicurus (342 – 270 BCE) who maintained that there was no afterlife, or no afterlife being who had some form of sensory input. A third would be the teachings of the Hellenist, Lucretius, (96 c. – 55 BCE), who adopted a similar position.

This can also be seen as a part of the protestantism of Protestantism. The humanists of the 15th, and 16th centuries, for instance, were people whom we would now regard as deeply religious folk, including, Giovanni Pico dela Mirandola, Erasmus, and Sir Thomas More.

19.2 The development of non-religious humanism

But as humanism developed it also allowed for the expression of those who wanted to reject religions, thinking religions to be inappropriate systems. Religious systems were sometimes regarded as systems that ignored the scientific method, and that claimed to be recipients of a revelation (a message from a supernatural source) that in some respects at least could not be rationally supported. That religious systems were held to be *in some respects rational* (that *some* doctrines of religions were rationally provable) and, in other respects, revelatory, is common among many theologians. (Thomas Aquinas, for instance, an out-and-out religionist, canonized by the Roman Catholic Church, and the thirteenth century architect of many positions often accepted since his time as central in articulations of the Christian worldview, maintained that many of the main views of Christianity could be supported by reason, but other rather important views, such as that the sacrifice of Jesus would effect human salvation, could not be and should be accepted on evidence-less faith.) The anti-religious humanists of the last three or so centuries wanted to counter the supposedly rational religious claims by presenting other reasons that go against the supposedly rational proofs. They also wanted to reject the revelatory claims; they regarded 'mere revelation' as an inadequate method to arrive at justifiable belief.

Some whose whole systems were based on elaborate argumentation were more or less on the borderline between being religious and being irreligious in the content of the system. Benedict Spinoza (1632 – 1677) may be regarded as having been on that borderline. He argued in his main work, the *Ethics* (posthumously published, since he was unwilling to release it in his own lifetime other than by manuscript to a very few individual readers, because of risk-factors generated by some its contents, denying that a personal God exists, for instance) that there is only one instance of a substance or true being. And he thought this being was God or Nature. A human being, and other everyday objects are, he said, merely modes (many think that modes are properties) of the one substance, God or Nature.

Some leaned toward vitriolic laughter about religious absurdities. Voltaire (the pseudonym of Francois Marie Arouet) (1694 – 1778) wrote many works poking bitter fun at religious ideas. Others were skeptical about God and substance. David Hume (1711 – 1776), for instance, a Scottish philosopher, wrote deeply inquiring, in fact, skeptical, works about religious views and some philosophical and some ordinary views.

But some rejected, or seemed to reject, the religious approach to reality altogether. Paul Henri D'Holbach (1723 – 1789), for instance, did so. And by the 19th century, some explicitly did so, including Friedrich Nietzsche (1844 – 1900), who is famous for having said via his character Zarathustra, "Has he not heard that God is dead?" (in *Thus Spake Zarathustra*). He wanted people to give up Christianity and other, similar, religions and to transform living so that one strived to be an 'Over-being,' or a 'Super-Being,' (an 'Übermensch').

9.3 The organization of non-religious or secular humanism

The first organizations of humanists were formed in the 19th century. By the 20th century, the atheist or non-theist humanists were organizing more frequently. Some of these began by thinking of humanism as a sort of religion. But by 1941 the American Humanist Association had been formed. It took a distinctly non-religious, and non-spiritual (meaning not religious-ish) line on things. In general, we can regard those who say that they are secular humanists as exponents of non-religion and non-spirituality where 'spirituality' means a religious-ish condition.

In April/May, 1976, there was a conference in State University of New York at Buffalo, which founded the Committee for the Scientific Investigation of Claims of the Paranormal. There are, then, two types of secular humanists, those particularly involved in the social non-religious non-spiritual organizations – often called 'the humanists', and those involved in the skeptical (inquiring) investigation of revelatory or pseudo-scientific claims – often called 'the skeptics.'[1] For convenience, we will include both in 'secular humanists.'

Secular humanists explicitly refer to the need for use of the scientific method (meant very broadly) in the development of justifiable views about things. Accordingly, there is ground for a strong support for physriology among secular humanists, and secular humanists would typically be disposed to fully accept physriology. We have noted that that acceptance logically requires the rejection of the eight (or nine) views mentioned in 19.0 (and reviewed many times earlier in this exposition), and also that physriology not strictly logically but strongly rejects other religious views. For that reason among others, secular humanists would tend to reject religion and spirituality.

19.4 The philosophical anti-religion/spirituality movement

We should also note that many philosophers over the last hundred years or so have been eager to reject religions and spirituality for the apparent lack of scientific methodology behind those movements and for the revelatory claims associated with religions and spirituality. As mentioned, the philosophers opposed to religions and spirituality movements reject the supposedly rational proofs as fallacious, and reject the revelatory claims as mere superstition.

---

[1] It is important to remember that 'skeptic' can mean either 'philosophical skeptic' who may be local or global in directing skeptical questions; or 'scientific skeptic' who is always local, and always looking at claims of paranormal or parapsychological events. As the term was just used, 'the skeptics' means 'the scientific skeptics.'

One such philosopher, who worked primarily in the first half of the 20th century, was Bertrand Russell. His anthology book *Why I Am Not A Christian* has been highly influential. He argued there against both the supposedly rationally defended claims in religion, and the non-rational or revelatory claims. One of the sources of appeal of Russell's approach is that Russell regarded himself as having the attitude of a mystic, while he also rejected the intellectual component of the various forms of mysticism. The development of the mystical attitude was personal for Russell. An account of a rapid transition in his attitudes is described in his autobiography. After being exposed to the deep pain of a friend, he said,

> Within five minutes, I went through some such reflections as the following: the loneliness of the human soul is unendurable; nothing can penetrate it except the highest intensity of the sort of love that religious teachers have preached; whatever does not spring from this motive is harmful, or at best useless; it follows that war is wrong, that a public school education is abominable, that the use of force is to be deprecated, and that in human relations one should penetrate to the core of loneliness in each person and speak to that.[2]

And shortly afterwards, he said, "At the end of those five minutes, I had become a completely different person. For a time, a sort of mystic illumination possessed me."[3] Russell, unsurprisingly, investigated the nature of mystical experience and belief. His view was that mystics accept (1) intuitive insight or revelation rather than sense, reason, and analysis; (2) that there is a unity beyond any divisions; (3) that time is unreal; and (4) that evil is mere appearance. He went on to show his many reasons for preferring sense, reason, and analysis over intuitive insight or revelation, the need for plural analyses over the impulse to an undivided unity, that although we should abandon certain irrational asymmetries in our experiences of time, we should continue to use temporal notions in our thinking, and that although belief in universal love and joy are important, these are moral notions and do not reflect the ultimate realities. "Good and bad, and even the higher good that mysticism finds everywhere, are reflections of our own emotions on

---

[2] Bertrand Russell, *The Autobiography of Bertrand Russell: 1872-1914:* 234.

[3] Bertrand Russell, *ibid:* 235.

other things not part of the substance of things as they are in themselves."[4]

Russell's notion, then, is that mysticism is, like other moral notions, based on an emotional attitude. Mysticism, he says or implies, like other moral notions, does not support rational or intellectual views, nor is it supported by rational or intellectual views, of how the world is in itself. Russell's opposition to religious views, then, is based both on reasons to reject the existence of God, the afterlife, and so on, and also on his more broad rejection of the notion that moral views reflect ultimate realities in the world. But he did have attitudes that we would often call moral attitudes, and, more particularly, mystical attitudes; and this combination, together with his verve and brilliance, was inspiring to many.

Other well known advocates of humanistic anti-religion are A. J. Ayer and Anthony Flew. In *The Humanist Outlook*,[5] Ayer showed that morality cannot be justified on a religious basis; there must be an independent source of the views of what is moral and what isn't. Ayer also maintained that moral propositions are neither true nor false; they are, rather expressions of attitudes. Anthony Flew has articulated many defenses of the atheist position, including the defense that atheism is to be assumed to be true unless it is shown to be false.[6]

Another thinker who has exposed something close to the phystriological point of view, a more recent thinker, is Paul Kurtz. He has written showing the difficulties in religious and paranormal beliefs, and has also participated in a central way in forming humanistic organizations.

Still another thinker, Daniel Dennett, has written a number of books suggesting the reasonableness of rejecting religion and arguing for the incorporation of religious views and attitudes into the objects of scientific study. Dennett's 1995 book *Darwin's Dangerous Idea* is by no means about religion *per se*; nonetheless, it not only makes reference to

---

[4] Bertrand Russell, *Mysticism and Logic*, London: Unwin Books 1974 [1917]: 27.

[5] A. J. Ayer, *The Humanist Outlook*, 1968, quoted in *Humanist Anthology*, ed. Margaret Knight, revised by Jim Herrick, London: Rationalist Press Association [1961] 1995.

[6] Anthony Flew in *The Presumption of Atheism*. Anthony Flew's recent remarks on a new openness to an afterlife were ambiguous; but to some extent they show his lack of absorption of the physically complete picture of the world.

the obvious conflict between Darwinism and creationism (the view that the world was created by God more or less as recorded in the book of Genesis), but also maintains that "Darwin's dangerous idea cuts much deeper into the fabric of our most fundamental beliefs than many of its sophisticated apologists have yet admitted, even to themselves."[7] Dennett's more recent *Breaking the Spell*, 2006, is explicitly about breaking the spell that holds it to be taboo to put religious views and attitudes into the scientific worldview. Many readers, however, would come to the conclusion that putting it into that scientific worldview will also break a different sort of spell, the spell of religion itself. Dennett makes remarks suggesting that had he been in a different cultural environment he might have been more outspoken in that way. He frequently mentioned his caution, a caution he took because, he said, he was working in the Unites States, where there are heavy pressures on public figures in regard to religious matters.

A more forthright author against religion, and, we might add, against spirituality (in our sense), though not a philosopher, but rather, a biologist, is Richard Dawkins. Dawkins' 2006 work, *The God Delusion*, pits the reasons for religion against the reasons to reject religion, and argues vociferously for such rejection. It is interesting to note that Dawkins is not explicit about what has been called physical closure since the 1960's, physical completeness since the 1990's, and is here being called phystriology. There is only one point in which a comparable position is taken, namely, that complexity comes about neither by mere chance nor by conscious design.[8] It is the lack of a suitable defense for the idea that complexity comes about either by mere chance or by conscious design that reflects the physically complete or phystriological result. Phystriology, of course, includes the notion that if there are any purposive beings, these purposive beings, including human beings, would be highly complex beings whose doings would be evolutionarily-produced sums of the goings-on of tiny non-purposively interacting physical particles or things.

Nonetheless, it is, as mentioned, interesting, and, not only that, it is indicative, that Dawkins does not mention physical closure (phystriology), nor its straightforward logical implications, nor its straightforward not strictly logical yet strong implications. Yet Dawkins is

---

[7] Daniel Dennett, *Darwin's Dangerous Idea*: 18.

[8] Richard Dawkins, *The God Delusion*: 113-4.

a fully read biologist. This indicates the need to explain why philosophers, who've known about physical closure (phystriology) for a long time, have been so quiet about getting the result known in the non-philosophical community. That, however, is a digression at this point. (The question will be taken up in Appendix 1).

Returning to the main point, we can observe that the Darwinian revolution has been thought to show grounds to reject the religious view. In what is here being represented as the accurate line to take, the Darwinian revolution ampliatively, but still modestly, suggested the anti-religious view. According to many thinkers, though, it did not ampliatively reject religion since it was logically open on vitalism, on British Emergentism, on William James's form of fideism, and, some would add, it was logically open on ontological interactive (or Cartesian) dualism. However, the revolution of phystriology, reached evidentially in one way of looking at it by about 1970, logically excluded the God who interacts with the world at the human or classical scale, the afterlife, and the others of the eight (or nine) views frequently mentioned, and given, for example, in 19.0. And phystriology strongly, though not strictly logically, rejects other views, such as that a personal God exists. And so those thinkers since the 1970's who have rejected religion have been at least subconsciously or semi-consciously influenced by the widespread acceptance of phystriology among philosophers who have, among other things, put together the physics, chemistry, and biology results.

For convenience, we can take the recent humanist and anti-religious, anti-spirituality views to be views as though developed through the recognition of phystriology. This may be slightly inaccurate, but that doesn't matter much to the task at hand.

19.5 What the recent humanist and anti-religion/spirituality movements may be ignoring

There is at least one position that the recent humanist and anti-religious/anti-spirituality movements seem to be ignoring. I will call this the 'natural scientific traditional religion/spirituality' response.[9] It seems

---

[9] '[T]raditional' is needed to distinguish the topic of the next Chapter from any topic that would include Sir Julian Huxley's view that humanism opens the door to a sort of new religion. That humanistic new sort of religion would not be a traditional religion or spirituality system. It can be seen as more affiliated with the 'reject the religions' views covered in this Chapter than with the views

necessary to review the natural scientific traditional religion/spirituality response to the conflict, and I will do that in the next Chapter. Those who reject traditional religion/spirituality on the grounds of recent scientific results should notice that the natural-scientific view of traditional religion/spirituality seeks to re-interpret canonical religious or spiritual texts so as to allow religion or spirituality to be consistent with the recent results of natural science.

There is another group of views, which I will label together as the 'it's all okay' group, to be discussed in Chapter Twenty One, which also needs to be reviewed. There is an implicit rejection of this group of views among the humanists and philosophical anti-religion/anti-spirituality exponents. Still, though, the issues need to be made a touch more explicit than they sometimes are.

And there is still another position, the mystical naturalist position, that I will then explore in Chapter Twenty Two.

Thus, as was earlier mentioned in 19.0, there are, in total, aside from any literalism, four positions that may be taken on the conflict between phystriology and religion/spirituality. I am putting aside the literalist position on account of what I take to be its implausibility: there are the many contradictions between different literalist views; there is no evidence for many views included in any one of them – each is revelatory in crucial doctrines; and, in addition, because they all go against phystriology. Someone might try to make out a pluralist literalism; but that position also seems to be not viable, for reasons just mentioned, and so I will ignore it. Finally, it is worth mentioning again that all responses – all four responses, or five, if literalism is included, and any other responses – come into play in the material of Chapter Twenty Three, which suggests a way for there to be a secular wisdom cultivating institution. In a secular wisdom cultivating institution none of the available positions would be institutionally rejected at all. The institution would welcome people of all available views as equal practitioners in the events of the institution.

---

covered in the next Chapter. But that is a subtle judgmental matter. Huxley's views may be on the border between the 'reject religions' view and the 'radically reinterpret religions' view.

Chapter Twenty: The Natural-scientific Religion/Spirituality View

20.0 The natural scientific religion/spirituality view adopts the easiest harmonization of spirituality/religion and phystriology that there can be. It fully accepts the view that hundreds of years of natural scientific work have resulted in a major change in our understanding of the natural world; *effectively*, this can be taken to mean that hundreds of years of natural scientific work have resulted in the phystriological picture of the world, the picture of the world in which small physical things have no inherent purposes, are governed by abstract mathematics, and there is no overturning of the rules, laws, or forces of physics. There is a bit added by that 'effectively,' namely, the specifics of the phystriological picture of the world, but that bit added seems to be fully consistent with the intent of the main natural-science authors, and so that addition will be adopted as an assumption.

At the same time, say the proponents of the natural-scientific attitude toward religions and spirituality, the natural-scientific approach to religion/spirituality allows traditional religious rituals, institutions, and central dogmas to be used more or less as they have been used, so long as they are interpreted in a natural-scientific manner, which means, here, in a phystriological manner. Just as religion/spirituality has adapted in many ways in the past (for instance, many forms of religion have accommodated Darwinian naturally selective evolution), so, too, according to proponents of natural-scientific religion or spirituality, religion or spirituality needs now to adapt in an equally strong way in the present, or, perhaps, an even stronger way in the present than it had to in the past.

All the viewpoints associated with a physically *incomplete* world must be given up. If one asks whether there is an interactive God at the human scale, an afterlife, a strong form of physics-overturning freedom, a hidden system of cosmic reward and punishment, and so on, the answer is, and must be, "No. The world doesn't work that way." The response can also be expressed more explicitly in terms of phystriology, saying something like, "All those views require that the world be physically incomplete. But the world is not physically incomplete. That has been established. Therefore, none of those views is correct." Questions will arise: "What do you mean, it has been established that the world is not physically incomplete?" and answers can be given. The ideas that there is no Providential higher power, no afterlife, and so on, are difficult to absorb, but they can be, gently, absorbed, according to the proponents of natural-scientific religion or spirituality.

However, the natural-scientific religion/spirituality view goes on to say that, "Just because all those views are incorrect does not mean that we must give up on religion or we must give up on attitudes that have been called spiritual attitudes. We can re-think the dogmas, doctrines or teachings that have traditionally been associated with religion and spirituality; we can re-interpret the traditional liturgies, rituals, affirmations, and so on, that we find in religious systems and systems upholding some form of spirituality. We will let those new forms arising from such re-interpretations become our new forms of religion and spirituality."

It seems to me that there were some anticipators of natural-scientific religion/spirituality prior to the 1970's and 1980's, and after that time, there have been two main implementations of something close to the natural-scientific religion/spirituality just described. I will mention two anticipators of the natural-scientific religion/spirituality view, and then, more centrally, I will review the two main recent, though different, expressions of the view that can be called natural-scientific religion/spirituality: those of Ralph Burhoe, and Willem Drees. And here, for good measure, as mentioned, we insert the specifics of phystriology into the natural scientific religion/spirituality view.

20.1 Two anticipators of natural-scientific religion/spirituality

In the first half of the 20th century, the Jewish theologian Mordecai Kaplan pioneered a form of Judaism in which belief in an interactive God was explicitly ruled out. "There is no God in the skies" was one quick way of putting Kaplan's important notion. Rather, according to Kaplan, all Jewish customs, traditions, rituals, stories, literature, and so on, were changing parts of a vast civilization that always had been changing and evolving. He also held that it is up to each individual to discover those rituals that are meaningful to that individual, and to engage in those rituals on account of their personal meaning. The Jewish law was not regarded as given as an authoritative system by God to Moses and from Moses to Joshua, and so on. Rather, the law was regarded as the expression of the leaders of the people from time to time as to how society should be organized. Kaplan was acutely aware of the changes brought about by the scientific revolutions beginning in the 17th century and continuing through till the time of his major investigations and writings in the first half of the 20th century. Kaplan took it that 'God' means the sum of all natural processes that allow for human fulfillment. Some interpret 'God' in Kaplan's system to mean the highest moral values, and some take those values to have a sort of independent existence.

In any case, though, returning to the development of Kaplan's thought, Kaplan died at the age of one hundred and two in 1983. He could have been clearly in touch with phystriology in the last decade or two of his life, but his main philosophical-theological work, *Judaism as a Civilization*, was written in the 1930's, and so his philosophy, and his movement in Judaism (Reconstruction Judaism) will be regarded here as a precursor of the natural-scientific religion/spirituality position.

In Christianity, a central theological view was espoused by Paul Tillich (1886-1965). According to Paul Tillich, God is the ground of being; every finite being with psychological states (including, in Tillich's view, each human being) is situated between the ground of being, which is beyond existence and non-existence, and the everyday finite realities. Hence, for Tillich, there is a source for religious and spiritual attitudes: the source is the yearning to orient toward the ground of being. For Tillich, the dogmas of a religious system can only be taken lightly. There is no authoritative source of religious revelation; all religious systems are metaphoric expressions of a human being's yearning to go beyond the finite to that which is beyond existence and non-existence. Uses of the term 'God', therefore, in Tillich's approach, point to what lies beyond metaphor and straightforward belief. We cannot see 'God' as a being (among beings) in any meaningful way at all, and the idea of Christ can be taken as an emblem of what a human being aspires to. Tillich's book, *The Courage To Be*, presented in the early 1950's, takes the view that it is idolatrous to take God to be a supreme Being among beings. Some would say that such a strong integration of existentialism and theology was, in some way, influenced by the scientific worldview. However, nowhere in Tillich's writings is there clear articulation of the implications of the natural-scientific world-view for the afterlife, and the others of the views rejected by phystriology. Accordingly, Tillich will be regarded here as an anticipator of the natural scientific religious view, though it is, to some extent, unclear whether he consciously anticipated that view.

One could undoubtedly go through many other examples, as well, of precursors or anticipators of the natural-science religious approach. However, the anticipators of phystriology went through their strongest development before, as it would generally be put, the time of completion of the evidence for phystriology. It is now many decades after the end of the usual gathering of the main evidence for phystriology, and so there is no need to further assemble the *anticipators* of the natural-science religion or spirituality view.

20.2 Ralph Burhoe's natural-scientific religion/spirituality view

Ralph Burhoe (1911-1997) was moved by two convictions: first, that scientific views and religious views must be compatible; and, second, that natural selection evolutionary science should not only be retained, but also that it should inspire positive religious and spiritual attitudes. If the naturally selective evolutionary process is itself a foundation of the way things take place in nature, then, one way or another, we can find the grains of religious or spiritual understanding in the natural worldview, or in a way that harmonizes with the natural worldview.

In Burhoe's view (as in everyone's view), there is a big difference between the behaviour of humans and that of other creatures. Burhoe emphasizes how in humans there is the potential for non-kin altruistic behaviour; it is this potential that shows the striking possibilities for human beings that are absent in other creatures, including the nearest apes and monkeys. The nearest apes and monkeys, like many other mammals, sometimes show altruistic kin or in-group behaviour, but not altruistic non-kin or non-in-group behaviour. Burhoe takes it that humans natural selectively evolved and that human languages, religions, and cultural forms give humans the abilities to behave and experience in ways that other animals cannot, including to engage in altruistic non-kin and non-in-group behaviour. There is, then, a sort of complementarity between the natural scientific evolutionary viewpoint, and the view that religion and other cultural forms give a unique capacity to human beings.

Of course some would emphasize that it is not uniquely religion that gives human beings these capacities; rather, some would say, it is the capacity for love – evolutionarily explicable – together with the capacity for language and cognition, also evolutionarily explicable – that gives rise to the capacity for recognition of all sentient beings as beings that can be humanly loved or valued. Religious systems may be the vehicle through which some, most, or even all, humans in the past acquired the capacity for non-kin or non-in-group altruism; but, some would say, it was non-religious factors that explain the development of such religious systems and that explain the unique capacities of human beings. They would say that the main non-religious factors would have been cognition and human emotional dispositions.

Some would also say that it is the capacity for cognition that gives ground for a strong form of philosophical skepticism; this would undo *one side* of the human capacity for non-kin, non-in-group altruistic attitudes, namely, the explicit expression of positive moral statements. However, *the other side* of the human capacity for non-kin, non-in-group altruistic attitudes would remain, namely, the behavioral side. And that would or could sustain Burhoe's project.

In any case, Burhoe's views accepted the natural scientific position. One would suspect that had he been clearly aware of the notion of phystriology he may well have accepted it. In fact, if we survey the main theses rejected by phystriology, we will not find any that is specifically endorsed by Burhoe. This strengthens the interpretation of Burhoe's position as one of natural-scientific religion and spirituality.

How, then, can religious or spiritual systems continue? Let us interpret Burhoe's position in as strong a way as it can be interpreted. Let us suppose, then, that in Burhoe's view, there is no interactive God at the human scale, nor, for ampliative reasons, is there an interactive God at the quantum scale, nor, more generally, is there a personal God or a supernatural intelligence. Also, there is no afterlife, no physics-overturning freedom, no hidden cosmic reward/punishment system, no mind-over-matter paranormal phenomena, no mystical ascent beyond the (gross) physical world, and no interactive dualism nor emanationism. How, then, in Burhoe's view, can a religious or spiritual system continue?

In Burhoe's view, first, one can find parallels between ancient religious notions and contemporary religious notions. Parallels, for instance, between some of Paul's views and the modern scientific views, Burhoe says, can be found.[10] Other parallels between the scientific view

---

[10] Ralph Burhoe, *Toward A Scientific Theology*: 22.

of natural selection, and various religious views are also pointed out.[11] Second, Burhoe uses the language of old-fashioned theology in indicating what lies behind the natural picture. For instance, he says "I see modern science as a new gift of revelation about the not-readily-discernible total reality which is our Creator and the Lord of our History – the larger environing reality that brought us into being and in which we live and move and have our being".[12] Burhoe's use of a term like 'a new gift of revelation' will be disturbing to some; he seems to be opening the door to unwelcome interpretations. Also, Burhoe is willing to think of the God behind the world in a somewhat intentional or subtly purposive manner: the "full meaning-purpose, and hope…are not…readily discernible by unaided common sense."[13] A more strict natural-scientific view might not agree with the last comment. Rather, it seems, the full acceptance of phystriology would, as I earlier stated, lead to thinking of the hidden meaning-purposes as a 'clutching at a straw' notion or a 'God of the gaps' where no gaps even exist. Third, Burhoe wants terms like 'God' and 'soul' to be used as symbols, somewhat metaphoric, one might add, in our interpretations of the world.[14] This enables traditional customs, rituals, liturgical affirmations, and so on, to be re-interpreted in accordance with modern scientific attitudes. This is evident, for instance, in Burhoe's view that "*God* [italicized by Burhoe to show that this is not the ordinary use of the term] is gracious to man; that is, without any merit on man's part, man has been raised up from the dust and perennially sustained and redeemed from his errancy and given the opportunity to be a conscious cocreator of *god's* evolving Kingdom of Life as long as man seeks, finds, and executes *god's* requirements."[15] In many passages, Burhoe interprets the natural system itself as an indicator of the Divine Nature.

It seems to me that two points are clear: First, the metaphoric discussion of God's grace, even italicized as *God's* grace or *god's* grace, in relation to human errancy, sounds so ambiguous that it may not be clear to many readers what Burhoe is saying in a more literal manner. Second, there is no explicit articulation in Burhoe's writings of what must be

---

[11] *Ibid*: 73-111.

[12] *Ibid.*: 22-3.

[13] *Ibid*: 23.

[14] *Ibid*: 117.

[15] *Ibid*: 125.

given up if the natural scientific results are to be fully incorporated into the religious/spiritual view of the world. That is, Burhoe's writings do not list the views to be rejected by the results of the last few centuries of the natural sciences. It is not surprising that this is so. Many of Burhoe's works were produced in the 1960's and 1970's, and so it is not to be expected that they would be fully informed of the phystriology result.

Some, therefore, would rather place Burhoe's views on the borderline between anticipation of phystriology and articulation of it. Alternatively, some would rather place Burhoe's views on the borderline between the natural-scientific approach to the problem, and the 'let science keep up with religion/spirituality' approach to the problem. That placement is consistent with Burhoe's willingness to say "sufficient unto the next millennium are the problems thereof,"[16] while not being aware of the details of phystriology, nor being willing to clearly say that however the problems of the next millennium are worked out – including the possibility that the thinkers in the next millennium will accept the eventual very long term (millions or billions of years) undoing of consciousness by entropy – that would be all right for the consistency of science and religion.

There are, then, several ways in which one wants to have a slightly clearer exponent of natural-science religion and spirituality. Perhaps Willem Drees is such a clearer exponent.

20.3 Willem Drees' natural-scientific view of religion

Another implementation of the natural-scientific approach to religion/spirituality is that of Willem Drees, centrally explained, for example, in *Religion, Science, and Naturalism*. Drees wants to accept the contemporary scientific view, and to do so in an entirely uncompromising way. As he puts it, "We need a view of science which avoids understatement as well as overstatement."[17] At the same time, Drees' position on the many views to be rejected by phystriology is not always clear. On the rejection of the non-physical or subtly physical mind created parapsychological phenomena, Drees says that such "rejection is not beyond dispute."[18] It's obvious that there are disputes; but such a

---

[16] *Ibid.* 133.

[17] *Ibid.* 237.

[18] Drees, *Religion, Science, Naturalism*: 242.

remark seems to endorse the grounds on both sides of the dispute, which is not entirely consistent with phystriology. Here, too, as with Burhoe's remarks, Drees' position is not as clear as one might hope it to be, even though Drees later disparages astrology, parapsychology, and so on.[19]

At the same time, he wants sciences that have "consistency, precision, fertility, avoidance of *ad hoc*-elements, and coherence with other knowledge."[20] This leads me to conclude that he is or should be willing to go as far as to accept the phystriological picture of the world.

In Drees' view, there are two key realms: the realm revealed by natural scientific study, and the realm of the transcendent, that which is not to be absorbed into the natural scientific view. It is the realm of the transcendent which somehow exhibits the notion of God. Once again, then, we accept the strongest interpretation of Drees' views – an interpretation in some ways indicated in his writings (for instance, he is against the interactivity of God[21]). According to this interpretation, and there may be a bit of injection or addition into Drees' position, there is no interactive God, no personal God, no conscious afterlife, no physics-overturning human freedom, and so on. Still, though, there is the transcendent realm, and, in Drees' view, we can, and would do well to, orient toward the transcendent realm. Such orientation is the exercising of the religious/spiritual attitude. And, he says, it can be done in religious systems.

Drees is himself, like Burhoe, a Christian, and interprets the traditional liturgies in such a way as to render them consistent with the natural scientific view of the world, and as to take them to indicate a somehow transcendent view. That involves jumping through a few hoops. But there is no obstacle toward such jumping. And phystriology does not itself deny that there is a realm inaccessible to the natural scientific view of the world. It is that realm toward which one orients in exercising the religious/spiritual attitudes. Drees provides reasons to think that there is such a realm.

How does one reach toward the transcendent realm? Drees first expounds many features of the natural world of space and time. Still, he says, one may also inquire into the nature of the Whole. This sort of

---

[19] *Ibid.* 243.

[20] *Ibid.* 243.

[21] *Ibid.* 248.

question brings one to what he calls the Limit Questions, questions about the Whole, about why there is something rather than nothing, about the order found in the natural world, and about the references between current conditions and the apparently fine-tuned initial conditions in our world. Pondering such questions itself does not yet integrate with religious or spiritual exercise, he says,[22] and so he goes on to describe how, he thinks, there can be an integration of contemporary natural science with religious and spiritual attitudes expressed in traditional cultural environments, such as a church, synagogue, mosque and so on.

Drees takes it that humans have limited initial cultural contexts, and that humans also are 'wandering and wondering' beings who expand their limited contextual ranges. In doing so, they can take the traditional customs, rituals, and myths and interpretively expand the context from literal beliefs in what is expressed to other beliefs consistent with current natural science. He says, for example, "I have found elements of value in this tradition [liberal Protestantism strongly influenced by the European Enlightenment] – in most of its parables and in some of its hymns, in a few of its representatives and in many articulations of ideals of justice nourished by it."[23] There is clear reference to a good deal of selectivity in response to the tradition in which Drees is situated. Although traditions change, they have aspects that are still worth preserving, according to Drees, because those aspects are "useful and powerful."[24]

When summarizing his integration of religious traditions with humans' capacity for inquiry into limit questions, Drees emphasizes a concern with mystery[25] and the apparent endless unclarity of the limit issues.[26] Bring the traditions together with a sense of mystery, says Drees, and there will not only be mystery, but also a sense of gratitude (or something like gratitude) in regard to one's existence. Perhaps there is, he says, a touch of mysticism in this, but that is not to be dismissed. In this way, we can see that Drees continues to articulate a way in which one could hold to phystriology, and still affirm somewhat traditional forms of religious or spiritual practice.

---

[22] *Ibid.* 274.

[23] *Ibid.* 277.

[24] *Ibid.* 278.

[25] *Ibid.* 280.

[26] *Ibid.* 281.

20.4 Natural scientific religion/spirituality re traditional religion/spirituality

We'll now note some key features of the relation between a natural-scientific approach to a religion or spirituality system and the traditional or somewhat traditional religious or spirituality systems. First, neither Burhoe nor Drees has a clear discussion about phystriology. This is a mild defect in both systems, though both authors, Drees especially, seem to be prepared to fully accept the results. Still, it can be complained that what has to be given up by acceptance of phystriology is not as clear and explicit as it should be.

Second, the central experiential features of the natural scientific religion/spirituality view are not unique to those favorable to religion or spirituality. This is a more important critical point. Burhoe's view that the scientific view of the world embodies deep mysteries is echoed, for example, in Chet Raymo's writings[27], yet Raymo is not writing in defense of religious systems, but, rather, for a merely science-based attitude of wonder and sense of mystery. A similar point can be made about Drees' views. Drees emphasizes the value of the sense of mystery,[28] but having a sense of awe and mystery at the glories of the universe is not found only in exponents of religion/spirituality.

Paul Kurtz, for example, who is, as we saw in the last Chapter, one of our time's central exponents of secular humanism (a view not in favour of religion nor of what is generally called spirituality) is very much in favor of art, literature, poetry, and science. He is a great defender of these forms of expression; and it is obvious that in much poetry, art, literature, and so on, there is a celebration of the mysteries of existence. Kurtz celebrated George Santayana, who, while "teaching at Harvard during it's Golden Age, one morning…reputedly observed, 'Gentlemen, it's spring,' and left the classroom never to return."[29] This reminds one of Whitman's well known work 'When I Heard the Learned Astronomer':

When I heard the learned astronomer,

When the proofs, the figures, were ranged in columns before me,

---

[27] Chet Raymo, *Natural Prayers*, Saint Paul: Hungry Mind Press, 1999; and *Skeptics and True Believers*, Toronto: Doubleday, 1998.

[28] Drees, *ibid*: 280.

[29] Paul Kurtz, *Transcendental Temptation*: 4.

When I was shown the charts and diagrams, to add, divide, and measure them,

When I sitting heard the astronomer where he lectured with much applause in the lecture room,

How soon unaccountable I became tired and sick,

Till rising and gliding out I wandered off by myself,

In the mystical moist night air, and from time to time,

Looked up in perfect silence at the stars.[30]

Obviously, Whitman made no mention of any traditional religion or anything like it. His sense of mystery in nature was powerfully conveyed as a response to a dry academic lecture. It is equally obvious that Paul Kurtz, a secular humanist, has as much access to the sense of mystery in nature as does anyone else. Accordingly, whether one needs traditional religious or spiritual systems to encourage the sense of mystery and other experiential benefits needs to be looked into.

Some would say, then, that the natural-scientific religion and spirituality is hardly a true form of religion or of any spirituality that is significantly different from general sensitivity. The proponents of another approach – the third in the presentation being given here – to the conflict between the natural sciences and religion or spirituality would step in at this point, and hold that more can be made of religion and spirituality than the natural-scientific approach allows. We'll now have a look at this third response to the current natural science versus religion or spirituality clash, which I will call the 'it's all okay' view.

---

[30] Walt Whitman, "When I Heard The Learned Astronomer," *50 Great Poets*, ed., Milton Crane, NY: Bantam: 407. Perhaps Kurtz would not like Whitman's use of the term 'mystical' though.

Chapter Twenty One: The 'It's all okay' Religion/Spirituality View

21.0 The 'It's all okay' religion/spirituality view

The challenge phystriology poses to spirituality is unmistakable. In Chapter Nineteen, we looked at the view that abandons organized spirituality. However, many would say that there must be a way to sustain some aspects of the religion/spirituality path even given the evidence for phystriology. Accordingly, in Chapter Twenty, we reviewed the natural-scientific response, and, as well, assumed or introduced acceptance of phystriology. We also reviewed several limits of the natural scientific response, one of which is that its preferred emotions are also preferred emotions of secular humanists, and a second of which is that there's a conflict between the natural-scientific worldview and the traditional religious materials. We'll now review the 'It's all okay' response, which tries to retain more of the traditional *doctrinal content* of the religions or of spirituality than does the natural-scientific response.

There are several forms of the 'It's all okay' approach. Here we'll divide it into four main groups: It's all okay because (a) the current leaps of faith in religion or spirituality are appropriate, (b) there are two *nonoverlapping magisteria*, or sources of authority, one scientific, and one religious, and since they are independent of each other, science and religion can survive together, (c) science can catch up to religious or spiritual wisdom, and (d) we can let the religious/spiritual institutions continue as they're now working, trusting that accommodations will subtly happen on their own. Of course someone who takes an 'It's all okay' approach need not be clearly placed in only one of these four groups; there may be combinations of them. In what follows, I will briefly review and criticize each of the four options.

21.1 We are licensed to make a leap of faith in religion and spirituality

We will look at four version of the licensed leap of faith approach: James's approach, Kant's approach, Pascal's approach, and the radical approach. To license a leap-of-faith approach is to say that a belief without an evidence basis for its acquisition is licensed or legitimate.

21.1.1 James's approach

William James, a U.S. founder of pragmatism in the late 19th century, put forward the idea in his lecture, "The Will To Believe," that a leap-of-faith system is legitimate, so long as the system is what may be called 'position relative': (i) the option for the leap-of-faith is a live option, which, in one way of reading it, requires that the evidence on the matter in question be wide open, at least on scientific matters, (ii) the option is momentous, and (iii) one can't help but take some kind of stand on the issue.[31] James took this to license evidence-less faith in the existence of the personal God.[32]

21.1.1.1 Criticism of James's approach

The time in which James presented his leap-of-faith system – the late 1800's – was a very different period from about 1965 or 1970, by which time the physicalization of chemistry and the physio-chemicalization of biology had taken place. These two processes, of course, had not been fulfilled and could hardly have even been barely indicated when James was working out his position.

The point could be put more strongly: the reaching of a high plateau level in each of the three processes occurred after 1910 (the last year of James's life). As was noticed before, the mathematization of physics process reached a high plateau level in 1918 with Nöther's Theorem; the physicalization of chemistry process reached a high plateau level by around the 1930's and was hardly yet in view during the period James was writing; and the physio-chemicalization of biology was far from being in evidential view in and around 1900 and reached a high plateau level either in the 1950's (allowing for a touch of prediction) or in the 1960's (when the predictions just mentioned were confirmed). By

---

[31] James's lecture, "The Will to Believe," was first published in 1897. James's fideism is a position-relative fideism, since it only applies when the user of it is in a certain position, namely, that the user has a live, momentous, forced option.

[32] James, *ibid*: 122.

1970 or so the evidence in all three processes was sufficiently clear so that each process had reached a plateau level from which there has been no retreat at all. Yet James was writing at the turn of the 20ᵗʰ century when the evidence had not yet come into view, and so, appropriately, there was much speculation, and one was entitled to say that the evidence was wide open. What was in 1900 a live option in which one could go this way (there are basically purposive beings, e.g., a personal God) or that way (there are no basically purposive beings, and so, there is no personal God) became by 1970, to anyone who looked at the evidence, no longer a live option in which one could go this way or that way. Anyone who looked at the evidence would have concluded that there are no natural objects that have basic purposes, so there are no basically purposive beings, and so there is no personal God.

The mathematization of physics process may have been reasonably clear to many after the conservation of mass law of the 18ᵗʰ century and the thermodynamic laws of the 19ᵗʰ century were articulated; but the physicalization of chemistry together with the physio-chemicalization of biology were still very much in process. And, of course, phystriology requires the results of those two processes, or some equivalent. Otherwise, for instance, vitalism would be an option in thinking about biology; British Emergentism, too, would be an option; even ontological interactive dualism could only be softly rejected by Darwinian evolution. On the physicalization of chemistry, around 1900 there was only the beginning of the discovery of electrons; there certainly wasn't the quantum theory of electromagnetism, nor its implications for atomic bonding; and on the physio-chemicalization of biology, the method by which reproduction occurred was not known, nor was it known how the body proteins and organs are built. And there were many in the 19ᵗʰ century who doubted the existence of atoms (Ernst Mach, for instance) until some time in the 20ᵗʰ century, after Einstein's 1905 work on Brownian motion.[33]

---

[33] In Einstein's paper submitted in May 1905 to the journal that published it that year, he demonstrated that microscopically visible things suspended in liquids would be pushed this way and that way by so many molecules, if molecules existed, that the zig-zagging motions of the suspended particles would be easily observed under a microscope. This provided a physical explanation for what had already been observed, that non-living particles suspended in liquids, moved this way and that way 'endlessly'. The motions had been called Brownian motions after Robert Brown, an English botanist, who had observed the motions, and had shown, in 1828, that the moving things were not living things.

Accordingly, what James licensed at the turn of the 20th century cannot be licensed by his own approach today. This is an important point to notice, since the Jamesian approach has been so widely accepted in religious culture and in general culture, too. Yet it is dependent on the view adopted by a philosopher prior to the fulfillment of the three processes that led to the result of phystriology. The lack of a justified Jamesian approach to the leap of faith in our time is, then, a crucially important point to notice.

This leads to our interest in the three other important leap of faith approaches to resolving the natural science versus religion or spirituality problem: the Kantian approach, the Pascalian approach, and the radical approach, the last of which may be thought of (perhaps historically inaccurately, which is not an issue of concern to us here) as the Tertullian approach.

21.1.2 The Kantian approach

Immanuel Kant (1724-1804) was deeply concerned with the implications of the Newtonian system. He was also, as he put it, awoken from his dogmatic slumber by the works (often skeptical) of David Hume. As a result of such an awakening, Kant accepted that there would be no adequate *philosopher's proof* for God's existence. However, Kant wanted to show the interrelations of the scientific view, the hope for human happiness, the requirements of morality, the hope for an immortal afterlife, and the belief in God, more or less, as God would have been usually understood at that time and place.

In his view, to have both a hope for human happiness and what he took to be necessary in morality, namely, a universal deontological (duty-based) moral system, one had to believe in a God who could harmonize the two realms, the realm of happiness, and the realm of morality. Hence Kant's approach was a hope-based approach to the existence of what amounted to a personal God. Many historians of ideas would place Kant's hope-based approach as marking a key turning point after which the non-evidential approach to God's existence took priority over the evidential approach.

21.1.2.1 Criticism of the Kantian approach

Kant's system was enormously influential. But Kant developed his system before physics was as fully mathematized as it became, and even longer before the empirical evidence for the physicalization of chemistry and physio-chemicalization of biology had assembled. (Nor was he aware of any equivalent to the conjunction of those three processes.) Hence hoping for a God who would harmonize happiness and deontology seems no longer up to date; for Kant, the afterlife would be part of God's harmonization; and Kant's God would, then, it seems, be an interactive personal God; and by now the interactive personal God at the human scale has been logically excluded by phystriology, and at the quantum scale has been strongly ampliatively (not strictly logically) excluded. Indeed, Kant's acceptance of the hope for an eternal afterlife directly goes against those three processes. So it may be fairly said, without any faulting of Kant, given the time period in which he worked, that the Kantian approach is not in touch with recent findings in the natural sciences.

21.1.3 The Pascalian approach

Blaise Pascal (1623 - 62) was a mathematician, a natural scientist, a philosopher, and a theologian. His leap-of-faith system is found in his collection *Pensées*[34], published only after his death. It is based on the view that we can wager on God's existence. In simple terms, the argument states that reason is inadequate in dealing with the Divine Nature. Consequently, we must take another approach to our theological, religious, or, we might say, spiritual attitudes. Believing in God is supposed to lead to a state of eternal bliss; disbelieving in God is supposed to lead to a state of eternal torment. In such conditions, maintains Pascal, there is every reason to wager on God's existence. If one dies, and there is no afterlife, the one who has wagered for God has lost little (considering the tiny lifetime of the person); if one dies, and there is no afterlife, and one wasn't a believer, there is little gain (given the tiny lifetime of the person); if one dies, and there is an afterlife, and one has been a believer, one gains an infinite benefit; if one dies, and there is an afterlife, and one has not been a believer, one loses an infinite loss (in hell). Consequently, by any 'wager calculus', the wager should be in favor of believing.

What if one accepts this calculus, but that doesn't lead to actual belief? Pascal suggested that one can change one's manner of living, so that one worships, prays, attends religious ceremonies, and these activities, he said, lead naturally to the arising of the religious beliefs.

21.1.3.1 Criticisms of the Pascalian approach

---

[34] Blaise Pascal, #223, "Pensees", in *The Essential Pascal*: 89-93.

There are several main criticisms of the Pascalian approach. Here we will focus on those objections most suited to our times. The first criticism holds that the Pascalian approach says that reason is inadequate in dealing with the Divine Nature; yet, after the evidence has accumulated for phystriology, there is no longer ground for this attitude toward what reason can logically reject, or not strictly logically but strongly reject. Even the philosophical skeptic will accept appearances, and so even the philosophical skeptic will recognize the appearances of the scientific evidence. Also the skeptic will not accept the Pascalian God.

In any case, the evidence shows, logically, that, for reasons just mentioned, no interactive God at the human or classical scale exists, and, ampliatively, that no purposive God exists at all. Similarly, there is no longer ground for belief in an afterlife; yet belief in an afterlife managed by a purposive (and interactive) God is part of the wager-consideration set-up in Pascal's argument. If one has no grounds for belief in the set-up of conditions for the wager argument, one can no longer take it that one is in any position to make the wager. The argument for making the wager is based on an unacceptable contrast about attitudes toward hypothetical conditions only one of which has evidential grounds in regard to it, namely, putting it sharply, that there is no afterlife. After all, what of the hypothesis of a mischievous world-creating spaghetti monster, who punishes the believers in Him, and rewards the disbelievers? There is no evidence for His existence, so any wager on the existence of the incomprehensible spaghetti monster has no pull on us. The Pascal wager itself requires belief in the existence of an afterlife. Yet, in the last few decades the phystriology position has been completed. So the Pascal wager has, or should have, no pull on us either.

This can be reinforced by an often-raised second objection. Pascal was immersed in a Christian culture. He knowingly ignored Jewish and Islamic forms of worship, and, perhaps, unknowingly ignored Hindu, Buddhist, Sikh, etcetera, forms of worship. Would his wager work equally well for those Hindus whose form of religious activities includes worship through idols and for Muslims whose form forbids worship through idols? Apparently some specific theoretical framework is required for the faith, or for the activities that might produce the faith; yet some Muslims claim that one who worships through idols will be punished at death; whereas Hindus often claim that one who appropriately relates to the idols will be rewarded after death in the reincarnation forms assumed. And so the Pascalian system comes apart at the seams when one takes a broader look at the plurality of occurring religious systems. Perhaps some would raise pluralistic interpretations of religious systems to get around this objection. This leads us to the final objection to the Pascalian approach to be presented here.

The way in which reason is regarded as being inadequate to the Divine Nature, and so reason is to be suspended, leaves a gap in our understanding of the Pascalian wager. Is the wager about something to which reason has so little access that it (the wager) cannot bring us into practical contact with religions or systems for cultivation of spirituality? Or is such practical contact to be allowed? Obviously, Pascal's wager requires practical contact to be allowed. If it is allowed, will the contact yield a pluralist or non-pluralist view of the religious systems? If it is non-pluralist, then, as we've just seen, the plurality of religious forms undoes the wager calculus. If it is fully pluralist, then it doesn't lead to non-acceptance of phystriology. Yet it is that conflict between phystriology and many forms of religious or spiritual views that we are considering. And phystriology excludes the existence of an afterlife, which Pascal's wager requires as a live option.

This returns us to the central objection for our time, which is the very first of the three: In Pascal's time, the background included the view that there is an afterlife. In our time, the evidence excludes such a view. So there is no ground in our time for making Pascal's wager.

The inadequacy of James', Kant's, and Pascal's approaches lead us to consider a more radical leap-of-faith-ism. We may associate that radical fideism with Tertullian, who lived roughly eighteen hundred years ago.

21.1.4 Radical leap-of-faith-ism

Tertullian (c. 160 – c. 220 CE) is famous, among other things, for his remark, "Indeed, what has Athens to do with Jerusalem?"[35] In Athens, of course, one finds philosophical reasoning; in Jerusalem, on the other hand, one finds revelation and scriptural authority, though the systems of revelation and scriptural authority differ, for instance, between Judaism and Christianity. Or so we would certainly say, today, and have been saying so for at least seventeen hundred years. In any case, we are interested in radical fideism or radical leap-of-faith-ism, which maintains that it doesn't matter what the evidence shows (what the Athenian approach leads to); according to radical fideism, there is an authoritative

---

[35] *De praescriptione haereticorum*, vii.

revelation or source of authority, and that is what should guide one's belief-formation process.

According to such a radical fideism, it shouldn't matter what the natural sciences have apparently shown; one can overcome the views according to the teachings of an authoritative source, and, one might add, this amounts to a radical leap of faith in that source of authority.[36]

21.1.4.1 Criticisms of the radical fideist approach

It is not difficult to spot the problem besetting the radical fideist approach. There are two ways to put it.

First, it licenses any of the many revelations and scriptural or prophetic authorities offering their counsel. One could be a moderate Muslim, Jew, Christian, Hindu, Buddhist, etc; but even the moderates find grounds for opposition to other moderate practices. We have already pointed to the contrast between the offense some Muslims found in idolatry, versus the approval some Hindus had and have for rituals observing some forms of idolatry (where 'idolatry' is used in the neutral sense of worshipping using idols). There are many other conflicts as well: for instance, some moderates – moderately, they would say – frown on the activities of homosexuality; other moderates – sensibly, I would say – approve of a freedom that openly permits homosexual activities. Radical fideism would also allow for approval of supposedly moderate or pluralistic affirmations of tricky gurus who deceptively engage in activities that are, unfortunately, criminal.

---

[36] One may, alternatively, invoke a philosophically skeptical defense of the leap of faith. If one is philosophically skeptical, why can't one make a leap of faith in favor of a religious system? The answer is, Because there will be endlessly many other leaps of faith with equally good or poor justifications as well to logically inconsistent systems. Yet one doesn't want a leap of faith for, say, Hindu apparent actions to be as unjustified as a leap of faith in favor of, say, Satanic apparent actions. Yet that is what one would be committed to. If a skeptic has a justification for acting in the apparent world as one would act if the apparent world is the real world, then one is to act as the scientific view allows. But the scientific view, since the 1960's or so, includes phystriology. And phystriology excludes the afterlife. This makes it unclear how skepticism is of any assistance. All in all, the skeptical approach to the leap of faith gives one no justification for any specific religious or traditional spirituality-oriented action. General, perhaps. But specific, no. And the radical leap of faith system would yield specific results.

This brings us to the second way of stating the criticism of radical fideism: There are not only moderate forms of Judaism, Christianity, Islam, Buddhism, Hinduism, etc., but also there are literalist forms of Judaism, Christianity, Islam, etc. In a literalist form, it is often the case that martyrdom by one or another means is approved; this can include (suicide) bombings. Yet if radical fideism supports any form and any interpretation of scriptural revelation, authority, etc., as it does, then it supports whatever behavior arises from any literalist form or interpretation of spirituality or religion.

To begin with, the literal Hindu has nothing to say to the literal Jew and vice versa. Both are supposedly protected by their authority, an authority invulnerable, it seems, to sharp criticism, according to the radical leap of faith approach. The literal Hindu has as much stance-legitimacy as the literal Jew, yet it is logically inconsistent to be both a literal Hindu and a literal Jew. Yet radical fideism's equal 'justifications' provide a ground for such an incoherent double system. Such incoherence cannot stand for long. If it is backed by some sort of harmless appearances, then phystriology has to be part of the harmless appearances; and phystriology would undo the literal Judaism and the literal Hinduism.

Also literalism of one sort or another permits bombings. This, too, entirely undermines the radical fideist approach. The sensible person will vigorously recoil at the wanton license of Tertullian authority or of the radical leap of evidence-less faith.[37]

21.1.5 The inadequacy of these four forms of leaps of faith, and the prevalence of leaps of evidence-less faith in our culture, together with the evidence for phystriology, shows how there has been a contrast between the rise of objective scientific results and, paradoxically, the disposition to accept, more and more, the leap of evidence-less faith approach. It is striking that in the ancient days, it was generally taken that there was good evidence for central religious doctrines. Nowadays, that sense, it seems, has very largely gone. Yet at the same time, the strength of what the natural sciences have established is unmistakable. Everyone accepts the results of the sciences. Perhaps the time has come for people to understand why the sciences have produced these results. And, it seems,

---

[37] For scholars, see Allen Wood, "The duty to believe according to the evidence."

the time has come for an abandonment of the leap of evidence-less faith approach.

21.2 There are *nonoverlapping magisteria*

Stephen Jay Gould, the evolutionary biologist who put forward the idea that there is punctuated evolution (several evolutionarily short time periods in which there was a lot of evolution), was a non-believer (an agnostic in regard to religion) who also said that there are two independent sources of general belief that people may have: the how-things-happen sources, and the why-things-happen sources. The sciences explain *how* things change. Religion and some branches of philosophy deal with *why* things are, and so this is intimately connected with our sense of meanings in life. Just as the Roman Catholic Church takes it that there are separate independent teachings or sources of authority, called *magisteria*, so, too, anyone can take it, according to Gould, that there is the scientific *magisterium*, and there is, independently, the religious *magisterium*. It follows, then, that the views of the sciences (and we can add phystriology, though Gould, notably, did not mention it through any of its currently used names) arise from the scientific *magisterium*, and they do not, therefore, interfere with the religious *magisterium*. The religious *magisterium*, however, includes the many views supposedly rejected by phystriology.

It is easy to see how attractive the double *magisterium* claim is. As Gould puts it:

> Unless at least half my colleagues are dunces, there can be – on the most raw and empirical grounds – no conflict between science and religion. I know hundreds of scientists who share a conviction about the fact of evolution, and teach it in the same way. Among these people I note an entire spectrum of religious attitudes – from devout daily prayer and worship to resolute atheism. Either there's no correlation between religious belief and confidence in evolution – or else half of these people are fools.[38]

Gould maintains the independence of the religious and of the scientific points of view even more clearly in "Noverlapping Magisteria." There he says:

---

[38] William Jay Gould, "Darwinism Defined."

I knew that Pope Pius XII (not one of my favorite figures in twentieth-century history, to say the least) had made the primary statement in a 1950 encyclical entitled *Humani Generis*. I knew the main thrust of his message: Catholics could believe whatever science determined about the evolution of the human body, so long as they accepted that, at some time of his choosing, God had infused the soul into such a creature. I also knew that I had no problem with this statement, for whatever my private beliefs about souls, science cannot touch such a subject and therefore cannot be threatened by any theological position on such a legitimately and intrinsically religious issue. Pope Pius XII, in other words, had properly acknowledged and respected the separate domains of science and theology.[39]

That the scientific and the theological approaches are independent, then, is the central claim of the *nonoverlapping magisteria* (sometimes symbolized as NOMA) view.

21.2.1 Criticism of the *nonoverlapping magisteria* approach

Gould, it seems, in the first of the two quotes, made a false dichotomy between scientists being dunces, on the one hand, and, on the other, there being no conflict between science and religion. Obviously, scientists are not dunces. And many of them accept religion. Ergo, he thought, there is no conflict between science and religion. However, there may well be severe conflict between scientific views and religious or spirituality-affirming views, a conflict that is not clearly recognized by those scientists. It may be, for instance, that the scientists in one or another science are only rudimentarily familiar with the way physics, chemistry, and biology fit together philosophically, so as to make for phystriology; and they may not be at all familiar with how acceptance of phystriology requires that an internally consistent position will reject each of the many views so often found in articulations of religious or spiritual approaches to the world.

---

[39] Stephen Jay Gould, "Nonoverlapping Magisteria", in <stephenjaygould.org/library/gould_noma.html>. "Nonoverlapping Magisteria" first appeared in *Natural History* **106**, March 1997: 16-22 and was reprinted in *Leonardo's Mountain of Clams and the Diet of Worms*, New York: Harmony Books, 1998, pp. 269-283.

There are good reasons for thinking not only that scientists are not the slightest bit dunces, but also that they don't know much about phystriology and its implications. It is philosophers, whose speciality includes integrating the results of several sciences, who have formulated the phystriological position. Furthermore, philosophers who have accepted phystriology have been unusually reluctant to publicize the phystriology result and its implications. There are few papers dealing with this topic (under physical closure or physical completeness), and even fewer on its implications;[40] it is no wonder, then, that the picture in the general community is unclear. For example, two readily available works on or relevant to phystriology – McLaughlin's of 1992[41], and Papineau's "Appendix" in his book *Consciousness* of 2002[42] – are at the senior/graduate student level in philosophy and beyond. They are scholarly works, rather than works for general consumption, as are all the others of the few discussions of phystriology. So it is not a wonder that phystriology is not yet widely known about outside of the senior/graduate-student-and-beyond philosophical level. As mentioned in Chapter Nineteen, even Richard Dawkin's book of 2006, *The God Delusion*,[43] summarizes the reasons for disbelieving in God, but doesn't mention the phystriological picture. Once again, this shows how reticent the philosophical community has been. (Explaining this reticence is part of the topic of Appendix 1.)

The second of the two quotes, the quote from "Nonoverlapping Magisteria," makes the mistake of ignoring phystriology in a bigger way. Gould says that "science cannot touch" the subject of an immaterial God putting a soul into a body. However, although it may be legitimate to say that no one science can approach this subject, the result of the three natural sciences of physics, chemistry, and biology, taken together as philosophers do take them together, does touch this subject. The result requires that there be no immaterial being interfering with the rules, laws, or forces of physics. Yet the placing of the soul in the body, and the

---

[40] To be more accurate, (of course excluding my own work) I am unaware of even a single paper on the topic of the implications of physical completeness for religious/spiritual beliefs.

[41.] "The Rise and Fall of British Emergentism."

[42] David Papineau, "Appendix" in *Consciousness*. This, with a few revisions, is similar to, Papineau's earlier "Rise of Physicalism."

[43] Richard Dawkins, *The God Delusion*.

activities of such a soul in a body, would interfere with the operations of the rules, laws, or forces of physics. So, on the most straightforward reading, there is an immediate logical conflict between the result of the three natural sciences taken together and the supposedly independent religious *magisterium*. One could hypothesize that God inserts the soul just by fiddling somehow with the quantum variables, but this is a 'clutching onto straws' sort of approach. Anyhow, would the soul do nothing during life? This was amply discussed in Part I. The impact of the religious views on the philosophically integrated scientific views and vice versa simply cannot be ignored. So the NOMA approach is incorrect.

The *nonoverlapping magisteria* (NOMA) approach cannot be maintained. It doesn't begin to face the logical clash, nor the not strictly logical but strong clash, between phystriology and the many views so common in articulations of religion or spirituality. Once again, it is the understandable failure to appreciate a not well-publicized philosophical integration of the three natural sciences that accounts for the error springing up in the thinking of a biologist.

21.3 The 'let science catch up with religious wisdom' approach

The third 'it's all okay' approach is in a sense the reverse of the natural-scientific approach to resolving the conflict between phystriology on the one side, and, on the other side, religion or spirituality. The natural-scientific approach accepts the results of the natural sciences, and attempts to reform religious practice accordingly. On the other hand, the 'it's all okay' approach, being a 'let science catch up with religious wisdom' approach, contrariwise, takes it that religious experiences and views and practices have a depth to them that is simply not matched in scientific investigations of any kind. For example, if it appears that philosophically integrated natural science has rejected the view that "some mystics ascend to a higher non-physical or only subtly physical reality," then, according to this point of view, so much the worse for science. According to this point of view, science must one way or another catch up with the wisdom of the various religious traditions.

There are several ways of expressing the 'let science catch up with religious wisdom'. I'll mention two of them. The first is what I'll call *The Templeton Approach*. In The Templeton Approach, it may be merely assumed that somehow the resolution will work out, and that it won't be by the rather strict acceptance of the natural-scientific results. Our example of an author working within the Templeton Approach will be the writings of Charles Taylor, winner of the Templeton award for 2007. Philosophical transpersonal psychologists give the second form of expression. Our example of this will be the work of the most philosophically minded exponent of transpersonal psychology, Ken Wilber.

21.3.1 Charles Taylor: hopes and omissions

For many years, an under-theme of Charles Taylor's work has been that we should, somehow, reconcile the religious sensibility and the scientific sensibility. This is a noble hope.

Yet there is also a big omission in Taylor's writings. Anyone who is looking for a specific proposal as to how to deal with the logical conflict between phystriology and the eight or nine spirituality views logically rejected by it, or how to deal with the not strictly logical conflict, but strong conflict, between phystriology and the many spirituality views rejected by it, including the general view that there is a personal God, will not find any such proposal in Taylor's writings. To begin with, Taylor nowhere exposes the content of the phystriological position, however it would be named. This is unfortunate. In the 1960's, when the phystriological position, called physical closure or completeness or something else, was just coming out as a real possibility, Taylor wrote *The Explanation of Behavior*, in which he championed future-directed teleological explanations over mechanistic ones. From the beginning, then, Taylor directed himself away from the phystriological point of view.

Similarly, in *Sources Of The Self*, published in 1989, Taylor has a chapter entitled, "The Conflicts of Modernity". Yet in this twenty-five page chapter, there is no mention of how the rules, laws or forces of physics seem not to be overturned by any other factor in or outside of nature, nor how religious or spirituality views require, or at least seem to require, that there be such overturning. On the other hand, at the end of the chapter, he says that there is a hope in Judeo-Christian theism.[44] However, no details at all are supplied as to what that hope is.

A more recent account by Taylor is *Varieties of Religion Today*, which reviews William James' thought on religion, especially James's *Varieties of Religious Experience*, which was published in 1902, exactly a century before the appearance of *Varieties of Religion Today*. However, in 2002 Taylor was apparently unaware of the difference between the

---

[44] *Sources of the Self.* 521.

evidential position of an author in 1902 and of an author anytime since, say, 1970. It is true that Taylor calls attention to James's focus on feelings rather than on teachings, or doctrines, or dogmas, or intellectual positions. But phystriology is *logically* inconsistent with many views – including: there is an interactive God at the classical scale, an afterlife or pre-life, a freedom that overturns the rules, laws, or forces of physics, a cosmic moral system tending to reward/deprivation, a non-physical mind-created paranormal power system, a mystical ascent in some people to a higher realm than the gross physical reality, an interactive dualism, and an emanationism. Post 1970, whether one accepts one of these eight views is no longer a mere "nuance of doctrine."[45]

Taylor's most comprehensive work on the relation of religion to contemporary culture is *A Secular Age*. The book is voluminous, elaborate, detailed, and tangled. It especially treats the relation between religion and social structures. However, from the very beginning of the book, Taylor makes it clear that he will not have much to say about the relation between the natural sciences and religion. Instead he will "shift the focus to the conditions of belief."[46] In explaining his motivation for providing this shift, he says that he doesn't see the strength of the clash between the sciences and religion. As he puts it, "I don't see the cogency of the supposed argument from, say, the findings of Darwin to the alleged refutation of religion."[47]

As we have seen, of course, Darwin's theory was about evolution, and not about *all* biological changes; it permitted vitalism, British Emergentism, Jamesian fideism, and was logically consistent with Cartesian dualism and emanationisms. So there is a huge difference between Newtonian physics plus Darwinian biology on the one hand, and, on the other hand, phystriology, which, according to the usual history, only appeared by around the 1950's or 1960's. Since 1970, Taylor seems, unfortunately, not to have absorbed what has been absorbed by just about all philosophers in (what has come to be called) mind-body theory.

This is puzzling, but it seems to be true. At the end of *A Secular Age*, Taylor expounds on various dilemmas he sees us as facing. There are, he says, the neo-Nietzscheans, the secular humanists, and the

---

[45] *Varieties of Religion Today:* 18.

[46] *A Secular Age:* 4.

[47] *A Secular Age:* 4.

pursuers of the good-beyond-life (the religious advocates, striving for transcendence). His theme is that all these groups are struggling among pressures. However, he doesn't see that his favored proposal – God's initiative is to love us, and our resistance is what weakens our religious affiliations – includes the idea of the interactive God or, more generally, the personal God.[48] This, however, is logically or not strictly logically yet strongly, excluded by phystriology.

Charles Taylor, like anyone else in our time, accepts the evidential results of physics and technology. Taylor would say, of course, that the earth is not at the absolute centre of the cosmos; rather, it orbits the sun. People who said that a few hundred years ago risked trial and imprisonment and, perhaps, death. Taylor wouldn't disagree with that at all. Yet anyone who wants to free us from a closed way of thinking, as Taylor does, has to be able to tell us when to accept the scientific results and when not to. Yet there is no way to figure out what accepting the scientific results means in this case.

In general, it is not unfair to say that Taylor offers no specific treatment of the clash between phystriology and standard and typical religious and spiritual views.

21.3.2 Ken Wilber's efforts to scientifically account for spiritual experience

We turn, next, to Ken Wilber's efforts at synthesis of science and spirituality or religion. Wilber's work is within transpersonal psychology. Transpersonal psychology affirms the scientific attitude of psychology, and also affirms the spiritual teachings of the world's religions. There are several ways in which the transpersonalism of transpersonal psychology arises, but the easiest way to suggest the spirit of transpersonal psychology is to say that it appreciates and lightly affirms the metaphoric side of exoteric religion/spirituality and wholeheartedly affirms the esoteric side of religion/spirituality in one or another literal, non-metaphoric interpretation. The transpersonalism can be interpreted in several ways. Here is one interpretation: If one affirms such teachings as "I am the all," or, "There is no self", or "There is only the partless One," or, "There is Nothing," then there are no more clear judgments about the difference between the underlying nature of one person and of another person, and so the system can be called a 'transpersonal' system.

---

[48] *A Secular Age*: 654-6.

Wilber's synthesis is based on what he calls a four quadrant holarchy. A holarchy is a system in which everything is a holon. A holon is a thing that has more than one part, and is a part, along with another part or parts, of a bigger thing. The four quadrants in the four quadrant holarchy are based on the four combinations of interior / exterior, and individual / collective. However, as I've shown elsewhere,[49] Wilber gives no adequate argument to the conclusion that the world is a holarchy, let alone a four quadrant holarchy. We need not go into the problems with Wilber's arguments for the holarchy here, since our central issue is phystriology and the challenge that presents to spirituality. So on the holarchy issue, I simply refer the curious reader to the work I've just cited.

On our more central topic, Wilber thinks that the elements of each quadrant causally interact with the elements of other quadrants: as he puts it, the elements of the quadrants "are all mutually determining. They all cause and are caused by" the other elements.[50] This is one of many ways in which Wilber adopts a physically incomplete model. Here is another way: Wilber says that we can accept the Great Chain of Being systems of Plotinus, Sri Aurobindo, and others "precisely as traditionally outlined."[51]

However, he doesn't realize that the Great Chain of Being systems conflict with phystriology, as is easy to show. Plotinus, for instance, wants the mind of the individual to reach upward toward the One, and he regards the One as distinct in some way from the gross physical realm. Hence there must be changes of motions of the atoms in the brain (in the modern view of things) enabling such reaching upwards to occur. But such reaching upwards is not something that happens through the rules, forces, or laws governing how things like rocks or parts of rocks interact. Wilber explicitly denies that the rules, laws, or forces governing parts of rocks can be the rules, laws, or forces governing purposive beings aspiring to the higher realms of the Great Chain of Being. He says, for instance, "I mean no offense to rocks, but by taking some of the dumbest holons in existence and making their study the study of 'really real reality', these physical sciences, we have seen, were largely responsible for the collapse of the Kosmos into the

---

[49] "Two Questions for Ken Wilber and the Wider Transpersonal Audience."

[50] *A Brief History of Everything*: 81.

[51] "An Integral Theory of Consciousness," above fig. 3.

cosmos."[52] Of course Wilber prefers the basically purposive Kosmos to the cosmos that is the sum of basically purposeless little things. In short, Wilber is against the phystriological result, and so is a member of the 'let science catch up with religious wisdom' approach.

Wilber's system is also flawed by some scandalously poor scholarship;[53] the point here, though, is that Wilber's efforts, in effect, miss the key problem. He doesn't mention what he should have called physical closure or physical completeness; he doesn't mention the content of the phystriological picture. He thinks he is integrating mysticism and science in a way that current thinkers can accept, yet, since he is denying phystriology, he is not doing so. The conflict between phystriology and the many beliefs celebrated by Wilber is not explicitly addressed. So it is that Wilber's grand synthesis is, in effect, unaware of the central problem that needs to be faced. This version, too, of the 'let science catch up with religious wisdom' approach does not work.

21.4 "Let the institutions carry on"

Finally, we consider a fourth "It's all okay" view. The fourth "It's all okay" view says that we should allow the religious and spiritual institutions to continue as they are going, since, in the end, they will accommodate the results of the natural sciences as they must. In the meantime, it's all okay.

21.4.1 Criticism of "Let the institutions carry on"

There is one sense in which this point of view is appropriate: we can't interfere with the operations of the institutions, other than by making comments of one sort or another. In this context, we have no powers or resources to do anything else. So, in this sense, we should allow the institutions to be. There is no option other than to make the comments we might want to make.

Still, there are the comments. It seems that for a long time (since Kant, or since James, or, if one is super-cautious, for the last few decades) the philosophical and intellectual dimension has more or less disappeared from within the religious/spiritual community. The mythic dimension is strong; the institutional dimension is strong; the ritual

---

[52] *Sex, Ecology, Spirituality*, 1st edition: 48; 2nd edition: 56.

[53] I show this in (2006b): 73-79.

dimension is strong; the experiential dimension is strong, or at least as strong as it has ever been. But the doctrinal dimension has been absorbed into the dimension of dogmatic imagery; doctrine has collapsed into imagistic myth. There has long been a dissonance between scientific results and earlier religious intuitions; since 1970 there has been not only a dissonance but also a logical conflict between phystriology and the eight or more central theses found in one or another combination group in religious or spiritual systems, and also there has been a strong, though not strictly logical conflict between phystriology and religious or spirituality views as well.

What the fourth variety of the "It's all okay" approach is saying is that we don't need to worry about any philosophical position to be taken. One way or another, people will function as they need to function, with or without a sound intellectual articulation of what is going on.

Those of a philosophical sensibility, however, will not be pleased by this approach. It is for such philosophically minded folk that one wants to go a little further; one wants to see if there isn't a better integration of phystriology and the religious/spiritual sensibility than has been articulated by the natural-scientific approach and than has been articulated by exponents of the 'it's all okay' approach. The position that I will offer in the next Chapter is that there is such a position, namely, mystical naturalism.

Chapter Twenty Two: Mystical Naturalism

22.0 I'll now outline a fourth response to the clash between phystriology and many important views in religion and spirituality, namely, *mystical naturalism*. This is the approach that I prefer, and so I will try to exhibit its advantages.

There are two central theses in this approach: first (putting philosophical skepticism about the external world aside) one entirely accepts phystriology;[54] second, one discovers as many specifics as one can for integrating phystriology with religion/spirituality. Unlike the natural-scientific approach to religion and spirituality, mystical naturalism states that more of religious phenomenology and doctrine can be integrated into phystriology than the mere phenomenology of awe, mystery, wonder, and such-like emotional attitudes towards natural selection evolution or incomprehensible features of reality. And unlike the "Let science catch up with religious wisdom" approach, and, more

---

[54] Once again, some people will wonder: What if one does adopt a skeptical attitude toward the external world? This problem was raised in 11.9 and elsewhere, but it might as well be addressed again. I am (more or less) a Pyrrhonian skeptic, and I find the question easy to answer: if one does adopt such an attitude, one still needs a rationale for acting in the ordinary way in the world. Suppose one has such a rationale. (It might be for harmony sake, for instance.) Then one would act as though the world were roughly as it seems to be. At that level, use of the results of the sciences, including phystriology, is mandated. The use could be colored by the base, whatever it would be. In mystical naturalism layered onto philosophical skepticism, the base would be imagistic-narrative. But the phystriology would still be there in one way or another. Rivals would not.

generally, the "It's all okay" approach, one tries to find specifics that will work in detail.

To put the main idea simply, we've already seen how awe, mystery, wonder, and such-like emotional attitudes are both religious/spiritual and consistent with current science; yet they, and belief in the objects of the emotional attitudes, are not distinctive to religion/spirituality. They may indicate a significant difference between humans and other animals, and they may be directed to what underlies the limit conditions of thought, but according to mystical naturalism there are specifically religious or spiritual phenomena that can be rescued. Mystical naturalism accepts awe, mystery, wonder, interpersonal sensitivities directed in the natural-scientific manner on the one hand, and also, on the other hand, esoteric experience and belief, so long as any aspects of those beliefs that are inconsistent with phystriology are rejected, and a new version of the belief is created so that the belief will be consistent with phystriology.

Accepting phystriology requires that one reject the five theses covered under exoteric religion and spirituality. Thereby, a lot of religious content *is* rejected; and it is rejected more clearly than one is likely to find in the writings of Burhoe or Drees. Rejected are the personal God (by ampliative reasoning from the logical rejection of the personal God interacting in the classical world), any supernatural non-mechanical intelligence, the standard afterlife, physics-overturning freedom, hidden cosmic karma, and paranormal occurrences. In addition to rejecting the five exoteric views, other views too are rejected in mystical naturalism: ontological interactive dualism and interactive emanationism. These philosophically phrased views about the world are rejected. And so is the usual content of process theology.

However, it is not clear from the outset if phystriology requires one to reject *all* of the esoteric doctrinal and experiential system. We have already seen that there is, at least, an important aspect of the esoteric system that is inconsistent with acceptance of phystriology. The usual interpretations of esoteric religion are excluded by phystriology. For instance, phystriology requires one to reject the idea that the mind can rise to a higher non-physical or subtly physical level through which the higher inherent or intrinsic unifications are achieved. Those would require interferences with the bottom-up governance of non-purposive physics-based rules, laws, or forces. Similarly, phystriology requires one to reject the idea of a *ch'i* like substance operating throughout nature. Further, phystriology requires one to reject the idea that ongoing bliss reflects the properties of a single person equally underlying, and in some sense, volitionally underlying, all parts of nature, or an immaterial person freed from appearance-entanglements. Looking at the last point from another angle, phystriology requires one to reject the idea that ongoing bliss reflects the higher properties of a mind in some sense separated from the gross physical world. The traditional interpretations of esoteric religious or spiritual experience and belief are, then, to be rejected.

On the other hand, the identification of the proper or genuine body of a person with the whole world – as is found, for instance, in some sections of the Upanishads, e.g., "I, indeed, am all this (world)"[55] – is not inconsistent with phystriology. Moreover, phystriology provides grounding for the view that the intuitive body boundary does not correspond to any genuine natural boundary. Some Buddhists, Taoists, and others also use the universal-self language. (Suggestions of the notion of the universal self occurred in Chapters Sixteen and Eighteen, and more direct examples of this will be given below in 22.2). The *ch'i* experience can be proprioceptive; it can be accomplished by something going on in the brain, and, perhaps, elsewhere in the ordinary body. In this way it wouldn't indicate anything spread through nature. And the ongoing bliss may be simply a feature of some form of brain reorganization. This, too, would be consistent with phystriology. The denial of the person's volitional control outside of the ordinary body can also be done. Hence the bearer of the ongoing contrastless bliss states does not require the usual interpretation of mysticism that is given.

22.1 I'll now offer many reasons that show that the intuitive human body boundary does not correspond to any genuine natural boundary. The investigation here is entirely philosophical, and so our focus shifts to the merely intellectual level of discussion.

To begin with, there are many borderline problems: It is hard, if not impossible, to find a way to say when a bit of dead skin falling off the surface of the skin is or is not a part of the body. Suppose such a bit of dead skin is just hanging by a cell or two, or that it became briefly free but then became entangled in the skin. The borderline seems unspecifiable.

---

[55] *Chandogya* VII: 25: I, Radhakrishnan trans.

Such borderline problems occur at a small scale. And they also occur at a large scale. What of the mostly invisible bits of skin floating far from the ordinary body? It seems clear that a fuzzy or by-degrees approach will not help here. Even if some dusty batch of skin of mine in the corner of my room should be, to some degree expressible in a percent, part of my body – say the batch of skin-dust in the corner is itself 3% part of my body, 97% not part of my body – a lot of troubling questions are left over. Does the percent change according to my distance from the room? If so, how? And so on.

Also, there are other large-scale borderline problems. It is, for example, seemingly arbitrary to say when an oxygen atom becomes part of the body during its inhalation, and inhalation involves atoms moving into the nostrils, then down the tracheal tubes, then into the trachea, then into the lungs, then into the blood. The transportation covers many inches of territory. Once again, a 'by degrees' approach does not help: consider days in which the wind is blowing away from the nostrils, or toward the nostrils. Do the degrees reflect the environmental conditions? That seems arbitrary. And there are other sorts of problems, too.

For instance, there are many conceptual problems as to what criterion might be used to determine whether something is or is not part of the body. For instance, there is not only the human DNA, but also the non-human mitochondrial DNA; there are the many bacteria in and around the (ordinary) body; the immune system is assisted by vaccines, but the vaccines on their way to the (ordinary) body seem to be as much part of the functional bodily system as is a vaccine in the (ordinary) body that for one reason or another will not fully protect. Similarly, nutritious food on the way to the (ordinary) body seems to be as much part of the functional body as non-nutritious food that is making its way through the intestinal system.

In addition, there is a strong analogy between vibration-transmitting things like natural fingernails in regard to touch sensation, artificial fingernails in regard to touch sensation, rulers held by the hand in regard to touch sensation, and light between distant objects and the eyes in regard to visual sensation. The analogy is built up as follows: the natural fingernails are parts of the intuitive body; the artificial fingernails might be regarded as parts of the intuitive body and might not be; the rulers transmit vibrations when held, just as do fingernails, natural or artificial, but they would not be regarded as parts of the intuitive body. Now, there seems to be no principled difference between the joined transmitters, as natural fingernails are, and the un-joined transmitters, as rulers are. Nor, therefore, does there seem to be a principled difference between the un-joined transmitters for touch on the one hand and for the light on its way to the eyes for the visual system on the other hand. Consequently we may as well treat the light on its way to the eyes as part of the body as not to do so, at least as far as sensory transmission is concerned.

Further, the agency language we customarily use includes much more than the intuitive body. Consider, for instance, "Leslie blew out the candles." Here the agent gets the air molecules to do the job. But then the air molecules are, or seem to be, as much part of the agent's body as are the hands according to "Leslie patted the dog."

And there's more: physical theories don't support the intuitive boundary notions. The human body is a mass object. But, according to physics, even as approximated in the Newtonian manner, the gravitational pull of the intuitive body goes far beyond the intuitive boundary of the body. The hints from general relativity certainly strengthen the sense that no future integration of general relativity and quantum physics will preserve the ordinary body boundary as far as the intuitive body's mass is concerned. The general relativity system sees mass as a bend in spacetime; the quantum theory would only undo a mass bend at the level of the Planck scale. Yet sufficient diminishment of the gravitational bend (judging by the approximative Newtonian force, just to get a sense of the problem) would have to occur only at some distance from the ordinary edge of the body to allow for the bend-disappearance by the Planck scale non-uniformities; that is, only a good distance from the intuitively picked out body would the gravitational bend diminish sufficiently so as to be swamped by the Planck scale oddities.

The external mind theorists find that there are elements outside the intuitive body that function in cognitive systems. Our question is, what is the extent of the body? How far out does it go? Now, whatever is in the cognitive *system* should count in establishing the extent of the body. But the cognitive *system* is very broad. It should include what is taken in cognition to be cognitively structured or cognitively represented as well as what is in the base of the process of cognition, the base being that part that enables something to be cognitively represented or to be cognitively structured. Yet all agree that the cognitive *system* so defined extends out into the environment of the ordinarily understood human body. We use notebooks, write math calculations out, and so on. Then, it seems, the body base should be regarded as extending into the environment of the ordinarily understood human body.[56]

Other difficulties for defining the ordinary body boundary as a genuine body boundary can be specified too.

However many such other difficulties there are, phystriology itself informs us that the rules of governance of, or laws or forces for, physics-based changes will not be overturned by any other forces, rules, or laws. This, too, tends to eliminate any purported natural boundary corresponding to the intuitive human body boundary.

22.2 Given these many ways of seeing the absence of a genuine natural boundary for the body, one of the key lessons of phystriology – a lesson to be absorbed by the scientifically minded as much as by anybody else – is that the intuitive body boundary is not a genuine boundary in nature. In this way, phystriology positively supports what may be called the contemporary philosophically mystical view according to which the ordinary body boundary is not an ontologically genuine boundary.

There are many examples that can be given to illustrate the historical sources or antecedents of such mystical views. The Advaita Hindus (on one interpretation of a remark as was quoted in 22.0) regard the genuine body as the whole world. The Buddhists deny that any ordinary body is substantial and this allows the genuine body to be the whole *pratityasamutpada* or realm of dependent origination. Indeed, some Buddhist authors use a 'True Self' vocabulary, and the universal self can be the best interpretation of such a vocabulary. This is seen, for instance, in "…the student must have the inner experience called satori by which he is reborn as the True Self."[57] The Taoists sometimes have the self 'embracing the world,' or being one with the world.[58] Jesus, in the Gospel of Thomas, is supposed to have said, "I am all."[59] This, perhaps, provides an account for sayings attributed to him in the canonical Gospels, for instance, that eating a piece of baked dough is eating his body. Other mystics (e.g., Rabbi Shneur Zalman) deny that there is any genuine

---

[56] For more on this, see "Quintuple Extension."

[57] Zenkei Shibayama, *Zen Comments on the Mumonkan*: 26.

[58] *Zhuangzi*, (Bk 25 "Zeyang" par. 6), translated by Hyun Höchsmann and Yang Guorong: 250.

[59] *Gospel of Thomas*, 77, in *The Gnostic Bible*: 63.

plurality: there is only a partless One.[60] Scholars will try to find a way to use contemporary set-theoretic logic to express the point.[61]

Accordingly, there is no intellectual opposition or clash between the teachings of many traditional mystics, on a suitable, though new, interpretation, on the one hand, and phystriology together with contemporary logical systems, on the other.

22.3 There is, then, a suitable intellectual framework for a reconciliation of phystriology and religious systems. The question that immediately arises is whether one can not only intellectually adhere to such teachings, but also experientially transform so as to see the world more or less as those known here as the philosophical mystics see it.

The religious traditions suggest that there is a way to experience such transformation. If the methods that are put forward by the philosophical mysticism generating religious schools are given a secular or myth-neutral interpretation, then the methods and instructions can easily stay away from emanationistic or interactive dualistic glosses of what's going on. There is no difficulty describing and practicing exercises of meditation and contemplation without reference to anything emanationistic or interactive dualistic. And when considering basic changes in the brain, the practices would be sufficiently deep as to avoid one intellectual reading or another. Accordingly, the joined hypothesis arises: (i) scientific naturalism and (ii) use of the esoteric or philosophically mystical aspect of religion and spirituality both intellectually, and practically. The intellectual and practical consistency of scientific naturalism and esoteric religion would be, and, as the rest of this Chapter attempts to show, is, the basis of mystical naturalism.

This will now be expressed in more detail. The main themes of esoteric spirituality are: that the ordinary body boundary is a fiction; that there is an ongoing contrastless bliss that is experienced by one who gives up the ordinary body boundary; and that there is a 'circulating light' or '*ch'i*' or '*shakhti*' sensation that accompanies such blissful experience.

---

[60] See Rachel Elior, "Habad": e.g., 163-4.

[61] To have a partless one, one can take terms referring to spacetime objects and re-cast them as predicates of the universal class. One can go farther; one can have a language in which there are predicates, but no objects referred to in expressions, and so, under the theory, no objects, would be referred to.

As we've now seen, the first thesis is fully consistent with phystriology. So is the second, restricting direct volitional control to the ordinary body. The third thesis, however, presents small difficulties; these small difficulties, though, can be fully resolved.

As we saw above, the *ch'i* thesis is traditionally taken to be about *ch'i* throughout the universe; but the last few hundred years of science reject the notion that there is any *ch'i* phenomenon throughout nature. To rectify the problem, all that one needs to do is to maintain that the *ch'i* experience is proprioceptive or, as it would sometimes be put, an 'inner sensation', a sensation having nothing to do with goings on outside the intuitive body boundary. That renders experience of *ch'i* consistent with acceptance of the phystriological picture.

Some might wonder: how would a proprioceptive experience of *ch'i* within the intuitive body boundary allow for the experience "I am the whole world"? Isn't there a clash between the experience of something like *ch'i* but only in the ordinary body and the experience, "I am the whole world"? In response, ordinarily proprioceptive *ch'i* plus "I am the whole world" seems to be an odd conjunction; yet it is not logically nor metaphysically difficult. (Once again, 'metaphysics' is here the study of the structure of the world.) The proprioceptive experience of *ch'i* might well, for instance, be an experience produced by unusual stimulation of the brain homunculus (the brain homunculus accounting for ordinary body experiences, including 'phantom limbs'), these unusual stimulations having nothing much to do with the intuitive extent of the body at all. The loss of the intuitive body boundary would be both intellectually realized (through such factors as were reviewed in 22.1), and experientially realized through practices such as special re-structuring thought exercises, or long periods of stillness meditation, and it would be *accompanied by* the deeply engaging experience of 'inner light' or '*ch'i*'. The apparent oddity of the conjunction of the proprioceptive *ch'i* and the "I am the world" experiences is thereby seen not to be intellectually difficult.

The experience of ongoing contrastless bliss is consistent with phystriology. But whether it is plausible to think that there are such experiences should be looked into. How would it come to be? In answer, it would be regarded as the result of a brain- reorganization or, possibly, an input change from the rest of the body to the brain. It is important to observe that we have bliss experiences in appropriate circumstances (after long periods of running, after massage, after eating tasty food, during sexual activities, due to sexual climactic states, and so on). This grounds the intellectual view that there may well be brain reorganizations allowing for ongoing bliss experiences. Such bliss experiences, being ongoing, would be contrastless experiences. Nonetheless, the contrastless aspect of the bliss remains.

It also seems likely that there are three or four kinds of such possible experiences of ongoing contrastless bliss: (i) very little negativity and a lot of positive experience; (ii) experience of a loving invisible being in the proximity of the body; (iii) experience of something like sexual pleasure in an ongoing contrastless way; (iv) experience of the '*ch'i* phenomenon,' if it is different from (iii); and (v) experience of the world as pleasurable without a 'self vs. other' boundary. It could be important to distinguish awakening of these different forms of ongoing contrastless pleasurable experiences, and to note the advisable and unadvisable aspects of each. For instance, layering experiences of (ii) with the belief that such a being exists is unadvisable according to the proponents of phystriology, since beliefs in invisible interpersonal beings are to be rejected according to the proponents of phystriology. On the other hand, experiences of the other three or four sorts are not unadvisable in that way. In the (v) form, some might be psychotic, whereas others might not. That, too, would need some investigation.

Proponents of phystriology, then, would recommend some sorts, but not all sorts, of cultivation of ongoing contrastless bliss experiences. Whether there are phystriology-recommendable cultivations, in the absence of good neurological studies, can only be a matter open for individual discoveries, person by person. Neurological research in the coming decades may help, intellectually, to clarify the issue. The assessment of the mystical naturalist claim, then, is a bit individualistic at this point in time.

Assuming a positive result of such an assessment, a sub-question remains: Perhaps an individual can not only intellectually conclude a form of estoteric mysticism consistent with phystriology but also realize the experience of an esoteric mysticism consistent with phystriology; but can there be collective or organized institutional expressions, including religious expressions, of this mystical naturalist point of view? Can there be a Judaism, a Christianity, an Islam, a Hinduism, a Buddhism, a Taoism, a Jainism, and so on, that survives the phystriology challenge in this manner? The question applies also to the extent of institutional development of humanism in the mystically naturalist direction, though humanism easily accommodates phystriology. It is the implementation of a scheme to abandon the ordinary body-boundary for large proportions of people that is the issue here.

Unfortunately, it seems that this cannot be determined at this stage. The mystical naturalist position is to hope that such questions can be answered in the affirmative. But whether the many changes required are feasible cannot at this stage be clearly worked out. Perhaps the best that can be said is that only time will tell.

22.4 It can be observed that four meanings of the term 'God' have been so far employed. First, there is the personal God interacting with the world at the human, or, more broadly, classical scale, a being logically inconsistent with phystriology, and which, therefore, is rejected by mystical naturalism. Second, there are two other forms of the personal God: the personal God who interacts with the world only at the quantum scale, and the personal non-interactive Deist God. Either way, such a God would be a being whose existence is rejected on strong grounds by one who accepts phystriology. For strong reasons, then, all these forms are rejected by phystriology, and so the existence of the personal God is rejected in mystical naturalism. So, too, phystriology rejects the existence of a tiny variant on this, the supernatural intelligence. This, too, is rejected in mystical naturalism.

Third, there is the God that transcends the scientific view of the world, the God that is the mystery at the limits of consciousness. This God concept is used by Willem Drees in scientifically natural religion, and is not rejected by phystriology. Similarly, there is Burhoe's slightly earlier God concept, which, put one way, is the feature of the universe that enables human fulfillment to take place. Neither of these two concepts of God would be rejected in mystical naturalism. It should also be noticed, though, that although the sense of mystery is suitably emphasized by Burhoe and Drees, there is no equivalent in the currently advocated scientific-naturalist view of religion (by Burhoe or Drees) to the strong experiential transformations as are supported in Hinduism, Buddhism, Taoism, and so on, and are consistent with phystriology; whereas there is in mystical naturalism. Orientation to the third concept of God, then, may not satisfy many seekers.

Fourth, there is the view, suggested to be experientially realizable, that the body of each human being is properly understood as the world. The body of one person, then, *is* the body of any other person. Yet since each person is an organized system centred, roughly, in a certain (tiny) region of the world, one person can be differentiated from any other person with reference to the organizational centre of that personal being. Seeing the world this way would be very different from the ordinary way of seeing the world. In this view, to say that God exists is effectively to say that God is the world as seen by the person who experiences, in a non-psychotic way, the boundarilessness of the body supporting the person, and the boundarilessness of the body supporting any other ordinary object.[62]

22.5 It has been said before, for example, in Chapter One and in Chapter Twelve, that articulating matters of central human concern is very different from articulating a scientific result, and is very different, as well, from articulating the phystriological view. If a mystical naturalist view of the world is to be the basis for integrating phystriology and religion/spirituality, what would be said about matters central to human concerns?

Whether there will be groups of people for whom the abandonment of the exoteric dimension of religious life is practical is not clear. For instance, whether people can adjust to mourning the loss of others without references to an afterlife is not clear. There can be many approaches taken. Humanist groups are already engaged in such practices. But the humanist groups tend to be small in numbers. For this reason, how far the mystical naturalist approach is likely to go, and how quickly it will develop, is unclear.

22.6 This Chapter has briefly summarized an integrative view of spiritual practices, contemporary science, and various views and teachings. Two messages were given to each of the two main groups in our conversation, the scientifically minded group, and the religion or spirituality minded group.

---

[62] The human body works as does the body of any ordinary object. Just as there are many reasons to deny that the human has a naturally grounded small boundary, so, too, there are many reasons to deny that any ordinary object has a naturally grounded small boundary (for the details on which, a careful reader may consult, for instance, Peter Unger, 1980). So every ordinary (spacetime) object, too, properly understood, is the world. The type term we use in referring to it picks out which properties of the world we are focusing on.

To the scientifically minded group the two messages are, first, to notice how phystriology requires acceptance of the view that the ordinary body boundary is not a genuine body boundary (since, it could be simply put, the rules, laws, or forces of physics apply equally everywhere in spacetime), and second, to notice how consistent the boundariless body notion is with traditional esoteric phenomenological religious experiences.

To the religion-and-spirituality minded group, the two messages are, first, to explicitly give up the five theses associated with exoteric religious experience, and second to re-conceive the claims associated with esoteric religion so as to allow religious forms to survive in a worldview that accepts phystriology.

This means that the religionists should also accept that the humanists can be involved in the very same enterprise, but using a different set of cultural practices. Mystical naturalism, then, is as sympathetic to the humanist goals as to the religious goals; and, going a bit further, claims that the humanist goals need now to expand a bit, to include something parallel to esoteric religionism. Mystical naturalism hopes for the development of both revised institutional humanism and revised institutional religions.

I have also suggested ways that the mystical naturalist view improves on each of the three previous views. Bertrand Russell, for instance, had a mystical feeling, but took it that the mystical worldview was without merit; yet the mystical feeling persisted. The mystical natural approach, though, favors a stronger form of mysticism than that theorized about by Bertrand Russell, and in addition finds intellectual grounding for that stronger form of mysticism in phystriology. For this reason, the acceptance of the mystical natural approach, which includes the philosophical mystical approach, might have more to it than the 'reject religions altogether' view associated, for instance, with Russell. The scientific naturalist approach to religion was based on attitudes common to religious and secular humanist groups; but the traditional texts, it would seem, would be too hard to constantly reinterpret. The 'it's all okay group' do not confront the centre of the problem, namely the strong clash between phystriology and advocacy of spirituality; hence their approaches lack central merit. Yet these problems seem to be addressed in the mystical naturalist approach. The difficulty is whether the mystical naturalist approach, both humanist and religious, can ever develop a broad-based practical appeal to a wide enough number of people. On that question, (and on whether canonical texts can be reconceived for the mystical naturalist purposes) it seems, only time will tell.

In the next Chapter, I will outline one important way there can be not only a new integration of religion/spirituality/secular humanism and contemporary science, but also a new sort of institute for cultivation of spirituality (where 'spirituality' is meant in a fully broad way) in an entirely secular environment.

Chapter Twenty Three: The Secular Wisdom Institute

23.0 Introduction

We have seen four main ways to respond to the conflict between phystriology and the various forms of religion and spirituality. Every reader will prefer some response, perhaps one within these four, or, perhaps, from elsewhere. I have given my own response in the last Chapter; and, of course, it will be controversial in various ways. In this Chapter, there will be no attempt to establish preferences between the four responses just reviewed or any other responses to the main challenge between contemporary natural science and religious and spiritual views. We live in a world with a multiplicity of attitudes and responses to religion, spirituality, and science. The point that I will be offering here is that a new relationship between science and spirituality has emerged, a relationship that enables the development of a new sort of collective enterprise, a collective enterprise that has never been implemented in world history. This is an exciting promise. It shows us to be at a new level in the history of the practical-intellectual endeavours of the human community.

The rise in the sciences parallels the rise in secularism, and it is in this way that the development of the possibility of a new sort of collective enterprise arises from the parallel development of science and secularism.

23.1 Secularism

I take it as obvious, and not in need of any historical defense, that in the last few hundred years we in Europe, North America, and many other locations, have been living in highly (though not perfectly) secularized societies. Many of our universities and colleges are partly publicly funded and are secular in their orientation; and many private universities and colleges are also secular in their orientation. A main feature of an ideal secular institution is that all students are welcome, regardless of their cultural background, regardless of their religious or spiritual beliefs or disbeliefs, regardless of the focus of their dreams. In an ideal secular institution, it is taken for granted that some students are strong atheists; some are strong theists; some are spiritually oriented, but not affiliated with any organized religion; some are moderate in their religious or spiritual stance; some are literalists in their religious or spiritual stance; some are agnostic on all matters having to do with religion and spirituality; some are skeptics in some skeptical tradition; some are Marxists; some are liberals; some are capitalists; some are anti-capitalists; … the list goes on and on. And, by and large, our public universities and colleges are secularist institutions to this extent at least.

This ideal secularist model requires that those who want to facilitate encounters between proponents of a wide range of rival intellectual views – which means, primarily, philosophers, though students in many other fields bring rival intellectual views into their studies, as well – must be secularists in the classroom. That is, they should not require, as a sort of pre-admission standard, or a graduation pre-requisite, that students accept one or another belief on any of the hot controversies of the time. Rather, they should encourage students to appreciate the many sides of an issue, and they should encourage students to become familiar with the various reasons people have for preferring one or another position. Once a student has become somewhat familiar with the various reasons for preferring one or another position should the student develop, at some appropriate level of detail, his or her own view and articulation of the reasons for that view.

Let's contrast this with the way education occurred in the ancient period (600 BCE to 300 CE, say). There were, of course, educational institutions in the Mediterranean world, in India, and in China during this time period. Pythagoras started his educational community. Plato founded the *Academy*. Aristotle founded the *Lyceum*, also known as the *Peripatetic* school. The Epicureans had their *Garden*; the Stoics had their *Stoa*. In India, there were the Jain institutions; there were what we now call the Hindu institutions; and there were the institutions of the Buddhist *sangha*. In China, there were, after 200 BCE[63] or so, the Taoist

---

[63] This may be taken, roughly, as the time when the 'hundred schools,' a loose grouping, became 'the six schools' or 'the nine schools.' See A. C. Graham: 377.

schools, the Confucian schools, the Mohist schools, the Legalist schools, and several others.

These were not, however, secularist schools. Each school had its approach to the nature of the universe and the nature of human or social fulfillment. Each potential student had a choice as to which school to attend, and the choice was often a difficult one. This is made especially clear in Lucian's dialogue, *Hermotimus*. Written in the second century CE, the dialogue is between a skeptic, Lycinus, and a Stoic, Hermotimus. Lycinus reminds Hermotimus of how many schools there are, of how many different views they espouse, and of how arbitrary it is to choose one or the other school. By the end of the dialogue, Hermotimus agrees that he may as well, and, indeed, will, give up being a Stoic. This is a triumph of the skeptical approach over the Stoic approach. It is not, however, a triumph of the secularist approach over any other approach.

In fact, a dialogue at that time exhibiting a triumph of the secularist approach could not have been written, because there was no opportunity in those days for the development of a secularist institution, and so there was no opportunity for a victory of the secularist approach. There was no method whereby a teacher could say anything like, "This institution takes no stand on the important controversy of whether there is an afterlife. We all listen to the debates and come to our own conclusion." There simply was no opportunity for the secularist neutrality to be taken in facilitation of a debate between students.

On the contrary, the skeptics were skeptics, and, one way or another, they had to live as skeptics; the Epicureans lived as Epicureans; the Jains were Jains; the Buddhists were Buddhists; the Taoists were Taoists, while the Confucians were Confucians. Wang Ch'ung, in China about nineteen hundred and thirty years ago, was an eclectic thinker. One conclusion he reached was that there is no afterlife; but he didn't found a school; anyway, if he had founded a school, it would not have been, indeed, it could not have been, a secularist school. In the ancient world, there was no secularist 'cover' or mask to be worn in classrooms in an educational institution. So the schools were formed along the lines of the leading thinkers of the time. Each school promoted its own line of thinking or its own attitude toward living.

In the last few hundred years, the secularist institution developed, and it has now reached a reasonably strong level. In philosophy classes, professors are reasonably well trained in allowing students to debate issues. This is particularly true in the United Kingdom, Canada, Australia, and in most parts of the United States. It is, perhaps, a little less true of a few parts of the United States, where particular 'lines' are heavily pushed by the public, and so the debates are not as vigorously followed as they might be. In what follows, though, I will, through ignorance, overstep the bumps in secularism in such places as the United States, and sidestep post-secondary educational institutions in the non-English speaking communities. In short, I will simplify the situation in regard to supposedly secular, including private supposedly secular, universities and colleges anywhere in the world, taking them to be fully secular.

23.2 The contrast between ancient philosophy and modern philosophy

There is a striking difference between philosophical work in the ancient period and philosophical work today. In the ancient period, being a philosopher meant being engaged in *philo-sophia*, that is, being engaged in the pursuit of wisdom, or ultimate fulfillment. The terms for wisdom in the languages of the ancient period were, of course, different from each other. Nonetheless, it is reasonably clear that in the ancient world, to attend one of the schools we are considering, was to be in pursuit of one or another form of ultimate fulfillment.

Nowadays, however, to be a philosopher is a different sort of thing. To be a philosopher is to be one who attempts to find satisfactory positions on some important fundamental theoretical controversies. This is a pursuit of truth, or a pursuit of justified opinion, or a pursuit of an adequate worldview. It is conceptually highly distinct from the pursuit of ultimate fulfillment. For instance, the areas in which there are important fundamental controversies are very much compartmentalized. There is logic, epistemology, metaphysics, ethics, aesthetics, philosophy of science, and so on.

Also, the practices of the contemporary philosopher are primarily thinking, reading, presenting points of view, discussing, debating, and writing essays. However the practices of the ancient philosophers, some of whom were the Pythagoreans in the Greek-Hellenistic world, some of whom were the Buddhists in Asia, some the Confucians in China, and so on, included not only those practices, but also practices like pressing out the wrinkles on the blankets or sheets on rising, eating only vegetarian food, dressing in certain sorts of clothing that marked which school one was attending or to which community one belonged, being prohibited from speaking for several years, chanting various formulaic statements, and, sometimes, sitting in silent meditation.

23.3 The current opportunity: a secular wisdom institute

There are two advantages that may come to mind through our exploration so far. The first advantage will be attractive to readers who have a distinct preference in regard to the accounts in Chapters Nineteen, Twenty, Twenty One, Twenty Two, or to any rival account. We'll see soon enough how any of these alternative views will find a special role (an optional role, and not in the slightest way a mandatory role) within the secular fulfillment institute. Proponents of one of the positions articulated in Chapters Twenty through Twenty Two in response to the challenge of phystriology is likely to think of the institute as a secular wisdom institute. Others would only be discovering what forms of fulfillment are possible. The term 'secular wisdom institute,' then, means no more than 'secular fulfillment institute.' For that reason, the latter is the phrase that will be used in what follows in this section, and will tend to be used sometimes after as well.

The second advantage does not require preference of one of the approaches of Chapters Nineteen through Twenty Two. It is consistent with preference of the atheist or religion-rejecting view, consistent with the natural-science spirituality, consistent with the "it's all okay" approach, and consistent with mystical naturalism. And it is consistent with the "I'm still thinking about this," approach, or the "I think Chapters Nineteen through Twenty Two approaches have left out a crucial angle" approach, or the "I haven't got a clue," approach. Whatever approach one takes to the clash between phystriology and religion or spirituality, one can see the value of a new sort of institute, namely, a secular fulfillment institute.

Here are some underlying features of a secular fulfillment institute.

First, there already are some people well trained to facilitate what is required in a secular fulfillment institution, since they've gone through (graduated from) the highest level of education in a secular institution in a department in which students debate (from the introductory to the highest level) all matters of fundamental controversy. These people are called philosophers. For this reason, it is possible to have a group of facilitators for the events at a secular fulfillment institute, namely the professional philosophers who are moved to be such facilitators.

Second, the commitment of such facilitators will be to preserve the secularism of the secular wisdom institute. This is a new kind of commitment, since the practices to be engaged in not only include the practices of a typical classroom in a secular university or college – reading, thinking, presenting points of view, discussing, debating, presenting essays – but also other practices. The next section will outline the different practices that can be used in a secular fulfillment institute. Here, some mere illustrations will be given, some to be used, some not to be used, often drawn from practices used in the ancient schools.

To begin with, here are some illustrations of practices that might be used: thought examination, switching perspectives as something like an imaginative art, silent contemplation or meditation, so long as those practices are stripped of specific doctrinal colorations, and so long as the practices do not presuppose a particular controversial view.

On the other hand, pressing out the wrinkles in blankets and sheets, for instance, seems to presuppose some reason for doing so; but it is not controversial to say that there is no good reason for doing so; so the practice of pressing out the wrinkles in blankets and sheets would carry too much controversy if it were to be an established practice of a secular fulfillment school. But various forms of imagination could be used, so long as doctrinal colorations were stripped off the instructions. It is not forbiddingly difficult to accomplish such strippings; the secularist background is already available, and the doctrinal colorations for practice instructions tend to be rather thin.

The only possibly difficult points to work out would be how to facilitate growth, or the cultivation of whatever ultimate fulfillment there might be, or any advantage that can be cultivated, within a secular atmosphere. Would one work for relatively small-scale advantages or benefits alone, or work for those in conjunction with large-scale transformations? That is a question that each practitioner could work out for himself or herself; yet no explicit direction in regard to that question needs to be taken by a facilitator at a secular fulfillment institute. And that provides the method of work. One cannot tell from someone's being a participant in a secular wisdom institute whether he or she has a long-term commitment to that sort of practice, or something more short term. (Of course one can inquire into the person's history, but that's another matter.)

The choices available through a secular wisdom institute would parallel choices already available to people everywhere, including in the secular institutions. For example, some students will stay away from a third year level or graduate level logic class, merely because they don't want to go through "all that" as they might think of it. Similarly, someone who is not attracted to the sorts of practices being offered at a session of a secular fulfillment institute could simply not enroll in that session. On the other hand, there can be sessions that offer practices that are more attractive to that student. The only suggestion is that practices be mentioned beforehand. And the only requirement is that the practices being offered at any session are practices that require no adoption of one side of a controversial belief.

23.4 A variety of secular practices are available for a secular fulfillment or wisdom institute

It happens that there are many secular practices available for work at a session of a secular fulfillment or wisdom institute in addition to those practices already in place in the secular universities and colleges. The practices already in place in the secular universities and colleges are, as mentioned above, reading, thinking, presenting points of view, conversing (that is, discussing and exploring ideas), debating, and presenting essays.

Here are some of (not all of, merely some of) the secular practices. Only some of these are of a sort that is already in place, though, mostly, in place for registered credit course students, which would not be the case for a secular fulfillment or wisdom institute. Others are new sorts of practices entirely consistent with secularism, yet leading to fulfillment or wisdom interpreted openly.

First there are physiological practices that can be recommended, or, in sampling sorts of ways, engaged in, at the sessions of a secular fulfillment or wisdom institute: some stretching or aerobic exercises, or other exercises as people in therapeutic recreation programs, for instance, are familiar with. These programs are already available through secular institutions, so they wouldn't be main focuses at all in a secularist fulfillment or wisdom institute. Similarly, although this is not very different from discussions already present in the classroom, views can be expressed about dietary approaches, and there can be discussions of those views. (There need be no dietary regime followed in the sessions of a secular fulfillment or wisdom institute, since such sessions need not include meals. And if they do include meals, secular institutions already do put on meals in various ways, and a secular fulfillment or wisdom institute could do so.)

Second, there can be recommendations for psychological exercises of the sort positive psychologists recommend. These can be used by anyone, regardless of his or her other beliefs or background. The recommendations can be to help be aware of and cultivate 'virtues', though it is important to be aware of the difference between the positive psychologists' views of virtues and the philosophers' views of virtues. The positive psychologists – Martin Seligman for example – see the activities of the sadomasochist who savors serial killing, the hit man who kills for cash, and the terrorist who plans or executes bombings as activities that allow them to lead, respectively, the pleasant life, the good life, and the meaningful life.[64] I know of no philosophers who would say so, and of course Martin Seligman after saying so, in one way of looking at it, takes it all back. He doesn't really mean what he said; he was only speaking as a neutral scientist. Philosophers, however, want to understand the relations of facts and values. This is a quick indication of the need for philosophy rather than for a science that hides behind a supposed neutrality on difficult questions. In any case, positive psychologists provide various exercises that can be employed.

Third, there are many exercises that have not been well developed to date; yet they are potentially very useful; and they are fully secular in focus. For instance, the psychologist Paul Ekman has identified seven universally recognized facial expressions: those of sadness, fear, disgust, contempt, anger, surprise, and joy. Making these faces (while facing the wall, say, so as not to be performing) can be very useful. Similarly, there are similar exercises that are well developed. There are now many laughter groups, for example; and introducing a minute or two of laughter into a secular fulfillment or wisdom group can be worthwhile.

Fourth, there can be unusual and readily accessible ways of engaging in aesthetic creativity: for instance, there can be one word-per-line sonnet writing, or a bit of informal drumming for rhythm sense.

Fifth, there can be various outlines of the variety of philosophical views on basic issues plus opportunities for participants to figure out

---

[64] See Seligman's *Authentic Happiness*, NY: Free Press, 2002: 249 and endnote 303. As mentioned in the text, Martin Seligman, the person, would not endorse what he says merely as a supposedly value neutral scientist. But, either way, he would give no philosophical exposition of his views.

their own views. This wouldn't be very different from the sort of information that is already available in philosophy classrooms, but it could be helpful for people who are not enrolled in a credit-course base philosophy program.

Sixth, there can be various thought experiments that people can engage in for whatever benefit they may bring. For instance, there are some collections of philosophical thought experiments, some of which can be gone through; there can be intimate task-relation idealizing exercises to engage in. These are, of course, personal and private exercises, though they can be facilitated in secular fulfillment sessions.

Seventh, there can be entirely secular forms of postural and non-postural meditation. These were traditionally given in various ancient schools of fulfillment, though the instructions given then were not secularly given. In a contemporary secular fulfillment institute, the instructions would be fully secularly given, and the practices, too, would not be in the least overlaid with mythic or doctrinal ingredients.

And eighth, there could be community-building exercises that are entirely secular in their expression. In our society, typically, people who belong to religions or to a secular humanist group take pride in the commonality of views found, to some degree, among members of that institution. A secular institution, however, equally welcomes people of radically opposed views. Yet a secular institution is a community. Accordingly, a secular wisdom institute could have a ritual in which, well after oppositions of views have been identified, everyone greets everyone else and exchanges thoughts in a chatty friendly way. The greeting and exchange would be a spontaneous building of community; it would express the fact that differences in intellectual views don't matter as far as harmonious community, and personal friendship, too, is concerned.

There is only one other recommended feature for a secular fulfillment institute, and it is an easy recommendation to fulfill. It has already been suggested. This is that some practices to be engaged in for any given session should be one way or another announced in advance.

23.5 The importance of a secular fulfillment institute

There are several ways in which we can understand how important the opening of secular fulfillment institutes would be for the contemporary secular university and college.

For one thing, such an institute would close the gap that is now found between religious/spiritualist institutions on the one side, and secular institutions on the other side. In other words, it would be possible for one to be engaged in fully secular activities, and also to be engaged in the project of developing oneself in whatever way is possible. There is a large gap at the moment in the public world; how to develop oneself is regarded as a private matter; yet there are public secular institutions. Why not allow the public secular institution to facilitate the development of each individual in a public way? It seems to be time for the secular institutions to do so.

Two cautionary notes: Non-philosophers sometimes think that they are more aware of what is required for secular discussion than they are. For this reason, it is best to ensure that facilitators at a secular wisdom institute be professional (Ph.D.) philosophers. Such philosophers typically have taught courses in which they have become exposed to how many views there are on any given topic; such philosophers can be relied on to stay farther away from (unintentionally, no doubt) providing biased approaches to difficult questions than others would be likely to.

Also, the secular wisdom institute should be a strictly and entirely non-credit institute. If it were to be mixed up with credit-gaining, then there would be scores of confusing conflicts of interest. The means of testing would be arbitrary and often unrelated to the intrinsic merits of a long and unpredictable process. Complaints would arise; confusions would result; the process would be anything but fulfillment-expressive or wisdom-expressive.

Let's return to the main topic, the importance of the development of a public secular fulfillment or wisdom institute. A public secular fulfillment or wisdom institute associated with or directly part of a secular university or college would enable the facilitators of such an institute – once again, those philosophers who are interested in the project – to return to what was the centre of their discipline in the ancient period, yet has more or less disappeared from it at the present time.[65] In other words, there is a need for old-fashioned philosophy

---

[65] Some philosophy professors maintain that their philosophical class activities promote the cultivation of wisdom; but then again, many don't. Also, the classes of those who do maintain this include only reading, discussing, giving or listening to lectures, and such like activities; they do not include six of the eight sorts of exercises mentioned in 23.4. And the class activities are restricted in

(meaning philosophy as the cultivation of the most sort of fulfillment that there can be); once again, there could be focus on ethics, on metaphysics, and on epistemology, all in ways accessible to newcomers, yet of interest to old hands; and there is a way for many forms of old-fashioned philosophy, and some new forms of what was old-fashioned philosophy, to reappear now within the secular atmosphere. This is an exciting opportunity for philosophers as practitioners and facilitators, for non-philosopher academics as practitioners, and for the public at large as practitioners.

Third, there are opportunities for atheists, anti-religionists, and self-described anti-spirituality folk to discover underlying methods of growth or transformation to whatever extent religionists can find such methods of growth or transformation as well. This, too, provides for an exciting system.

As the reader may have guessed, I have begun such a wisdom institute at my College (Douglas College in BC, Canada). It has been operating now for several years, with, at the moment, many one day secular wisdom workshops. I would be happy to answer any questions that may arise about it.

---

many ways in regard to enrollment as well. Participation in a secular wisdom institute would not be. The difference between current classroom activities in philosophy and what happens in a secular wisdom institute is significant.

Appendix I: Phystriology Was Presented, But Why So Reticently?

A1.0 The following may be useful to two groups: those interested in the 20th century development of the phystriology position, and those interested in accounting for the odd reticence among philosophers during the last half century or so about so important a result as phystriology.

A1.1 D'Arcy Thompson published *On Growth and Form*, first in 1917, then in a second edition, 1942. It begins with an introductory chapter that exposes the need for an integration of mechanical explanations with purposive or teleological explanations in organisms. Perhaps it was because he had no access to the distinction between theoretical reductions and token ontological reductions that his remarks are a touch unclear. Yet there is in Thompson's work an anticipation of the phystriological result. It is not, however, clear just how strong that anticipation was. On the one hand, Thompson says, "Of how it is that the soul informs the body, physical science teaches me nothing...,"[1] which, in one way of reading it, undercuts what was to result from phystriology. On the other hand, he says,

> When physical science falls short of explaining the order which reigns throughout these manifold phenomena...men hasten to invoke a guiding principle, an entelechy or call it what you will. But all the while, so far as I'm aware, no physical law, any more than gravity itself, not even among the puzzles of "stereometry"

---

[1] D'Arcy Thompson, *On Growth and Form*: 8; (2nd edition pg. 13).

or of physiological "surface-action" or "osmosis," is known to be transgressed by the bodily mechanism.[2]

That already showed a strong leaning toward the phystriological position. But there is more: In the second edition, Thompson removed, "so far as I'm aware," showing the distance that had been travelled from 1917 to some time in the 1930's or early 1940's. In any case, in the light of both sorts of remarks, D'Arcy Thompson, although working along forward-leading paths, to some extent, still, sat on the fence.

Perhaps one of the earliest articulations of something close to the phystriology thesis is the famous remark made by Ernest Rutherford sometimes reported as: "All science is either physics or stamp collecting."[3] This suggests that any efforts in chemistry, biology, and other sciences do not overturn the rules, laws, or forces found in physics, and, presumably, assumes the mathematization of physics. That amounts to the two central phystriology theses. But this was reported merely as a remark made, and it is not clear how far it goes evidentially.

The Encyclopedia Britannica of the 1930's has an article by E. S. Goodrich on "Evolution" which holds that an organism is a "physico-chemical" complex mechanism.[4] Perhaps this should be regarded as a statement as to what was regarded as highly probable, rather than as a statement as to what had been established by the evidence beyond any reasonable doubt. Although it might be said that it had been pretty fully established (by 1930 or so) that there are no fundamental chemically complex configurations of particles with special motions, nonetheless, it had not yet been pretty fully established that there were no fundamental biologically complex configurations of particles with special motions. That was only established by 1953 with the discovery of the DNA structure, or by some time in the 1960's, with the confirmation of the predictions – some of them by Francis Crick and James Watson – of the ways DNA and related chemicals would account for the reproduction of

---

[2] Thompson, *ibid.*: 9; 2nd edition, without "so far as I'm aware": 13.

[3] This quote is frequently offered, but without citation or without an indication of the date. David Wilson, in *Rutherford: Simple Genius*, lists other examples of Rutherford's disparagement of chemistry and other sciences in the early 1930's, pg. 564. The quote is, apparently, to be found in J. B. Birks, *Rutherford at Manchester*, NY: W. A. Benjamin, 1962.

[4] Goodrich, Edwin, 1938, "Evolution," *Encyclopedia Britannica*: 917, 928.

organisms, reproduction of cells, the creation of proteins, and the creation of organs and their interrelations.

A good history of the last few hundred years of science, *Science Since 1500*, by H. T. Pledge, was published in 1939, and then given a second edition in 1959. The period from 1939 to 1959 includes the major turning point from a time in which the evidence for phystriology has often been taken to be incomplete to a time in which it was, for all practical purposes, complete. However, Pledge's "Prefatory Note" for the second edition made it clear that no fundamental revisions were undertaken during this period. The original work did not expound, nor mention the possibility of, phystriology, even though the book is organized around developments in mathematics, physics, chemistry, and biology.

In 1944, Erwin Schrödinger published *What Is Life?* which anticipated the development of molecular biology, a movement arising in the 1940's, '50's and '60's. Schrödinger's *What Is Life?* in one sense pioneered the token union of physics and biology. *What Is Life?* was, avowedly, not a deeply entrenched biological work, but rather the work of a great physicist thinking about biological forms of stability and order, and speculating on results in physics and chemistry, particularly statistical results, that, he thought, would account for the biological order we have. Schrödinger already accepted the physicalization of chemistry, as is clear from various references he makes in his fourth Chapter on "Quantum Mechanical Evidence." In large part, the intention behind the book seems to have been to show many reasons to anticipate the physio-chemicalization of biology.

There are, however, several ways in which the book is internally incoherent if it is taken to anticipate the full development of phystriology. To begin with, phystriology is logically inconsistent with the traditional metaphysics of the Advaita Vedantins. The Advaita Vedantins traditionally take it that there is a reincarnation system, such that (in the vocabulary of the Yoga school) the *purusha*-mind frees itself from the entanglements of the *prakriti*-matter enmeshments, and such that the unity of the mind is discoverable in experience. All these elements, and more in the traditional Advaita Vedantin view, go against the requirements of phystriology.[56] Yet Schrödinger, in the Epilogue to *What*

---

[5] See, for example, P. T. Raju, *Structural Depths of Indian Thought*, Ch's IX and XI.

Is Life? adulates the Advaita Vedantin metaphysical system. Further, the picture he offered of the Advaita Vedantins is that their position is consistent with the conclusion he wanted to draw. The conclusion is that anyone who would like to reconcile contemporary mechanism with the interior sense of freedom would be forced to agree with the view that "'I'…am the person, if any, who controls the 'motions of the atoms' according to the Laws of Nature."[7]

There are, one might say, four problems with Schrödinger's conclusion. First, the phrase 'if any' nullifies the direction of the conclusion. What if there is no such person? Is there still a 'control' of the motions of the particles? If there is, but it is not in a higher sense of 'control,' then the Advaita Vedantin position is gone. (If there is, and it is in a higher sense of 'control', then Schrödinger did not anticipate phystriology.) Second, removing the 'if any' phrase, the 'control' notion suggests that the conclusion moves against the argument from phystriology whose result is that a person is, or is supervenient on, a complex sum of atoms moving according to the laws, rules, or forces of physics. Then there should be no postulate of a person transcendent of such sums controlling the motions according to the laws of nature. (Perhaps Schrödinger didn't take a person to be transcendent in the usual sense, though. One could defend Schrödinger's view in this way. But then his defense of the Advaita Vedantins is puzzling.) Third, the Advaita Vedanta position and other related positions affirmed by Schrödinger go against the fulfillment of the Laws of Nature as conceived under phystriology. (The evidence for phystriology was reached only after the writing of *What Is Life?* but here we are merely assuming that Schrödinger was anticipating its development.) Fourth, Schrödinger neglected the well-known compatibilist view of freedom, pioneered, for example, by Thomas Hobbes in the 17th century. All in all, the degree to which Schrödinger fully anticipated the development of phystriology is unclear.

Similarly, the remarks of general systems theorists,[8] first presented in 1940 by its founder, Ludwig von Bertalanffy, do not clarify the distinction between the two sorts of emergence reviewed in 11.6: strong emergence, which overturns the rules, laws, or forces of physics, and is the sort of emergence postulated by the British Emergentists, and weak emergence, which does not overturn the rules, laws, or forces of

---

[7] Erwin Schrödinger, *What Is Life?* 93.

[8] See, for example, Ludwig von Bertalanffy, 1968, *General System Theory*.

physics. Consequently it is extremely difficult to say whether the views of the general systems theorists support those of the British Emergentists, or those of many contemporary exponents of phystriology. Yet the distinction is a crucially important one (and it should be generalized too, so that 'strong emergent change,' for instance, becomes 'strong change,' thus avoiding any controversy over the type anti-reductionism brought in by the term 'emergent'). Phystriology is logically inconsistent with eight views often reviewed above – the God interacting with the world at the human scale, the afterlife, etcetera – but British Emergentism is consistent with those eight views.

Probably, Paul Oppenheim and Hilary Putnam gave the first clear and detailed exposition of a physically closed model of the natural sciences in 1958.[9] The terms they used were 'the unity of science' and 'micro-reductions.' Their 'unity of science' was an ideal notion, a notion only realized in trends within the sciences. This enabled them (over-ambitiously) to include psychology and the social sciences. Also, their micro-reduction hypothesis was over-ambitious. Their system doesn't show how the philosophically significant phystriology thesis needs no more than physics, chemistry, and biology, but, rather, extended the model through psychology and the higher sciences. They did present many empirical details underlying their "working hypothesis" to the professional audience. However, their working from biology to psychology and beyond, most philosophers would say, was not justified. The distinction between token ontological reduction and theoretical reduction was not used at this stage (since, once again, it had not yet been developed), and their theory was based on methodological or explanatory reductions going right through the sciences. Their system was also highly compositional. They maintained that: atoms sometimes make cells; cells sometimes make organisms; some organisms have psychological features; some psychologically featured organisms make societies; some societies...etc.[10] However, although compositionality in biology is easy, at some level, to accept, there are strong objections to the compositionality reduction view of the contents of states studied in, for example,

---

[9] In "Unity of Science As A Working Hypothesis."

[10] See Oppenheim and Putnam, *ibid*.: 9-10. Interestingly, this does not interfere with compositional reductions within all natural objects – although objects with psychological states are natural objects – down to classical physical objects such as atoms interpreted classically, or statistically down to groups of quantum physical objects.

psychology to states studied in biology.[11] Consequently, Oppenheim and Putnam's theory was subject to many objections. Also, they said nothing explicitly about what is here being called the mathematization of physics.

A1.2 The period from 1958 to the early 1990's lacked a well developed exposition of phystriology from physics through biology-only, despite the fact that the evidence for such a phystriology was more or less all done (and was entirely done by a decade later, 1968, say), and despite the rapid acceptance of the phystriology thesis, on mostly implicit bases, by a vast majority, indeed, a consensus, of the philosophers called mind-body philosophers, and of non-constructivist philosophers of science during the 1970's and after. Peter Medawar in 1958 made a passing note that "it is…the belief of almost every reputable modern biologist, that this act of integration [putting together the higher level (biological) changes from our knowledge of its constituent parts] is in fact possible." This remark was made in his comments on D'Arcy Thompson's *On Growth and Form*.[12]

In 1962, Wilfrid Sellars contrasted the manifest image of the world that people have with the scientific image of the world, and said that "the scientific image presents itself as a closed system of explanation."[13] Some have, loosely, interpreted this as a reference of sorts to a causally closed system;[14] that shifts the content of Sellars' remark a bit, but it does indicate the softness in the early expressions of phystriology. We will return below to Sellars' undetailed rejection of phystriology about two decades later.

Coming back to the 1960's, Richard Feynman, in *The Character of Physical Law*, a record of lectures given in 1964, saw the nesting relation between biological phenomena and physical phenomena. He said, for

---

[11] E.g., "The Present Status of the Innateness Controversy" in *Representations*, Jerry Fodor, Cambridge Mass: Bradford MIT Press, 1981.

[12] Medawar's review was published as "Postscript" in Ruth D'Arcy Thompson's *D'Arcy Wentworth Thompson*, London: Oxford University Press, 1958; it is also found in Medawar's collections *The Art of the Soluble*, 1967, and, *Pluto's Republic*, (but only partially in my copy) Oxford: Oxford University Press, 1984. The quote in *Pluto's Republic* is on pg. 235.

[13] Wilfrid Sellars, "Philosophy and the Scientific Image of Man," VI, 4th to last par.

[14] James R. O'Shea, *Sellars*: 19.

instance, "Probably the most powerful single assumption that contributes most to the progress of biology is the assumption that everything animals do the atoms can do, that the things that are seen in the biological world are the results of the behaviour of physical and chemical phenomena with no 'extra something'."[15]

Also, there was a good paper in 1966 by Gerald Feinberg, "Physics and the Thales Problem." Feinberg there spoke mostly about the recent physics results. Still, it is clear on the physicalization of chemical relations that had already been shown to be true,[16] and expresses a sort of hope that biological relations will prove to be no exception to the dominance of physics-rules, laws, or forces that had already been found.[17]

In the late 1950's and 1960's the type-to-type identity theories developed by J. J. C. Smart, U. T. Place, and David Armstrong accepted phystriology, as is clear from off-hand and secondary remarks made in their arguments.[18] However, they did not explicitly use phystriology as a primary premise. Armstrong, for instance, after noting the strong likelihood of the biology to chemistry to physics reductions, stated that it would be difficult – too difficult, he thought – to take it that psychological states would not be similarly reducible. Still, this didn't make physics through to biology a major premise in his argument.

We can also notice some other, perhaps defective, factors in the reasoning. Armstrong seems to have been ignoring some features of psychological states. Moreover, he did not state what he could have, namely, illustratively, that a poet who writes down the mentally appearing words of a poem, is a biological creature, and that that is sufficient to ensure that the laws, rules, or forces governing the motions of the fingers of the poet are the (already discovered) laws, rules, or forces of physics (in contexts of discovery in which hands are moving to write poems) so long as they are taken as approximate results, and applied for short term time periods. Epistemically possible objections occur; there might be

---

[15] Richard Feynman, *The Character of Physical Law.* 165.

[16] Gerald Feinberg, 'Physics and the Thales Problem': 10.

[17] Gerald Feinberg, 'Physics and the Thales Problem': 14.

[18] For example, J. J. C. Smart, "Sensations and Brain Processes"; and Armstrong, D., *A Materialist Theory of the Mind.* David Papineau comments on this in the Introduction to his "Appendix" to *Thinking about Consciousness*: 233.

potential to actual and actual to potential transitions that cancel each other out in small scale regions; but by the 1960's such objections had become so extremely implausible as to be discountable. Nonetheless, had the type-type identity theorists not accepted phystriology from physics through biology, they would very likely not have been led to postulate the identity theories they did postulate.

Still, one may wonder as to why they were not clearer in regard to their acceptance of phystriology from physics through biology. Armstrong, for instance thought that evidence for the paranormal might justify the exception of the mental states from such reductions. He partially countered the notion by upholding the view that some physical system might underlie the apparently paranormal performances.[19] To many, this will seem too ad hoc. It seemed ad hoc to Armstrong too, and so, he concluded that "the claims of psychical research are the small black cloud on the horizon of Materialist theory of mind."[20] Still, the more obvious point, that humans were biological creatures descended by naturally selective evolution, seems to have been missed. If it were not missed, then psychological states would make no difference, or not much difference on this point.

One might also say that the evidence, even by 1968, was stronger for phystriology than Armstrong exposed. There was the phystriological point of view, but it was not much focused on. Perhaps, one might think, the absence of extended discussion was due to the methodological emphasis for *all* the sciences in Oppenheim and Putnam's view of 1958. For instance, had Smart, Place, and Armstrong not accepted phystriology from physics through biology, they would very likely not have been led to postulate the type-to-type identity theories they did postulate. Oppenheim and Putnam's 1958 view was, from this perspective, a distraction from what might have been, but wasn't, done. To avoid the distraction, Smart, Place, Armstrong, and suchlike philosophers let their views on mind-body identity hang on other theoretical issues, issues to a degree independent of the broad methodological views of Oppenheim and Putnam. We will come back to this thought in the next section of this Appendix.

It was philosophy of mind workers who expressed the phystriology notion in somewhat more full forms. Donald Davidson in

---

[19] Armstrong, *ibid.*: 362.

[20] Armstrong, *ibid.*: 364.

1970 said that physical theory "promises to provide a comprehensive closed system" for "every physical event..."[21] That was phrased merely in 'promise' terms. Two years earlier, David Armstrong had taken an equally confident line: "It seems increasingly likely that biology is completely reducible to chemistry which is, in its turn, completely reducible to physics."[22] His notion of 'reduction,' given the time period, was unclear; however, his focus on biology, chemistry, and physics was on the mark as to the notion of phystriology, unfettered, as it is, by the relation of psychological states to biological, chemical, or physical states.

On the other hand, there is an important difference between phystriology notions and reduction notions. The mental states seem to have causal relations with other mental states and with physical states, for instance. If there is reduction of mental states to physical states, then the micro-states seem to sum to have such causal relations, and, some will say, the micro-states themselves have such causal relations. But there has been a very strong tendency to adopt the hypothesis of time reversal invariance in physics, and causes in the everyday sense – especially mental causes – resist the idea of sequence reversibility. So there is everyday language resistance to the hypothesis of such microcausation. Davidson's phystriology notion is, notably, not expressed as a physical *causal* closure notion. But by the 1990's, as we will see, phystriology became physical causal closure. This was probably, in part, due to the continued use of the 'causation' term by physicists who accepted time reversal invariance. There was, then, a revision of the everyday causation notion in these uses. (The content of a statement like, "Darcy decided to leave the building; that decision then caused Darcy to leave the building" cannot be readily reversed; if so, it would be the unintelligible, "Darcy left the building; that leaving then caused Darcy to decide to leave the building.") In any case, it is noteworthy that the phystriology 'ism' only says that there is no overturning of the rules, laws, or forces of physics. It does not make clear how reversible causality operates.

Returning to the narrative, little was written between 1958 and the 1990's in favor of phystriology, aside from a line or two here and there, as we found in Armstrong and Davidson above. And rarely, there

---

[21] Donald Davidson, 1970, "Mental Events," quoted in D. Spurrett, *The Completeness of Physics*, PhD thesis: 2. Why "promises"? For one thing, because relativistic gravity was not (and still is not) integrated with quantum physics.

[22] David Armstrong, *A Materialist Theory of The Mind*: 49.

were objections to it: Wilfrid Sellars, for instance, in "Foundations for a Metaphysics of Pure Process,"[23] in 1981, 3rd section, denied the autonomy of the mechanical realm, and hypothesized additional causes in the British Emergentist (or strong emergentist) style. Another renowned opponent of phystriology was Karl Popper. He postulated three worlds, the physical world, the mental world, and the mental-expressional or knowledge world.[24] Items in the latter two worlds, according to Popper, causally impact the physical world, producing changes that otherwise would not have occurred. If any such strong emergentist change existed, which Popper claimed do exist, the claims of physriology would be broken. The neurobiologist Roger Sperry adopted an anti-physriological approach as well.[25]

However, despite the few who opposed physriology, the supervenience notion developed during the 1970's. After 1975 or so most everyone working in mind-body philosophy either accepted an identity thesis or a supervenience thesis. This showed, effectively, a consensus on physriology. However, a physical causal closure notion, where 'causal' is unclear as to whether it is everyday-causal or revised-causal, conjoined with a causal exclusion principle, has been said to produce strong tensions within supervenience theories.[26]

John Haugeland's work on supervenience[27] is a good example of the sort of discussion that went on in the 1970's and 1980's. On the one hand, his remarks on history in discussion of "The Way The Wind Blows"[28] did not mention the basic structure of the evidence for the triple nesting of biology in chemistry in physics; he also did not note the difference between psychological and higher complexity states on one side, and, on another side, biological states, chemical states, and physical

---

[23] Sellars, The Carus Lectures, *The Monist*, **64**: 3 – 90.

[24] See, for instance, "Three Worlds," Tanner Lectures on Human Values, University of Michigan, April 7, 1978, on line, and other works by Karl Popper ≥ 1972.

[25] E.g., Roger Sperry, *Science and Moral Priority*, 1983: 116-7.

[26] For more recent articulations of supervenience theories, see Kim, J., 1993, "Concepts of Supervenience," or, for the tensions, *Physicalism or Something Near Enough*: 13-22.

[27] John Haugeland, 1984, "Ontological Supervenience."

[28] Haugeland, *ibid*: 4.

states. On the other hand, his notion of 'completeness' was accurate; he says that "Strict completeness means only that physics brooks no intrusions on its own turf; it does not mean that physics is the only explanatory game in town…"[29] We can also note the use of the term 'completeness,' showing its use, along with 'closure,' at that time.

A1.3 There is a worthy task, to explain the unusual quiet in the philosophical world about so important a result as phystriology. There are many explanations one might propose. (And these factors may well go beyond 1990 to the present time as well; I'll return to the more recent period below.)

The first is the focus of Kuhn's work in *The Structure of Scientific Revolutions*, 1962, and the way in which that focus became central in a large discussion that, effectively, eye-framed many philosophers who were writing about *controversies* in the philosophy of science. The focus Kuhn studied was the history of individual sciences, and most particularly, the history of physics. Kuhn did not discuss the relationships between physics, chemistry, and biology. Since a large controversy surrounded his description of radical changes within single sciences, a note of strong caution was struck, which may have prevented a well-oriented discussion on the relations between the three natural sciences of physics, chemistry, and biology.

This was part of the reason that the major shift in understanding of the natural sciences reviewed through Part I, especially Chapters Two through Nine, was not much focused on. It has been fashionable, since Kuhn's work, to emphasize the radical changes in the meanings of special terms in the sciences. What has been, in some quarters, unfashionable is an emphasis on how the radical new meanings of terms preserve, at least approximately, any established measurements (over short term time periods, to avoid chaotic results) of the older quantified theories in the original contexts of discovery. 'The original contexts of discovery' needs to be mentioned on account of Kuhn's correct comment that approximation theories that leave out the contexts fail.

I predict that the view that there is short term time period context-restricted preservation of old quantified theories will spread beyond some circles in philosophy to a much larger group, both in and

---

[29] Haugeland, *ibid*: 8.

outside of philosophy, in the next half century or so. The quantification of theories has this result, and, as is well known, quantified measurements arose in physics from around 1600, in chemistry from the late 18th century, and in biology from, perhaps, the early 17th century. The no-turning back point happened in the 1950's and 1960's. Accordingly, some will say that during the fifteen years in which Kuhn was working out the details of *The Structure of Scientific Revolutions*, he missed noticing the take-over of what many will regard as the most important philo-scientific revolution in the last few thousand years. His work in the conceptual revolutions within a science will continue to be fruitful, but it will be absorbed into a larger description of the non-dropping or non-overturning of the quantized results, regarded as approximate results over short term time periods for original contexts of research, in biology, chemistry, and physics. That's a prediction, and only the future will reveal how well it comes true.

Returning now to the task at hand, let us think of the many objections to the 1958 Oppenheim-Putnam unity of the sciences view as the second element in the explanation of the absence of explicit discussion of phystriology from physics through biology during the 1960's till the 1990's.

There are also other possible explanatory factors. The third might be the natural distraction encouraged by the criticisms of the type-type identity theory. Ironically, it was Putnam who made these criticisms.[30] They noted the multiple realization possibilities for any functional type. Accordingly, the type-type identities would not work. On account of the apparent failure of the type-type identities, there was a great deal of work in the creation of token-token identity and supervenience theories to account for the higher level notions.

Simultaneously, it became recognized how difficult if not impossible it would be to develop theoretical reductions of the Ernest Nagel[31] sort, not only from psychological states to biological-chemical-or-physical states, but also from biological or chemical states to physical states.[32] During the period in which phystriology from physics through biology evidentially developed (1910's to 1960 or '70 or so), the

---

[30] Putnam, Hilary, 1967, "Psychological Predicates," in W.H. Capitan and D.D. Merrill eds, *Art, Mind, and Religion*.

[31] Ernest Nagel, 1961, *The Structure of Science*.

[32] See, for instance, Jerry Fodor's "Special Sciences," in *Representations*.

theoretical reduction model was developed. But in the period afterward, it was abandoned as unsatisfactory, and so it may be that the phystriology that had been established from physics through biology, relying only on *token* ontological reduction, although occasionally articulated[33], was not explicitly articulated as much as it might have been.

Also, advocating one or another of the many rival schools of thought in mind-body relations that developed since the 1960's, but within phystriology, may have distracted philosophers from explicit discussions of the evidence for phystriology from physics through biology only. Since so many philosophers took that evidence to be non-controversial, it would only be to exhibit to the religious philosophers what the evidence is that would motivate the expositions. But too many philosophers, for one reason or another, have not been enthusiastic in regard to debating religious positions. And so the number of those who might focus on phystriology has been limited. Whatever draws philosophers to mind-body study and philosophy of science may, in addition, frequently draw them away from intellectual defense of religious attitudes. And it is between religious philosophers on the one hand, and mind-body philosophers or most philosophers of science, on the other, that the gap is to be primarily found. That, too, would explain some lack of interest in exposing the evidential bases of phystriology.

Perhaps we can say that there was an element of social caution. Phystriology threatened many standard religious views; and pointing this out seemed to some to be incautious. It was left to someone else to point that out. As it happened, however, no one took up that task. And John F. Post, for instance, asserted that the postulation of God's existence is logically consistent with the results of the natural sciences, thus, unfortunately, ignoring the *logical* implications of phystriology in regard to any interactive God at the classical scale, and ignoring the strong though not strictly logical implications against any other form of the personal God.[34] From the late 1950's through to the early 1990's, there was a large, lamentable, gap in the literature, which I reviewed elsewhere.[35]

A fifth factor is that many thinkers were – how to put it? – glancing at, but not being clear about this enormously important result.

---

[33] For example, in "Special Sciences": 130.

[34] John F. Post, 1987, *The Faces of Existence*: 332.

[35] As in Ch 11 first note: "Compositional science and religious philosophy," *Religious Studies*, **41**: 130-1.

For instance, Noam Chomsky, in 1968, expressed the view that the term 'physics' could or would come to encompass results that might "emerge at only higher levels of organization".[36] This takes seriously British Emergentist fundamental complexity. Similarly, Ned Block said, in 1980, that it is "conceivable that there are physical laws that 'come into play' in brains of a certain size and complexity…"[37] Neither Chomsky nor Block were clear on whether the laws would be fundamental or not, and this only allowed for a confusion between causal closure issues and type-reductionism issues.

A sixth factor is the controversy between strong physicalists and moderate physicalists. This contrast can be construed in various ways. Here is one of them: A strong physicalist holds that everything, whether concrete or abstract, is supervenient on the domain of physics-based objects. A moderate physicalist restricts what is supervenient on a physical subvenient base, and holds that everything that occupies spacetime is supervenient on the domain of physics-based objects or facts; this allows for the existence of universals; universals may be in, or be transcendent of, spacetime. W. V. O. Quine, for instance, was a strong physicalist. In 1979, for example, he said that physics provides the supervenience base for everything.[38] But many theorists moderated one or another aspect of strong physicalism. D. M. Armstrong, for instance, accepted universals in spacetime.[39] Entering this controversy allows one, incorrectly, to think that there is an equivalent controversy between the phystriology permitted easily by moderate physicalism, and the difficulties a strong physicalist supposedly has accommodating both phystriology and apparent universals. This distracts one away from an adequate definition of phystriology, which, accepting that all changes are weak changes, is not vulnerable to the supposed difficulty.

Finally, as a result of the few thinkers (some already mentioned, born in 1902, 1912, 1913, and such like dates) who explicitly rejected phystriology post 1970, and of philosophers sometimes classified as irrealists who commented, like Richard Rorty, in 1979[40], that it is

---

[36] Noam Chomsky, *Language and Mind*: 83.

[37] Ned Block, 1980, "Troubles with Functionalism."

[38] W. V. O. Quine, "Facts of the Matter": 163-4.

[39] D. M. Armstrong, e.g., *A World of States of Affairs*.

[40] In *Philosophy and the Mirror of Nature*.

"Whiggish" to review history from one or another all-inclusive angle, it may be that more status came to the idea that there was some controversy lurking in support of the phystriology notion, though, as Chapters Two through Nine, and Chapters Ten and Eleven showed, and Appendix 2 will show, there wasn't. That partially undermines, but doesn't completely undermine the question, "Why wasn't the scientific build-up of the phystriology result elaborated close to when that build-up became completed, in the 1960's or 1970's?"

This much can be certainly said: there were many distracting issues preoccupying philosophers from 1970 to 1990.

A1.4 Brian McLaughlin in 1992[41] described the rise and fall of British Emergentism. This provided him with an opportunity to emphasize the recent history of phystriology, though he didn't use any such term. Rather, he talked about the British Emergentist positions on emergent causal powers, downward causes, and fundamental configurational forces (where a configuration is a configuration of particles). In any case, his main point was to emphasize that the a priori status of British Emergentism suffered no downfall; rather, it was the empirical results – here, I've called them the results of mathematized physics, of physicalized chemistry, and of physio-chemicalized biology – that undid the British Emergentist hypothesis. It is interesting to note that McLaughlin (and, it seems, all writers we've been reviewing on the topic) missed the mostly a priori way of obtaining the phystriology result: Nöther's Theorem is mostly a priori. Interestingly, Nöther's Theorem implies Darwinian natural selection. In any case, Nöther's Theorem, alone, implies phystriology.[42]

By the way, as mentioned in a note in Chapter Ten, it is to require that there are no British Emergentist processes in a phystriological system that the third statement in the definition of phystriology given in Chapter Ten was included. As McLaughlin makes clear 'physics' could refer only to the sum of micro-physics processes; or it could refer to both that and British Emergentist physics as practiced by physicists, if there were such a thing, which there wasn't. A merely verbally tricky use of

---

[41] McLaughlin, Brian, "The Rise and Fall of British Emergentism."

[42] See 10.4, note 173.

statement two in the definition is prevented by inclusion of the third statement in the definition.

McLaughlin refers to the key developments in the first half of the 20th century that clinched the tale of the rise of phystriology (quantum explanations of chemistry, and some key results in biology including uncovering the DNA structure).[43] But he doesn't go back in any detail to the history over the last few hundred years. He referred (briefly) to some versions of vitalism as different from British Emergentism. But he did not discuss the mathematization of physics. (That topic was outside his range.)

It was still rather quiet on the nature of the phystriology theory in the early 1990's. David Papineau explicitly characterized the completeness of physics notion in 1993; as he exposed it, "we need never look beyond the realm of the physical in order to identify a set of antecedents which fixes the chances of every physical occurrence."[44] Papineau then used cause and effect language in place of 'antecedent' and 'consequent' language. Causal relations between mental states and physical states were discussed in other contexts, and soon enough, the physical completeness claim refers to physical effects,[45] which calls to mind causal relations. This gave rise to the question about what the physical is; and that was discussed occasionally, for example, by Tim Crane and, later, in response, by David Papineau.[46] There also was the development of the notion of the causal exclusion argument, which effectively uses the phystriology result, e.g., by Jaegwon Kim in 1992.

David Spurrett in 1999 completed his PhD project on the completeness of physics, and he reviews such discussions. However, his investigation was almost entirely on the completeness of physics in relation to various academic themes in the philosophical literature; he briefly touches on the scientific evidence for phystriology (in Chapter 2 section 7), but his focus is mostly on highly theoretical academic philosophical questions. Spurrett did not go into the important implications of phystriology in regard to religion and spirituality at all. He also makes it seem as though there must be something controversial

---

[43] McLaughlin, *ibid*: e.g., 54.

[44] David Papineau, *Philosophical Naturalism*: 13; the quote: 16.

[45] Papineau, *Philosophical Naturalism*: 30.

[46] David Papineau, *Philosophical Naturalism*: 1.9.

about the empirical-scientific evidence for phystriology; otherwise why bother with the detailed theoretical work? However, as I tried to show in Chapters Two through Nine, in Chapters Ten and Eleven, and will fill out in more detail in Appendix II, there is no significant doubt to be offered in regard to the empirical-scientific evidence for phystriology from physics through to, and stopping at, biology. Once we have insight into the three processes – the mathematization of physics, the physicalization of chemistry, and the physio-chemicalization of biology – possible doubts are overleaped. As mentioned before, (11.1,11.13), this is reinforced by other factors such as Nöther Theorem (see, e.g., above, 10.4, n. 172) and what I elsewhere called 'the demarcation problem,' which itself will be reviewed in A2.1. I will return to the shortage of insight into the structure of the processes involved in the gathering of the scientific evidence below.

A1.5 We return now to the task of A1.3, explaining the lack of exposure of the phystriology result and the evidence behind it. We found some factors possibly explaining that absence from 1950's to 1990, but now we have been looking at the results of the 1990's, in which there was another factor. This was Alvin Plantinga's 1993 exposition at the end of his *Warrant and Proper Function* of an argument whose conclusion is that evolutionary naturalism is inconsistent with belief in the reliability of cognitive outputs. A vast number of philosophers took this argument to be interesting, and to require responses; consequently, very many responses to this argument were given.[47] But, at the same time, it should be noted that this added to the distractions away from considering the integrated results of the ordinary sciences. It is the philosopher's job to show such integrations, and so we have another explanatory factor for what seems to be the over-hesitance of philosophers.

A1.6 Still, not all philosophers have entirely shied away from the phystriology topic. David Papineau in 2001 reviewed much of what is involved in the notion of phystriology.[48] There were a few details he was not satisfied with. In 2002, Papineau gave a short but comprehensive

---

[47] See, for instance, *Naturalism Defeated?*, edited by James Beilby, and the many articles referred to by Alvin Plantinga in note form at the beginning of his "Reply to Beilby's Cohorts," 204-275.

[48] Papineau, David, "Rise of Physicalism."

review of how phystriology notions – called notions of the completeness of physics – developed.[49] He began with some work in the 17th century, and proceeded through to the middle of the 20th century; the discussion is pitched to scholars. Also, he revised some details he had given in his 2001 presentation. The review given in Chapters Three through Nine of this book picks out a rather different set of events to focus on, generally more accessible elements, whereby introductory readers may grasp the empirical work that led to acceptance of phystriology by so many philosophers. Also, the mathematization of physics was not explained (though it was, effectively, assumed) in these works of Papineau.

Neither Papineau nor McLaughlin mentions the importance of the Darwinian evolution theory in undermining interactive dualism. Oppenheim and Putnam in 1958 do, however, though briefly, and so, for example, does Patricia Churchland, also briefly, in 1986, and Paul Churchland, 1988,[50] and many others.

Natural selection evolution theory, as mentioned earlier, is important in the development of phystriology since, according to some, it shows the gross implausibility of any physically incomplete system that satisfies Newtonian (or post-Newtonian) mechanism in the third sense (as defined in Chapter Three), or a current strictly mathematically governed physics for humans. And the evidence for natural selection evolution is overwhelming, as many of the works of Richard Dawkins, for instance, make clear. But a crucial point needs to be emphasized: natural selection in evolution still left open the possibility of a British Emergentist, or, alternatively, a vitalist, system for organisms. Some would add the position-relative Jamesian form of fideism it allowed; it is important to add that, since Jamesian fideism is logically impossible under phystriology; phystriology makes the issue not 'live' to one who looks at the evidence. And some would add that Cartesian interactive dualism could also be considered; there was no logical exclusion of it under Darwinian evolution, though there was under phystriology.

Darwinian evolution, then, was a vitally important indicator of what would come; but since it still left the field open in three or four main ways, it did not yet accomplish the result that phystriology did. Darwinian evolution was only about the evolutionary process – whether

---

[49] Papineau, David, "Appendix" in *Consciousness*.

[50] Oppenheim and Putnam, *ibid.*, pg. 25; Churchland, Patricia, 1986, *Neurophilosophy*: 320; Churchland, Paul, *Matter and Consciousness*, revised edition.

there was a species evolutionary process, and by what means, if there was a species evolutionary process, it occurred. It was not about *all* biological changes.

It is also important to see that vitalism and British Emergentism are still consistent with the law of conservation of energy, through use of both potential and non-potential energy sums.[51] If Copernicus (supplemented by Galileo, and others including Newton) established the Copernican revolution, and Darwin, alone, or with Wallace, established the second, Darwinian revolution, then there was also a third revolution, established by the vast number of physicists, chemists and biologists (and, it seems, philosophers, too) whose work added up to the phystriology result.

Another background point: some pure philosophical factors are used, though they are mostly implicit in the summary of Chapters Three through Nine, in development of the evidence for phystriology, and as this was described, for instance, by McLaughlin, and Papineau. For example, there is the simplicity principle. It is conceivable that a non-physical mind causes physical changes and that all the evidence found is nonetheless incorrect. But the simplicity principle leads us to reject such a hypothesis. (This also reminds us that philosophical skepticism about the external world of the Academic or Pyrrhonian sort is put aside in this discussion; but it needn't be – and it wasn't in 11.9. Even the Pyrrhonian skeptics follow appearances. Why? Perhaps for non-evidential reasons, e.g., harmonies. But that doesn't matter; behaviour will still follow appearances.)

Yet though the philosophical principles such as Occam's razor are at work, the extraordinary confluence of the developments in the natural sciences provides grounds for a not strictly logical argument denying what otherwise would be the logical possibilities. The concepts of purpose, goal, and so on, were in use for scores of thousands of years, but only in the last few hundred years have we discovered that all purposive beings are evolutionarily, and natural selectively, produced sums of purposeless things. Then came the phystriology result by around 1970; we use it logically and nearly logically since then. Hence the logical possibilities are undone.

---

[51] This is briefly explained, for example, in Brian McLaughlin's "The Rise and Fall of British Emergentism," *ibid.* 72.

Further on background, Papineau's story given in 2002 effectively ends at around 1960, though he speaks briefly, though only in a footnote on pg. 255, about later questioning of the phystriology result on the basis of quantum physics. However, as will be reviewed at the beginning of Appendix II, there are five views about how one might specifically be able to deny phystriology that have been offered since around 1960, not just one. It has become necessary to answer the other four views and to elaborate on the first as well. This will be done in Appendix II; and this, partially, explains the comic gap in communications between exponents and rejectors of phystriology referred to above.

A1.7 A discussion of material on phystriology should also note that the absence of clear explanatory materials on the rise of phystriology created an important absence in the understanding of religious philosophers. As just mentioned, I've elsewhere shown how big that absence, or gap in understanding, has been. Here, though, I'll note how important scientists have effectively been prevented from having a clear understanding of the situation by the over-caution of philosophers. The over-caution of philosophers has led to the masking of over-caution in supposed reasonableness, as is found in scientists.

An excellent example is the work of Francis Crick, a powerful scientist whose efforts were crucial in uncovering the bio-chemical material from which phystriology was drawn. A notable chemist, he was certainly aware of the electromagnetic accounts of atomic bonding; accordingly, he was aware of the material from which the physicalization of chemistry can be drawn. In 1953, he and James Watson discovered the structure of DNA; they both speculated on the importance of this discovery for cell reproduction, organism reproduction, protein construction, and organism construction. The conjectural predictions they made were confirmed later in the 1950s, in the 1960's, and after. Accordingly, Crick was central in the development of the material from which the physio-chemicalization of biology result has been drawn. And, of course, like more or less everyone, Crick was aware, one way or another, of the mathematization of physics. Later, Crick decided to work on the problem of the relation between mental states and biological states. In *The Astonishing Hypothesis*, he presented the results he had been able to reach to the time of publication of the book (1994).

It is evident, though, that Crick was (unsurprisingly) not aware of the difference between a worldview in which phystriology is found and a worldview in which it is not found. For instance, he says that someone might complain that he, Crick, said nothing about creative mental states and 'my relationship with God'; Crick responds, saying, "Such criticisms are perfectly valid at the moment, but making them in this context would show a lack of appreciation of the methods of science" (259). Anyone familiar with phystriology would say that not only are the methods of science in tension with remarks about 'my relationship with God', *but also*, after the 1960's, it was the results of the natural sciences, when uncontroversially though philosophically integrated, that were *logically incompatible* with there being any such relationship as traditionally understood. (The only exception would be a relationship established between God working only at the quantum scale and humans, too, working only at the quantum scale; that would be so strongly ampliatively absurd as to be close to, though not quite, logically ruled out.) Accordingly, as notably well read, and as central a scientist in the development of the phystriology picture as was Francis Crick, could not help but be unaware of phystriology, due, no doubt, either to the extreme hesitancy of the philosophers after 1970 or so or to their being distracted by so many other factors.

To see how hesitant or distracted philosophers were, it is useful to note a brief remark by Jeff Poland, also in 1994. In the development of the core ideas and values of physicalism, he said that there are gratuitous associations with it. One of them, he said, is 'anti-religion'. The reason it is gratuitous to say that physicalism is anti-religious is because, Poland says, anti-religion, among other views, "is not evidently implied by the core ideas and values"[52] of physicalism. However, the core ideas and values of physicalism state, according to Poland, that everything is, or is supervenient on, the physical.[53] Yet there are eight views widely found in religions that are logically eliminated by everything in spacetime being supervenient on the laws, rules, or forces of physics. Poland's remark, here, shows how blind physicalists have been to its implications. A defender of Poland might say that Poland only wanted to allow religious beliefs to remain for their instrumental uses; but that, oddly, ignores straightforward logical contradictions.

The hesitancy of so many philosophers has had unfortunate consequences. I've already noted this in the cases of Francis Crick, just

---

[52] Jeff Poland, *Physicalism*: 41.

[53] Poland, *ibid.*: 15.

above, and, earlier, how the biologist, Richard Dawkins, by 2006, canvassed the reasons against believing in an interactive God, and did not seem to be aware of how by 1970 or so, it was the results of the natural sciences that *logically excluded* the interactive God at the human or more broadly classical scale.

Even some philosophers, Wilfrid Sellars, Karl Popper, as reviewed above, and Charles Taylor, as reviewed in 21.3.1, who, in the 1960's, supported purposive accounts of mechanical relations, did not catch up to results that were, in some sense, widely available. Now, in the 21st century, Taylor continues to ignore what has been available for many decades.

A1.8 The phystriology result, to put it simply, is the most important philo-scientific result, or revolution, of the last two and a half millenia. Yet, all in all, there have been few, indeed, expositions of the development of phystriology. The conjunction of the following three features should be a topic for further explanation: (i) phystriology has spread so widely within mind-body philosophy and among most (among, I guess, all non-constructivist) philosophers of science since the 1960's or so, (ii) phystriology has been hardly ever explicitly discussed, (iii) in the few occasions in which it has been explicitly discussed, it was not discussed for general consumption, but rather for upper level undergraduate or for graduate and beyond philosophical consumption, and (iv) its consequences for religious and spiritual beliefs were not, in the past, (the author's writings aside) carefully reviewed anywhere.

I have given some explanations of the initial shortage of expositions of phystriology, but there may well be more explanations to offer, especially in regard to the last few decades. It is relatively easy to see why phystriology has been ignored by so many religious philosophers, even in the last few decades. On the other hand, could it have been largely social caution that led to the ignoring of so huge a discovery? Or was it largely inattention (to the difference between physics, chemistry, and biology on the one hand, and physics, chemistry, biology, psychology, etcetera) on the other hand? Or was it distraction? Or was it the plurality of pseudo-issues? Or was it fear to discuss a tendency given human conceptual structures?

My own view is as follows: All those explanatory factors count. But so does one more factor, in my mind a more telling factor, too. Since philosophy began twenty seven hundred years ago or so, it was a field in which different figures established different viewpoints. As was mentioned in Chapter One, every position, aside from positions about logical derivations, was 'up for grabs.' On the other hand, mathematics is a field in which no theorem generally accepted by mathematicians at one time was later rejected by the consensus of mathematicians. There were occasionally conceptual refinements or restrictions, but the theorem still stood after the refinements or restrictions were made. After the 17th century, through the mathematization of physics, the non-overturning of mathematics came to be seen as applying, though through approximations, restrictions to original contexts, and only in short term time periods, to the physical world. Phystriology is the result of a few hundred years of subsequent research.

But the discovery of the world being phystriological is a combinatorial and therefore a philosophical discovery. This means that an enormous change has occurred in the nature of philosophical work. Whereas until the two thirds point in the 20th century, every position in philosophy, logical derivations aside, was controversial, it is now turning out that a truly important position in philosophy is not substantively controversial. It is this feature – the lack of substantive controversy about so important a thesis – that has, oddly, led philosophers to shy away from the topic. Perhaps phystriology should come to be known as the thesis that mathematized philosophy.

Philosophers needn't worry though. Although to say that the world is phystriological is not substantively controversial, whether to abandon religion, as in Chapter Nineteen, or to reform it, as in Chapter Twenty, or to champion it, saying "It's all okay," as in Chapter Twenty One, or to generate a mystical naturalism, as in Chapter Twenty Two, is highly controversial. And there are many other controversies, too, altogether untouched by phystriology.

All in all, though, it may be said that by now it's no longer useful or helpful (if it ever was!) to avoid explicit discussion of what many would regard as the most important result reached by scientific philosophy over thousands of years.

Appendix II: Scholarly Objections Against Phystriology

A2.0 In Chapter Eleven, I reviewed thirteen objections that might be raised against phystriology, and showed that they are readily answered. The objections were found to be mere pseudo-objections. I mentioned that more objections, scholarly objections, could be raised or have been raised, as well, and that they would be considered in Appendix 2. That, then, is the topic here, to show that the more scholarly objections are mere pseudo-objections.

A2.1 The five specific physically incomplete theories

It is one thing to object in principle to phystriology. It is another thing to propose a specific way in which the world might turn out to be not phystriological. Since the nineteen sixties or so, there have been, roughly, five views about how one might specifically be able to deny phystriology. These five will be looked at here.

First, there is the view based on informational or causal input often employing some features of quantum physics. One form of this view has been recently suggested, though tentatively, by David Chalmers.[54] Second, there is William Hart's version of the expanded energy-exchange conservation system.[55] Third, there is Tim Crane's system in which there could be multi-causal results, where some of the causes are the physics-based causes and others are non-physical mental causes.[56] Fourth, there is continuation of the British Emergentist view

---

[54] David Chalmers, "Consciousness and its place in nature." See pg. 126.

[55] Hart, William, *The Engines of the Soul.*

[56] Crane, Tim, *Elements of Mind.* 64-5.

(that there are special fundamental chemical, biological, or psychological forces or laws), as may be recently exemplified by Roger Sperry[57], though there are other ways of interpreting Sperry's view. (If one interprets his view in another specific way, it will fit into one of the other four approaches.) And fifth, there is the view, as advocated, for example, by the popular thinker Ken Wilber[58], that there are subtle intrinsically noetic (informational, intentional, conscious, or cognitive) bodily objects that are in interactive causal relations with lower level or gross bodily objects. Each of these authors has implicitly or explicitly suggested that his method gets around the evidence for phystriology.

Exponents of phystriology would say that, for many reasons, these methods do not work. I will first show this in six ways for quantum approaches; and then broaden it to cover all the proposals to specifically generate a physically incomplete system.

First, although some have wondered about what seems to be a subjective framework in the use of quantum formulas, the objective accuracy of these formulas is as great as, or greater than, the accuracy of any other formulas in physics or anywhere else.[59] Also, in a recent account, there are six *interpretations* of what is called the measurement problem (however the measurement problem is described), and only one interpretation of one of them developed in the late 1920's,[60] the Copenhagen view, accepts the subjectivity of observation states as crucial in understanding quantum physics. (In addition, it is important to note the objectivist as well as the subjectivist interpretation of the Cophenhagen view; we have to beware of the term 'observer': observers would not report anything different from machine reports.)

Second, the unusual probabilities in quantum relations are realized in an objective mathematical manner. When systems are large-scale systems, like the system in the human brain, for instance, there is a canceling of the probabilistic bases, aside from a 'noise' element that remains. The functional system, consequently, very much seems to be as

---

[57] Sperry, Roger, *Science and Moral Priority*: 96-117.

[58] Wilber, Ken, 2000, "Waves, Streams, States, and Self."

[59] See Steven Weinberg, *Dreams of a Final Theory*: 90-91. He says of a twelve decimal place accuracy, "The numerical agreement between theory and experiment here is perhaps the most impressive in all of science."

[60] Roger Penrose, *The Road To Reality*: 785-791.

non-purposive at the base as it is in a classical (that is, a non-quantum) system.

It would be absurd to think that if a car engine is quantum physics-based, then its quantum level transitions are intrinsically purposive. Similarly, it would be absurd to think that the quantum level changes underlying a human brain are intrinsically purposive. To put it another way, the quantum level changes underlying a human brain cannot be distinguished from the quantum level changes an inch away (in any direction) from any spot in the human brain. For one thing the uncertainty relations prevent there from being any such boundaries, except statistically. But statistical boundaries cannot be plausibly provided for any part of the brain. It seems that the only conclusion to draw is that wherever one finds the quantum events, there are only intrinsically non-purposive tiny physical processes leading to the outcomes.

Third, the subjectivity cannot be regarded as a human-based causal factor for outcomes. In any common sense picture of the world, there was a time without the sorts of subjectivity connected to the human race; there was a time with no (ordinarily thought of) conscious beings. So using any form of subjectivity seems too far fetched.

Fourth, the question needs to be looked at in the context of the results of the physicalization of chemistry, and the physio-chemicalization of biology. Given these two results, the urge to find fundamental purposes in the physical interactions is enormously undermined.

Fifth, quantum physics has, of course, challenged the basic classical notions, and it is also sometimes said that even the very idea of causality must be eliminated from elementary physical relations. Some might hope that this will enable purposes to function again through the mysterious quantum relations. In response, though, there are many factors that need to be put together: Intuitively, one can still see causality in human-scaled object relations. Many would say that the statistical effects of the probabilities would yield the causal relations. Then the causal relations at the large scale would sometimes yield the purposive beings, including human beings; it would be the sum probabilities that would be accomplishing such results. And such surface-wise time irreversible causality, at one level, doesn't reach down to the quantum objects; at another level, it does. But no purposes are brought down to the quantum level by those means.

If (unusually) one rejects causality at the human-scaled level, one would only be emphasizing what we are referring to as the mathematization of physics. One would not in any way be supporting physical *in*completeness. Once again, the unusual qualities of quantum physics do not support physical *in*completeness.

Sixth, some physicists say that they are anti-reductionists; more specifically, they think that unprepared non-local correlations, as seem to have been empirically confirmed, show that we can no longer adopt the view that the operations of small things in a big thing exclusively govern the operations of the big things that include them. The non-local correlations are themselves correlations occurring at great distances, and so the correlations can't be viewed as the effects of small-scale things inside the big things.

In response to this, however, it should be noted that the difficulties here seem to have little, perhaps nothing, to do with consciousness, which seems to be local in its origin and manifestation. However difficult it is to figure out what is going on with unprepared non-local correlations, invoking some purposive consciousness seems to be out of the ballpark; there was a time when there were no animals on earth, for instance.

Also, the sort of reductionism being purportedly undermined here is unclear; it may be mereological reductionism over time for all objects; it may be some form of type reductionism; but, in any case, exponents of phystriology would say that eliminating some kinds of reductionism would not put purposes back into the basics of reality. In other words, such anti-reductionism does not go against phystriology. Similarly, a many-worlds quantum approach doesn't bring purposes back into the base level.

Consequently, however one interprets quantum problems, there seems to be no genuine threat to the mathematization without intrinsic purposes in physics including quantum physics.

The quantum physics approach doesn't work. The matter can also be discussed more generally as well.

Take, for example, the last of the five main approaches we're looking at in this section, the idea that there are subtle noetic bodies that causally interact with gross bodies, as was put forward by Ken Wilber, among others. Many will hold that there is no observational evidence of the intrinsically noetic subtle physical objects; there is no evidence of the effects of such bodies; the hypothesis does not integrate with the

Darwinian evolutionary theory, nor with the broader lines including the mathematization of physics; and the proposal (for intrinsically noetic subtle physical objects and against phystriology) is within philosophical traditions generated at times in which there was no exposure to the contents and results of the last four centuries of natural science. Accordingly, exponents of phystriology would say, this proposal has little, if any, current plausibility.[61]

Similar remarks could be made about the other approaches. The Darwinian evolutionary evidence, particularly, makes them highly implausible. The physicist Henry Stapp has tried to figure out how evolutionary processes might have allowed for the development of what amounts to a physically incomplete system; but his central notion includes the Wigner-theory that mind is not emergent from the physical world, but is built right into the quantum world. This seems highly unlikely for reasons some of which are stated above, and more will be stated below in A2.3. The main problem is that the mathematical principles of physics include no desire-like purposes as features governing change. That is enough to show that the overall system seems to be extremely implausible. Perhaps Stapp was nobly grasping at straws.[62] In reviewing the evolutionary evidence it is helpful to keep in mind the two levels at which the evidence operates – the macro-level that notices the macro- or large-scale processes, and the detailed "here's how it happens" level. As was mentioned in 9.5, Darwin had no theory of any chemical or physical or other means through which properties of parents are transmitted, with variations, to offspring. Yet he didn't include that problem in the list of serious problems for his theory, a list that he was diligent in presenting in a thorough way at the end of *The Origin of Species.* Perhaps one reason he didn't include that problem would be that he was reasonably confident that the variations are both positive, for reproductive fitness, and negative, against reproductive fitness. So whatever theory, physical/chemical, or otherwise, filled in the details

---

[61] See also Chapter Twenty One, where Ken Wilber's views are reviewed as representative of the group who hold that science should one way or another catch up with religious/spiritual wisdom. And, once again, for a broader, articulation of this critique of Ken Wilber's views, see my "Two Questions for Ken Wilber and the Wider Transpersonal Audience."

[62] See Henry Stapp, "Attention, Intention and Will in Quantum Physics," and "The Hard Problem: A Quantum Approach." Both refer to his *Mind, Matter, and Quantum Mechanics,* Heisenberg: Springer-Verlag, 1993.

wouldn't matter. When it turned out that the biology is ordinary chemistry, and that the physical electromagnetic force accounts for the chemical changes, then this emphasized the smoothness of the causal processes in a remarkably strong way.

It should also be reflected at this point that a vitalist view, a British Emergentist view, and a Jamesian fideist view, were each consistent with natural selective evolution; all the first two needed to do, re natural selection evolution, is provide a means for, or allow for, both positive and negative variations in the likely-to-reproduce underlying properties of offspring. Hence, incidentally, once again[63] we see the importance of closure in physics over and above the success of Darwinian natural selection. Darwinian evolution included human beings in biological creatures, but it did not eliminate such views as British Emergentism and vitalism.

There is also another factor that has hitherto been mostly implicit, and only rarely explicit,[64] that can be mentioned in regard to the five post-1960 approaches against phystriology. This factor may be called *the demarcation problem*. I have summarized it elsewhere,[65] and it will be useful to review it here. The basic idea is that for any biologically complex system, there is a basic smoothness in the relations between cells, their parts, and their environments. There is no sharp boundary at which one can say, for example, 'this is exactly the boundary of the brain'. There are nerves going into the brain and coming out of the brain. The nerves have their intuitively or informally or conventionally determined endings relatively far away from the brain. Different pictures of the brain show different boundaries of it (some include the eye nerves and retinas, some don't; where to end the brain stem is arbitrary, and so

---

[63] As we've already seen, phystriology is both *logically* inconsistent with eight views commonly found in religious or spirituality systems and strongly abductively inconsistent with other views central to religions and spirituality promoting systems, yet, prior to the development of phystriology, there was only a *soft abductive* (*soft interpretive*) question between, say, Newtonian mechanics, Darwinian evolution, and spirituality. The strength of both logic and some abductions is enormous compared to the strength of soft interpretive factors.

[64] It is hinted at in the third paragraph of Smart, J. J. C., 1959, "Sensations and Brain Processes." And it is explicit, although very briefly put, in Wilson, David, 1999, "Mind-brain interaction and violation of physical laws": 191.

[65] "Compositional Science and religious philosophy": 131-139.

forth[66]). In this way, one cannot plausibly establish a special region in which the special effects take place, and other regions in which those special effects cannot take place. Yet such boundaries are required, or there would be odd competitions between events wanted by one mind, but not wanted by another mind, say. Leslie wants the fork moved from the centre of the table to Leslie's place at the table, say, and Pat wants the fork moved to Pat's place at the table, so there would be competition over what happens to that fork at the centre of the table. But there are no such competitions without fingers at the fork. The demarcation problem cannot be solved under the quantum theory, the expanded energy exchange theory, the multi-causal theory, and the revived British Emergentist theory. The noetic object theory has already been shown to be so highly implausible as to be discountable. So the demarcation problem is effectively devastating to the four remaining approaches.

It is also useful to note that three views have so far been presented as strongly convergent toward phystriology: the nesting of the three main natural sciences, Nöther's Theorem, and the demarcation problem. One could find other convergent views, as well. These convergent factors go against not only the five specific theories mentioned here, but also the explicit objectors against phystriology whose views present no specific answers to these convergent factors, including the demarcation problem, namely, the views of Wilfrid Sellars, Karl Popper, and would-be revivers of the British Emergentist scheme such as Roger Sperry. They say something like "It isn't so," but never say in specific terms how the changes occur.

A2.2 There are some recent theories in which indeterminism in quantum physics is taken to provide a basis for the defense of a view of human freedom; this defense of human freedom could be put forward as an objection against phystriology, and this use of quantum physics is different from those already considered in A2.1. Quantum indeterminacy plus chaotic effects, it is claimed, allow for the notion of human freedom.[67]

---

[66] As before, see Patricia Churchland, *Brain-Wise*: 89, 138.

[67] See David Hodgson, "Quantum Physics, Consciousness, and Free Will", and Robert Bishop, "Chaos Indeterminism and Free Will," in Robert Kane's 2002 anthology.

In response, this view does not opt for a non-physical mental *overturning* of the physical outcomes; nor does it opt for basic physical interactions with intrinsic purposes built into them; and it does not opt for a highly complex physical configuration of particles that triggers a *fundamental* law concerning the motions, etcetera, of physical particles. (Once again, in our sense, a fundamental law, rule, or force would overturn the outcomes *hypothetically reached* by the operations only of laws, rules, or forces without that fundamental law, rule, or force; one could also define 'fundamental' in a parallel way in respect to *already found* laws, rules, or forces, so long as they are taken only in original contexts of discovery, are approximate, and over short term time periods.) Reviewing the way physics theoretically or hypothetically explains chemical relations is of particular assistance in showing how powerful are the mechanical features in physics in the third sense (the third sense as exposed in the latter parts of Chapter Three). The sophisticated conceptual speculations with regard to human freedom will not touch the power of the physical analysis in relation to chemical changes. And when chemical changes are also shown to be the basics of biological changes, the sophisticated conceptual analyses do not address the basic evidential grounding of phystriology. There are, it seems, no specific counter-responses to this reply to the objection. The objection, in form alone, is irrelevant to the phystriology claim.

A2.3 Paul Humphreys in 1997 put forward a model based on quantum emergence internal to physics, through which, or analogous to which, he says, some sort of psychological emergence might be found to occur.[68] We have to be patient, he says. Based on Humphreys' paper, an objection against acceptance of phystriology would simply advocate for patience on the issue.

In response, we should note that Humphreys is by no means explicitly advocating patience in regard to non-physical mental interaction with the physical world, nor in regard to British Emergentism. Similarly, his patience is not explicitly directed toward helping the religious philosophers and other closely related philosophers who advocate physical incompleteness. This presents the central problem for our context: Humphreys does not suggest how his system would help any

---

[68] Humphreys, Paul, "How Properties Emerge."

attempt to provide for physical incompleteness, that is to say, for an overturning of mathematized physics.

This central problem can be articulated in the following eight ways: A) There is no observational-theoretical basic evidence for a parallel of, or application of, quantum emergence to the psychological (or psychologically biological) level in such a way as to provide for physical incompleteness. B) There is no evolutionary explanation as to why such a phenomenon should be present. C) There is stochastic (statistical) evidence against a parallel of, or application of, quantum emergence for the functional requirements of the higher level given the apparent lack of opportunity for quantum coherence at the brain level. This does not go against there being important effects of quantum changes on functioning units; it only goes against such quantum changes being crucial parts of the functioning system. D) There are, apparently, objective decoherence processes[69]; this reinforces the notion that there are classical outcomes governing the biologically functional structure. E) There is what I have called the demarcation problem:[70] there need to be, but, apparently, there cannot plausibly be, any appropriate demarcations between where the emergence takes place at the psychological level and where it doesn't, if the emergence is supposed to yield incompleteness. F) There is the vast amount of ordinary neurophysiology according to which the functional effects of the agency system are accomplished by the classical structure. If so, again, quantum indeterminacies would be an important sort of noise in the system, but not a directly functional ingredient. G) There are several ways to see why things are phystriological, such as the data summarized in Chapters Three through Nine, a careful analysis of Nöther's Theorem, and the demarcation problem. And, finally, H) there are at least the beginnings of ruthlessly strong reductions of one sort or another from psychology to biology and lower, as shown in the work of John Bickle.[71]

Sometimes holding one's breath seems needless. I, for one, will be happy to change my mind when these factors are undermined, or some new strongly established empirical evidence for a parallel to, or an

---

[69] See Omnes, Roland, *Converging Realities*: 122.

[70] As explained in A2.1; for the original account, see note 66 in this Appendix.

[71] See John Bickle, *Philosophy and Neuroscience: A Ruthlessly Reductive Account*, and "Philosophy of Mind and the Neurosciences", *Philosophy of Mind*, S. P. Stich, and T. A. Warfield, (eds).

application of, quantum emergence to biological or psychological matters in such a way as to provide for physical incompleteness is present. The mere notion of emergence, even supposedly strengthened by Humphreys' desire for patience, should not provide a distraction for those attracted by the physically *in*complete claims such as that there is a causally interactive immaterial God, etc. The key point, then, is that Humphrey's emergence is not directed toward physical incompleteness, the overturning of the results of mathematized physics.

A2.4 Some take emergence to be true a priori, and from this it is possible to raise an unusual form of the emergence objection to phystriology. Roy Bhaskar, a founder of the critical realist school of thinking, has put forward the notion that there *must be* emergence in the sciences as one rises up in complexity. The question is whether the emergence put forward is emergence that overturns the rules, laws or forces of physics or not. As mentioned in Chapter Eleven, if it is of that overturning type, and is called, following the extant terminology[72] a 'strong emergence,' it goes against phystriology; if it is not, it is called 'weak emergence.' In assessing the evidence for phystriology we are only interested to find out if there is any strong emergence,[73] as that is the only emergence that would undo the phystriological picture. However, to argue for strong emergence on *a priori* grounds both seems, and is, without merit. To show that the sciences are emergent not only in requiring non-theoretically reducible terms, but also in requiring changed motions of the small constituent things (that is, in the strong emergent sense, not the weak emergent sense, as was defined in A1.1) cannot be done *a priori*. It can only be done through observation backed by theory. In fact, by 1918 there were good purely theoretical reasons to suspect or conclude the opposite, that there would *not* be any overturning systems (the symmetry notions in physics were shown to be deep). Hence arguing in the other direction, that there *must be* fundamental laws in which triggering of

---

[72] See M. A. Bedau, "Weak Emergence."

[73] 'Emergence' is typically taken to be an autonomous phenomenon, and to be not reducible (for which see Bedau, *ibid*: 375, 377). Accordingly, as mentioned in the last Appendix, to avoid the controversies over reductionism, one can merely talk about a terminologically simpler distinction between strong changes and weak changes. Alternatively, one can clarify that the sense of 'emergence' is what Bedau called 'nominal emergence' in Bedau 2003: 158, namely a property of a complex object that cannnot be found in its parts.

special kinds of motions or changes occur in some highly complex situations, could not stand on its own. Empirical backing was required to show this.[74]

An excellent exposition of the weak emergent property point of view is found in Robert Laughlin's *A Different Universe*. One of the striking features of Laughlin's exposition is that he by no means claims physical incompleteness. He maintains that the classical physical world is the collectively organized quantum physical world. Yet he also maintains that the view that the micro-world laws account for the macro-effects is a "believable, and I think, correct"[75] approach. This shows that Laughlin's view emphasizes the (nominal, that is, most broad) emergent feature at the macro-scale, yet does not undo phystriology as phystriology is being exposed here.

An example of writers who do not, but should, employ the crucial distinction between emergence that overturns the inaccessible natural laws, forces, or rules of physics and emergence that does not (that is, between emergence that is narrow and emergence that is broad, or between changes that are strong and changes that are weak) is Stuart Kaufman, the complexity theorist.[76] On the one hand, Kaufman claims to be developing a radical view of the sciences, a view that is based on many thitherto undreamt of premises. On the other hand, his view is entirely entrenched in *theoretical* work, the work for ever-better *theories*, without any apparent awareness of the need for the distinction between fundamental and non-fundamental laws (or rules, or forces, or whatever). Even in physics, the n $\geq$ 3 body gravitational problem shows that theoretical physical rules do not capture the natural physical rules, forces, or laws. Yet the theoretically expressible physical rules since Newton's rules *approximate* the natural results by successive pairings over short term time periods in original contexts of discovery. In this way, we need to distinguish the theoretically expressible results from the natural results. And given that there are natural results, we need to distinguish between nominally emergent properties (see n. 73) that do, and nominally

---

[74] See Roy Bhaskar, 1978, *A Realist Theory of Science* (2nd Edition): 74-79. A clear treatment of Bhaskar's claims, and their problems, is given in David Spurrett's on-line available PhD. thesis, *The Completeness of Physics*: 62-79, especially 72, and 72 n. 47.

[75] Laughlin, *A Different Universe*: 36.

[76] See Stuart Kaufman, *Investigations*: 35.

emergent properties that do not, overturn the (inaccessible) natural rules of physics. Thereby we have the distinction between a fundamental law (rule or force, or whatever) and a non-fundamental law (rule or force or whatever).

Kaufman wants to know if there is a fourth law of thermodynamics among biological entities in open systems, but doesn't distinguish between a fundamental law and a non-fundamental law[77]. This may seem like a small omission; but it makes for significant differences, given that a non-fundamental law would not oppose phystriology, whereas a fundamental law could. The difference between theoretical reduction (a reduction that does not occur according to current exponents of phystriology) and token ontological reduction from biology down to mathematical statistical physics (a reduction that does occur according to all exponents of phystriology) once again turns out to be a crucial difference. There is a debate over whether there is token reduction of psychological states down to biological states. But there is no debate over token reduction of biological states, when the type-definitions are forgotten, to chemical-physical states (by composition to classical physical states, and statistically to quantum physical states). Scientists as well as philosophers would do well to assimilate this. There may be radical changes in scientific theories in future, but the approximate results over short term time periods reached through the last four or five hundred years of the natural sciences of physics, chemistry, and biology would remain for original contexts of research.

This distinction between two forms of reductionism calls to mind a rather slippery objection to physical completeness on the grounds that many philosophers are anti-reductionists. This is true; many philosophers are anti-reductionists. But there are so many senses of 'reductionism'[78] that it is necessary to state to which sort of anti-reductionism the many anti-reductionist philosophers adhere. Unfortunately for those who want to retain physical *in*completeness, there are, it seems, no thinkers who are

---

[77] Kaufman, *Investigations*: 2-4, etc.

[78] Here are some kinds of reductionism: type ontological reductionism; token ontological reductionism; theoretical reductionism; methodological reductionism; mereological reductionism; nomological reductionism; branch of study *x* reductionism, e.g, psychological reductionism, semantic reductionism, epistemic reductionism, logical reductionism, metaphysical reductionism, and linguistic reductionism. Of course there are others as well (for instance, micro- and macro-determinative reductionism).

anti-reductionist in any way that would rescue or revive physical incompleteness. Some thinkers are token anti-reductionists for psychological states and more complex states; some, or all or almost all, thinkers are token anti-reductionists for chemical states in relation to quantum physical states. But the former doesn't help physical incompleteness, since all psychological beings are biological beings. And the latter doesn't help, because the irreducibility of a classical molecule into any quantum parts won't bring purposes back into the base level. It is only biological token ontological anti-reductionism that includes the governance of the relations between the lowest level tokens over time that would keep physical incompleteness alive; but, as Alex Rosenberg comments in a recent article on reductionism, "Antireductionism [in biology] does not dispute physicalism's metaphysical claim," which is that biological facts are fixed by macromolecular facts.[79] Of course macromolecular facts are themselves consensus-wise seen as fixed by the physical facts, as has been reviewed above. So antireductionism of the sort that is widespread is, effectively, theoretical anti-reductionism or *type* ontological anti-reductionism, or, in various ways, token anti-reductionism at the complexity level of psychology and higher, and none of this disturbs the phystriological thesis.

This last point can be improved with a bit of clarification. The question is, Can one forget about type-definitions? In the important sense for this inquiry, one can. As far as phystriology goes, the only way the type-definitions count is if the changes in a large thing undo or overturn the changes that would be reached by nothing but the sums of the forces or laws or rules or whatever of the smallest things, e.g., the things studied by physicists. But if the large objects don't overturn etc., those changes, then the type definitions can be forgotten.

To put it technically, as far as phystriology goes, all that counts is what may be called, adapting D. M Armstong's vocabulary,[80] somewhat thin token identity; and somewhat thin token identities are not disputed by anyone, nor have they been for decades. For natural objects, A is somewhat thinly identical to B iff A ongoingly occupies (statistically if necessary) the same spacetime region as B; the changes in B do not violate, overturn, undo, etcetera, the sums of the rules, laws, forces, or whatever, that make the changes in A; and if $A \neq B$, B's properties are

---

[79] Alex Rosenberg, "Reductionism In Biology": 349.

[80] See *A World of States of Affairs*: 123 – 6.

more complex or at a higher level than *A*'s properties. This shows the irrelevance of type ontological antireductionism to phystriology. It is only thin token ontological antireductionism, an antireductionism which is not upheld by any current theorists for biological, nor chemical things, that would be relevant to deny phystriology. (Once again, one uses composition in the classical realm; and one bridges the classical and quantum realm statistically.) Nobody disagrees with thin identity, and we do not need to undo a theory that nobody holds and that everyone who has looked into it rejects.

Given that thin token identity is not at all controversial, the split between the level of the sums of physics things and the sums carrying chemical, biological, psychological, social, economic, etc., properties or characteristics can be made out. It is at such levels that type properties or characteristics may or may not be (type) reducible. The difference between the two kinds of sums shows the irrelevance of whether or not there are type reductions to whether or not the world is phystriological.

A2.5 Some philosophers advocate anti-realism or critical realism; some advocate instrumentalism; and some advocate pragmatism. Each of these might be thought to support physical *in*completeness.

In response, any view that anti-realism, critical realism, instrumentalism, or pragmatism supports physical incompleteness is mistaken. None of such views supports physical incompleteness.

Advocacy of anti-realism (which will hereafter include forms of critical realism not covered in the last section), instrumentalism, or pragmatism doesn't help any case for physical incompleteness. The instrumentalists, pragmatists, and anti-realists need the measurements to come out the same as the measurements come out in the realist interpretations; so instrumentalism, pragmatism, and anti-realism won't help in establishing physical incompleteness. For hundreds of years since the beginnings of third-theory mechanism (as defined in Chapter Three), there have not been quantified theories exhibiting intrinsic purposes at the physical micro-base. And there has been the overwhelming evidence for the understructure relationship between physics, chemistry and biology, however this is interpreted in regard to realism and anti-realism.

Physical analysis has exhibited the physical bases of chemical changes. Those in favor of anti-reductionism of chemistry to physics, like

J. van Brakel, for example,[81] are *theoretical* anti-reductionists; they hold that the theories we create cannot have referring terms for which there are or can be substitutions by the referring terms of lower level theories. In this case, the antireductionist claim centrally includes the idea that chemists need theories that use chemical terminology. We cannot say all that we want to say using talk whose referring terms refer to subatomic particles only. But this point of view is already typically accepted by exponents of phystriology.

It is true that exponents of phystriology frequently maintain that the events or processes or force interactions or operations of the laws of nature *themselves* are not overturned by anything (e.g., chemistry or biology or psychology or sociology) outside physics. And that sounds realist. Also, it's true that exponents of phystriology frequently maintain that it is the relations of the subatomic particles to the extent that they can be considered classically that constitute the relations among the larger more complex chemical items. And it would be good to think that since our symbols classify reality a certain way, it will follow that our theories lock us into our symbols, and cannot directly refer to the events, processes, force interactions, operations of the laws of nature *themselves*.

However, once one sees that it is the measurements that yield the physically closed results, whatever conceptual intrusion one accepts is pretty much irrelevant. The motions of the fingers of a poet on a keyboard typing a spontaneously occurring poem will still be governed (at least approximately over short term time periods if what follows is accessible) by the applications of the (sometimes inaccessible, sometimes accessible) rules, laws, or forces of physics; and there won't be, for example, special fundamental animate forces to include in the physical rules such as conservation of energy. Phystriology will be a part of the conceptual system that we use whether or not some form of realism obtains. Anti-realism, instrumentalism, or pragmatism, then, contribute little, if anything, to the assistance of physical incompleteness.

To put this another way, the vigorous debate between realists and anti-realists is independent of the evidence for phystriology. No matter how anti-realist or instrumentalist one's theory is, one needs some notion to cover the (sometimes) inaccessibility of theories one way or another. Accordingly, the realist versus anti-realist debate is independent of the (empirical or observational-theoretical) grounds for phystriology.

---

[81] J. van Brakel, *Philosophy of Chemistry*.

Nancy Cartwright's objections to phystriology may also be discussed in this section, since her views were sometimes associated with anti-realism. It's true that she did not regard her view as directed against realism; she argued for realism;[82] and many are clear on that; David Spurrett, for instance, regards her view as "patchwork realism".[83] However, the discussion that follows doesn't rely on any anti-realism in her work; and so, the following comments on Cartwright's views can be moved to another section if that would be better.

Cartwright's view is that the theoretical attitudes one might adopt on the sciences are three: fundamentalism ('fundamentalism' being her term, and it is supposed to include phystriology), strong emergentism ('emergentism' is her term, and it is only strong emergentism that interests us; also 'emergentism' can be interpreted in our context as a nominal or broad emergentism, for which see n. 74 this Appendix), and patchwork-ism. If one position is true, then the other two are not; and Cartwright's view is patchwork-ism.[84] Laws, she says, are lies; and so both foundationalism and emergentism (strong or weak) are false, and we have only patchwork-ism.[85] A good coverage of the way in which Cartwright's arguments do not go against the completeness of physics (Spurrett's term) was provided by David Spurrett in 1999. Here I'll provide another way of countering her objection (of sorts) to phystriology. The counter given here picks up on one comment that Spurrett makes. He says that she puts "the epistemological cart before the ontological horse."[86] He shows this in one way; I will show it in another way.

Cartwright keeps referring to our need for models that do what they need to do. This suggests that Cartwright's views are restricted to our theories about the world. If so, Cartwright's position is entirely epistemological. Some would say, though, that we need to also think about how things are in nature itself; she would agree with that, since she is a realist; and that raises the relation between the epistemological

---

[82] Nancy Cartwright, "Fundamentalism vs the Patchwork of Laws": 279.

[83] David Spurrett, *Completeness of Physics*: 140.

[84] "…nature is governed in different domains by different systems of laws not necessarily related to each other in any systematic or uniform way: by a patchwork of laws" Cartwright, *ibid*: 288-9.

[85] This runs through *How the Laws of Physics Lie*; *Nature's Capacities and Their Measurement*; "Fundamentalism vs. the Patchwork of Laws."

[86] D. Spurrett, *ibid*: 170.

perspective and the ontological perspective. We will begin by exploring that relation and then come back to the epistemological point of view.

Earlier it was recognized that there is a difference between the natural truths and the theoretically expressible truths. The n ≥ 3 body gravitational problem shows this: we have theories about pairs of objects in gravitational relations; and nature works with more objects than two in measurable gravitational relations. Yet our theoretical formulas for pairs of objects can be tested to see whether they account, approximately, for the n ≥ 3 gravitational relations in general. If they do, then everyone with realist attitudes toward nature, including Cartwright, would have to agree that there are natural, as yet non-theoretically expressed, truths. If they don't, it would only be because there are special factors context by context, and in some contexts they do, whereas in other contexts, they don't. But still, for the contexts in which they do, realistically speaking, there would be natural, non-theoretically expressed truths. Now, if there are such truths, either they are governed by rules, laws, forces, principles, or whatever, of some sort, or they are not. Once again, though, the empirical-theoretical evidence, context restricted, has shown that they are governed by rules, laws, forces, principles, or whatever, of some sort; after all, our results for two bodies in gravitational relations, in some contexts at least, approximate what happens when these two bodies are in a larger group (in original contexts of research, over short term time periods). So there are natural rules, laws, forces, principles, or whatever, of some sort, in some contexts.

Next, consider that the choice between phystriology and strong emergence is exclusive. ('Emergence' here, once again, is nominal emergence. And for our purposes here phystriology and strong emergence are both theories about the natural truths.) The question that follows is, Can we ontologically get away from *both* phystriology and strong emergence?

Cartwright's patchwork-ism requires that we can get away from both of them to understand context relations. But she also says that mechanics is true for any context in which laws can be found.[87] Yet that shows that we cannot get away from both of them in looking at the relations of contexts. The patchwork-ism approach would say that we

---

[87] "mechanics is true… for all those motions whose causes can be adequately represented by the familiar models that get assigned force functions in mechanics." "Fundamentalism vs. the Patchwork of Laws": 284.

have many contexts. In each context with theories, they are mechanical theories; there is only epistemologically, context restrictedly, weak emergentism. But overall, there is no necessary relation between contexts in any systematic lawfully organized way; yet, remarkably, each context is mechanical, without any strong emergentism. Then patchwork-ism can only be about our perspective; it cannot be ontological. This allows phystriology as an ontological position to survive in a natural context restricted way.

True, that doesn't yield phystriology as an epistemological position; but its survival as an ontological context-restricted position is a good enough beginning. Now, add on to this that in whatever contexts mechanics holds, the theories discovered remain as approximately true in short term time periods in original contexts. Accordingly, it becomes entirely reasonable to say that phystriology survives not only as an ontological context restricted view, but also as an epistemological context restricted view.

There are two interpretations now of 'phystriology': (a) that it can be context restricted; (b) that it cannot be. If (a), then Cartwright's patchwork-ism is undone; if (b) then an explanation is needed as to why each context is mechanical. But, I'd maintain, the contexts overlap, are not theoretically specifiable, and so on. Consequently, no such explanation can be given. Accordingly, Cartwright's patchwork-ism is undone.

To put it as simply as possible, Cartwright's position requires that there be no necessary laws, rules, or whatever to distinguish the contexts. But then it would make no sense if phystriology is to be context restricted. And if phystriology is not conceptually context restricted, and the last four hundred years of the natural sciences are as they have been, then Cartwright's patchworkism position, too, cannot survive.

A2.6 There are contemporary efforts to undermine phystriology that (like some others already considered) proceed from an entirely conceptual point of view. For example, Trenton Merricks, in *Objects and Persons*[88] argues against a phystriology point of view on conceptual grounds. Merricks bases his argument on the *assumption* that if a person is a

---

[88] Trenton Merricks, *Objects and Persons*: Ch. 6.

genuine object, then the person is the human organism.[89] But this makes it difficult to claim that there are physical property outcomes overturned by the operations of the organism. The conceptual assertion that the organism is a real object will not undermine the view that the atoms in the organism all work according to the laws or rules or forces of physics, even if the properties of the organism are, in some sense, e.g., nominally, emergent. Since there is no sharp boundary between the organism and its environment in regard to the outcomes of physical laws, rules, or forces, the atoms will not behave differently within the organism from the way they will behave just outside the organism, however that is defined. Consequently, his argument does not undermine phystriology. If there is any emergence it is merely a weak emergence.

This point is similar to the point that 'top down causation' or 'downward causation' are used ambiguously. Sometimes such a phrase is only used for strong (nominally emergent) causal changes as in McLaughlin's work in 1992; sometimes such a phrase is used to include, and, perhaps, be restricted to, weak (nominally emergent) causal changes of a special kind, as is in Theo Meyering's work in 2002.[90] Sometimes it is a bit unclear. Merrick's point might be put by saying that there is downward causation, but then downward causation would only be the initiation of weak (nominally emergent) causal changes of a special kind. Once again, unfortunate ambiguities can be confusing.

A2.7 An objection could be put this way: Surely, some authors directly and vigorously argue for a contemporary version of interactive dualism. Interactive dualism goes against phystriology. Probably the most extended such analysis was provided in 1991 by John Foster in *The Immaterial Self*. What, if anything, was wrong with his approach?

Indeed, John Foster's approach was extensive and comprehensive. It is particularly instructive to note that the vast bulk of his analysis was devoted to showing that all the various forms of *mental* reductionism had difficulties. He showed this for eliminativism, analytical behaviorism, analytical functionalism, type identity theories, non-anomalous monist token identity theories, metaphysical reductionist theories, anomalous monist token-identity theories. And the discussion

---

[89] Merricks, *ibid*: 85-7.

[90] Theo Meyering, "Physicalism and downward causation in psychology and the special sciences" *Inquiry* **43**, 2000: 181-202.

was full; in page numbers, it went from pg. 16 to pg. 185. It was only after this useful, long discussion that, in one paragraph, he simply asserted that any physically complete views about the brain causal processes are indirect, and "all that we pre-scientifically know about ourselves suggests that the mind, qua mind, has a causal influence on our behaviour..." Consequently, he says, "the rational conclusion to draw is that the brain is subject to certain non-physical influences which do not affect the other physical systems which science investigates" (200).

If only it were as easy as this to hang onto pre-scientific intuitions! Here are four major problems. Each one in itself is sufficient to undo Foster's effort; but taken together they make for an overwhelming case against his approach.

First, showing difficulties in mental reductionism is easy to do. The difficulties have fuelled debates since the 1960's. There are many positions to go through, and so the extensiveness of Foster's discussion is natural. But – and this is a big 'but' – mental reductionism is only secondarily at issue. The biology-physics-chemistry relationship was established without centering on human beings who have (or, as a few would say, since Descartes' time, seem to have) minds. Natural selection evolution also fits into the picture. If the biological items evolved via naturally selective processes, then the differences between earthworms, bees, lizards, birds and mammals gradually evolved. This applies, too, within mammals. The differences between apes and humans, also, gradually evolved. So, *prima facie* at least, what we say about earthworms as biological entities – their changes are complex chemical and physical changes – will also apply to human beings, unless we can provide excellent reasons to think that humans are sufficiently different as to get away from phystriology. And Foster hasn't even tried to confront the evolutionary problem.

Natural science has shown us that token biological things are chemical things and chemical things, statistically, are physics-based things. If one is to get away from that for human beings, one has to tackle the extraordinarily difficult problem of showing how human beings as biological creatures are sufficiently different from apes and so on to allow something other than phystriology to occur. Foster ought to have faced the evolutionary problem, but he didn't.[91] This in itself undoes Foster's work.

Second, we can't talk about things happening to *the brain* that don't happen in other physical systems which science investigates. 'The brain' is a notion that has no clear boundaries. Some brain theorists include the retinas, some don't[92]. And no one can say exactly where the afferent and efferent nerves are or are not parts of the brain. The boundary of the brain is an entirely conventional notion. So to hope that somehow there is a real objective boundary in which the objective physics-ish laws of nature exclusively operate, and beyond which they do not exclusively operate, or in which a non-physical mind operates and outside of which it doesn't operate, is peculiar. More accurately, it makes little sense.

Third, there are other options for the reductionist mental theorists. One might accept one of the reductionist theories that Foster rejects. Alternatively, one might reject those reductionisms and still accept physriology. It could be that 'cause' is systematically ambiguous, for example. Then one wouldn't get away from physriology. Yet Foster doesn't talk about some possible future theory that could make better sense of the mental-physical claims than does his adherence to the notion of a real objective boundary in the brain, or elsewhere in the human body.

Fourth, there is the demarcation problem. This is close to the problem raised as the second problem. But regardless of classification of the objections, there is no evidence at all that Foster can escape from the demarcation problem. He has to be able to get away from that problem, or there will be no fruit to the theory of physical incompleteness. Yet he doesn't tackle the demarcation problem at all. Once again, he hasn't tried to do what is necessary to do successfully to defend physical incompleteness.

All in all, Foster in *The Immaterial Self* has done a thorough but, unfortunately, off-target job.

---

[91] He didn't even mention the natural selective evolutionary problem in dealing with "non-human animals" 236-7. He said he didn't "regard the issues as unimportant," but that hardly is credible, given the absence of any discussion of the problem.

[92] As above: Patricia Churchland, *Brain-wise*: e.g., 89, 138.

A2.8 It is not at all unusual to find philosophers who emphasize the tension between naturalism on the one hand, taken to be associated with various forms of physicalism, and, on the other hand, some requirement of clear thinking expressed philosophically, such as rules of logic, principles of truth, or our apparent linguistic use of universals and/or properties.[93] For convenience, I will first look at the relation between naturalism and universals or properties, and then speak more generally about naturalism, physicalism, and philosophical concerns.

Many philosophers maintain that naturalism requires that whatever exists is spatiotemporally located, and so there cannot be abstract atemporal, nonspatial entities that instantiate in spacetime occupying objects. Yet universals, and in some versions, properties, would be such things, and it is hard to get away from postulating the existence of such things that instantiate in particular objects. From this it is often taken to be the case that naturalism fails, and the failure of naturalism is often taken to be the failure of physicalism. Furthermore, the thesis of phystriology is sometimes regarded as a central thesis of physicalism. It seems, then, that phystriology is undone by any fully realist view of universals.

The easiest way to deal with this objection is to distinguish between two kinds of physicalism. A physicalism that states that there are no abstract objects of transcendent sorts is one kind of physicalism. Another kind of physicalism accepts phystriology, but is open to a variety of theories on abstract objects; in one sub-theory they exist immanently only; in another sub-theory they exist transcendentally; in still another, they don't exist, but, rather, they merely occur. And there are still other theories and sub-theories. Of course, if they do exist, and if phystriology is a thesis that is accepted, then another problem needs to be solved: how can we come to have justifiable beliefs concerning abstract entities?

Let us allow that some who accept phystriology and accept universals need to address this problem. What is most important from our point of view is to observe that no one who raises the tension between naturalism and acceptance of universals gives any argument

---

[93] See, for instance, *Naturalism: A critical analysis* eds., W. L. Craig and ˙ Moreland. This is an anthology of articles against naturalism specifical]' against many forms of physicalism, sometimes implicitly, and so⌐ explicitly.

against the vast amount of evidence over the last four hundred years from which, for example, the triple process resulted, namely, the mathematization of physics, the physicalization of chemistry, and the physio-chemicalization of biology. For this reason, the tension over naturalism and universals does not constitute a specific objection against phystriology.

The problem (and the resolution of the problem) could be cast in a different garb. Suppose one takes it that there are causal relations among universals. However, it is not the least bit unusual to hold that whatever effects occur at the human-scale level are (hypothetically at least) perceivable by us. Hence there seem to be causal relations among universals that are perceptually accessible to us. Yet the universals are identical though placed in many regions at once. The two notions – perceivable to us, and yet causally interrelated while outside the realm of particulars – seem to go against phystriology. That is the new garb for the problem.

In response to this, though, the exponent of phystriology only needs to say that one should have a theory about accessible causality, universals, and particulars. The phystriology result is not challenged by the need for such a theory. If it ends up with perceptual causal changes interrelating universals without affecting particulars, so be it. If it abandons causal interrelations among universals, so be it. Still, the phystriology result itself is not challenged. In short, arcane metaphysical issues are important; and they can be addressed, while recognizing that four hundred years of natural scientific work has accomplished some stunning results.

This shows that the tension between naturalism (associated with physicalism, and thus associated with phystriology) and universals does not really threaten phystriology. There are, as mentioned, other tensions surrounding various forms of naturalism; principles of truth, laws of logic have been mentioned. In addition, there are concerns with what it is that bears representations, and, as will be discussed below, there are arguments against the coherence of cognitive reliability and evolutionary naturalism. However, one can't use difficult philosophical problems to get away from hundreds of years of natural science work, nor to get away from phystriology. To generalize what was mentioned above, if phystriology must accept abstract items, so be it. If it need not, so be it. The central result of the last four hundred years of natural scientific work nds either way. In short, philosophical discussions need to both assimilate the main natural science result, and to do what needs to be done philosophically.

Let us look now, briefly, at the argument against evolutionary naturalism presented by Alvin Plantinga, for example, at the end of *Warrant and Proper Function*, in 1993. His main argument is that if evolutionary naturalism is true, then cognitive output is not based on truth, but on adaptation. If it is not based on truth, then the acceptance of the reliability of our cognitive output is undermined. Hence the naturalism part of evolutionary naturalism, says Plantinga, must go. In its place is the purposive design of cognitive function, as would be given by God. As mentioned in Appendix 1, this argument has been much discussed in the literature.

There are many responses to it. The reader can look, for instance, at *Naturalism Defeated?* edited by James Beilby, as referred to above, which contains many critical analyses. A general response to Plantinga's argument is to say something like, "Let's follow the results of any philosophical integration of the ordinary natural sciences. That yields phystriology. Let's worry about truth versus merely adaptive reliability afterwards. In doing such worrying, many will find that truth survives anyhow. One way or another, it may be that some work has to be done to assimilate the new results of the philosophical integration of the ordinary natural science conclusions. The integration is the result of hundreds of years of research. We can't avoid it, even if much other philosophical work arises. And even if we're ignorant of that philosophical work now, we cannot be distracted away from accepting the conclusions of the ordinary sciences, conclusions that require us to refine our notion of 'purpose,' 'design,' and so on, so that they mean only evolutionarily summative phenomena where the tiny elements have no inherent purposes or inherent purpose-like designs." That seems to be a fine response to Plantinga's approach. Indeed, that Plantinga has not noted that all changes in nature are weak changes is rather striking. Yet to note that is very important.

A2.9 Summary

Including Chapter 11, I have briefly reviewed many objections against phystriology. *All* of them seem to be mere pseudo-objections. There are many angles from which one might try to get rid of phystriology, but, as I tried to show in this Appendix, all of them fail. The phystriology result, as appropriately defined, stands untouched. And, as I've shown, the phystriology result is enormously intellectually important.

Works Cited:

Al-Khalili, Jim, 2003, *Quantum*, London: Weidenfeld & Nicolson.

Alston, William, 1991, *Perceiving God*, Ithaca: Cornell University Press.

Angel, Leonard, 1994, *Enlightenment East & West*, Albany: SUNY.

Angel, Leonard, 1994b, "Empirical Evidence for Reincarnation? Examining Stevenson's Most Impressive Case," *Skeptical Inquirer*, **18**: 5 (Fall): 481 – 487.

Angel, Leonard, 2002, "Reincarnation All Over Again – A review of Ian Stevenson's Reincarnation and Biology," *Skeptic*, **9**: 3: 86-90.

Angel, Leonard, 2002b, "Mystical Naturalism," *Religious Studies*, **38**: 317 – 338.

Angel, Leonard, 2004, "Universal Self Consciousness mysticism and the physical completeness principle," *International Journal for Philosophy of Religion,* **55**: 1-29.

Angel, Leonard, 2005, "Compositional science and religious philosophy," *Religious Studies*, **41**: 125 – 143.

Angel, Leonard, 2006, "An Interview With LA Universal Self," *Sophia*, **45** 1: 79 – 93.

Angel, Leonard, 2006b, "Two Questions for Ken Wilber and the Wider Transpersonal Audience," *Journal for Transpersonal Psychology*, **38**: 73-94.

Angel, Leonard, 2008, "An Overview of the Work of Ian Stevenson (1918-2007)," *Skeptic*, (UK), 21: 1 Spring: 8-14.

Angel, Leonard, 2009, "Quintuple Extension," *Zygon*, (forthcoming).

Aristotle, c. 330 BCE/1941, *Basic Works of Aristotle*, edited by Richard McKeon, NY: Random House.

Armstrong, David, 1968, *A Materialist Theory of The Mind*, London: Routledge and Kegan Paul.

Armstrong, David, 1997, *A World of States of Affairs*, Cambridge UK: Cambridge University Press.

Atkins, Peter, 1987, *The Second Law*, NY: W. H. Freeman.

Atkins, Peter, 2003, *Galileo's Finger*, Oxford: Oxford University Press.

Avila, Vernon, 1995, *Biology*, Boston: Bookmark, 1995.

Ayer, A. J., 1968, *The Humanist Outlook*, quoted in *Humanist Anthology*, ed. Margaret Knight, revised by Jim Herrick, London: Rationalist Press Association 1995.

Bedau, M. A., 1997, "Weak Emergence," *Philosophical Perspectives, 11, Mind, Causation, and World*, Oxford: Blackwell: 375-399.

Bedau, M. A., 2003, "Downward Causation and Autonomy in Weak Emergence," in *Emergence*, ed. by M. A. Bedau and P. Humphreys, 2008, Cambridge Mass: Bradford MIT: 155 - 188; *Principia Revista International de Epistemologica* 6 (20003): 5 – 50.

Beilby, James, ed., 2002, *Naturalism Defeated?* Albany: Cornell University Press.

Berlinski, David, 2008, *Infinite Ascent*, NY: Modern Library.

Beyerstein, Dale, 1996, "Satya Sai Baba", in Stein, G., ed., *The Encyclopedia of the Paranormal*, Prometheus Press: 653-657.

Bhaskar, Roy, 1978, *A Realist Theory of Science* (2nd Edition), Sussex: The Harvester Press.

Bickle, John, 2003, *Philosophy and Neuroscience: A Ruthlessly Reductive Account*, Dordrecht: Kluwer Academic Publishers.

Bickle, John, 2003b, "Philosophy of Mind and the Neurosciences", *Philosophy of Mind*, S. P. Stich, and T. A. Warfield, (eds), Oxford: Blackwell Publishing Ltd.: 322-351.

Bishop, Robert, "Chaos Indeterminism and Free Will," *Oxford Handbook of Free Will*, ed. Robert Kane, Oxford: Oxford University Press: 111-124.

Blackmore, Susan, 1986, *The Adventures of a Parapsychologist*, Buffalo NY: Prometheus Press.

Blackmore, Susan, 1996, "Out of Body Experiences," in *Encyclopedia of the Paranormal*, ed. G. Stein: 479, 482.

Block, Ned, 1980, "Troubles with Functionalism" in *Readings in the Philosophy of Psychology*, ed., N. Block, Cambridge Mass: Harvard University Press.

Brooke, John Hedley, 1991, *Science and Religion*, Cambridge: Cambridge University Press.

Burhoe, Ralph, 1981, *Toward A Scientific Theology*, Belfast; Christian Journals Limited.

Calder, Niger, 1979, *Einstein's Universe*, NY: Penguin.

Cartwright, Nancy, 1980, *How the Laws of Physics Lie*, Oxford: Clarendon Press.

Cartwright, Nancy, 1989, *Nature's Capacities and Their Measurement*, Oxford: Clarendon Press.

Cartwright, Nancy, 1994, "Fundamentalism vs. the Patchwork of Laws," *Proceedings of the Aristotelian Society* **94**: 279 – 292.

Chalmers, David, 1996, *The Conscious Mind*, Oxford: Oxford University Press.

Chalmers, David, 2003, "Consciousness and its Place in Nature" in *Philosophy of Mind*, ed. by S. Stich and T. Warfield, Oxford: Blackwell: 102 – 142.

Chomsky, Noam, 1968, *Language and Mind*, NY: Harcourt Brace and World.

Christopher, Kevin, 2002, "'No effect' Prayer Study", *Skeptical Inquirer* **26** (2) March/April: 5.

Churchland, Patricia, 1986, *Neurophilosophy*, Cambridge: Bradford-MIT Press.

Churchland, Patricia, 2002, *Brain-Wise*, Cambridge: Bradford-MIT Press.

Churchland, Paul, 1988, *Matter and Consciousness*, revised edition, Cambridge Mass: Bradford MIT Press.

Churchland, Paul, 1996, *The Engine of Reason, The Seat of the Soul*, Cambridge Mass: Bradford MIT.

Cohen, I. Bernard, 1960, *The Birth of a New Physics*, NY: Doubleday.

Cohen, I. Bernard, 1985, *Revolution in Science*, Cambridge: Harvard University Press.

Collins, Robin, 1999, "A Scientific Argument for the Existence of God" in Murray, Michael (ed), *Reason for the Hope Within*, Grand Rapids: Eerdmans: 47-95.

Confucius, <400 BCE/1979, *Analects*, introduction and trans. D. C. Lau, NY: Penguin.

Cooney, Brian, ed., 2000, *The Place of Mind*, ed., Brian Cooney, Belmont CA: Wadsworth.

Craig, William Lane, and Moreland, J. P., eds., 2000, *Naturalism: A critical analysis*, London: Routledge.

Crane, Tim, 2001, *Elements of Mind*, Oxford: Oxford University Press.

Crick, Francis, 1994, *The Astonishing Hypothesis*, NY: Simon & Schuster.

Crick, Francis, and Christof Koch, Christof, 1995/1998, "Why Neuroscience May Be Able To Explain Consciousness" *Explaining Consciousness: The Hard Problem*, ed. J. Shear, Cambridge MA: Bradford MIT: 237-9; reprinted from *Scientific American* **273** (6) Dec. 1995: 84-5.

Darwin, Darwin, 1859/1872 6th edition/1962, *The Origin of Species*, NY: Collier.

Davidson, Donald, 1970, "Mental Events" in L. Foster and J. Swanson (eds.) *Experience and Theory*, Amherst, Mass: University of Massachusetts Press, 291-303; quoted in D. Spurrett, 1999, *The Completeness of Physics*, PhD thesis (available academically on-line): 2.

Dawkins, Richard, 2006, *The God Delusion*, Boston: Houghton Mifflin Company.

Dennet, Daniel, 1991, *Consciousness Explained*, London: Little, Brown, and Company.

Dennett, Daniel, 1995, *Darwin's Dangerous Idea*, 1995: NY: Simon and Schuster

Dennett, Daniel, 1996, *Kinds of Minds*, San Francisco: Basic Books.

Dennett, Daniel, 2005, *Sweet Dreams*, Cambridge, Mass: Bradford MIT Press.

Dennett, Daniel, 2006, *Breaking The Spell*, NY: Viking.

Dijksterhuis, E. J., 1961, *The Mechanization of the World Picture*, trans. C. Dikshoorn, London: Oxford University Press.

Drees, Willem, 1996, *Religion, Science, and Naturalism*, Cambridge UK: Cambridge University Press.

Edwards, Paul, 1967, "Life, Meaning and Value of" in *The Encyclopedia of Philosophy*, ed., Paul Edwards, vol. IV, NY: Macmillan: 467-477

Einstein, Albert, 1905/2005, "On a Heuristic Point of View Concerning the Production and Transformation of Light," in *Einstein's Miraculous Year*, ed. John Stachel, trans. T. Lipscombe, A. Calaprice, S. Elsworthy, J. Stachel, Princeton NY: Princeton University Press: 177-198; originally in *Annalen der Physik* 17 (1905): 132-148.

Einstein, Albert, 1906/1989, "The Principle Of Conservation Of Motion Of The Center Of Gravity And The Inertia of Energy" §1, in Doc. 35 in *Collected Papers of Albert Einstein, vol. 2 1900-1909*, Anna Beck Translator, Peter Havas, Consultant, Princeton University Press: 200-202; originally in *Annalen der Physik* 20, 1906: 627-633.

Einstein, Albert, 1906, "Zur Theorie der Lichterzeugung und Lichtabsorption," *Annalen der Physik*, 20, 199-206.

Einstein, Albert, 1916/1961, *Relativity*, NY: Wings.

Einstein, Albert, and Infeld, Leopold, 1938/1966, *The Evolution of Physics*, NY: Simon & Schuster.

Elior, Rachel, 1987, "Habad" in *Jewish Spirituality II*, ed. Arthur Green, NY: Crossroad: 157 – 205.

Ellis, Brian, 2002, *The Philosophy of Nature*, Montreal & Kingston: McGill-Queen's.

Feinberg, Gerald, 1966, "Physics and the Thales Problem," *The Journal of Philosophy*, **63**: 5-17.

Feuerstein, Georg, 1990, *Encyclopedic Dictionary of Yoga*, NY: Paragon.

Feynman, Richard, 1965, *The Character of Physical Law*, Cambridge MA: MIT Press.

Flew, Anthony, 1975, *The Presumption of Atheism*, The Rationalist Press Association.

Flynn, Thomas, 1996, "Thoughtography," *Encyclopedia of the Paranormal* ed. G. Stein, Prometheus Press: 522.

Fodor, Jerry, 1981, "Special Sciences," *Representations*, Cambridge Mass: Bradford MIT: 127 – 45.

Fodor, Jerry, 1981, "The Present Status of the Innateness Controversy," *Representations*, Jerry Fodor, Cambridge Mass: Bradford MIT Press: 257 – 316.

Forman, Robert, 1999, "What Does Mysticism Have to Teach Us About Consciousness?" *Models of the Self*, ed. S. Gallagher and J. Shear, Thorverton UK: Imprint Academic: 361- 377.

Foster, John, 1991, *The Immaterial Self*, London: Routledge.

Freud, Sigmund, 1927/1985, *Future of An Illusion*, in *vol. 12, Sigmund Freud, Civilization, Society and Religion*, edited Albert Dickson, London: Penguin: 179 – 241.

Frazier, K., ed., 1991, *The Hundredth Monkey and other Paradigms of the Paranormal*, Buffalo NY: Prometheus Press.

Galileo, 1638/1974, *Discourse on Two New Sciences*, trans. S. Drake, Madison: University of Wisconsin Press.

Gardner, Martin, 1981, "The Extraordinary Mental Bending of Professor Taylor", in *Science Good, Bad, and Bogus*, NY: Avon.

Gardner, Martin, 1996, "Eyeless Vision," *Encyclopedia of the Paranormal* ed. G. Stein: Prometheus: 259.

Gardner, Martin, 1996, "Leonara Piper", *Encyclopedia of the Paranormal*, ed. G. Stein, Prometheus: 538-9.

Gilovich, Thomas, 1991, *How We Know What Isn't So*, NY: The Free Press.

Gödel, Kurt, 1931/1962/1992, *On Formally Undecidable Propositions of Principia Mathematica and Related Systems*, trans. B. Meltzer, NY: Dover.

Gogineni, Babu, 1999, "Godman of India," *Skeptic* vol. 7 No. 4.

Goodrich, Edwin, 1938, "Evolution," *Encyclopedia Britannica*.

Gould, William Jay, 1987, "Darwinism Defined," *Discover*, January: 64-70, 68, quoted in Daniel Dennett, *Darwin's Dangerous Idea* NY: Simon & Schuster 1995: 310.

Gould, Stephen Jay, 1997, "Nonoverlapping Magisteria," *Natural History* **106**, March 1997: 16-22; reprinted, 1998, in *Leonardo's Mountain of Clams and the Diet of Worms*, New York: Harmony Books: 269-283; and is on-line at <stephenjaygould.org/library/gould_noma.html>.

Graham, A. C., 1989, *Disputers of the Tao*, La Salle Ill: Open Court.

Greene, Brian, 1999, *The Elegant Universe*, NY: Vintage.

Grene, Marjorie, and Depew, David, 2004, *The Philosophy of Biology*, Cambridge: Cambridge University Press.

Gribbin, John, 1998, *Q is for Quantum*, London: Orion Books.

Griffin, David Ray, 1997, *Parapsychology, Philosophy, and Spirituality*, Albany: SUNY.

Hacking, Ian, 1984, *The Emergence of Probability*, Bristol: Cambridge University Press.

Hart, William, 1988, *The Engines of the Soul*, Cambridge: Cambridge University Press.

Hall, Trevor, 1984, *The Medium and the Scientist*, Buffalo NY: Prometheus Press.

Hankinson, R. J., 1995, *The Skeptics*, London: Routledge.

Hansel, C. E. M., 1989, *The Search for Psychic Power*, Buffalo: Prometheus Books.

Harold, Franklin, 2001, *The Way of the Cell*, NY: Oxford 2001.

Haugeland, John, 1984, "Ontological Supervenience," *Southern Journal of Philosophy*, **22**: 1 – 12.

Hesse, Mary, 1967, "Action at a Distance and Field Theory" *Encyclopedia of Philosophy*, ed. Paul Edwards, NY: vol. 1.

Hick, John, 1999, *The Fifth Dimension*, Oxford: Oneworld Publications.

Hodgson, David, 2002, "Quantum Physics, Consciousness, and Free Will", *Oxford Handbook of Free Will*, ed. Robert Kane, Oxford: Oxford University Press.

Hope, Terri, (April) 2007, "Spirituality Without Religion," *Canadian Humanist* BC

News, ed. by B. Broderick, Ottawa: Humanist Association of Canada.

Humphrey, Nicholas, 2000, "The Power of Prayer," *Skeptical Inquirer*, **24** (3): 61.

Humphreys, Paul, 1997, "How Properties Emerge," *Philosophy of Science* **64**: 1-17.

Jackson, Frank, 1986, "What Mary Didn't Know" *Journal of Philosophy* **83**: 291-295.

Jaffe, Bernard, 1957, *Crucibles: The Story of Chemistry*, NY: Simon and Schuster.

James, William, 1897/1956, "The Will to Believe" in *The Will to Believe and other essays on popular philosophy*, NY: Dover, 1956.

James, William, 1897/1956, "Psychic Research," in *Will To Believe and other essays on popular philosophy*, NY: Dover.

Jammer, Max, 1957, *Concepts of Force*, Mineola NY: Dover.

Jammer, Max, 1961, *Concepts of Mass*, Cambridge: Harvard University Press.

Jammer, Max, 1999, *Einstein and Religion*, Princeton NJ: Princeton University Press.

Jesus (of Nazareth), ancient/2003, *Gospel of Thomas*, *The Gnostic Bible*, edited by W. Barnstone, M. Meyer, Boston: Shambhala.

Kane, Robert, ed., 2002, *The Oxford Handbook of Free Will*, Oxford: Oxford University Press.

Kapleau, Philip, ed., etc., 1967, *The Three Pillars of Zen*, Boston: Beacon Books.

Kaufman, Stuart, 2000, *Investigations*, NY: Oxford University Press.

Keneally, Christine, 2007, *The First Word*, NY: Penguin.

Kim, Jaegwon, 1992, "'Downward Causation' in Emergentism and Non-reductive Physicalism," in *Emergence or Reduction?* edited by A. Beckermann, H. Flohr, J. Kim, Berlin: Walter de Gruyter: 119 – 138.

Kim, Jaegwon, 1993, "Concepts of Supervenience," *Supervenience and Mind*, Cambridge: Cambridge University Press; first in *Philosophy and Phenomenological Research*, **45**: 153-76.

Kim, Jaegwon, 1996, *Philosophy of Mind*, Boulder: HarperCollins.

Kim, Jaegwon, 2005, *Physicalism or Something Near Enough*, Princeton: Princeton University Press.

Kokol, Peter, 2000, "Is There More Than One Kind of Non-Constructed Mystical Experience? *Sophia* **39**: 64-77.

Kuhn, Thomas, 1959, "Energy Conservation As An Example of Simultaneous Discovery," in *Essential Tension*, Chicago: University of Chicago Press, 1977: 66-104.

Kuhn, Thomas, 1970, *The Structure of Scientific Revolutions*, 2nd Ed., 1970, Chicago: University of Chicago Press.

Kuhn, Thomas, 1984, *Black-Body Theory and the Quantum Discontinuity 1894-1912*, Chicago: University of Chicago Press.

Kurtz, Paul, 1986, *Transcendental Temptation*, Amherst NY: Prometheus Press.

Lao Tzu, (author of *Tao Te Ching*), < 350 BCE, *Tao Te Ching*, trans. D. C. Lau, NY: Penguin (1963); *The Gate of All Marvellous Things,* trans. G. C. Richter, South San Francisco: Red Mansions Publishing (1998).

Laughlin, Robert, B., 2005, *A Different Universe*, NY: Perseus Books.

Le Poidevin, Robert, 2005, "Missing Elements and Missing Premises," *British Journal for the Philosophy of Science* **56**: 117-134.

Leibniz, Gottfried, *Leibniz, Philosophical Papers and Letters*, translated, edited, and with introduction by Leroy E. Loemker, vol. 1, Chicago: University of Chicago Press.

Lewis, David, 1983, "New Work for a theory of Universals," *Australasian Journal of Philosophy*, 61: 343-77.

Lovejoy, Arthur, 1936/1964, *The Great Chain of Being*, Cambridge MA: Harvard University Press.

Loy, David, 1988, *Nonduality*, Atlantic Highlands NY: Humanities Press.

Ludlow, Peter, Nagasawa, Yujin, and Daniel Stoljar, Daniel, eds, 2004, *There's Something About* Mary, Cambridge Mass: Bradford MIT.

Mach, Ernst, 1893/1960 *The Science of Mechanics*, Introduction #1, 6th American edition, La Salle Ill: Open Court.

Mackie, J. L., 1977, *Ethics*, Reading: Penguin.

Mascaro, Juan, trans., etc., ancient/1973, *The Dhammapada*, Harmondsworth: Penguin.

Malhotra, Ashok, trans., 1999, *Bhagavad Gita*, Upper Saddle River NJ: Prentice Hall.

McGinn, Colin, 1999, *The Mysterious Flame*, NY: Basic Books.

McLaughlin, Brian, 1992, The Rise and Fall of British Emergentism," in *Emergence or Reduction?* edited by A. Beckermann, H. Flohr, and J. Kim, Berlin: Walter de Gruyter: 49 – 93.

Medawar, Peter, 1958, "Postscript," *D'Arcy Wentworth Thompson*, Ruth D'Arcy Thompson, London: Oxford University Press.

Works Cited

Mencius, ancient/ 1970, *Mencius*, D. C. Lau trans., NY: Penguin.

Merricks, Trenton, 2001, *Objects and Persons*, Oxford: Clarendon Press.

Meyering, Theo, 2000, "Physicalism and downward causation in psychology and the special sciences" *Inquiry* **43**: 181-202.

Micklos, David, and Freyer, Greg A., 2003, *DNA Science: A First Course*, 2nd edition, Cold Spring Harbor NY: Cold Spring Harbor Laboratory Press.

Miller, Alexander, 2003, *An Introduction to Contemporary Metaethics*, Cambridge UK: Polity Press.

Milton, Julie, and Wiseman, Richard, 1999, "Does Psi Exist? Lack of Replication of an Anomalous Process of Information Transfer," *Psychological Bulletin* **125** No. 4: 387-391.

Muktibodananda Saraswati, Swami, commentary, c. 1000/1985, *Hatha Yoga Pradipika*, Munger: Bihar School of Yoga.

Nagel, Ernest, 1961, *The Structure of Science*, New York: Harcourt, Brace & World.

Newton, Isaac, 1600's, early 1700's/1995, *Newton*, I. B. Cohen and R. Westfall (eds) NY: W. W. Norton.

Nietzsche, Friedrich, 1884/2007, *Thus Spake Zarathustra*, selections, in *Nietzsche and the Death of God*, translated and edited, Peter Fritzsche, Boston: Bedford St. Martin's: 79 – 121.

Nöther, Emmy, 1918/1971, "Invariant Variation Problems," trans. M. A. Tavel, *Transport Theory and Statistical Mechanics* **1** (3) 186 – 207.

Omnes, Roland, 2005, *Converging Realities*, Princeton NJ: Princeton University Press.

Oppenheim, Paul, and Putnam, Hilary, 1958, "Unity of Science As A Working Hypothesis", *Concepts, Theories, and the Mind-Body Problem, Minnesota Studies in the Philosophy of Science, vol. II*, ed. H. Feigl, M. Scriven, and G. Maxwell, Minneapolis Minn.: University of Minnesota Press: 3-36.

O'Shea, James R., 2007, *Wilfrid Sellars*, Cambridge UK: Polity Press.

Pais, Abraham, 1986, *Inward Bound*, NY: Oxford University Press.

Papineau, David, 1993, *Philosophical Naturalism*, Oxford: Blackwell.

Papineau, David, 2001, "Rise of Physicalism," *Physicalism and Its Discontents*, ed. Carl Gillett and Barry Loewer, Cambridge: Cambridge University Press: 3 – 36.

Papineau, David, 2002, *Consciousness*, Oxford: Clarendon Press.

Pascal, Blaise, [posthumous > 1662.]/1966, #223, "Pensées", in *The Essential Pascal*, translated by G. F. Pullen, Toronto: Mentor-Omega: 89-93.

Patanjali, Bhagwan Shree, ancient/1938, *Yogasutras* (*Aphorisms of Yoga*), translated by Shree Purohit Swami, London: Faber and Faber.

Penrose, Roger, 2005, *The Road To Reality*, NY: Alfred A Knopf.

Pickover, Clifford, 1999, *Surfing Through Hyperspace*, Oxford: Oxford University Press.

Pigliucci, Massimo, 2002, "Hypothesis Testing and the Nature of Skeptical Investigations," *Skeptical Inquirer* November/December **26**: 27 – 30; 48.

Plantinga, Alvin, 1993, *Warrant and Proper Function*, Oxford: Oxford University Press.

Plantinga, Alvin, 2000, *Warranted Christian Belief*, Oxford: Oxford University Press.

Pledge, H. T., 1939/1959, *Science Since 1500*, NY: Harper Torchbooks.

Plato, c. 350 BCE/1961, *Collected Dialogues*, edited by Edith Hamilton, Huntington Cairns, Princeton NJ: Princeton University Press.

Poland, Jeff, 1994, *Physicalism*, Oxford: Clarendon Press.

Polkinghorne, John, 2000, "Profile: Conversations with John Polkinghorne: The Nature of Physical Reality" *Zygon* **35**: 4: 933-953.

Poncé, Charles, 1980, *Kabbalah*, 2nd edition, Wheaton Ill: Quest.

Popper, Karl, 1972, *Objective Knowledge*, Oxford: Clarendon Press.

Popper, Karl, 1978, "Three Worlds," *Tanner Lectures on Human Values*, University of Michigan, April 7, www.tannerlectures.utah.edu/lectures/documents/popper80.pdf

Popper, Karl, and John Eccles, 1977, *The Self and Its Brain*, NY: Springer Int'l.

Post, John, F., 1987, *The Faces of Existence*, Ithaca: Cornell University Press.

Pullman, Bernard, 1998, *The Atom in the History of Human Thought*, trans. Axel Reisinger, NY: Oxford University Press.

Putnam, Hilary, 1967, "Psychological Predicates," in W.H. Capitan and D.D. Merrill eds., *Art, Mind, and Religion*. Pittsburgh: University of Pittsburgh Press: 37-48.

Quine, W. V. O., 1979, "Facts of the Matter," *Southwestern Journal of Philosophy* 9: 155-69.

Radhakrishnan, S., ed., etc., 1953, *The Principal Upanisads*, London: George Allen & Unwin Ltd.

Raju, P. T., 1985, *Structural Depths of Indian Thought*, Albany: SUNY.

Rawcliffe, D. H., 1952/1959, *Illusions and Delusions of the Supernatural and the Occult*, NY: Dover (originally published as *Psychology of the Occult*, London: Derrick Ridgway).

Raymo, Chet, 1998, *Skeptics and True Believers*, Toronto: Doubleday.

Raymo, Chet, 1999, *Natural Prayers*, Saint Paul: Hungry Mind Press.

Rees, Martin, 1997, *Before the Beginning*, Reading Mass: Addison Wesley.

Rees, Martin, 2000, *Just Six Numbers*, NY: Basic Books.

Rhys David, T. W., trans., ancient/1963, *The Questions of King Milinda 2 vol.'s*, New York: Dover.

Ridley, Matt, 1999, *Genome*, NY: HarperCollins.

Rigden, John, 2005, *Einstein 1905*, "March" Cambridge: Harvard University Press, 2005: 19-39.

Rorty, Richard, 1979, *Philosophy and the Mirror of Nature*, Princeton NJ: Princeton University Press.

Rosenberg, Alex, 2007, "Reductionism In Biology" in *Philosophy of Biology*, ed. M. Matthen and S. Stephens, Amsterdam: Elsevier.

Russell, Bertrand, 1917/1974, *Mysticism and Logic*, London: Unwin Books.

Russell, Bertrand, 1951/1967, *The Autobiography of Bertrand Russell: 1872-1914*, Boston: Little Brown and Company.

Russell, Bertrand, 1957, *Why I Am Not A Christian*, London: George Allen & Unwin Ltd.

Sacks, Oliver, 1985, *The Man Who Mistook His Wife for a Hat and other clinical tales*, NY: Summit Books.

Sambursky, S. 1956, *The Physical World of the Greeks*, London: Routledge and Kegan Paul.

Sayama, Mike, 1986, *Samadhi*, Albany: SUNY 1986.

Sapp, Jan, 2003, *Genesis: Evolution of Biology*, Oxford: Oxford University Press.

Schrödinger, Erwin, 1934/1964, "What Is An Elementary Particle?" in *Space, Time, and the New Mathematics*, ed. Robert Marks, NY: Bantam, 1964: 100-115.

Schrödinger, Erwin, 1944/1967, *What Is Life?* Cambridge: Cambridge University Press.

Schuon, Frithjof, 1975, *The Transcendent Unity of Religions*, 1948, trans. Peter Townsend, NY: Harper and Row.

Sellars, Wilfrid, 1962, "Philosophy and the Scientific Image of Man," in *Frontiers of Science and Philosophy*, ed., Robert Colodny, Pittsburgh: University of Pittsburgh Press: 35 – 78.

Sheldrake, Rupert, 1995, *Seven Experiments That Could Change The World*, NY: Riverhead Books.

Shibayama, Zenkei, 1974, *Zen Comments on the Mumonkan*, Sumiko Kudo translator, NY: New American Library.

Silver, Brian, 1998, *The Ascent of Science*, NY: Oxford University Press, 1998.

Smart, J. J. C., 1959, "Sensations and Brain Processes", *Philosophical Review*, **68**:141-56.

Smart, Ninian, 1969, *Religious Experience of Mankind*, NY: Scribner's.

Smith, Quentin, and Jokic, Aleksandar, eds, 2003, *Consciousness*, Oxford: Clarendon Press.

Smolin, Lee, 2001/2, *Three Roads to Quantum Gravity*, NY: Perseus Books.

Sperry, Roger, 1983, *Science and Moral Priority*, NY: Columbia University Press.

Spurrett, David, 1999, *The Completeness of Physics* (PhD thesis), http://cogprints.org/3379/.

Srivastava, Sheela, and Shrivastava, PS, 2003, *Understanding Bacteria*, Norwell MA: Kluwer Academic Publishers, 2003.

Stace, Walter, 1960, *Mysticism and Philosophy* NY: Macmillan.

Stachel, John, and Torretti, Roberto, 1982, "Einstein's first derivation of mass-energy equivalence" *Am J. Phys* **50** (8).

Stapp, Henry, 1993, *Mind, Matter, and Quantum Mechanics*, Heisenberg: Springer-Verlag, 1993.

Stapp, Henry, 1996, "The Hard Problem: A Quantum Approach," *Journal of Consciousness Studies*, **3**, 1996: 194-210; and in *Explaining Consciousness: The Hard Problem*, ed. Jonathan Shear, Boston: Bradford-MIT, 1998: 197-215.

Stapp, Henry, 1999, "Attention, Intention and Will in Quantum Physics" *Journal of Consciousness Studies* **6**: 8-9.

Stein, Gordon, ed., 1996, *Encyclopedia on the Paranormal*, Amherst NY: Prometheus Press.

Stenger, Victor, 2008, *God: The Failed Hypothesis*, Amherst NY: Prometheus.

Stevenson, Ian, 1966/1974 2nd edition, *Twenty Cases Suggestive of Reincarnation*, Charlottesville: U of Virginia Press.

Stevenson, Ian, 1997, *Reincarnation and Biology*, 2 vol., Westport CT: Praeger.

Stewart, Ian, 2007, *Why Beauty is Truth*, NY: Perseus Books.

Stokes, Douglas M., 2001, "Parapsychology's File Drawer Problem," *Skeptical Inquirer*, **25**: 3: 22-25.

Susskind, Leonard, 2006, *The Cosmic Landscape*, NY: Little, Brown, and Co.

Sykes, J. B. ed., 1982, *The Concise Oxford Dictionary*, Oxford: Clarendon Press.

Taliaferro, Charles, 2000, "Naturalism and the Mind", in *Naturalism: A Critical Analysis*, W. L. Craig and J. P. Moreland (eds.) London: Routledge.

Taylor, Charles, 1964, *The Explanation of Behavior*, London: Routledge and Kegan Paul.

Taylor, Charles, 1989, *Sources of the Self*, Boston: Harvard University Press.

Taylor, Charles, 2002, *Varieties of Religion Today*, Boston: Harvard University Press.

Taylor, Charles, 2007, *A Secular Age*, Boston: Harvard University Press.

Tessman, I., and Tessman, J., 2000, "Efficacy of Prayer," *Skeptical Inquirer* 24 (2): 31-33.

Thompson, D'Arcy, 1917, *On Growth and Form*, London: Cambridge University Press.

Torretti, Roberto 1999, *The Philosophy of Physics*, Cambridge: Cambridge University Press.

Unger, Peter, 1980, "The Problem of The Many," *Midwest Studies In Philosophy V, Studies In Epistemology*, ed., P. French, T. Uehling, Jr., and H. Wettstein, Minneapolis: University of Minnesota Press.

van Brakel, J., 2000, *Philosophy of Chemistry*, Leuven: Leuven University Press.

von Bertalanffy, Ludwig, 1968, *General System Theory*, NY: George Braziller.

von Laue, Max, 1951, "Inertia and Energy" in *Albert Einstein*, ed. by P. A. Schilpp, NY: Tudor Publishing.

Wainwright, William, 1981, *Mysticism*, Brighton: Harvester, 1981.

Watson, James D., 1968, *The Double Helix*, NY: New American Library.

Weinberg, Steven, 1993, *Dreams of a Final Theory*, London: Hutchison Radius.

Westfall, Richard, 1971, *The Construction of Modern Science*, NY: John Wiley and Sons.

Whitman, Walt, c. 1870/1961 "When I Heard The Learn'd Astronomer," *50 Great Poets*, ed., Milton Crane, NY: Bantam: 407.

Wilber, Ken, 1995 1st edition/2000 2nd edition, *Sex, Ecology, Spirituality*, Boston: Shabhala.

Wilber, Ken, 1996, *A Brief History of Everything*, Boston: Shamhala.

Wilber, Ken, "An Integral Theory of Consciousness" *Journal of Consciousness Studies,* **41**: 71-92.

Wilber, Ken, 2000, "Waves, Streams, States, and Self," *Journal of Consciousness Studies* 7, No 11-12, pp 146-76; also in *Cognitive Models and Spiritual Maps* ed. by J. Andresen and R. Forman, Torverton UK: Imprint Academic, 2000.

Wilhelm, Richard, ed., etc., 1931/1962/1984, *The Secret of the Golden Flower*, London: Arkana reprint.

Williams, W., 2000, "Crookes, Sir William," *Encyclopedia of Pseudoscience,* NY: Book Builders/ Facts on File Inc: 66-67.

Wilson, David, 1983, *Rutherford: Simple Genius,* Cambridge Mass: MIT Press.

Wilson, David, 1999, "Mind-brain interaction and violation of physical laws," in *The Volitional Brain,* ed., Libet, Freeman, & Sutherland, Thorverton: Imprint Academic: 185-200.

Witkowsky, Jan, ed., 2005, *The Inside Story,* NY: Cold Spring Harbour Press.

Wood, Allen, 2008, "The duty to believe according to the evidence," *International Journal for the Philosophy of Religion,* **63**: 7-24.

Zhuangzi, ancient/2007, *Zhuangzi,* translated by Hyun Höchsmann and Yang, Guorong, NY: Pearson.